Understanding
Toni Morrison's
Beloved and *Sula*:

Selected Essays and Criticisms
of the works by the
Nobel Prize-winning author

Understanding
Toni Morrison's
Beloved and *Sula*:

Selected Essays and Criticisms
of the works by the
Nobel Prize-winning author

edited by

Solomon O. Iyasere
Marla W. Iyasere

Whitston Publishing Company
Troy, New York
2000

For our beloved children

Christiana, Solomon, and Julia—

To them we owe who we are.

Contents

Acknowledgements

"Belonging and Freedom in Morrison's *Beloved*: Slavery, Sentimentality, and the Evolution of Consciousness" by Howard W. Fulweiler in *The Centennial Review* 40.2 (Spring 1996). Reprinted with permission of *The Centennial Review*.

"Toni Morrison's *Sula*: A Black Woman's Epic" by Karen F. Stein in *Black American Literature Forum* 18.4 (Winter 1984). Reprinted with permission.

"A Blessing and a Burden: The Relation to the Past in *Sula, Song of Solomon* and *Beloved*" by Deborah Guth in *Modern Fiction Studies* 39.9 (Fall-Winter 1993). Reprinted with permission of Johns Hopkins University Press.

"The Bonds of Love and the Boundaries of Self in Toni Morrison's *Beloved*" by Barbara Schapiro in *Contemporary Literature* 32.2 (Summer 1991). Reprinted with permission of The University of Wisconsin Press.

"The Force Outside/The Force Inside: Mother-Love and Regenerative Spaces in *Sula* and *Beloved*" by Laurie Vickroy in *Obsidian II: Black Literature in Review* 8.2 (Fall-Winter 1993). Reprinted with permission of *Obsidian II: Black Literature in Review*.

"Giving Body to the Word: The Maternal Symbolic in Toni Morrison's *Beloved*" by Jean Wyatt in *PMLA* 108.3 (May 1993). Reprinted with permission.

"'will the parts hold?': The Journey Toward a Coherent Self in *Beloved*" by Betty Jane Powell in *Colby Quarterly* 31.2 (June 1995). Reprinted with permission of *Colby Quarterly*.

"Who Cares? Women-Centered Psychology in *Sula*" by Diane Gillespie and Missy Dehn Kubitschek in *Black American Literature Fourm* 24.1 (Spring 1990). Reprinted with permission.

Toni Morrison:

Selected Works

1970   *The Bluest Eye*, Novel, Published by Holt.

1974   *Sula*, Second Novel, Published by Knopf.

1977   *Song of Solomon*, Third Novel, Published by Knopf.

1981   *Tar Baby*, Fourth Novel, Published by Knopf.

1985   Premier of *Dreaming of Emmett*, a play.

1987   *Beloved*, Fifth Novel, Published by Knopf.

1992   *Jazz*, Sixth Novel, Published by Knopf.

1992   *Playing in the Dark: Whiteness and the Literary Imagination*, Harvard Press.

1998   *Paradise*, Seventh Novel, Published by Knopf.

Introduction

Toni Morrison:
Bearing Witness for the Voiceless

Our silence has been long and deep. In canonical literature, we have always been spoken for. Or we have been spoken *to*. Or we have appeared as jokes or as flat figures suggesting sensuality. Today we are taking back the narrative, telling our own story.   —Toni Morrison[1]

The problem I face as a writer is to make my stories mean something. You can have a wonderful, interesting people, a fascinating story, but it's not about anything. It has no real substance. I want my books to always be about something that is important to me, and the subjects that are important in the world are the same ones that have always been important.
                                                      —Toni Morrison[2]

Toni Morrison is an important novelist. . . . Part of her appeal of course lies in her extraordinary ability to create beautiful language and striking characters. However, Morrison's most important gift, the one which gives her a major author's universality, is the insight with which she writes of problems all humans face. . . . At the core of her novels is a penetrating view of the unyielding, heart-breaking dilemma which torments people of all races.   —Elizabeth B. House[3]

I am really happy when I read something, particularly about black people, when it is not so simple minded . . . when it is not set up in some sociological equation where all the villains do this and all the whites are heroes, because it just makes black people boring, and they are not. I have never met yet a boring black person. All you have to do is scratch the surface and you will see. And this is because of the way they look at life.   —Toni Morrison[4]

When Toni Morrison was awarded the Nobel Prize for Literature in 1993, the world's most prestigious literary recognition, she was the first African-American writer, male or female, to be so honored. She is also one of only two American women ever to win the award; the other was Pearl Buck in 1938. Surely, winning this coveted literary prize earned Morrison the recognition she deeply deserved. Nadine Gordimer, the last woman before Morrison to win the Nobel Prize in Literature, affirms, "The Nobel Prize in Literature is not awarded for gender or race. If it were, many thousands of mediocre writers might qualify. The significance of Toni Morrison winning the prize is simply that she is recognized internationally as an outstanding, fine writer."[5] Commenting on the quality of her works, the Nobel Prize Committee writes, "[Ms. Morrison] gives life to an essential aspect of American reality in her novels characterized by visionary force and poetic import."[6] Morrison's reputation soared internationally; she was no longer regarded only as a prominent contemporary American novelist but also as a major figure in contemporary world literature.

Toni Morrison's literary career has been astonishing. Since 1970, when she published her first novel, *The Bluest Eye*, she has published seven widely acclaimed and award-winning novels. *Sula*, published in 1974, was nominated the next year for the National Book Award in fiction; *Song of Solomon*, published in 1979, won the National Book Critics Circle Award, the American Academy and Institute Award, and was named a Book of the Month Club selection, "the first book by a black writer to receive such an endorsement since Richard Wright's *Native Son* in 1940."[7] *Tar Baby* (1981), on *The New York Times* Best Sellers List for four months, prompted *Newsweek* to feature Toni Morrison on its cover that year. Nancy J. Peterson reminds us Morrison became the first black woman since Zora Neale Hurston in 1943 to achieve that level of recognition.[8] *Beloved*, which appeared in 1987, is regarded by most literary critics as Morrison's masterpiece, the publication that brought her to the forefront of American letters. As might be expected, *Beloved* became Morrison's most honored novel: It was nominated for the National Book Award and the National Book Critics Circle Award; it received the Pulitzer Prize for Fiction, the Robert F. Kennedy Award, the New York State Governor's Arts Award, and the Washington College Literary Award. In 1998, because of the novel's vision and its popularity, Oprah Winfrey produced

and starred in a film version of the novel. Morrison also published two other widely acclaimed novels, *Jazz* in 1992 and *Paradise* in 1998. She has extended her writing into drama and
scholarly writing as well; her play, *Dreaming Emmett*, appeared
in 1986; *Playing in the Dark: Whiteness and the Literary Imagination*, a scholarly work based on lectures delivered at Harvard,
came out in 1992.

Producing such a substantial body of award-winning work
in such a short time (28 years) is indeed an extraordinary literary
achievement, one that catapulted Morrison to international
prominence. This achievement becomes even more inspiring
when we consider the challenges and hardships that marked her
career. For example, she faced the unrelentingly negative attitudes of many critics toward her work because, and she herself
explains, critics lack understanding of the culture, the world, the
given quality out of which she writes. In her essay, "Rootedness:
The Anecdote as Foundation," she remarks, "My general disap-
pointment in some of the criticism that my work has received
has nothing to do with approval. It has something to do with
the vocabulary used in order to describe these things. I don't like
to find my books condemned as bad or praised as good, when
that condemnation or that praise is based on criteria from other
paradigms. I would much prefer that they were dismissed or
embraced on the success of their accomplishment within the culture out of which I write." Morrison's work has also been less
than favorably received at times and because she is an African-
American woman. According to Deborah McDowell, "When
black women writers are neither ignored altogether nor merely
given honorable mention, they are critically misunderstood and
summarily dismissed."[9] Further, she was a single mother raising two young boys and working full time as an editor at Random House.

Awards are not the only important measure of Morrison's
literary success. The burgeoning popularity of her works among
diverse audiences (the Book of the Month Club recently mar-
keted all of Morrison's novels in hard cover editions with their
original dust jackets) and the extensive scholarship devoted to
studying her life and her art confirm Morrison's place as a leading voice in American letters. David Middleton elaborates, "The
sheer quantity of scholarly work done on Morrison is indeed
impressive, appearing in small circulation, ethnic magazines
and journals, in mainline publications in America and abroad,

in collections of essays and in books, monographs and even the inevitable dissertations. . . ."[10] While there will always be those myopic views which assert that "in no way is the literature Morrison creates supported by the academic world,"[11] the fact is that Morrison's works are vigorously endorsed by the academy and appeal to students across disciplines such as contemporary American literature, African-American literature, women's studies, and multiculturalism in universities both within the United States and abroad. Journals such as *Modern Fiction Studies* have devoted special issues to critical studies of Morrison's works, and discussion of Morrison has dominated conferences of major literary associations, including MLA. Nancy J. Peterson provides an apt summary of the Morrison's stature, ". . . [I]t is not only in the field of literature that Morrison has become the touchstone; as her winning of the Nobel Prize suggests, she has become the symbol of African-American, of human struggle against various kinds of oppressions, of a global longing for liberation. . . . Since the publication of *Beloved*, 'Toni Morrison' has become the name around which debates of considerable significance to American literature, culture, and ideology have amassed. . . ."[12]

Sula

With the publication of *Sula* in 1974, following *The Bluest Eye* in 1970, Toni Morrison established herself as a skillful and formidable novelist. *Sula*, a complex novel, interweaves the themes of love, friendship, good vs. evil, violence, racism, the quest for selfhood, and the role of the family and community in shaping an individual's values. In treating these themes, Morrison employs a variety of advanced narrative techniques, such as shifting perspectives and points of view, resonant images via flashbacks, and cascading ironies to explore the contradictory world of "the Bottom" and its "ordinary" inhabitants. The most important of these are Sula, Nel, Shadrack, and Eva Peace. The novel's involved structure, striking characterizations, and poetic language attracted considerable attention, and the work quickly became the subject of critical reviews and scholarly attention. Although *Sula* did not achieve the immediate success of *Song of Solomon* (1977), a number of critics extolled the novel as bold,

vital, and rich. Consequently, it was nominated for the National
Book Award and excerpted in a major American literary anthol-
ogy, *The American Tradition in Literature*, and in the popular
women's magazine, *Redbook*.

Though simpler in conception and execution than *Beloved*, *Sula* is nevertheless a complex and moving work. *Sula*'s
multiplicity of meaning is summarized by **Maureen T. Reddy**:
"*Sula* can be, and has been, read as, among other things, a fable, a
lesbian novel, a black female *bildungsroman*, a novel of heroic
questing, and an historical novel that captures a crucial change
in black patterns of living. . . ." To synthesize these various
strands into a critical whole, Professor Reddy argues, one theme
interrelates to and interconnects all the rest. Her analysis
examines *Sula* as an anti-war novel, with the term "war" encap-
sulating the three principal types of conflict which beset the
characters—armed warfare of nation against nation; the legal,
economic, and social war of American against its black citizens;
and the pervasive hostility toward black women, especially from
black men. These types of warfare shape the lives and personalities of all three protagonists, Shadrack, Sula/Nel, and the black
community that lives in the Bottom. Tying the development of
the novel to key dates/events in recent Black American history
enables Morrison to rework that history and dramatize, through
Sula, the anguish of seeking to define one's sense of personal
self and worth except in the context of that larger framework.

The question of whether or not a woman's sense of self
can be defined away from or outside of one's community is discussed on a theoretical as well as textual level by **Diane Gillespie**
and **Missy Dehn Kubitschek**. Setting their analysis within and
against the corpus of inquiry concerning woman-centered psychology, Professors Gillespie and Kubitschek apply Carol Gilligan's paradigm, which defines female maturation as occurring
in three stages. These stages "are characterized by unique definitions of moral responsibility to others: first, an unsocialized selfishness; second, submersion in others; third, an authenticity in
relationship." Although Morrison's work predates Gilligan's by
eight years, "Morrison's depiction of the Wright women's progression is almost a textbook illustration of Gilligan's critique of
the second stage of women's moral development, degenerative
goodness." Gilligan's paradigm is likewise applied to the development of Sula and Nel, each insufficient without the other, for
"Moral authenticity requires both truth [Sula] and empathy

[Nel]. Without truth, degenerative goodness coopts empathy in the service of control. Without empathy, truth destroys the possibility for connection."

Karen Stein approaches *Sula* via Morrison's use of two narrative devices, ironic structuring and character pairing. Because her heroes are black women, rather than the white men of western literary tradition, Morrison uses "ironic reversals of epic expectations to create a new definition of heroism that will encompass the lives of black women." Ironies are compounded when "it is the drab and ordinary Nel rather than the more flamboyant Sula . . . that achieves heroic stature." Juxtaposing Sula and Nel empowers both to "grow in self-knowledge and understanding through their links to each other." Ironic structuring and character pairing define the novel's vision and the true heroism that arises only in confrontation with the self.

Beloved

The astonishing achievement of *Beloved*, like that of other great works of literature, exfoliates with a different variation to each reader and upon each rereading. *Beloved* speaks to us singularly, as individuals who bring a unique perspective and set of expectations to the experience of reading, and collectively, as human beings who endeavor to grasp what William Faulkner termed "the old verities of the human heart." So, too, the figure of Beloved interacts with each of the main characters differently, and fulfills in each a distinct human need, whether for passion (Paul D), sisterhood (Denver) or redemption (Sethe). Simultaneously the embodiment of the combined unconscious of all who were engulfed by the Middle Passage, the incarnation of "crawling already baby," and an escaped sex slave, like Ella, Beloved is at once elusive and all-encompassing. The critical essays included in this volume have been selected to help us understand who/what Beloved is and to apprehend the multiple levels of form, structure, rhetoric, imagery and meaning of the novel as a whole.

The structure of the novel is a key issue for **Eusebio L. Rodrigues**. "*Beloved* is a triumph of storytelling," he writes. "Toni Morrison fuses arts that belong to black oral folk tradition with strategies that are sophisticatedly modern in order to create the blues mode in fiction and tell a tale thick in texture and richly complex in meaning." The structure of this "blues mode" is thus "aural," musical rather than spatial in its architecture. In demonstrating the unique structure of this complex and powerful novel, Professor Rodrigues deftly analyzes key patterns in *Beloved*, emphasizing the significance of the three types of narrator, the two focal regions for the setting, the method of telling history through "rememory," the uses of repetition and food imagery, the narrators' technique of circling, as well as the animal imagery associated with killing and with love. Morrison's expert handling of these narrative elements endows the novel not with a "Hemingway translucence" but with a "Faulknerian density."

For all the novel's richness, its "presence," it is primarily, as **Caroline Rody** demonstrates, an "exercise in the poetics of absence." Professor Rody incisively examines Morrison's prose to show how the narrative style represents the multiple shades of loss and absence the slaves/former slaves experienced. Through modes of haunting, memory, and storytelling, Morrison defines a "landscape of loss" in which her pensive heroine, Sethe, struggles with facing and reclaiming her personal history. Sethe's personal history is as well kaleidoscopic, both embracing and serving as emblem of the lost history of all African-Americans. Dr. Rody summarizes, "In the dialectic between the lost past and rememorying function of narrative love, *Beloved* reconceives the historical text as a transformative space: a space in which the present takes the past in a new and transforming embrace, constructed for mutual healing."

To accomplish its postmodern narrative practice, *Beloved* draws deeply upon multiple literary traditions. **Howard Fulweiler** measures Morrison's achievement against these literary forebears, including Victorian sentimental fiction, such as Charles Dickens' *Hard Times* and Thomas Hardy's *The Mayor of Casterbridge*; the epic journeys of Odysseus and Aeneas; the tragedies of *Macbeth*, *Hamlet* and *Oedipus Rex*; and the biblical themes of Edenic existence, belonging *versus* freedom, salvation, humility, and service. Professor Fulweiler argues, both perceptively and persuasively, that the novel's richness and complexity, its deepest structures, are in sympathy with epic, with tragedy and with the rhythms of scripture. Through interweaving these multiple elements, *Beloved* has opened the way for a new American "rememory" for all races.

That process of rememory centers on Beloved, whose fragmented character is emblematic of the splintering which has devastated the lives of all former slaves, as **Betty Jane Powell** explains, "Morrison's major characters are spiritually and physically fragmented individuals who are disconnected from themselves, from each other, and from community." This dissociation leaves nothing but emptiness where the self should be and is so profound "that the characters cannot see or recognize their own bodies." One way to begin the healing process and work toward coherence, Dr. Powell demonstrates, is through "the coupling together of the pain from the past and the hope for the future through the art of storytelling." Beloved's presence both precipitates and threatens Sethe's attempt to reclaim ownership of her freed self.

Creating a sense of self and then claiming ownership of that self are almost impossible tasks for former slaves, because, as **Barbara Schapiro** clarifies, "For Morrison's characters, African-Americans in a racist, slave society, there is no reliable other to recognize and reaffirm their existence." Even the most fundamental means of self-recognition, the bond between mother and child, has been rent beyond repair by the multiple violations of slavery. Because the result, "psychic death," is far more horrible than physical death, Sethe slays Beloved to spare her this anguish, "'If I hadn't killed her she would have died and that is something I could not bear to happen to her.'" The only possible escape from psychic death, Dr. Schapiro elaborates, depends "on the loving response and recognition from another" that will lead to "the experience of one's cohesiveness and reality as a self."

Patterns of biblical imagery are another element vital to Morrison's narrative reality. Focusing on the most prominent and most powerful of these images as Morrison "refigures three gospel stories which are central to Christian hermeneutics," **Carolyn A. Mitchell** explores how Morrison transforms "the carrying of the Cross (the tree on Sethe's back), the parable of the Good Samaritan (Amy Denver's healing of Sethe), and the call to preach the Gospel (the ministry of Baby Suggs)" as they are realized in the history of African-American enslavement. Dr. Mitchell's thoughtful and elegant discussion enables us to "understand the concept of the Spirit still working in human life and history as a partial key to the complexity of Morrison's narrative."

Carl D. Malmgren addresses the effect of slavery on self-hood, showing that "the institution perverts the relation between Self and other, master and slave, by thoroughly dehumanizing both parties." Professor Malmgren's analysis confirms, "A sense of self is thus contingent upon personal freedom and autonomy." His focus is on the structural development of the novel in addition to the personal development of the main characters. The structure of the novel owes to a number of different forms, including ghost story, historical novel, love story and slave narrative. Ultimately, "It is the institution of slavery that supplies the logic underwriting the novel, the thematic glue that unifies this multifaceted text."

Part of what is required to achieve a coherent sense of self is some way of transcending the "paradox of the unspoken." For the characters in *Beloved*, explains **Andrew Schopp**, the unspoken is tied directly to issues of safety, "Of course, to speak the unspeakable, to articulate the culturally repressed, is to threaten the inherent 'safety' provided by the maintenance of dichotomies such as speakable/unspeakable, known/unknown." Plumbing the unspeakable inevitably leads each character to confront the horror of the past as "they strive to produce meaning by articulating a repressed past." At the same time, reconstruction of the past is essential if the characters are to be able to reconstruct any sense of self, one of the many agonizing paradoxes Morrison engages to create her "postmodern" narrative.

Morrison's linguistic inventiveness in finding ways to express the ineffable is the subject of **Jean Wyatt**'s essay, "Giving Body to the Word." The challenge Morrison defines for her novel inevitably requires that she take language and the novel form itself to new levels. "The project of incorporating into a text subjects previously excluded from language causes a breakdown and restructuring of linguistic forms," Dr. Wyatt explains; "to make room for the articulation of alternative desires, Morrison's textual practice flouts basic rules of normative discourse." Professor Wyatt measures Morrison's achievement against the paradigm set forth by Jacques Lacan "to point out Morrison's deviation from dominant language practices and from the psychological premises that underlie them" and coins the phrase *maternal symbolic* "to discuss not only an alternative language incorporating maternal and material values but also a system that, like Lacan's symbolic, locates subjects in relation to other subjects."

Like Eusebio Rodrigues, **Kristin Boudreau** turns to the blues tradition, not for elements of structure, but principles of meaning to understand the nature and purpose of pain and suffering as presented in *Beloved*. Dr. Boudreau explores the novel's "unmaking" of language and of memory as aspects of the unmaking of self, the only real outcome of pain. Thus, pain is "ineffable" and "the experience of vivid pain dismantles language itself, so that pain results in the impossibility of any intelligible utterance." Professor Boudreau shows how *Beloved* contradicts the romantic tradition of the valorization of pain; always destructive, pain "cannot make us real." To become "fully human," then, requires far more than the vivid experience of searing pain. The centerpiece of that healing is not, as Sethe endeavors, "to begin the day's serious work of beating back the past" (73). Rather, *Beloved* teaches us, healing can emerge only from recalling, confronting, making peace with and growing beyond the past, even one so hideous as slavery.

Beloved and *Sula*

Rachel Lee's essay examines the "slippage of words" as Morrison attempts to "indulge two seemingly contradictory gestures: to make 'Peace' a longing, and to make people 'at rest' with this longing piece." The slippage of words in *Beloved* places "emphasis on absences and indeterminate meanings" which "cast an interpretational bone in the direction of readers and critics who transform absence into presence." The resulting ambiguities in the novel signify "an unattainable desire for stable definitions and identities." Through broken speech and missing words Morrison thus "implies how historical realities perpetuate a system that precludes intimate contact." The brokenness of language thus emblemizes the brokenness of the lives of the slaves, "Anybody Baby Suggs knew, let alone loved, who hadn't run off or been hanged, got rented out, loaned out, bought up, brought back, stored up, mortgaged, won, stolen or seized" (*Beloved* 23). The truths about slavery and what slaves endured are too horrible for language to express, so Morrison suggests and intimates, giving the reader just enough to be able to conceive the inconceivable.

In *Sula*, Morrison's linguistic inventiveness "broaches the subject not only of semantic integrity . . . but also of epistemological integrity." Slips of language, and their attendant missed meanings, occur between characters in their conversations, within an individual character's mind in a dialogue with self, and between narrator and reader in what is intimated but cannot be expressed. When language fails, what alternatives exist to define and convey meaning? Professor Lee's deft analysis enables us to apprehend more fully how both novel and novelist explore this dilemma.

Of all the failed relationships in *Sula* and *Beloved*, the most crucial are those between mother and child and between individual and self. When oppressive external forces of slavery, racism, and poverty threaten their children's very survival, Eva Peace and Sethe respond in similar ways. Morrison's depiction of Eva's and Sethe's fierce love for their children "is fraught with irresolvable conflicts and difficulties," writes **Laurie Vickroy**. Because these women and the families they struggle so hard to protect are always at risk, neither Eva nor Sethe has the opportunity to see [her] children as separate [from herself] or to enjoy them as autonomous individuals." Professor Vickroy analyzes how Morrison employs spatial metaphors to measure "the possibility of individuals to achieve different degrees of autonomy through escape, refuge or growth."

Deborah Guth offers a contrastive study of the relationship to the past in three novels, *Sula*, *Song of Solomon* and *Beloved*. Morrison's purpose in exploring this relationship to the past is to "dramatize the complex interaction between a present in search of itself and a past that appears sometimes as nurturing cultural foundation, sometimes as a restrictive tradition to be fought off, and sometimes—in *Beloved*, for example—as a frightening nightmare that imposes itself between the present and a future of freedom and renewal." In *Sula*, "the past serves as suppressed model, juxtaposed with the present in order to assess the nature of failure." In *Beloved*, a far more complex relationship is involved. Professor Guth carefully delineates how the more recent novel "dramatizes the intersection of two warring impulses towards the past, the imperative to remember and the desperate need to forget, and encodes them in a tale where one woman's attempt to defy the encroachment of the past culminates in a truly symbolic bond between the present, imaged as haunted mother, and the past, represented in the form of her murdered and resurrected child."

Recovery of that terrible past is crucial, argues **Carolyn Jones**, if Sethe and Sula are to find ways to transcend their reenactment of the myth of Cain. "Both Sethe and Sula commit Cain's act," writes Professor Jones, "although they do not act out of jealousy as Cain does. . . . They also bear Cain's mark, a mark that sets each woman apart both from personal identity and from community and each must undergo mourning and re-memory to find and define the self." Dr. Jones explores the dimensions of the Cain myth as it helps define the degree to which each woman is able to grow beyond her role as rejected human soul.

These essays enrich our experience of Morrison's work, and we offer them here to deepen each reader's understanding and appreciation of *Sula* and *Beloved*. Nothing can take the place of the literary work or art itself; thus, the purpose of this collection is to encourage you to revisit Morrison's novels again and again, using these essays as a means of discovering a new insight to treasure or passage to savor with each rereading of *Sula* and *Beloved*.

Notes

[1] David Gates. "Keep Your Eyes on the Prize." *Newsweek* 18 October 1993: 89.

[2] Susan M. Troskyeded. "Morrison." *Contemporary Authors* 42 (Detroit: Gale Research, 1994): 327.

[3] Elizabeth B. House. "Toni Morrison." Ed. Karen L. Rood. *Dictionary of Literary Biography Yearbook 1981* (Detroit: Gale Research, 1982): 118.

[4] Toni Morrison. "Behind the Making of *The Black Book*." *Black World* 23 (1974): xxx.

[5] Gates, 89.

[6] Toni Morrison. "Lecture and Speech of Acceptance, Upon the Award of the Nobel Prize for Literature." *The Nobel Lecture in Literature*. New York: Alfred A. Knopf, 1994.

[7] Nancy J. Peterson. "Introduction: Canonizing Toni Morrison." *Modern Fiction Studies* 39: 3&4 (Fall/Winter 1993): 462.

[8] Peterson, 463.

[9] Deborah E. McDowell. "New Directions for Black Feminist Criticism." Ed. Elaine Showalter. *The Feminist Criticism* (New York: Pantheon Books, 1985): 187.

[10] David L. Middleton. "Introduction." *Toni Morrison: An Annotated Bibliography* (New York: Garland Publishing, Inc., 1987): vii.

[11] Barbara Christian. "The Race for Theory." *Cultural Critique* 6 (1987): 61-62.

[12] Peterson, 464-465.

The Tripled Plot and Center of *Sula*

Maureen T. Reddy

> With the same disregard for name changes by marriage
> that the black people of Medallion always showed,
> each flat slab had one word carved on it. Together
> they read like a chant: PEACE 1895-1921, PEACE 1890-
> 1923, PEACE 1910-1940, PEACE 1892-1959.
>   They were not dead people. They were words. Not
> even words. Wishes, longings.   (171)

Toni Morrison's *Sula* begins and ends with death: the
"prologue" to the novel tells of the death of both a neighborhood and its characteristic way of life, and the "epilogue," from
which the above is quoted, is set in a cemetery where Nel
Wright Greene is finally beginning to mourn the death of her
friend Sula Peace, twenty-five years after the fact. These deaths,
as Nel's thoughts about the grave markers suggest, are linked to
wider scenes of death, to war and to the longing for peace, and,
significantly, to freedom through the formal structure of the
novel. The untitled prologue describes the settling of the Bottom by a freed slave, thereby calling up associations with the
Civil War, and of its destruction a century later in order to make
way for a golf course, calling to mind the aftermath of Lyndon
Johnson's War on Poverty, which often seemed more like a war
on the poor, with its massive urban renewal (removal) projects
that displaced many black people. The epilogue is titled "1965,"
reminding us of both the war in Vietnam and the Civil Rights
Movement. The novel's other chapters are also titled with
years, with the first, "1919," recalling World War I and the last,
"1941," World War II. Each of the ten major chapters includes a
death, sometimes metaphoric but more usually actual: "1919"
describes the death of a nameless and quite literally faceless sol-

dier in war and Shadrack's founding of National Suicide Day. "1920" includes the death of Cecile Sabat; "1921," the burning of Plum Peace; "1922," the drowning of Chicken Little; and "1923," the burning of Hannah Peace. The next three chapters focus on metaphoric deaths: "1927," the death of Nel's inner self through her marriage to Jude Greene, who thinks that he and Nel "together would make one Jude" (83); "1937," the death of Nel's and Sula's friendship; and "1939," Sula's fantasized destruction of Ajax. In "1940" we have Sula's death and in "1941" the last National Suicide Day, which culminates in the deaths of many townspeople, all of them black. In examining here the ways in which Morrison's narrative technique continually pushes the reader to refer outward from the ostensible subjects of *Sula*, I want to argue for a broader reading of the novel than is usually offered.

Critics of *Sula* frequently comment on the pervasive presence of death, the uses of a particular cultural and historical background, the split or doubled protagonist (Sula/Nel), and the attention to chronology in the novel. However, as far as I am aware, no one has presented a reading of *Sula* that explores the interrelatedness of these elements; yet it is the connections among them that most usefully reveal the novel's overall thematic patterns. *Sula* can be, and has been, read as, among other things, a fable, a lesbian novel, a black female *bildungsroman*, a novel of heroic questing and an historical novel that captures a crucial change in black patterns of living;[1] all these modes are certainly discernible in the test. One approach that has not been taken is to read *Sula* as a war novel, or, more precisely as an anti-war novel.

The phrasing of Nel's musings at the cemetery demands that we work out the distinctions she makes among words, wishes, and longings. Her commentary on the grave markers moves from the concrete to the abstract, a movement that accentuates the way in which the "chant" Nel reads is an assertion of hope, not a description of reality, for in fact there has been no peace from 1895-1921 or 1890-1923 or 1910-1940 or 1892-1959—not in the world, not in the black community, not in the individual lives of the people now decaying in those graves—unless we think of Peace strictly as a surname designating the now-dead people, a possibility Nel immediately negates. The word is more concrete than the wish it gestures toward, the signifier always simplifying the signified. Nel rejects even wishes, though, ending by deciding that the four repetitions of Peace are "longings," a word which implies deeply felt but inchoate and largely ineffable desires for some remote or even unachievable object. The longing for peace encoded in the novel's structure is a response to the several different kinds of war in which the novel's characters are caught up: actual armed conflict among nations; legal, economic, and social war against black people by the society in which they live, sometimes taking the form of armed (on one side) conflict; and hostility toward black women, so palpable that it forces them to discover in early childhood that "they [are] neither white nor male, and that all freedom and triumph [is] forbidden to them" (52).

Despite its title, *Sula* actually has three protagonists: Shadrack, Sula/Nel, and the community of black people who live in the Bottom. These three protagonists are at the centers of different but overlapping and intricately interconnected plots that in turn convey various aspects of the anti-war theme. To be more explicit, Shadrack represents the impinging of the outside world on the black people of Medallion through war, the army being "the first of capitalism's modern industrial machines to incorporate black men" (Willis 276), and his plot concerns the futile attempt to control death and chaos. The Sula/Nel couple—the two sides of a "Janus' head" that together would make one woman (Parker 253)—are the center of the plot about female friendship and female development and represent the effects of internalized racist stereotypes and the multiple oppression of black women. The community as a whole enacts the recent history of black people in the United States and represents some possible responses to social otherness. This tripling of plot, center, and theme is announced in the final sentence of the novel's prologue: "They [the black people of the Bottom] were mightily preoccupied with earthly things—and each other, wondering even as early as 1920 what Shadrack was all about, what that little girl Sula who grew into a woman in their town was all about, and what they themselves were all about, tucked up there in the Bottom" (6). The role of the reader of *Sula* is to share this preoccupation with "earthly things" and to wonder, with the townspeople, what is Shadrack all about? what are Sula and Nel all about? what are the townspeople all about? These questions guide our reading of the novel, in which Morrison offers not answers, but ways of developing our responses to the central questions.

The many deaths in *Sula* reinforce the anti-war theme, as each is linked to one or more of the novel's centers. The deaths of the nameless soldier and of Plum Peace are results of World War I, as the blame for Plum's death rests not on Eva, who soaks him with kerosene and lights the match, but on those horrors he experienced in war that drove him to seek oblivion through heroin. The actual deaths of Cecile Sabat, Chicken Little, Hannah, and Sula; the metaphoric deaths of Nel's inner self and of Sula's and Nel's friendship; and Sula's fantasy of murdering Ajax are linked to the social war on black women. Cecile's death is important less for Cecile's sake than for Nel's, as the train journey to New Orleans teaches Nel about the humiliations in store for any black woman, no matter how beautiful or how well-bred, who ventures into the wider world. Three years after this trip Nel acts out her fury at her position in life, and especially at the mother's role by acting to gain some kind of freedom as she and Sula taunt Chicken Little, who slips out of Sula's hands and plunges into the river to his death: Nel wanted to be free of him, and now she is. Hannah burns while tending to a conventionally feminine task, preserving fruit. Sula dies, I would argue, because death seems her only option for freedom; she and the townspeople together seem to will her death. The death of Nel's inner self and the death of her friendship with Sula are both attributable to externally imposed limitations on black women's lives, while Sula's desire to destroy Ajax is part of a pattern of danger resulting from the denial of creative agency. The other deaths—of the people on National Suicide Day in 1941—are linked both to the racist war on black people in the U.S. and to armed conflict, as it is Shadrack who established National Suicide Day upon his return from war. In no chapter can we escape death and destruction. This is what war is, the novel seems to say, and it is not so limited as conventional definitions would have it, or is it ever glamorous, romantic, or heroic: It is everywhere, and it is terrifyingly ugly.

The chapter that immediately follows the prologue focuses on Shadrack, "blasted and permanently astonished by the events of 1917" in France (7), where he saw a soldier's face blown off and his faceless body continue to run into battle—or perhaps away from battle: This was Shadrack's first encounter with "the enemy," and he wasn't sure whether his company was advancing or retreating. Suffering from what usually is euphemistically referred to as shell shock or battle fatigue but here is clearly presented as actual madness, the only possible response to the horrors of war, Shadrack is rapidly discharged from a veterans' hospital after an episode of violence. The chaos he has witnessed in the world seems to have invaded even his own body; he thinks that "anything could be anywhere," and imagines his hands growing to monstrous proportions (9).

War has formed a vast, unbridgeable divide in his life, permanently separating his old self from what he now is: "Twenty-two years old, weak, hot, frightened, not daring to acknowledge the fact that he didn't even know who or what he was . . . with no past, no language, no tribe, no source, no address book, no comb, no pencil, no clock, no pocket handkerchief, no rug, no bed, no can opener, no faded postcard, no soap, no key, no tobacco pouch, no soiled underwear and nothing nothing nothing to do . . . he was sure of one thing only: the unchecked monstrosity of his hands" (12). This definition by negation, with its almost ritualistic chanting of "no," its insistent affirmation of what is absent, places Shadrack the returning soldier in relationship to his enslaved ancestors; just as slavery brutally attempted to strip people of past, language, tribe, possessions, so does war. Shadrack's story, then, functions as a modern slave narrative, even repeating the structure of slave narratives, which usually describe a series of journeys—from the ancestral land to slavery in the Southern United States to freedom, of sorts, in the north.[2] Each part of the slave's journey includes an attempt to reconstitute a tribe or community under adverse circumstances, which is what Shadrack attempts to do in the Bottom. In important ways, Shadrack is much like the questing figure of romance and therefore is linked to Sula, whose journey, like Shadrack's, is a quest for self; each of these quests is complicated by social, political, and economic forces over which the quester has little control, symbolized here by Shadrack's perceived lack of control over his own body. Unlike his Biblical namesake, this Shadrack has not been saved whole from the fire.

The journey motif inaugurated in *Sula* by Shadrack's largely unsuccessful attempt to retrieve the self blasted by World War I is an ironic comment on conventional quest tales, in which the male protagonist frequently fulfills his desire for adventure and achieves adulthood through physical combat. Many of the male characters in *Sula* leave the Bottom in search of adventure or to prove their manhood in ways denied them at home. Plum, like Shadrack, fights in the First World War; all we know of his experiences is that they were so horrific that he sought oblivion through heroin. Morrison structures Plum's story to parallel his response to war with Shadrack's: Both National Suicide Day and heroin addiction represent rejections of the world as it is and futile, self-defeating attempts to reorder that world, to make it less chaotic and less terrifying. Although Plum at last remembers his immediate past and his source— after trying to forget them by staying away from home upon his return from war—he attempts to eradicate his present through heroin, which enables him to effect the regression to a comparatively safe childhood he so desperately desires. Eva's murder of Plum, which she defends as an effort to save him, cuts off his retreat to infancy and echoes the motives behind infanticide during slavery.[3] There are intimations that Ajax's quest for freedom and adventure will end in his destruction as well. The novel leaves him in 1939, setting off for Dayton to gaze at his beloved airplanes, a love that may plausibly lead him to enlist to serve in World War II.

With the exception of Nel's father, who nevertheless spends almost no time at home due to the demands of his job as a cook on a Great Lakes line that puts him in port only three days out of every sixteen (17), all of the male characters in *Sula* are in flight from the traditional responsibilities of adulthood, although several paradoxically see themselves as proving their manhood. Eva's husband Boy Boy abandons his wife and three children to seek adventure in the city, returning home many years later with a symbol of his success, a woman in a flashy dress, to display in Eva's yard. Even his name, the redundant remark on a kind of eternal childhood, places Boy Boy outside adult life. At the same time, though, by echoing a racist epithet for adult black males, this name reminds the reader of the circumstances that entrap black men in an economic dependency that replicates childhood. The three Deweys, whose abnormal shortness (four feet) mirrors their stunted emotional and intellectual growth, are the novel's most extreme versions of childish men. They remain unable to care for themselves for as long as they live, expecting Eva and then Sula to provide their food, shelter, and clothing—to mother them, in short, a task Sula accepts only briefly, during her infatuation with Ajax.

The mothering Jude expects from Nel is of a more complicated variety, but it is mothering nonetheless. Jude marries Nel when his hopes of proving his masculinity through building the New River Road are dashed by racist hiring policies. Jude thinks of building the road as "real work. . . . He wanted to swing the pick or kneel down with the string or shovel the gravel. His arms ached for something heavier than trays, for something dirtier than peelings; his feet wanted the heavy work shoes . . ." (81-82). When he realizes that he is permanently barred from such work due to race, he turns to Nel for solace. Morrison is explicit about Jude's motives for marrying: ". . . it as rage, rage and a determination to take on a man's role anyhow that made him press Nel about settling down. He needed some of his appetites filled, some posture of adulthood recognized, but mostly he wanted someone to care about his hurt, to care very deeply. Deep enough to hold him, deep enough to rock him. . . . And if he were to be a man, that someone could no longer be his mother" (82). In turn, Nel marries Jude because she realizes that he needs her; that is, she colludes in the eradication of her self in a marriage in which she is meant to be a part of Jude.

The marriage of Nel and Jude demonstrates the crippling effects of several types of oppression: Both are victims in the racist war against black people, but Nel doubly so because Jude sees the only escape from oppression as residing in the oppression of another. Both have internalized the racist and sexist attitudes of the white capitalist society that says that one's value as a man is determined by one's work and by that work's economic rewards, including ownership of a woman and children, and that one's value as a woman is determined by one's ability to attract a man and then to provide that man with children. Many black male writers have written about the determined, programmatic emasculation of black men by white capitalist society, but Morrison, along with other black women writers, redefines the problem. James Baldwin, to offer just one example, bitterly condemns the racism that figuratively, and frequently literally, castrates black men, asserting in *No Name in the Street*, a text contemporaneous with *Sula*, that "a man's balance depends on the weight he carries between his legs . . . the word *genesis* describes the male, involves the phallus, and refers to the seed which gives life" (64). "The slave," adds Baldwin, "knows, however his master may be deluded on this point, that he is called a slave because his manhood has been, or can be, or will be taken away from him. To be a slave means that one's manhood is engaged in a dubious battle indeed. . . . In the case of American slavery, the black man's right to his women, as well as to his children, was simply taken from him" (62).

In *Sula*, Morrison tacitly argues that the terms in which such protests are couched betray the tragic fact that black men remain trapped in the white man's nightmare. To think of relations between men and women as "the black man's *right* to *his* women" (my emphasis) is to enlist on the side of the oppressors by agreeing to participate in a system that perceives women primarily as the objects of exchange between men, with the effect of poisoning relations between black men and black women.[4] The passage quoted from Baldwin defines the slave as a male, both by the use of the male pronoun and by the emphasis on "manhood," ignoring the fact that black women also were enslaved while focusing exclusively on what slavery meant to men. This focus eclipses black women's history, doing to black women something close to what war did to Shadrack and what slavery tried to do to all black people: leaving them with "no past, no language, no tribe, no source." To the extent that Baldwin's phrasing of the problem is representative of texts written by black men in the 1960s and early 1970s—and I think that it is—it illustrates the ways in which black women are multiply oppressed, by the dominant culture and, far more painfully, by their own brothers, fathers, sons. *Sula* shows the men of the Bottom, with the sole exception of Ajax, turning to women for support, but offering very little support or even acknowledgment in return.

Early in her life, Sula sees a problem between men and women but is unable to articulate it until she returns to the Bottom from her mysterious ten-year journey. When she is twelve, her response to Shadrack's "always" is sheer terror, because this seems to condemn her to a future in which nothing changes, and she longs for change, since she does not want to live as the women of the Bottom do, in thrall to male needs, male desires, male rules. This is the day on which she determines to lead "an experimental life," the day on which she and Nel enact a rite of passage into adult sexuality through their ritualistic digging in the earth with twigs (58), the day "her mother's remarks [that she loves but does not like Sula] sent her flying up those stairs," the day "her one major feeling of responsibility had been exorcised on the bank of a river with a close place in the middle" (118). At twelve, she learns that "there was no other that you could count on" and "that there was no self to count on either" (118-119). Her travels, particularly her experiences with men, make her realize that "a lover was not a comrade and could never be—for a woman" (121). Sula thinks of Nel not as an "other," but as a second self, but Nel betrays her by choosing a man and marriage over their friendship (Jude over the self, in other words).

When Sula walks away from Nel's and Jude's wedding "with just a hint of a strut" (58), not to be seen again in the bottom for ten years, she is embarking on a foredoomed quest for types of friendship and of selfhood that she finally discovers to be impossible. In college, and in Nashville, Detroit, New Orleans, New York, Philadelphia, Macon, and San Diego, Sula is looking for a replacement for Nel, who has been to Sula "the closest thing to both an other and a self" (119), but she learns "that no one would ever be that version of herself which she sought to reach out to and touch with an ungloved hand" (121). Sula makes the double mistake of thinking that other places are different from Medallion in ways that would significantly affect her personal possibilities and of believing that she will be able to find a self by exploring the wider world. Her disillusionment is expressed in an apparently enigmatic comment to Nel, who tells Sula that she has been away for too long. "Not too long, but maybe too far," Sula replies (96). Nel finds this incomprehensible, and Sula is either unable or unwilling to explain herself further, but her reasoning is not very difficult to follow: She has traveled too far, seen too many places, to retain any hope that somewhere, in some place as yet unknown, she might find the object of her quest. Her journey has convinced her that every city "held the same people, working the same mouths, sweating the same sweat" (120)—there is no promised land of freedom to look toward.

Although Sula eventually scorns Nel's rootedness and respectability, thinking that Nel is now like the other townspeople who fear being truly alive (120), Sula's deepest desire is to *be* Nel. In childhood, Sula loved Nel's oppressively neat house and seemed to want to change places with her friend. It is Nel who draws Sula back to Medallion, and Nel who keeps her there, despite their estrangement. As she is dying, Sula reflects on her badly managed attempt to imitate Nel, which "always ended up in some action noteworthy not for its coolness but mostly for its being bizarre" (141). The wish to be Nel is what drives Sula into her sexual experimentation with Jude, which she later describes as an attempt to fill up "this space in front of me, behind me, in

my head" (144).   The space Sula confronts is her absence of a
"center, [a] speck around which to grow" (119); she had no true
inner core of self and tries to appropriate Nel's by doing what
Nel does, including having sex with Jude.   Morrison at one
point refers to Sula as an "artist with no art form," whose "craving for the other half of her equation was the consequence of an
idle imagination" (121).   Nel, then, substitutes in Sula's life for
paints, clay, music, or even words, serving as the material out of
which Sula tries to create both a self and a way of expressing that
self.   This absence of a creative outlet seems linked to Sula's status as a black woman, for black women's artistic desires and tal-
ents were often driven underground by the hostility of the dominant culture, as Alice Walker so movingly details in "In Search
of Our Mothers' Gardens."   Then, too, Sula grows up in a community in which a woman's art is her domestic work, her care of
family and home.   In a weird way, Jude and then Ajax become
the subjects of Sula's experiments with Nel-like domesticity; if
Nel can find a self through a relationship with a man—as it appears to Sula—then Sula is willing to try to do so as well.   In
spite of her deathbed claim that she "sure did live in this world"
and her insistence that she owns herself (143), Sula never
reaches real self-understanding because she has no abiding self to
understand nor any way of creating a self.   She needs Nel to verify herself and to be whole, as her post-death musings (surely the
oddest feature of the novel) suggest: "Well, I'll be damned . . . it
didn't even hurt.   Wait'll I tell Nel" (149).

     Nel finally does reach self-understanding, and it is Sula
who leads her to it; her recognition of her true feelings provides
her with that speck around which to grow, symbolized by the
scattering of spores from the gray ball that has previously hov-
ered in her peripheral vision.   Just as Sula wanted to be Nel, Nel
once wanted to be Sula, preferring Sula's family and home to
her own and needing Sula to verify her feelings.   However, unlike Sula, Nel gives up this wish when she surrenders herself by
allowing her "response to Jude's shame and anger select . . . her
away from Sula . . . greater than her friendship was this new feeling of being needed by someone who saw her singly" (84).   Here
Nel makes an interpretative error equivalent to those that sent
Sula away from Medallion: Jude not only fails to see Nel singly,
he fails to see her at all, seeing only "himself taking shape in her
eyes" (83).   Nel becomes the center around which Jude and the
children grow, herself adopting a conventionally feminine role

of self-abnegation and self-sacrifice. She eventually loses the ability to know her own feelings and, like Sula, tries to fill up space with another, in this case her children.

From the moment that she banishes Sula and Jude, Nel is haunted by "something just to the right of her, in the air, just out of view. She could not see it, but she knew exactly what it looked like. A gray ball hovering just there. Just there. To the right. Quiet, gray, dirty. A ball of muddy strings, but without weight, fluffy but terrible in its malevolence" (108-109). This gray ball is a physical manifestation of her own feelings, which she is afraid to examine, choosing instead to attribute her grief to a conventionally understood and accepted source. Nel convinces herself that it is Jude she will miss, Jude who knew her, and Jude whose departure leaves an emptiness in her, but it is actually Sula. Nearly three decades later, after Eva tells Nel that she and Sula were "Just alike. Both of you. Never was no difference between you" and then calls her "Sula," as if to emphasize their interchangeability (169), Nel is finally able to face the real source of her grief. As she stands at Sula's grave, the gray ball breaks and "scatter[s] like dandelion spores in the breeze," and Nel cries out, "All that time, all that time, I thought I was missing Jude" (174). This epiphany comes at the very end of the book and provides the most optimistic ending of any of Morrison's novels with the exception of *Beloved*, leaving open the possibility that Nel may now grow, freed from the lies in which she has held herself prisoner, and may discover the inner peace that has thus far eluded her.[5]

Both Nel and Sula are influenced in adult life by their maternal inheritances, each enacting to an extreme degree the meaning of adult womanhood that her mother has shown her. Despite Nel's early rejection of her mother and attraction to her disreputable grandmother, Nel follows her mother into conventionality, her wedding to Jude serving as "the culmination of all [Helene] had been, thought or done in this world" (79). Sula easily takes and just as easily discards new sexual partners, following Hannah's old pattern but without Hannah's affection for the men involved. Nel merges with the community; Sula becomes its center.

Sula becomes the speck around which the townspeople grow, at least temporarily, in reaction to her having violated their most basic rules, chief among them the dicta against sexual relationships with white men and against disrespecting the elderly. Town gossip holds that Sula has done the unforgivable, slept with white men; this is a sin against the belief that black men "own" black women, that a woman's sexuality is not her own to control. Sula's placing Eva in a nursing home violates the community value of taking care of one's own. Hannah may have slept with married men and Eva may have cut off her own leg for money and killed her son, but neither was ostracized by the folk because neither treated community standards contemptuously—both remained "womanly." Sula's real crime is her complete disregard of her womanly responsibilities, as denied by her community; Sula steps outside the circle of community and becomes a pariah. Convinced that Sula is evil, the townspeople united against her, making her the scapegoat for all their many troubles: "Once the source of their personal misfortune was identified, they had leave to protect and love one another. They began to cherish their husbands and wives, protect their children, repair their homes and in general band together against the devil in their midst" (117-118). Sula is not, of course, the source of the townspeople's problems, but she is certainly a convenient scapegoat, far easier to fight against than would be the complex, faceless, virtually unknowable social system of exclusion that oppresses them. Sula may even represent this social system to the townspeople, as her behavior is "white" by their standards. The possibility of running Sula out of town and thereby solving their problems never occurs to the people of the Bottom, although such banishment is part of American mythology and indeed American history. The novel describes mob actions like lynching as peculiar to whites, simultaneously implying that black ethics are superior to the looser moral code holding sway in the dominant culture: "There was no creature so ungodly as to make them destroy it. They could kill easily if provoked to anger, but not by design, which explained why they could not 'mob kill' anyone" (118).

Religious faith, residing in a version of Christian mythology that reinterprets the Trinity as a quartet, with the fourth face of God being Satan, informs the lives of the Bottom's people. Morrison's depiction of folk belief in *Sula* insists that Christian faith offers only an explanation of evil and of God's apparent indifference to black suffering, not a justification for that suffering. However, Christian belief defines freedom as loss of self, teaching that one may find the Lord only through abandonment of the self; furthermore, it instructs believers to regard earthly suffering as a small price to pay for the joys of the afterlife and to perceive death not as an end, but as a beginning. *Sula* does not comment directly on Christian theology, but the promised freedom of the afterlife does seem to undergird the people's refusal to lose faith. They are determined "not to let anything—anything at all: not failed crops, not rednecks, lost jobs, sick children, rotten potatoes, broken pipes, bug-ridden flour, third-class coal, educated social workers, thieving insurance men, garlic-ridden hunkies, corrupt Catholics, racist Protestants, cowardly Jews, slaveholding Moslems, jackleg nigger preachers, squeamish Chinamen, cholera, dropsy or the Black Plague, let alone a strange woman—keep them from their God" (150). This list, a stylistic device of which Morrison is fond, has the rhythm and the imaginative energy of a particularly stirring sermon, at once asserting the enormity of the sufferings that black people have endured and reducing them by diminishing the differences among them: Accidents of nature and premeditated human evil are equated as potential barriers between a people and their God, and are treated as challenges that must be met for the sake of both spiritual and physical survival. The "Black Plague" that serves as the penultimate item on the list seems both a hyperbolic comment on the visitations of evil the people will overcome and an ironic summation of what comes before it: a plague striking at blacks, a war on black people. The faith stressed here is reinforced, even vindicated, by the Bottom's outlasting Sula.

Once Sula dies, the Bottom ceases to be a cohesive community. Her death brings first general relief and then "restless irritability":

> . . . mothers who had defended their children from Sula's malevolence (or who had defended their positions as mothers from Sula's scorn for the role) now had nothing to rub up against. The tension was gone and so was the reason for the effort they had made. Without her mockery, affection for others sank into flaccid disrepair. . . . Wives uncoddled their husbands; there seemed no further need to reinforce their vanity. And even those Negroes who had moved down from Canada to Medallion, who remarked every chance they got that they had never been slaves, felt a loosening of the reactionary compassion for Southern-born blacks Sula had inspired in them. They returned to their original claims of superiority.   (153-154)

The people of the Bottom require something or someone to define themselves against, some common enemy to bind them to each other, a situation analogous to the surge of patriotism countries experience in war time. With Sula alive, they unite; with Sula dead, they divide against each other again. The common enemy that they fail to identify correctly in this case is the Depression, which we are told came late to the Bottom, but which also affected black people as a whole far more severely than it did whites, given the impoverished conditions under which many blacks already lived. The Bottom's people indulge in self-hatred and self-blame when they make Sula a pariah; scapegoating Sula is a very particular enactment of the multiple oppression of black women, as Sula is blamed for conditions under which she also suffers. Turning rage inward, striking at the self or at those nearest to the self instead of at the real oppressor, is one possible, and extremely dangerous, response to oppression.

Ultimately, many of those who hated Sula reveal their despairing self-hatred when they join in Shadrack's National Suicide Day. It is the middle of the most difficult winter in memory, and they don't know what to do. They attempt to strike back at the nameless, faceless system of exploitation that is responsible for their current predicament by killing "the tunnel they were forbidden to build" (161), but this futile gesture causes their own destruction when the tunnel collapses and many die. The tunnel is a symbol of the repeatedly awakened and repeatedly dashed hopes of the people, the place "where their hope had lain since 1927. There was the promise: leaf-dead" (161). It is another awakening of those hopes that leads people to join Shadrack's bizarre parade. The hope the people share is actually a hope for freedom from oppression—for peace—which enables them to endure that oppression. It is "the same hope that kept them picking beans for other farmers; kept them from finally leaving as they talked of doing; kept them knee-deep in other people's dirt; kept them excited about other people's wars; kept them solicitous of white people's children; kept them convinced that some magic 'government' was going to lift them up, out and away from that dirt, those beans, those wars" (160). Although *white* appears in this list only once, I think it must be read into each recurring "other" as well: It is white farmers for whom black people sharecropped, white people for whom black women worked as domestics, white people who started those wars, and white people, most damningly, who run the dubious "government" that has failed to "lift them [blacks] up." It is white people in general who wage war against black people. The people who die at the tunnel and those who will die in World War II are equally victims of other people's wars; they share in dreams deferred and promises repeatedly broken by the ruling class. The three centers and plots of *Sula* connect here as the anti-war theme is most forcefully presented in a chapter set on the eve of American engagement in the Second World War, with responsibility for the destruction of many black people laid firmly on the white ruling class, the very same people who run the government and start the wars. There are no important white characters in *Sula*, no individualized white people, but when we do see white people in the text—instead of hovering just outside its borders, like Nel's gray ball—they are consistently shown as sharing the dominant culture's hatred of blacks, from the conductor who humiliates Helene on the train to the three boys who threaten Sula and Nel to the barge operator who mistreats Chicken Little's corpse.

The leaving that the people are said to have spoken of in the passage quoted above is probably of two sorts: leaving the Bottom for an industrial, more northern city, paralleling the migration of many black people throughout this century but most especially in war time, and leaving the United States for Africa. This last is suggested by the dating of the death of hopes in 1927, the year that Marcus Garvey was deported to Jamaica, effectively ending a vibrant Black nationalist movement until its revival in the 1960s. The last, devastating National Suicide Day takes place in 1941, the year many black men would be called to fight in another one of those wars and would respond to that call with hope that after *this* war, full civil rights would be theirs, while other black men and women would fight discrimination in the defense industry (Giddings 237).

Sula effectively ends in 1941, with the final chapter functioning as an epilogue that brings us up to 1965. The intervening twenty-four years have proved the end of the Bottom as Nel and Sula knew it. Black people have abandoned the Bottom, which is rapidly becoming a wealthy white area; the black people who made some money during World War II moved to the valley, now considered less desirable by whites. The epilogue begins ominously: "Things were so much better in 1965. Or so it seemed" (163). The obvious implication is that things are *not*

any better in 1965 than they were in 1941, or in 1919 for that matter, the recent Civil Rights Movement and rebirth of Black Nationalism notwithstanding. Nel notices black people holding
jobs from which they were previously excluded—dime store
clerk, junior high school teacher—but the new young people
remind her of the Deweys, a damning comparison that consigns
the young to eternal youth and that calls into question the value
and permanency of those rights gained between 1941 and 1965.
By 1965, the year that saw the assassination of Malcolm X, the
Civil Rights Movement was splintering into many different
movements, each responding differently to the recognition that
legal rights were not in themselves likely to end centuries of oppression. Nineteen sixty-five was the year that Watts burned,
beginning two years of violence in urban ghettoes, events which
seem foreshadowed in *Sula* by the riot at the tunnel and which
force us to see that believing things to be better in 1965 than in
1941 is falling prey to delusion. The third of the three interconnected plots of *Sula*, the one that centers on the black residents of
the Bottom, is a story of collective, externally imposed stasis, designed to be read as a corrective to illusory hope. The novel implies that all growth is personal and that all true hope must
therefore reside in the personal and in extensions of the personal—that is, in cooperative action rooted in personal relationships, not in faith in the magical possibilities of a government or
even of a movement.

I do not mean to suggest here that *Sula* is in any sense a
complete history of black people in the U.S. or even that the
novel at any point corresponds exactly with a particular moment
in that history. Morrison uses dates of chapters and comments
on social changes to gesture toward history which serves as a
context for events in the novel. In many important ways, *Sula*
operates as a mythological reworking of recent black American
history, with the title drawing attention to the one character
most determined to break free of that history, refusing all the
roles and limitations thrust upon her. Sula, though, rejects not
only external limitations but also love and community, thereby
severely restricting her own potential for growth, engaging in a
personal war with the world. Unloved and unloving, dead finally of a mysterious wasting disease similar to those that pun-
ished unconventional nineteenth-century heroines, Sula is the
hero of the novel, a solitary seeker trying to make her own self.
This is not to say that Sula is the most admirable character in the

novel; Morrison calls into question the whole concept of the hero while placing Sula in the hero's position in the text. *Sula* suggests that a traditional hero is not a very desirable thing to be, showing the hero to be isolated, lacking in self-understanding, unable to acknowledge needs of self or of others and, not incidentally, dead young. The tripled center of the novel implies another possibility, redefining the hero and the self: Just as the real hero of this text is a composite creation, comprising Shadrack, Sula/Nel, and the townspeople, so the self is revisioned as communal, not solitary. Morrison's novel ultimately asserts the value of communality, of love against death, of peace against war, as we see Nel at Sula's grave accepting the past, her love of Sula, and her own weaknesses, an acceptance that may lead her to peace and to freedom.

Notes

[1] Fable, Christian 153 ff.; lesbian novel, Smith 168-185; *bildungsroman*, Abel, Hirsch, and Langland 11; heroic quest, Stein 146; historical novel, Willis "Eruptions of Funk" 263-284.

[2] I am indebted for this parallel to Susan Willis's discussion of women writers' use of slave narratives ("Black Women Writers" 219-220). *Beloved*, in which Morrison returns to *Sula*'s central themes, also repeats the structure of a slave narrative, with Paul D. and Sethe telling their stories of life in slavery, escape, and illusory freedom in Cincinnati.

[3] For reports of infanticide during slavery, see Giddings 44-46. A mother who attempts to save her child from a life that seems worse than death is placed at the center of *Beloved*. Sethe, a runaway slave, sees slavecatchers coming toward her house and instantly begins killing her children, succeeding in slashing her daughter's throat before others intervene to save the three remaining children. Like Eva, Sethe acts out of love; unlike Eva, Sethe is rejected by her community for this action and legally prosecuted. The dilemma Morrison treats is clearer in *Beloved* than in *Sula*: Sethe may have done the right thing, yet she has no right—morally or legally—to do it.

[4] Giddings incorporates discussion of this issue within her overall analysis of black women's history, and I am indebted to her treatment of this issue and to her work generally.

[5] Like all of Morrison's endings, though, the close of *Sula* is ambiguous. It is possible to see Nel's cry not as the beginning of a discovery of peace, but as what Spillers calls "The onset of a sickness-unto-death," provoked by a remorse that can never again be escaped (311).

Works Cited

Abel, Elizabeth, Marianne Hirsch and Elizabeth Langland, eds. *The Voyage In: Fictions of Female Development*. Hanover: University Press of New England, 1983.

Baldwin, James. *No Name in the Street*. New York: Dial, 1972.

Christian, Barbara. *Black Women Novelists: The Development of a Tradition, 1892-1976*. Westport: Greenwood, 1980.

Giddings, Paula. *When and Where I Enter: The Impact of Black Women on Race and Sex in America*. New York: Morrow, 1984.

Morrison, Toni. *Sula*. New York: Knopf, 1974.

Parker, Bettye J. "Complexity: Toni Morrison's Women—An Interview Essay." *Sturdy Black Bridges: Visions of Black Women in Literature*. Ed. Roseann P. Bell, Bettye J. Parker and Beverly Guy-Sheftall. New York: Anchor, 1979. 251-257.

Smith, Barbara. "Toward a Black Feminist Criticism." *The New Feminist Criticism*. Ed. Elaine Showalter. New York: Pantheon, 1985. 168-185.

Spillers, Hortense J. "A Hateful Passion, A Lost Love." *Feminist Studies* 9 (1983): 293-323.

Stein, Karen F. "Toni Morrison's *Sula*: A Black Woman's Epic." *Black American Literature Forum* 18 (1984): 146-150.

Walker, Alice. "In Search of Our Mothers' Gardens." *In Search of Our Mothers' Gardens*. New York: Harcourt, 1983. 231-243.

Willis, Susan. "Black Women Writers: Taking a Critical Perspective." *Making a Difference: Feminist Literary Criticism*. Ed. Gayle Greene and Coppelia Kahn. New York: Methuen, 1985. 211-237.

—. "Eruptions of Funk: Historicizing Toni Morrison." *Black Literature and Literary Theory*. Ed. Henry Louis Gates, Jr. New York: Methuen, 1984. 263-283.

Who Cares?
Women-Centered Psychology in *Sula*

Diane Gillespie
and
Missy Dehn Kubitschek

In the 1970s and 1980s, an explosion of creativity in Afro-American fiction has made famous Ernest Gaines, David Bradley, Toni Morrison, Alice Walker, and Gloria Naylor, to name only a few. As the last three names suggest, this "second renaissance" of fiction has a strong female component. In these same decades, a new psychology of women has emerged, in part, through the research of Nancy Chodorow, Carol Gilligan, and the Stone Center psychologists at Wellesley College. In that it focuses on women's rather than men's experiences and derives its interpretative categories from women's own descriptions of their experiences, this body of research may be described as women-centered. These researchers have listened to and analyzed women's voices; as part of this exploration, they have turned to literature by and about women, where emerging psychological conceptualizations of female development are, as Carol Gilligan notes, well represented ("Moral Orientation" 29). Women-centered psychologists have found caretaking and its associated values of empathy, affiliation, nurturance, and a collective vision of social life to be central to female experience. This new psychology of women challenges the traditional male idea of the self-in-relationship. In order to explore this self-in-relationship, women-centered psychology has privileged the continuing mother-daughter relationship, an important expansion of the male model of the self. This new paradigm in turn requires expansion.

As yet, most of the literary models used in women-centered psychology have been of middle- or upper-class Euro-American origin (for example, see Jean Wyatt's analysis of *Mrs. Dalloway*). Minority literature offers women-centered psychology another expansion of the female self beyond the Euro-American mother-daughter or friend-friend dyad; Afro-American literature often explores a self-in-community. The mother-daughter relationship is certainly crucial in the development of the female self, but powerful social and economic forces affect that central relationship and female development as a whole. In their depiction of female characters, minority women authors delineate experiences and psychological processes described in the new women-centered psychology; they also challenge its limited assumptions about self-in-relation.

Toni Morrison's *Sula*, a contemporary novel about female friendship, offers a view of female psychological development that defies traditional male-centered interpretations of female development and calls out for an expansion of the women-centered paradigm. Both the novel's subject (minority experience) and its treatment implicitly critique the psychology's usual focus on the experiences of middle-class white women, who are often bound by conventional social relationships. Nancy Chodorow's theory of the reproduction of mothering, Carol Gilligan's work on women's moral and psychological development, and the continuing work of the Stone Center offer a paradigm through which to perceive the novel, while *Sula*'s exploration of women's experiences fleshes out the still emerging psychological schema of these researchers.

Sula demonstrates the inadequacy of traditional male-centered psychology's idea of the self by showing that men raised to be autonomous, contained selves become alienated and unhappy; though the women's lives do not run smoothly, they are raised to be selves-in-community and, except for Sula, have more fulfilling lives. In showing these two modes of self-definition, the novel anticipated the findings of women-centered psychology. Nancy Chodorow's *The Reproduction of Mothering* provided the basis which women-centered psychologists have since used to discuss the origins of gender-identity differences between men and women. Significantly, although Chodorow explores individual psychological development, her theory explicitly rests on the social fact of women's having been the primary caretakers of children. Like Toni Morrison, she sees the construction of an individual, gendered self as the result of inescapable social context.

In her groundbreaking 1981 essay on female friendship in five novels, including *Sula*, Elizabeth Abel disputes the sufficiency of Chodorow's theory of the reproduction of mothering. Chodorow argues that, because women, historically, have reared children, boys have had to differentiate themselves from their mothers in order to establish firm gender identities. In contrast, girls have identified with their mothers, and the resulting attachment has established the basis for empathic understanding of others' needs and experiences. Critical to the girl's preoedipal experience is her mother's double identification. In "Family Structure and Feminine Personality," Chodorow states, "A woman identifies with her own mother and, through identification with her child, she (re)experiences herself as a cared-for child" (47). In addition, a girl forms her gender identity by observing female role activities that are "immediately apprehensible in the world of her daily life" (51). She does not have to repress or reject this preoedipal identification with her mother in developing. Instead, she continues to identify with her mother and other women in her social world after the preoedipal period: "Sex role training and social interaction build upon and reinforce the largely unconscious development" (54) so that girls become relationally oriented.

In her analysis Abel identifies and describes a common underlying psychological process or emotional pattern that, she argues, transcends "the diverse cultural situations" of the several novels. She criticizes Chodorow's theory for overestimating the degree of mother-daughter identification and undervaluing the role of women's friendships in "fulfilling the desire for identification" (418). In this framework, several of the friendships exemplify women's tendency toward identification as a source of personal growth. *Sula*, in contrast, exemplifies "the tensions generated by the conflict between identification and autonomy" (426); the novel highlights this issue of "ambivalence and separation" in female friendships (443).

Abel presents a thoughtful case for the importance of identification in female friendships, largely unexplored terrain at the time of her essay. Her approach, however, has a fundamental weakness which limits her interpretation: Her analysis decontextualizes female friendship. The scope necessary for a psychological theory of engenderment has been the occasional subject of feminist critical exchanges. Literary critic Judith Gardiner pointed out immediately that Abel's analysis isolated Nel and Sula's relationship. Psychologist Harriet Lerner criticizes feminist psychoanalytic theory from a family systems perspective which attempts to restore social context.

Overlooking the context of female friendship particularly distorts *Sula*, the only Afro-American novel in Abel's analysis. In limiting her discussion to Nel and Sula, she assumes *a priori* that *Sula* centers on self-in-relation rather than self-in-community. The Afro-American tradition has, however, always been steeped in context, assumed self-in-community (Levine, Genovese). Hazel Carby, for example, distinguishes the nineteenth-century Afro-American women's tradition in fiction from the Euro-American women's tradition on just these grounds: "But [Iola Leroy's] future was perceived as social, a transformed individual committed to a definition of self in relation to community" (75). *Iola Leroy* was, of course, long thought to be the first novel by an American black woman; *Sula*'s immersion in social context partakes of a long tradition. Morrison refuses to privilege the individual female in relation to any particular other. For female residents of the Bottom, the self exists in relation to the entire community; there is no alternative.

Abel's exclusive focus on the friendship makes invisible or uninteresting two major components of the novel: first, the interaction of male and female perspectives and, second, the social and economic influence on female identity. Relocating the critical focus from the dyad of a friendship to this social context reveals *Sula*'s exploration of the interaction between traditional male and female visions of sociality and hence of the self. It recognizes *Sula*'s challenges to current women-centered psychology limited by class and race: What happens when rigidly held social conventions, such as those characteristic of the middle class, determine the course of female psychological development? What happens to female psychological development when poverty and racism intervene in the process of mothering?

Nel and Sula's friendship forms part of an interchange between male and female versions of the community. A return to Chodorow's theory offers a means of analyzing *Sula*'s presentation of the traditional male vision of sociality. In her postulation of two very different gender-determined visions of the self, Chodorow concludes that "masculine personality . . . comes to be defined more in terms of denial of relation and connection . . . whereas feminine personality comes to include a fundamental definition of self in relationship" (169), a perception borne out in Gilligan's *In a Different Voice* and Jean Baker Miller's *Toward a New Psychology of Women*. Because boys must successfully separate from the mother, individuation becomes the overriding issue in the development of masculine identity, while connection and involvement with others are denied. Not surprisingly, then, male-centered developmental theories, such as those of Freud and Erikson, designate the achievement of separation as a prerequisite for intimate relationships.

    Sula's narrator clearly finds this separation inimical to personal fulfillment, but she depicts male sociality, as she does female sociality, in the total social context of the novel. An interpretation like Abel's decontextualizes the girls' friendship not only from the other women in the novel but from the men also. A holistic interpretation of gender must admit and analyze *Sula*'s interactive, transformative interchanges between male and female visions.

I.
The Male Vision of Community

    Women-centered psychologists cast doubt on the assertion "that separation leads to attachment and that individuation eventuates in mutuality" (Gilligan, *Different Voice* 155). The narrator's depiction of male characters in *Sula* shares their skepticism. In achieving identity through maintaining distance, the males experience a diminished capacity for intimacy and interdependence. Nel's father's occupation becomes a synecdoche for his position in the family—rarely at home, he's "a seaman." When their relationships become troubled, BoyBoy, Jude, and A. Jacks[1] leave Medallion. Such a need to distance themselves fits with Chodorow's assumption that "for boys, identification processes and masculine role learning are not likely to be embedded in relationship with their fathers or men but rather to involve the denial of affective relationship to their mothers" (177). In *Sula*, with the single exception of A. Jacks, men who do not physically remove themselves from their mothers or mother surrogates cannot maintain their identities. The Deweys' individual identities dissipate completely to merge into one, and they not only stop growing physically but remain boys in mind,

"mischievous, cunning, private and completely unhousebro-
ken" (73). Tar Baby and Plum "lose" themselves in alcohol and
heroin, respectively. In this women-centered portrayal, nearly
all men are impoverished in their ability to relate to others.
Separation "dislocates" men, dissipating the community; closeness suffocates them, dissipating the self. In contrast to other
male characters, Shadrack does participate in the community, albeit from a distance. Unlike his Biblical namesake, Shadrack
emerges from his inferno, WWI, neither personally nor socially
triumphant. He is alienated, "with no past, no language, no
tribe, no source, no address book . . ." (10). The community recognizes his distance by considering him crazy. A self, "a grave
black face" unconnected to anyone else, he alone of the male
characters "struggle[s] to order and focus experience" (12) and in
so doing stakes out "a place for fear" so that he can control it.
His ordering principle, National Suicide Day, becomes a recognized ritual in the community.

Though Shadrack's degree of alienation differentiates him
from the other characters, his thinking nevertheless shows two
traits which Gilligan considers central supports for the male
model of a completely independent and detachable self: an extreme respect for others' autonomy and an overarching abstraction as the basis for all moral action. Shadrack only once directly
interacts with another member of the community (with Sula, after Chicken Little's death). The annual National Suicide Day parade welcomes any participant but requires none; its form is
fixed whether it involves only Shadrack or half the town.
Shadrack thus lives a vision which requires nothing of others, a
position which links him to the men of Gilligan's study: "By
limiting interference, [men tend to] make life in community
safe, protecting autonomy through reciprocity, extending the
same consideration to others and self" (*Different Voice* 37-38). In
expressing fear through his ritual, Shadrack fulfills his responsibility to himself; by allowing others to participate, he extends it.
By remaining physically isolated, he cordons off aggression in
himself and limits any possible interference with his own or
others' autonomy. Shadrack thus sustains somewhat tenuous
connections rather than severing them, as BoyBoy and Jude do;
in absorbing this man and his bizarre insight, the Bottom co-
heres as a community.

This alienation perhaps of necessity makes Shadrack's
moral vision abstract. When Sula stumbles into his shack after

Chicken Little has drowned, Shadrack sees "the skull beneath" Sula's face—a truth which abstracts from the context of Chicken Little's death (with which Sula is preoccupied) to the human condition. Shadrack understands that the presence of death makes human connections fragile, ever-changing, dangerous, especially if one attempts to live in proximity to others. In this same scene the narrator sets the background for contrasting the morality of abstraction with the morality of social connection. Shadrack attempts to comfort Sula with a single word, "always"—without further context, a cryptic abstraction of maddeningly contradictory meanings. Sula, on the other hand, discovers Shadrack as an individual through an empathic response to his situation; unlike the rest of the town, she sees a neat, orderly, unthreatening person whom she dubs "Shad." Because she recognizes him as an individual, her visit leaves an impression on him. As women-centered psychologist Janet Surrey might explain, through Sula's presence, Shadrack recognizes his "need to be seen . . . for who [he] is and [his] need to see and understand the other with ongoing authenticity" (9). Shadrack treasures his only post-war experience of self-in-relationship.

Shadrack's impersonal truth transcends his social context until Sula's death, when the certainty of "always" crumbles and the narrator exposes the depth of his loneliness. Complete autonomy and its guardian abstract morality have been made bearable by the complementary experience of being "recognized and seen" by Sula. Deprived of the hope of continued relationship, Shadrack cannot maintain his role. In the canonical American novel, Shadrack's type of independence, with its concomitants of alienation and abstraction, has been privileged; its accompanying loneliness has in fact been valorized (Chase, Baym). In the usual pattern, Shadrack's moral vision and its development would dominate and Sula's would recede. The narrator of this women-centered novel, however, portrays Shadrack's world view in a reciprocal interchange with a female vision of moral connection.

II.
The Female Experience of Community

As Chodorow emphasized the source of different male and female conception of the self, Carol Gilligan has traced the processes of this gender development. Complemented by Stone Center research, Gilligan's paradigm offers an illuminating vocabulary for a beginning discussion of *Sula*'s female characters. At the same time, *Sula* delineates moral problems and paradoxes for which women-centered psychology has as yet no language, limited as it has been by its focus on the white middle class.

Working from interviews with women about moral dilemmas in their lives, Gilligan traces a distinctive development in the moral thinking of her female subjects quite different from that identified in dominant developmental theories based on studies of boys and men. Whereas the male models value individuality and abstract principles, such as "justice," which apparently safeguard it, the female voice emergent from these interviews speaks of the primacy of emotional connection and its preservation. Women's concern for this continuity leads them to exercise care in their interactions with others to make decisions not on the basis of abstractions but with regard to a particular context. Outside of psychology, discussions of "particular context" have frequently used different terminology, "community" being the most common. The centrality of this concern to Afro-American fiction is apparent from Susan Willis's remark on "the single most common feature in fiction by black women writers: that of return to the community" (116). In her discussion of selfhood in Paule Marshall's 1959 *Brown Girl, Brownstones*, Mary Helen Washington accents the contextual model and its implications for individual identity: "Selfhood is not defined negatively as separateness from others, nor is it defined narrowly by the individual dyad—the child and its mother—but on the larger scale as the ability to recognize one's continuity with the larger community" (159).

Women developing this ethic of care progress through three stages, Gilligan suggests, which are characterized by unique definitions of moral responsibility to others: first, an unsocialized selfishness; second, submersion in others; third, an authenticity in relationship. Self-centered and isolated, a woman in the first stage conceives of morality as imposed from without; in this unsocialized state, her primary concern is survival. In the second stage, she selflessly immerses herself in other people; defining morality by social conventions and traditional feminine goodness, she concerns herself with service. Selfishness is equated with immorality, with not "being good." In the third stage, a woman includes responsibilities to herself as well as to others, an inclusion which forms the basis for authentic emotional connections.

After Chodorow, most women-centered psychologists recognize the preeminent influence of the mother-daughter relationship, its quality an important determinant of the young girl's successful passage through Gilligan's stages of moral development. This primary relationship is widely recognized in feminist (or womanist, to use Alice Walker's term) writing and criticism (Christian, Walker and Rich). Several prominent Black women novelists have attributed their artistic successes to their mothers' and grandmothers' empowering influences (Washington). These real-life stories, of course, embody the extraordinary rather than the usual life. Gloria Wade-Gayles speaks movingly of black women's ambivalences in reading fiction about the mother-daughter relationship, indicating that they are

> often disappointed by the recurring image of the cold, distant and domineering mother. We want to see mothers embracing their daughters—loving them openly and unashamedly. We want to see mothers and daughters sharing laughter and bearing [sic] their souls to each other in moments of intimacy. And yet, we want the truths of our mothers' lives, even if those truths are sometimes 'cruel enough to stop the blood.' We must see them first as persons with dreams and needs no less important than ours, and then as mothers who sacrificed their dreams in order to put our hands on the pulse of freedom and self-hood.   (12)

Wade-Gayles's comment reiterates Chodorow's social concern: The social context of the mother-daughter relationship structures female personality and relational capabilities. Toni Morrison has consistently delineated the results of mother-daughter relationships damaged by racism and poverty. In *The Bluest Eye*, Pauline Breedlove psychically abandons her daughter Pecola, who goes mad; in *Song of Solomon*, First Corinthians becomes whole despite her mother; the heroine of *Tar Baby* is a deracinated orphan; in *Beloved*, Sethe's household is haunted by an unresolved mother-daughter relationship. *Sula* explores the mother-daughter experience in the Bottom's equivalent of the middle class, the Wrights' milieu, and in its poorest sector, the household of the young Eva Peace. Further, the novel's portrayal of the mother-daughter relationships is firmly contextualized in the larger society.

Women-centered psychological interpretations of female experience emphasize the web-like nature of women's social relationships. The connections represented in the web, interdependence and affiliation, are critical to the emergence of a secure sense of female self. As Gilligan notes, "The ideal of care is . . . an activity of relationship, of seeing and responding to need, taking care of the world by sustaining the web of connection so that no one is left alone" (*Different Voice* 62). Partially because male psychology and literature have denigrated women's caretaking roles as impositions on male autonomy (consider Sigmund Freud, Erik Erikson and James Thurber), women-centered psychology has tended to reclaim caretaking by focusing on its empowering, generative aspects. The dangers of a self-image based upon a morality of care, however, have not been extensively explored from within a women-centered framework. True, feminist literary critiques of caretaking have often focused on the degenerative aspects of this role for the women themselves, their stunted personal or artistic growth. This criticism, however, has generally been rounded on conceptions of the self more in line with the independent male model than the self-in-relationship.

The greatness of *Sula* lies partially in its commitment to the complexity of women's experience of caring. Exploring the degenerative and generative versions of female morality, *Sula* exposes the paradoxes of women's individual efforts to participate in the collective life. Predating Gilligan's work by eight years, Morrison's depiction of the Wright women's progression is almost a textbook illustration of Gilligan's critique of the second stage of women's moral development, degenerative goodness. *Sula* simultaneously shows the development of empathy possible within such financial security—a condition for eventual authentic selfhood—and the hibernation of the female self in the middle class.

Wrighteousness:
The Middle Class and Degenerative Goodness

Sula traces through the Wright women the complexities of the second stage of women's moral development. Taking on responsibility for others to the exclusion of the self, a woman with this perspective venerates the feminine conventions of self-sacrifice and martyrdom. As Gilligan states, "The woman at this point validates her claim to social membership through the adoption of societal values. Consensual judgment about good-ness becomes the overriding concern as survival is now seen to depend on acceptance by others" (*Different Voice* 79). The ten-sion between responsibility to others and responsibility to self, however, creates a feeling of duplicity in relationships, an "un-derground world" (53) where opinion and judgment are re-served. In reserving the self, the woman fails to develop her own adult voice. Without a reconciliation between femininity and adulthood, the conflict between self and other "cannot be re-solved. The 'good woman' masks assertion in evasion, denying responsibility by claiming only to meet the needs of others, while the 'bad woman' forgoes or renounces the commitments that bind her in self-deception and betrayal" (71). Women gen-erally cannot articulate these degenerative aspects of caring be-cause caring constitutes the whole social definition of their being good; they are psychically unable to forego social approval and to imagine alternatives which are "not good."

For most of *Sula*, the adult Nel Wright personifies the de-generate aspects of conventional female morality; her mother largely shapes this lengthy phase of Nel's development. Helene Wright epitomizes the immorality of conventional feminine "goodness." Her many social concerns are not genuine; rather, her unconscious aim is to control by "manipulating her daugh-ter and her husband" (16). When Helene smiles at the white conductor who has just insulted her integrity, Nel sees the "cus-tard" which social propriety masks. Helene represents the melt-down of the self that occurs when women unconsciously adhere to social convention. She is the spider "blind[ed] to the cobalt on [her] own back" (104), unaware of her own nature and capabili-ties. Helene fears her repressed self—for example, her "rage at the folded leaves she had endured" (23) after relieving herself during her train trip home. Her fear of the social truths of her past—her "much handled" mother, "who never said a word of greeting or affection" (23)—prevents her from developing a moral perspective. Acting from this fear, she stifles the threatening development of her daughter's self. Her insistence on clothespinning Nel's nose symbolizes her powerful need to channel her daughter's development in socially acceptable directions. Her ostensible attention to others' needs is motivated by her own need for social approval. This option of conforming through service is, however, available only to a woman with sufficient income. Eva, trapped with three hungry children and no money, must make a genuine sacrifice as opposed to Helene's bogus productions. Eva gives of herself, literally, to secure food for her children, while Helene feeds on her child. Middle-class status thus allows the development of patterns of caring, which, carried to an extreme, blind one to the authentic needs of the self. Poverty and racism, on the other hand, often prevent predictable social patterns from developing or recurring, as the Peace women's experiences demonstrate.

From her mother, Nel learns middle-class self-righteous immersion in others. From the time that she meets Jude Greene, Nel embodies the limitations and paradoxes of such immersion. As Gilligan makes clear, this goodness, ostensibly freely offered to others, is in fact a bargain: "Childlike in the vulnerability of their dependence and consequent fear of abandonment, they claim to wish only to please, but in return for their goodness they expect to be loved and cared for" (*Different Voice* 67). Nel's husband shows an awareness of this social contract, and his image of wifely subordination indicates one of its usually unspecified costs: "Whatever his fortune, whatever the cut of his garment, there would always be the hem—the tuck and fold that hid his raveling edges; a someone sweet, industrious and loyal to shore him up. And in return he would shelter her, love her, grow old with her" (*Sula* 71). The obliteration of the serving woman's personality becomes explicit in his complacent forecast: "The two of them together would make one Jude" (71). The marriage bargain breaks down, of course, when Nel discovers Sula and Jude having sex. After several years Nel confronts Sula with what she defines as Sula's betrayal, protesting, "'I was good to you, Sula, why don't that matter?'" (124). Sula's reply exposes the diseased motivation in Nel's reasoning: "'It matters, Nel, but only to you. . . . Being good to somebody is just like being mean to somebody. Risky. You don't get nothing for it'" (124-125). But the traditionally good woman expects something for all that she has given up.

Nel's concept of goodness damages her and those she serves. To ensure that her husband remains dependent on her goodness, that he needs her, Nel encourages his worst traits. Morrison's diction indicates her disgust with the male childishness and female manipulation engendered by this process:

> [Jude] told them a brief tale of some personal insult done him by a customer and his boss—a whiney tale that peaked somewhere between anger and a lapping desire for comfort. He ended it with the observation that a Negro man had a hard row to hoe in this world. He expected his story to dovetail into milkwarm commiseration, but before Nel could excrete it, Sula said that she didn't know about that—it looked like a pretty good life to her. (88-89)

Sula's humorous rejoinder that the whole world is obsessed with his privates makes Jude aware of a viewpoint other than his own and moves him toward self-recognition as Nel's coddling can never do.

When Nel discovers Sula and Jude on the floor of the bedroom, she approaches the acceptance of her own needs which characterizes moral maturity and authenticity:

> Hunched down in the small bright room Nel waited. Waited for the oldest cry. A scream not for others, not in sympathy for a burnt child, or a dead father, but a deeply personal cry for one's own pain. A loud, strident: 'Why me?' She waited. The mud shifted, the leaves stirred, the smell of overripe green things enveloped her and announced the beginnings of her own howl.
> But it did not come. (93)

Nel's inability to admit her needs and feelings takes a terrible toll. Deprived of her husband, Nel focuses on her children, and here too the narrator's judgment of traditional goodness is unsparing: "But it was a love that, like a pan of syrup kept too long on the stove, had cooked out, leaving only its odor and a hard, sweet sludge, impossible to scrape off" (142). Or, again, Nel's overwhelming intensity toward her children is "bear-love" (119). Destructive because of its dishonesty, this love enables Nel to evade her responsibilities toward understanding her own experience; consequently she preserves an immature and incomplete saintly self-image based on a denial of her real self.

Nel's submerged needs are embodied in a gray ball of fur floating just outside her field of vision, and "that was the terrible part, the effort it took not to look" (94). Repression devours Nel's energy, but Morrison's portrayal, while sympathetic, neither excuses nor evades Nel's motivation, which is cowardice: "It was so nice to think about their [her children's] scary dreams and not about a ball of fur. . . . It just floated there for the seeing, if she wanted to. . . . But she didn't want to see it, ever, for if she saw it, who could tell but what she might actually touch it, or want to, and then what would happen . . ." (94). The hair ball represents an extreme of the repression which Nel has practiced all her life to preserve a self-image of goodness which has a nasty flavor of complacency. Sula challenges this assumption with her deathbed statement, "'About who was good. How you know it was you? . . . I mean maybe it wasn't you. Maybe it was me'" (126). At this point, self-deluded by a "vision of an innocence attained by the denial of self" (Gilligan, *Different Voice* 145), Nel cannot admit that Sula's point has any validity; preoccupied with her own goodness in overcoming selfish resentment of the betrayal, Nel glories in being the only woman in town willing to visit the dying Sula.

Eva's much later reiteration of the same idea forces Nel to a self-recognition because Eva includes specific details which Nel cannot refute. Again enveloped in a glow of self-approval, Nel visits Eva in the nursing home as an act of charity. Instead of conforming to the social conventions of being grateful for Nel's sacrifice, Eva rudely demands, "'Tell me how you killed that little boy'" (144) and refuses to accept Nel's disclaimer with "'You. Sula. What's the difference? You was there. You watched, didn't you? Me, I never would've watched'" (145). Eva identifies the same image of passivity characteristic of the second-stage women of Gilligan's studies, women "drawn unthinkingly . . . by the appeal of avoiding responsibility by sinking [like Nel] into an 'ice age of inactivity'" (143).

Eva jolts Nel into remembering that she did in fact watch as opposed to merely seeing; that is, she did in some way enjoy the excitement of the event: "All these years she had been secretly proud of her calm, controlled behavior when Sula was uncontrollable. . . . Now it seemed that what she had thought was maturity, serenity and compassion was only the tranquillity that follows a joyful stimulation" (146). Immediately after this recognition, she becomes very angry with Eva, considering her a bad woman, mean and spiteful. Her self-image has been shaken, however, and revisiting Sula's grave provides the psychic impetus necessary to her self-recognition and acceptance:

> Leaves stirred; mud shifted; there was the smell of overripe green things. A soft ball of fur broke and scattered like dandelion spores in the breeze. 'All that time, all that time, I thought I was missing Jude.' And the loss pressed down on her chest and came up into her throat. 'We was girls together,' she said as though explaining something. 'O Lord, Sula,' she cried, 'girl, girl, girlgirlgirl.'   (149)

In this scene, the last of the novel, Nel abandons the conventional fiction of her supreme attachment to her husband to mourn her greater losses, Sula's friendship and Sula herself. No longer oversimplifying her experience and denying her feelings and her own needs. Nel has the potential to attain moral maturity and enjoy authentic relations with others.

Nel breaks out of the conventional vision of goodness, which, in its preoccupation with propriety, fails to nurture truthfulness necessary to relationships that clarify the self. Nel's socialization, however, does teach her to empathize with others so that she can serve them. Her capacity for empathy extends to situations that fit conventional social dictates—an older woman in a nursing home, children, a sick friend. Her empathy reaches its limit when another's actions are unconventional—a friend sleeping with her husband.   Nel's early friendship with Sula provided her with an alternative vision of the good which, in Sula's absence, she could not sustain on her own—until the end. The models of women-centered psychology can comfortably accommodate the Wright women; the Peace women, however, in their experiences of poverty, challenge the presumed universality of the self-in-relation model, as Sula insists on an expansion to self-in-community.

The Peace Women:
Necessary Experimentation

As with Nel, Sula's relationship with her mother psychically structures her conception of morality and self. In the Peace household three generations of mother-daughter relationships work out their responsibilities to themselves and others in nontraditional terms. Because these women are largely indifferent to social convention, they can articulate an honest self-in-relation which avows responsibility for action; such honesty promotes mutuality that eventuates in self-knowledge, knowledge necessary to achieve the authenticity of Gilligan's final stage. In taking responsibility for their actions, however, the Peace women struggle with developing emotional connections to other people and to each other. They tell social truths that cut through illusory, fragile, or superficial   connections; these truths force redefinition of the self-in-relationship, as with the mothers who suddenly parent their children in Sula's presence. But in this process the Peace women fail to develop empathy, a capability necessary to harness truth with care.

Unlike the middle-class Helene Wright, Eva does not turn to custard in order to survive, but maintains an integrated self-in-relation with other people. In the poverty which constructs her reality, the survival of Eva's children is constantly threatened, and her emotional connections with them are thus frequently heightened (hence the fiery nature of her relationships). Paradoxically, in order to deal practically with this threat, Eva must distance herself (hence the ice imagery which also characterizes her). In order to feed her children after Boy Boy's desertion, for example, Eva leaves town for eighteen months. This physical separation is sign and symbol of an analogous emotional distance, for Hannah asks at one point, "'Mamma, did you ever love us?'" (58). In indignant reply, Eva demands to know if she "'was supposed to play rang-around-the-rosie'" while her daughter was "'shittin' worms'" (60). To Eva, the knowledge that she made herself live in order that they might live should suffice without softer manifestations of love. Eva bequeaths to Hannah, and Hannah in turn bequeaths to Sula, a capacity for emotional distance which allows for the creation of a female self. Through Eva, Morrison delineates the paradoxes of a morality of care when self and relations are threatened by social and economic annihilation.

For much of her life Eva embodies and evangelically promotes conventional service to others. Thus, she sacrifices her leg for insurance money to feed her children and throws herself out a window in a vain attempt to smother the flames killing her daughter Hannah. Eva's efforts extend from her immediate family to the larger community. Indeed, Eva's house becomes a kind of extended family when she takes on the matriarchal role of demanding that the young married women rooming there prepare timely suppers for their husbands and otherwise pay attention to conventional niceties. The house becomes a kind of social center for men, who leave intellectually and emotionally refreshed. Further, Eva takes in homeless waifs. In all these ways she becomes a connective force in the community, her traditional goodness a generative force for those around her.

The models of women-centered psychology do not yet include this expanded caretaking which does not erode the caring self. The Stone Center researchers do, however, suggest an explanation for the fate of three of the waifs. Three boys of disparate ages, races, and temperaments under Eva's tutelage gradually merge into one entity. Seeing them in her house for the first time, when their differences are still evident, Eva names each one Dewey. Questioned about how others will be able to tell them apart, Eva answers, "'What you need to tell them apart for? They's all deweys'" (32). This chilling obliteration of individuality permanently stunts the boys: Not only do they become physically indistinguishable, they stop growing at 48 inches and never learn toilet training. Like Sula's later attempt to manipulate A. Jacks, Eva's mangling of the Deweys grotesquely parodies Nel's "good" treatment of Jude. This suffocation of individuality through a conventional maternal morality reinforces male fears of intimacy. Eva's care of the waifs, lacking an understanding of their individuality, lacks empathy, a crucial element in completing the process of female development.

Women psychologists at the Stone Center have just begun to elucidate the role of empathy in the morality of care. In working out a psychology of women, they assume that the self develops "in relation" with other people, that psychological growth occurs by "participating in and fostering the development of others" (Miller, "The Development" 13). In these researchers' view, "Relationship implies a sense of knowing oneself and others through a process of mutual relational interaction and continuity of 'emotional-cognitive dialogue' over time and space" (Surrey 10). Mutuality and reciprocity in relations lead to an unfolding of intersubjective worlds in which the self is seen and clarified; in a sense, there is no self apart from relationship.

Critical in the development of the relational self is the capacity for empathy, "the central organizing concept in women's relational experience" (Surrey 2). In "Empathic Communication," Alexandra Kaplan identifies two dimensions in accurate empathic responses, the cognitive and the affective. Affectively the empathic experience is one of interconnection, "an interpenetration of feeling" (14). Once one has perceived affective cues in the other, one "surrenders to affective arousal in oneself—as if the perceived affective cues were one's own" (Jordan, "Empathy" 3). The cognitive part of empathy recognizes that the self is separate from the other and from what has happened in the momentary identification. Both dimensions must coexist if "a genuine sense of understanding and being understood" (Jordan, "Empathy" 3) is to occur. The one experiencing empathy has her experience validated by the affective response from the other yet feels her differences accepted. As Jordan states, "Growth occurs because as I stretch to match or understand your experience, something new is acknowledged or grows in me" ("The Meaning" 7). But Eva's lack of empathy does not allow for growth or change.

Unlike Helene and Nel Wright, however, Eva maintains a self in her relations with others. Her autonomy and her independence of others' judgments rest on ability to perceive and admit truth about herself and her relations. Her morality, then, extends beyond conventional definitions of self-sacrifice. Remaining within the network of her family, friends, and community, she takes responsibility for her choices, a critical component of a morally mature vision: "To be responsible for oneself, it is first necessary to acknowledge what one is doing. The criterion for judgment thus shifts from goodness to truth when the morality of action is assessed not on the basis of its appearance in the eyes of others, but in terms of the realities of its intention and consequence" (Gilligan, *Different Voice* 83). Eva alone, of all the female characters, demonstrates this commitment to a sometimes very painful truth. Unlike Shadrack, who distances himself on the basis of his knowledge, she both weaves the filaments of the communal web and lives among them.

This truthful dimension of Eva's morality appears most strikingly when she discusses her decision to kill her drug addict son Plum. Eva's shocking action has, in the absence of critical analysis of the psychology of caretaking, given rise to some odd interpretations. Philip Royster refers to "Eva's *fantasy* that her son, Plum, an alcoholic [*sic*] veteran of World War I, wanted to return to her womb" (161-162, emphasis added), while Barbara Christian calls Eva's homicide "presumptuous" and opines that Eva has recurrent dreams of incest with Plum (160). Critics have by and large simply ignored Eva's own rationale (for exceptions, see Faith Pullin and Elizabeth Ordonez). This rationale refuses to temporize about Plum's degeneration, a threat both to Eva's individual self and to the community of the household:

> 'There wasn't space for him in my womb. And he was crawlin' back. Being helpless and thinking baby thoughts and dreaming baby dreams and messing up his pants again and smiling all the time. I had room enough in my heart, but not in my womb, got no more. I birthed him once. I couldn't do it again . . . and he'd be creepin' to the bed trying to spread my legs trying to get back up in my womb.'   62)

Eva's language hardly expresses sexual desire, nor does the metaphor of returning to the passivity of the developing fetus seem fantastic when applied to the parasitic junkie. (Plum has regressed completely; almost entirely passive, he becomes active only to steal from everyone in the house.) At his bedside, Eva identifies the contents in a soda bottle as blood and water—a birth image connected, of course, with Plum's attempted re-entry. Eva claims that her own needs must be primary, that she cannot again take on the all-sustaining maternal role which she has already performed for Plum. Eva's refusal to accept an adult baby is reminiscent of Edna Pontellier's less articulate summation in Kate Chopin's *The Awakening* that she would give up her life for her children but not her self. Eva's consideration of her own needs as well as Plum's indicates that at this point her connections are authentic, based on a solid self rather than the need to serve.

    The critical disapproval of Eva's perception of Plum stems, we believe, not only from her action but from the critics' discomfort with the notion that extreme circumstances warrant extreme reactions to defend the individual self—Malcolm X's "any means necessary"—when that self is female. Although Eva's actions in sacrificing her leg for insurance money and throwing herself out a window in a vain attempt to save Hannah are as violent as her murder of Plum, they do not occasion the same attacks because they defend *others*, Eva's children rather than Eva herself. The critics imply that Eva's action arises from thinking characteristic of Gilligan's first stage, where all attention is focused on individual survival and amoral perception makes external punishment the only brake on behavior. Eva mourns Plum, however, before she burns him, grieving that her child's personality has died. Her consideration and her decision simply do not seem the act of a panicked and selfish individual lightly denying another's rights. Crucially, when Hannah asks why she has killed Plum, Eva does not lie. Unlike Nel, Eva forces herself to recognize the truth of her own needs, to act on them, and to communicate the truth when asked.

Of the three Peace women, Eva has the most capacity for authenticity in caretaking. The extremity of her early life as a caregiver forced her to recognize her own as well as others' needs. She neither leaves the community permanently nor compromises herself in her relation with others. In large measure she dictates the terms of social life in the community for young married couples, the Deweys, and the men who come to court her. Only Sula is sufficiently independent to rebuff her prescriptions. When Eva asks Sula about plans to marry and have children, Sula replies, "'I don't want to make somebody else. I want to make myself.'" Eva inveighs with the verdict used against women who do not conform: "'Selfish. Ain't no woman got no business floatin' around without no man.'" Ironically, as Sula points out to her, "You did" (80). And in fact Eva has, like her daughter Hannah and now her granddaughter, made herself without depending on others, but at the expense of supportive emotional connections that allow for the expression of a full range of intersubjective experiences.

Whereas Nel must distance herself from her mother's dominance and shallow social vision to gain her identity, the Peace daughters must find some way to connect with each other, to close distances between them that vary with the generations and have variant effects. Although Hannah is not a fully developed character, the reader notices a continuity between Eva and her daughter—after her husband Rekus's death, Hannah eschews a definite commitment to any one man. She does, however, move back into Eva's house "to take care of it and her mother forever" (35), precisely the commitment which Sula refuses both when her mother burns and when she sends Eva to the nursing home. This difference may reflect Hannah's and Sula's divergent experiences with their mothers. Hannah may have been in doubt about Eva's feelings for her, but Sula learns early the true state of her mother's affections, having overheard Hannah say that she loves her but cannot like her. This rejection unfits her for conventional female morality, which assumes that care irrevocably connects individuals through empathic understanding. The distance between Peace mothers and daughters in *Sula*, then, allows the daughters considerable freedom in creating a self, but it restricts the daughters' capacities for emotional nurturing, empathy, and connection.

A true ethic of care, in women-centered psychology and moral development, requires reciprocity between the person cared for and the person who cares. Eva rarely experiences being cared for, i.e., being interdependent; generally, she performs the caring activities, i.e., is depended upon. As she withdraws more and more, her daughter and granddaughter learn few caretaking skills. The clumsiness of the untrained caretaking impulse is noticeable in one of the few links between Eva and Sula: As Eva sacrifices her leg to feed her children, so Sula slashes her finger to protect Nel, but Eva's desperate solution is appropriate to desperate circumstances while Sula's is wildly disproportionate to the threat—ordinary means are simply not part of Sula's vocabulary because she has not experienced traditional care. Unlike Nel, who has inherited from her mother what Gilligan terms "the conventional feminine voice" (*Different Voice* 79), Sula has inherited an unconventional feminine voice for which there is no consistent, understanding audience. As a result of growing up in Eva's chaotic household where she is "never scolded or [given] directions," Sula "could hardly be counted on to sustain any emotion for more than three minutes" (45). Sula will thus have difficulty in sustaining connections, a difficulty foreshadowed when Chicken Little, having "slipped from her hands" (52), drowns. This inability to experience connection is most obvious in Sula's experience of sex, which she pursues in order to feel most intensely her loneliness and isolation. Although free, Sula lacks nurturance and the training to care for others, experiences which could give her freedom connected meaning. Morrison clearly identifies the two most formative events for Sula as hearing Hannah's avowal of dislike for her and losing Chicken Little's grip: "The first experience taught her there was no other that you could count on; the second that there was no self to count on either" (103). Sula thus lacks both the terms necessary to any ethic of service; without either a coherent self or a consistent other, the exchange of caring cannot exist. Sula's moral voice develops out of a shock of recognition of her separateness from others. Unlike Nel, who cannot differentiate sufficiently (first from her mother and later from her children), Sula experiences fortified boundaries, both with her mother and with the community as a whole. Thus the intersubjective worlds of other women do not unfold for Sula, except, of course, briefly during her relationship with A. Jacks and more continuously in her adolescent relation with Nel.

Women-centered psychology has discovered the importance of empathy and described the process of its growth; its next task is to confront the effects of poverty and racism on caretaking and its necessary precursor, empathy. Morrison's social vision does not, however, show poor women as crushed, with nothing to offer, even if they are not empathic. In fact, partially because poverty has forced social experimentation and made conventional falsities impossible, poor women may provide middle-class women (and researchers) with impetus toward self-recognition. Their unconventional voices do not, in Morrison's view, become masculine: Unlike BoyBoy and Jude, Eva returns for her children; unlike Shadrack, Sula returns to Nel. The unconventional female voice remains essentially female—and essential.

III.
Nel and Sula:
Mutually Creative Selves-in-Relation

The friendship between Sula and Nel in many ways nurtures both girls by supplying the lacks in their mother-daughter relationships. Nel, for example, finds support for her nascent separation from her mother: Basking in Sula's approval, she stops using the clothespin which her mother hopes will reshape her "too-broad" nose. Sula, on the other hand, finds companionship to replace the distance in her family; Nel sees her fully. The attachment to Nel prevents Sula from operating totally out of unsocialized selfishness, Gilligan's first stage. Without Nel, she would be, to use Gilligan's terms, "constrained by a lack of power that stems from feeling disconnected and thus, in effect, all alone" (*Different Voice* 75). Although Sula considers Nel and herself identical, Nel is at crucial moments aware of their boundaries. When Sula sacrifices the top of her finger to scare off hoodlums frightening the two girls, Nel notices as they walk away that Sula's face is "miles and miles away" (47).

In their childhood friendship, Nel's and Sula's antithetical strengths and weaknesses assure them mutual dependency and thus equality of participation. Sula's preservation of her self allows Nel to limn boundaries between herself and her mother; in turn, Nel's attention to details of connection and her calm consistency allow Sula's rigid boundaries to become more fluid, as when they work together digging holes in the earth or when Sula empathically discovers "Shad." In describing the relationship, the narrator points to the development of individuality necessary to any moral maturity: "In the safe harbor of each other's company they could afford to abandon the ways of other people and concentrate on their own perceptions of things" (47). After identifying with each other in the areas they define as fundamental (Abel), they, nevertheless, complement each other in a way which anticipates the possibility of a mature moral vision; both Sula's freedom of self-expression and Nel's consistent regard for others are necessities for authenticity. Their friendship empowers them until the end of their adolescence, when caretaking must be extended to the adult world of love and work.

This marvelous friendship does not exist in a social vacuum, however, and just as the girls' images of themselves are modified by the surrounding society, so is the course of the friendship. Although Sula and Nel value each other highly, they realize that their valuations are eccentric—they know that they are not white or male, the social elites. As the surrounding society beam in, they internalize social contempt. While buying ice cream, they are deemed "pig meat" (43), a phrase replete with the ambiguous compliments of a sexist society. Afterwards, they dig circular holes with sticks, enlarge the holes so that they join in a larger circle, and then fill the entire "grave" with trash (50). The scene shows clearly their subconscious recognition of their femininity in their construction of the yonic symbols and their conception of themselves as one (either defined by gender or joined sexually—for an interpretation of *Sula* as a lesbian novel, see Barbara Smith). Unfortunately, they cannot rejoice in this unity; their actions recreate the social trashing of their female identity. The surrounding society impinges on the friendship in another way. Nel's conventional response to Jude causes her first lasting divergence from Sula, who has not been trained in the usual ways of keeping a man. In a heterosexual society, Nel is expected to refocus her commitments from her female friend to her husband, an expectation so strong that Nel thinks for years that she has done so.

The primary force that raptures the friendship is not the direct impact of the surrounding society, however, but Nel's and Sula's conflicting modes of moral perception. The confrontation occurs in a particularly damaging way because neither woman is aware even of potential divergence. Nel thinks that talking with Sula has always been like talking to herself (82), while Sula thinks of "Nel as the closest thing to both an other and a self" (103). In Sula's ten-year absence, Nel has developed into the very conventional feminine voice "proclaiming its worth on the basis of the ability to care for and protect others" (Gilligan, *Different Voice* 79) for which her family has trained her. Sula, in contrast, has learned to take care of only herself and to take responsibility for her actions. Working from this conceptual framework of independence, Sula objectively evaluates degenerative goodness in a critique resembling Gilligan's description of women in the second stage of moral development. Although Sula has not learned conventional caretaking behaviors, she has "scrutinize[d] the logic of self-sacrifice in the service of a morality of care" (Gilligan, *Different Voice* 82), a capacity critical to authenticity, in which "the morality of action is assessed not on the basis of its appearance in the eyes of others, but in terms of the realities of its intention and consequence" (83). Sula's lack of interest in social appearance unfits her for social conversation "because she could not lie" (*Sula* 105). Significantly, among the lies that she cannot tell are those denying the costs of women's self-sacrifice in their service to husbands and children (105).

Some truths also escape her, notably, the possibility of authentic connections in which neither individual is forced to mirror the other. Thus, Sula cannot conceive of the possibility of hurting Nel if Sula herself is pleased, and she has sex with Jude with no idea of the likely consequences to her friendship with Nel. Nel, on the other hand, sacrifices her real feelings for those socially expected and earns Sula's disgust for her dishonesty. As Gilligan notes of the two modes of self-definition, "These divergent constructions of identity, in self-expression or

in self-sacrifice, create different problems for further development—the former a problem of human connection, and the latter a problem of truth" (*Different Voice* 157). Nel joins with the
community to view Sula as a "pariah" (105), a "selfish" woman
who has only her own interest at heart. Sula, for her part, judges
Nel as "one of *them*. One of the spiders whose only thought was
the next rung of the web. . . . It had surprised her a little and
saddened her a good deal when Nel behaved the way the others
would have" (103-104). Exposing both modes of perception to
the scathing critique of the other, Morrison refuses to sentimen-
talize or deny their inherent limitations: Both necessary to authenticity, they remain in their isolated states, destructive to
both themselves and their community.

Nel's rejection of Sula is a microcosm of the community's
rejection, for the Bottom's judgment of a woman living an experimental life is severe. Sula's functions as scapegoat (Royster)
and as negative definition for the community (Christian, Ogunyemi, Pullin) have often been the subject of critical commentary.
The quality of life in the community improves when Sula becomes the embodiment of a threatening evil and individuals
unite to defend themselves. The community might, however,
have adopted another means of incorporating Sula, that of listening to her insights. Instead, Sula's actions speak louder than
her words; that is, the community reacts to its definition of her
actions while her voice, speaking its radical re-definition of her
own acts and those of others, remains inaudible. As Nel reflects
in remembering Sula's effects, Sula "simply helped others define
themselves" (82).

The community cannot listen to Sula because she does
not care for it, either literally or figuratively. Sula's general failure to develop empathy—temporarily accepting another's perspective as one's own—leaves her moral vision incomplete and
inaccessible to the community. Remaining incapable of em-
pathizing with real individuals (the trapped Nel, the aged and ill
Eva, Hannah on fire), Sula weeps instead "for the deaths of the
littlest things" (106), like children's cast-off shoes and wedding
rings in pawn shops, sentimental representations unconnected
to known individuals.

Empathy by itself, of course, does not guarantee the integrity of a moral system or its use to the community. Without
reciprocity, it becomes a tool of pity or venom. As Nel's degenerative goodness clearly indicates, empathy may be used to bind

another in dependency. In one of her few empathic moments, during her relationship with A. Jacks, Sula feels "flooded with an awareness of the impact of the outside world on Ajax" (115). Instead of using this insight to understand his subjective truth, though, Sula says the fatal "'Lean on me'" (115). When A. Jacks bolts from this blatant attempt to violate his independence and make him into another Jude, Sula recognizes her own failure, as Nel never does: "'I did not hold my head stiff enough when I met him and so I lost it just like the dolls'" (117). Earlier Sula muses on women's difficulties with emotional boundaries while making love with A. Jacks: *"I will water your soil, keep it rich and moist. But how much? How much water to keep the loam moist? And how much loam will I need to keep my water still? And when do the two make mud?"* (113). Caring or others, whether individually or communally, requires a giving of one's self and "selfless" effort to experience with the other, yet these very acts can both entrap the self in the "restriction [they] impose on direct expression" (Gilligan, *Different Voice* 79) and exploitatively convert the vulnerability of another into dependency. Moral authenticity requires both truth and empathy. Without truth, degenerative goodness coopts empathy in the service of control. Without empathy, truth destroys the possibility for connection.

Morrison's exploration of the female voice struggling toward maturity and authenticity climaxes in Sula and Nel's discussion at Sula's deathbed. There they confront the limitations of their respective moral visions. Frightened by Sula's detachment, even in the face of death, Nel is unable to hear Sula's truth; irritated by Nel's self-sacrifice in the name of conventional goodness, Sula fails to appreciate Nel's pain. In their final actions, Sula and Nel openly and reciprocally care for the other in a recognition of interdependence: *After* Sula dies, her first thought is to tell Nel of the experience; years after Sula's death, Nel feels her presence and makes a crucial step toward authenticity. The emotional connections between Sula and Nel transcend the hostility of their immediate society and the vagaries of their conflicting moral perceptions. Death cannot sever the only genuine emotional connection which Sula experiences, nor can it obliterate the influence which moves Nel toward authentic emotional and moral maturity.

IV.
Collaborative Conclusions:
Toward Selves-in-Community

In *Sula* the moral work of the women caretakers—work ignored or devalued by the male world—sustains both personal and community identity. Yet as the tunnel scene suggests, none of the conventional caretaking has prevented damage to individuals or ultimately obliteration of the Bottom community. Unlike Sula, Nel, and Shadrack, many in the Bottom hoped for someone else to save them from the grips of racism and poverty. (For discussion of this passivity, see Lounsberry and Hovet.) Thus, conventional caretaking encouraged passivity rather than mature activity: Hoping for abatement of their pent-up anger, the townsfolk crawl into the tunnel-womb, and like Plum in his desire to retreat to the safety of total dependency, they suffocate. However, Nel's final synthesis of the two necessary constituents of authentic selfhood, empathic caring and self-assertion, argues for actual individual growth and potential interdependence among members of a community. Morrison hopes to create a different community, one composed of the readers of her novels ("Rootedness" 341). Thus, the exchanges between women-centered psychologists, minority women writers, and readers of both might constitute the speech of a new community.

Significantly, this community is not solely female. *Sula* shows damage done to both male and female characters: the isolated Shadrack and Jude, the conglomerated Deweys, the melted Helene, the lonely Sula. Furthermore, A. Jacks and Nel, the only two successfully integrated personalities, represent both genders. The end of the novel, often read solely as Nel's recognition of her bond with Sula, in fact also shows a continuing dialogue between male and female points of view: Just before Nel's recognition, she passes Shadrack (the male who reminds her of Sula); just before she articulates her insight, she smells "overripe green things," surely a reference to Jude Greene. Female bonds do not exist in isolation but in a community which necessarily includes men.

Both the community within the book and the community of readers outside the book communicate in an erratic and flawed manner, of course—witness the broken relationships of the novel, on the one hand, and the gap between women-centered models of middle-class white female development and

Eva's experiences, on the other. Morrison demonstrates how much she values these attempts at communication, however, by contrasting the imperfect community of the Bottom with its replacement, the archetypal symbol of white suburbia—the golf course. Nel recognizes the loss when she thinks, "Maybe it hadn't been a community, but it had been a place. Now there weren't any places left, just separate houses with separate televisions and separate telephones and less and less dropping by" (143). This separation has resulted from the monologue of the controlling voice in the Western social context, a male definition of sociality in search of abstract principles to guarantee individual autonomy and freedom. Morrison suggests that dialogue with the female perspectives of self-in-relation and self-in-community will both empower women and offer a chance for stronger communities. The dialogue between women writers and women psychologists, therefore, not only elaborates theoretical moral perspectives for women's experiences, but also takes on particular urgency in a society operating largely on abstraction, separation, and detachment.

Note

[1] In a crucial scene, Sula discovers from his driver's license that the man whose name she has always heard as "Ajax" is in fact named "A. Jacks." The novel offers some justification for literary critics' unanimous choice to use "Ajax"—"Ajax" occurs not only in Sula's consciousness but once in the narrator's usage *after* Sula's death (page 139 lists among the victims of the tunnel disaster "some of Ajax's younger brothers"). Morrison often depicts the interaction of myth with quotidian reality, and in *The Bluest Eye* the myth is specifically Greek. The mythological implications of "Ajax," however, seem a poor fit with this character, who does not resemble either of the *Iliad*'s two Ajaxes. Barring the discovery of another Ajax to offer enriching characterization, then, the critics' preference for "Ajax" ignores Sula's discovery.

On the large scale, this usage obscures Morrison's exploration of ambiguities in language; on the smaller, it devalues Sula's self-examination and screens Morrison's connection of Eva and Sula. Morrison begins here a concern which figures more prominently in her next novel, *Song of Solomon* (the double meanings of "You can't just fly off and leave a body" and "Sing"). The whole incident offers a fascinating opportunity for discussing the complex interactions of oral and print traditions: Sula accepts a printed document's correction of her oral understanding of her lover's name, but that oral understanding was based on the printed version of an originally oral epic poem.

Within the context of *Sula*'s characterization, "A. Jacks" underlines the limitations of both Sula's and Eva's characters. Contemplating why she has lost her connection with Albert Jacks, Sula considers her misidentification of his name as emblematic of her inability to know and respect his true self. As this essay argues later, Eva's misnaming of the Deweys indicates a similar failing, her inability to perceive and value their separate selves.

Works Cited

Abel, Elizabeth. "(E)Merging Identities: The Dynamics of Female Friendship in Contemporary Fiction by Women." *Signs* 6.3 (1981): 413-435.

Bayre, Nina. "Melodramas of Beset Manhood: How Theories of American Fiction Exclude Women Authors." *The New Feminist Criticism.* Ed. Elaine Showalter. New York: Pantheon, 1985. 63-80.

Carby, Hazel. *Reconstructing Womanhood.* New York: Oxford University Press, 1987.

Chase, Richard. *The American Novel and Its Tradition.* Garden City: Anchor, 1957.

Chodorow, Nancy. "Family Structure and Feminine Personality." *Woman, Culture, and Society.* Ed. M. Z. Rosaldo and L. Lamphere. Stanford: Stanford University Press, 1974. 43-68.

—. *The Reproduction of Mothering: Psychoanalysis and the Sociology of Gender.* Berkeley: University of California Press, 1978.

Christian, Barbara. *Black Women Novelists: The Development of a Tradition.* Westport: Greenwood, 1980.

Gardiner, Judith Kegan. "The (US)es of (I)dentity: A Response of Abel on '(E}Merging Identities.'" *Signs* 6.3 (1981): 436-442.

Genovese, Eugene. *Roll, Jordan, Roll.* 1974. New York: Vintage-Random, 1976.

Gilligan, Carol. *In a Different Voice: Psychological Theory and Women's Moral Development.* Cambridge: Harvard University Press, 1982.

—. "Moral Orientation and Moral Development." *Women and Moral Theory.* Ed. Eva Feder Kittay and Diana T. Meyers. Totowa: Rowman, 1987. 19-33.

Homans, Margaret. "Her Very Own Howl: The Ambiguities of Representation in Recent Women's Fiction." *Signs* 9.2 (1983): 186-205.

Jordan, Judith. "Empathy and the Mother-Daughter Relationship." *Women and Empathy: Implications for Psychological Development and Psychotherapy.* Ed. Jacquelyn H. Hall. Works in Progress 82-02. Wellesley: Stone Center for Developmental Services and Studies, 1983. 2-5.

—. "The Meaning of Mutuality." Works in Progress 23. Wellesley: Stone Center for Developmental Services and Studies, 1986.

Kaplan, Alexandra. "Empathic Communication in the Psychotherapy Relationship." *Women and Empathy: Implications for Psychological Development and Psychotherapy.* Ed. Jacquelyn H. Hall. Works in Progress 83-02. Wellesley: Stone Center for Developmental Services and Studies, 1983. 12-16.

Lerner, Harriet G. *Women in Therapy.* Northvale: Aronson, 1988.

Levine, Lawrence. *Black Culture and Black Consciousness.* Oxford: Oxford University Press, 1977.

Lounsberry, Barbara and Grace Ann Hovet. "Principles of Perception in Toni Morrison's *Sula*." *Black American Literature Forum* 13 (1979): 126-129.

Miller, Jean Baker. "The Development of Women's Sense of Self." Works in Progress 12. Wellesley: Stone Center for Developmental Services and Studies, 1984.

—. *Toward a New Psychology of Women*. Boston: Beacon, 1976.

—. "What Do We Mean by Relationships?" Works in Progress 22. Wellesley: Stone Center for Developmental Services and Studies, 1986.

Morrison, Toni. *Sula*. 1973. New York: Bantam, 1974.

—. "Rootedness: The Ancestor as Foundation." Black Women Writers (1950-1980). Ed. Mari Evans. Garden City: Anchor, 1984. 339-345.

Ogunyemi, Chikwenye Okonjo. "*Sula*: 'A Nigger Joke.'" *Black American Literature Forum* 13 (1979): 130-133.

Ordonez, Elizabeth J. "Narrative Texts for Ethnic Women: Rereading the Past, Reshaping the Future." *MELUS* 9.3 (1983): 19-28.

Pullin, Faith. "Landscapes of Reality: The Fiction of Contemporary Afro-American Women." *Black Fiction: New Studies in the Afro-American Novel Since 1945*. Ed. A. Robert Lee. New York: Barnes, 1980. 173-203.

Rich, Adrienne. *Of Woman Born*. New York: Norton, 1978.

Royster, Philip M. "A Priest and a Witch against the Spiders and the Snakes: Scapegoating in Toni Morrison's *Sula*." *Omoja* 2 (1978): 149-168.

Smith, Barbara. "Toward a Black Feminist Criticism." *The New Feminist Criticism*. Ed. Elaine Showalter. New York: Pantheon, 1985. 168-185.

Surrey, Janet. "Self in Relation: A Theory of Women's Development." Works in Progress 13. Wellesley: Stone Center for Developmental Services and Studies, 1985.

Wade-Gayles, Gloria. "The Truths of Our Mothers' Lives: Mother-Daughter Relationships in Black Women's Fiction." *Sage* 1.2 (1984): 8-12.

Walker, Alice. "In Search of Our Mothers' Gardens." *In Search of Our Mothers' Gardens*. New York: Harcourt, 1983. 231-243.

Washington, Mary Helen. "'I Sign My Mother's Name': Alice Walker, Dorothy West, Paule Marshall." *Mothering the Mind: Twelve Studies of Writers and Their Silent Partners*. Ed. Ruth Perry and Martine Watson Brownley. New York: Holmes, 1984. 142-163.

Willis, Susan. *Specifying*. Madison: University of Wisconsin Press, 1987.

Wyatt, Jean. "Avoiding Self-Definition: In Defense of Women's Right to Merge (Julia Kristeva and *Mrs. Dalloway*)." *Women's Studies* 13 (1986): 115-126.

Toni Morrison's *Sula*:
A Black Woman's Epic

Karen F. Stein

In Toni Morrison's novels of black American life, appearance and reality, the magical and the real, the tragic and the comic are continually juxtaposed. Irony operates on many levels, as the hopes and plans of Morrison's characters are frustrated by their white neighbors and by fate.[1] The author plays with a variety of viewpoints as whites and blacks, husbands and wives, parents and children observe and misunderstand each other.[2]

Perhaps Morrison's multi-layered vision has been shaped by her complex relationship to literary traditions: As a black woman author, she is a double outsider in our patriarchal, white culture—a position which allows her to criticize both the white and the black worlds.[3] But whatever the source of her unique vision, the result is her books' complex literary and moral texture. As we are drawn into her stories, we must shed our misconceptions and question our judgments until we arrive at the core of truth.

Morrison typically frames her tales within mythic narrative structures, thus creating a heroic context for her themes and characters. At the same time, she develops a rich irony by juxtaposing heroic expectation with mundane reality. Furthermore, by pitting contrasting figures against one another, Morrison repeatedly reverses the reader's expectations. It is Morrison's use of these two devices, ironic structuring and character pairing, that I wish to examine in discussing her 1973 novel *Sula*.

The central figures in the novel, Nel Wright and Sula Peace, are diametric opposites whose lives are linked by bonds too powerful for either to resist. Ultimately hero and villain change roles, as their relationship grows into a larger selfhood.

Using heroic conventions as a structural basis for her novel, Morrison creates layers of irony and multiple perceptions that add depth to her analysis of contemporary black women. Although the characters' lives in an impoverished rural community, tellingly named "the Bottom," contrast markedly with the epic figures whose names they bear (i.e., Ajax, Helen, Eve, and Judas), Morrison's characters are measured by the heroic yardstick. And true heroism does flourish here, in the most unlikely soil, as the book's hero painfully comes to terms with her own evil.

Almost all American novelists have written tales of questing heroes, creating characters of heroic stature whose journeys lead to tragic destruction or comic renewal. But these heroic myths have tended to be cast in androcentric terms. Joseph Campbell's well-known *Hero with a Thousand Faces* (Princeton University Press 1949), for example, traces the literary journeys of male heroes who overcome dangerous foes, mate with symbolically significant women, and return to restore order to their kingdoms. Because traditional heroic patterns describe male characters, the lives of questing female heroes are often anomalous.[4] Living in a culture that sets limits on acceptable female behavior, they often face constraint rather than enhancement of life. To some readers, their actions may seem aberrant, more suited to punishment than reward.

To combat such traditional attitudes, women writers frequently use irony and parody and invert traditional motifs. Thus, we find Morrison grounding *Sula* in the epic tradition, but using ironic reversals of epic expectations to create a new definition of heroism that will encompass the lives of black women. Unlike the stock epic tale, in which the hero, driven by inner compulsion to leave society in search of knowledge and power, undertakes a dangerous but successful journey and returns in triumph to transform a fallen world, *Sula* presents a tale of courage in the face of limitations and powerlessness, of self-knowledge wrested from loss and suffering, of social amelioration eked out of hatred and fear. Because it is the drab and ordinary Nel rather than the more flamboyant Sula, with whom Nel is paired, that achieves heroic stature, the book dramatizes the inwardness of the quest. Most of the characters in *Sula* misinterpret the novel's two central figures, permitting Morrison to emphasize the private nature of heroism and the complexity of moral judgment.

Epic in scope, rich in Biblical allusions, the book's vision, like that of the heroic tale, is of human life played out against a background of natural and supernatural forces. The novel's mythic elements—repeated deaths by fire and water, rituals of naming, signs and dreams, the mysteries of human motivation and behavior—are held in balance by irony; chronological structure; a taut, objective narrative style; and harsh realism. A recurring rhythm of birth, death, and rebirth structures the novel, every chapter describing an actual or symbolic death. To compound the irony, death is often seen as positive, as in Eva's burning of Plum, a ritual of release and purification.[5] Unlike many traditional epics, which depict the founding of a civilization or its restoration to proper order, *Sula* begins with the razing of the Bottom to make room for a whites-only golf course. This destruction, which sets the book's tone of hovering doom, is both example and symbol of the steady erosion that the black community and its members suffer. The contrast of fertile life and sterile machinery[6] reenacts the black struggle to survive in the face of white oppression, the epic struggle between life and death. Economically and politically powerless, the black community is vulnerable to white society's exploitative self-aggrandizement. By the book's ambiguous conclusion only one character—Nel—will enact the epic promise of renewal.

Set in a small Ohio town during the years 1919 to 1965, *Sula* chronicles the fortunes of the women in two matriarchal households within the black community, particularly Nel Wright and Sula Peace, whose lives represent the range of choices possible for black women in modern America. As we watch them grow to maturity, the heroes learn about sexuality, evil, power, love, and, primarily, about the prospects and limits of their lives, the difficulties of survival in an inimical world. Sula and Nel represent opposite approaches to the epic tasks of self-discovery and integration into society. Whereas the questing hero is traditionally an embodiment of a culture's noblest values, the rigid Nel is too bound by convention to undertake a journey, and the adventurous Sula appears to be the antithesis of her society's codes. Further, although Sula's quest appears to be a failure, her return brings an unexpected, albeit short-lived, boon to the Bottom. Although Sula is shunned and feared as a reprobate, paradoxically, her negative example spurs others to greater virtue, and she inspires the psychological growth of the friend she betrays. Thus, a seemingly failed quest has unexpectedly positive ramifications.

At the book's heart is the tale of the friendship between Nel Wright and Sula Peace. Beginning when they are adolescent girls and continuing as they mature, the friendship changes in nature but remains the deepest attachment and most profound influence on both of their lives. Although the two girls share dreams of adventure and unfolding selfhood, their approaches to the task of maturation are diametrically opposed. Nel casts her visions in traditional romantic fantasies and sacrifices her independence to conventionality, while Sula, insisting on her independence, becomes isolated from society; she is free but directionless.

Obedient, quiet, and repressed, Nel first experiences herself as an individual apart from her family when she gazes in a mirror and dreams of traveling in the world beyond the Bottom. "But," the narrator interjects at this point, "that was before she met Sula . . ." (p. 25). The introduction of Sula at this crucial birth of Nel's self-awareness highlights the link between the two girls. In fact, it is her sense of her nascent identity which gives Nel the strength to defy her mother's prohibition and establish a friendship with Sula. Yet it is to be Sula, rather than Nel, who eventually realizes Nel's dreams of a journey and of independent selfhood.

As is frequently the case in epics, dreams play a significant role in the story. Dreams build the initial link between Sula and Nel, and foretell their different paths of self-expression. In her daydreams, Nel fantasizes "lying on a flowered bed, tangled in her own hair, waiting for some fiery prince" (p. 44) like the passive fairy-tale heroine. When Nel later marries, her life becomes one of passive limitation and stagnation, described in terms of spider web imagery suggestive of the entanglement in her own hair. Sula's fantasies, by contrast, are actively sensuous ones in which she gallops "through her own mind on a gray-and-white horse tasting sugar and smelling roses" (p. 44). Resisting human ties, she is the daring, sensuous, active woman, seeking to experience life and her own being to the fullest. In her isolation, Sula is free, but she is directionless. Because neither of these two paths leads to personal fulfillment and social regeneration, the novel dramatizes the ironic contrast between epic expectation and actual achievement.

The process of self-development carries with it the hope of fulfillment and achieving selfhood. Again, *Sula* depicts reality frustrating expectation. Instead of enlarging their worlds and achieving contentment and fruition, Nel and Sula repeatedly find experience constricting their lives and bringing the bitterness of death and betrayal. This ironic reversal is epitomized in the chapter entitled "1922," which begins with the girls' sexual awakening and ends with a funeral. The book's single use of lush natural description heralds their rite of passage:

> Then summer came. A summer limp with the weight of blossomed things. Heavy sunflowers weeping over fences; iris curling and browning at the edges far away from their purple hearts; ears of corn letting their auburn hair wind down their stalks.   (p. 48)

Nature's fertile ripening evokes the ripening sexuality of the friends. Yet, as the description of the personified natural world makes clear, ripening is simply a stage in the growth that leads inevitably to death and decay.

In this luxuriant Summer of 1922, Nel and Sula reaffirm their awareness of themselves as sexually desirable by passing an ice cream parlor where they receive the appreciative stares and comments of the lounging young men. But this sense of complacent well-being is shattered by two events which occur in rapid succession and blight the promise of Sula's life. The first crisis is Sula's overhearing her mother comment casually that she doesn't like her. The second is her accidental drowning of the young boy Chicken Little while playing with him near the river. This double disillusionment determines the subsequent course of Sula's life: "The first experience taught her there was no other that you could count on; the second that there was no self to count on either. She had no center, no speck around which to grow" (p. 103). Life's mysteries confound her; she learns poorly and too soon the lessons of death and of the essential untrustworthiness and isolation of human beings.

The chapter that begins in such delicious anticipation ends with the funeral of Chicken Little. Leaving the funeral together, Nel and Sula outwardly appear to be like "any two young girlfriends trotting up the road on a summer day wondering what happened to butterflies in the winter" (p. 57). The irony of this image highlights the tension between their apparent childlike innocence and their terrible knowledge of death.

The incidents of the chapter "1922" reflect a recurring pattern in the book. Repeatedly, an individual at the height of his or her powers dies or witnesses a traumatizing death. Sula is destroyed by her involvement in Chicken Little's drowning. Directionless, without a foundation of human trust, she is isolated, a pariah.

For Nel, sexual awakening also produces a kind of death: It leads her to a death of self in her marriage to Jude Greene. (As in the case with other names, Jude's is of ironic import: He will be Judas, betrayer of Nel's hopes.) Her marriage is described in the imagery of death. Ajax advises Jude that girls want to be miserable: "'Ax em to die for you and they yours for life'" (p. 71). Married women are seen as "folded . . . into starched coffins" (p. 105). In Jude's eyes, Nel is to become a part of him, "the hem . . . of his garment"; "the two of them together would make one Jude" (p. 71). This, of course, signifies the death of Nel's already fragile sense of self. An image which recurrently describes the contraction of Nel's life after marriage is that of the web (see pp. 82, 103-104). Caught in a trap of her own devising, Nel, spider-like, comes to occupy a small, but safe, space.

Nel's marriage separates her from Sula, who alone, of all the women in the Bottom, rejects the limits, the obligations and restrictions, of marriage and motherhood. Viewing marriage as compounded of convenience and caution, Sula avoids such ties. While her repudiation of these bonds renders her an outcast in the eyes of her community, she perceives herself as free, and therefore able, as none of the other women are, to be honest and to experience life and self fully. Her journey is the enactment of that freedom.

Most epics focus on the initiation phase of the hero's journey—with its dangerous, often fantastic adventures leading to participation in the sources of universal power. Because Sula's freedom is uncommitted, her journey is seen only briefly; nevertheless, her return will lead to enlightenment.

On Nel's wedding day, Sula, with an amused smile, leaves town, returning ten years later. Her quest for knowledge and experience is described only in retrospect. Her years at college, her travels and romantic liaisons are mentioned parenthetically; she remembers most as boring. The wisdom she attains is the cynic's. While the heroic journey is typically a source of power, this is not the case for Sula. Although Campbell defines a "mystical marriage" as the hero's "ultimate adventure," representing an increase of power and the attainment of "total mastery of life" (*Hero with a Thousand Faces* pp. 109-120), Sula's sexuality breeds only boredom and despair. She learns of the alienation she reaches in post-coital sadness, when she descends to a private core of loneliness and melancholy nostalgia. Sexual intercourse, rather than promoting human relatedness and mystic insight, increases her isolation and misery (*Sula* p. 106).

Described as an artist without a medium (p. 105), dangerous because undirected, lacking discipline or aim, Sula is free but empty. She never makes the existentialist's commitment, the surrender of freedom through attachment to an idea or person that de Beauvoir and others see as the truest hallmark of human freedom.[7] Her one human relationship of significance, the friendship with Nel, provides her with a center, a place she can call home: "Nel was the first person who had been real to her, whose name she knew, who had seen as she had the slant of life that made it possible to stretch it to its limits" (p. 103). Her need to reestablish her link to Nel brings her back.

It is consistently at the points of tangency to each other that the lives of Nel and Sula are most vitally lived. We remember that their friendship came into being in dreams before the two girls met each other. More significantly, Morrison's imagery suggests a kinship so close as to be a physical connection. In their girlhood, ". . . their friendship was so close, they themselves had difficulty distinguishing one's thoughts from the other's . . . a compliment to one was a compliment to the other, and cruelty to one was a challenge to the other" (p. 72). When Sula returns the ties remain strong. Nel's home-centered life is expanded and enriched when Sula returns to the Bottom. Her reappearance is described in physical terms. To Nel, her friend's return is "like getting the use of an eye back, having a cataract removed. . . . Talking to Sula had always been a conversation with herself" (p. 82). For Sula, lacking a central core, Nel is "the closest thing to both an other and a self" (p. 103); she thinks of them as "'two throats and one eye'" (p. 126). The imagery of physical connection suggests a more profound bond than friendship between the two women; they are two parts of one personality or, as Morrison has stated, "If they were one woman, they would be complete."[8] As doubles, they complement each other and, combined, make up a complete picture of the hero.

Although it is her connection to Nel that prompts Sula to return to the Bottom, she jeopardizes the friendship by refusing to acknowledge any ties as binding. Sula brings knowledge of a wider world, objective distances, a fresh, disinterested perspec-

tive that enables her to find humor in the everyday details of her
friend's domestic life. For a life time they recapture the sweetness of their adolescent companionship. Enjoying their shared
reminiscences, Nel is relaxed and happy; this is the only time we
see her laugh. However, this harmonious interlude is shattered
when Sula seduces Jude. For her, acting out of sheer restlessness
and habit, out of whim, out of a need to challenge the very fabric
of marriage itself, this liaison is as brief and unimportant as any
of her others. For Nel, it is a betrayal of friendship. Jude, discovered, leaves. Accusing Sula of disloyalty, Nel remains aloof,
although she thinks of her friend often. Without Sula and Jude,
with her children growing away from her as they grow up, Nel's
life contracts even further, narrowing into a loveless round of
duties and responsibilities, to job, children, and church.

Partly from a sense of duty, but more from a need to confront her directly and discover the reason for her betrayal, Nel
visits the dying Sula three years later. Sula, still interested in observing her own mind, is lying in bed, analyzing the sensations
of pain in its various stages, as she had earlier indulged in fantasies of savoring the sweetness of sugar and roses. Still wry and
quick-tongued, she teases Nel, challenging her belief that she is a
wronged victim: "'What you mean take him away? I didn't kill
him, I just fucked him. If we were such good friends, how come
you couldn't get over it'" (p. 125). Sula implies that it is Nel herself who has been the traitor. For when Nel married Jude, she
severed the ties of friendship that bound the special relationship
between the two girls and grounded Sula in the human community. Without Nel, Sula becomes an outsider.

Although the typical epic hero experiences a transforming
vision which he or she brings back to redeem society, Sula has
attained only a knowledge of her own sadness, alienation, and
loss. Now, however, at her death, half-joking, she articulates
her own tart apocalyptic vision of a Messianic era in which all
people will come to love each other:

> 'After all the old women have lain with the teen-agers;
> when all the young girls have slept with their old drunken
> uncles; after all the black men fuck all the white ones;
> when all the white women kiss all the black ones; when
> the guards have raped all the jailbirds . . . and Norma
> Shearer makes it with Stepin Fetchit; . . . then there'll be a
> little love left over for me.'   (p. 125)

Her comic sexual analogy to the promised Biblical period of peace and love stresses harmony, sexual passion, and equality between the powerful and the powerless. In the outrageousness of her vision, the novel ironically emphasizes the distance between the ideal of epic regeneration and the impossibility of redemption in the fallen world of modern America.

Sula's final speech asserts her own goodness, and questions Nel's assumption of righteousness. Nel leaves, "embarrassed, irritable and a little bit ashamed" (p. 126). After her words of triumphant self-justification, Sula curls up in a fetal position and dies, thinking of a comforting return to a permanent womb-like sleep. At the very moment when breath and heartbeat cease, Sula, always aware of her experiences, and thinking of her one friend, notes, "'. . . it didn't even hurt. Wait'll I tell Nel'" (p. 128). Acting out her childhood dream of exploring her mind and tasting sensuous pleasures, Sula has lived hard, made no compromises and now dies young.

Sula's death is interpreted by her community as a sign of approaching good fortune. Because of her wanderings and estrangement from the usual human ties, the townsfolk believed her to be a witch. Signs and portents were attributed to her: Her return was accompanied by a "plague of robins" (p. 77). Yet, ironically, her negative example was a warning which inspired others to greater goodness. Her blessing to her community is achieved indirectly; it lies in the improved behavior with which others respond to her presumed evil:

> Their conviction of Sula's evil changed them in accountable yet mysterious ways. Once the source of their personal misfortune was identified, they had leave to protect and love one another. They began to cherish their husbands and wives, protect their children, repair their homes and in general band together against the devil in their midst.   (p. 102)

Contrary to expectation, bad luck follows her death. Rumors that blacks will be hired to build the tunnel on the New River Road prove false. Severe frost kills the fall crops and strains the limited resources of the Bottom. Epidemics of croup and scarlet fever erupt. But worse, with Sula gone, her neighbors relapse into their former lackadaisical ways. The increase of energy and virtue with which they reacted to her seeming evil disappears with her death:

> The tension was gone and so was the reason for the effort they had made. Without her mockery, affection for others sank into flaccid disrepair. Daughters who had complained bitterly about the responsibilities of taking care of their aged mothers-in-law had altered when Sula locked Eva away. . . . Now that Sula was dead and done with, they returned to a steeping resentment of the burdens of old people. Wives uncoddled their husbands; there seemed no further need to reinforce their vanity.   (p. 132)

Accordingly, Sula's boon to her society is achieved by her negative model, and lasts for only a short time. But for Nel, the person to whom she was closest, Sula's impact is more intense.

To Nel, Sula brings not only loss and pain, but also, even after her death, an enlarged self-awareness. Although Nel leads a restrained, constricted life, she survives. Through her involvement with Sula she learns about herself, attaining greater openness and emotional capacity. She comes to realize that caution had led her to accept limitations too readily and that moral smugness had blinded her to her own potential for evil.

Believing herself morally superior to Sula, Nel realizes later her own complicity in Chicken Little's death. When Nel makes one of her charity visits to the old people's home, Sula's grandmother Eva confuses her with Sula and asserts that she was involved in the drowning. Nel is upset by the accusation. She has always been careful to think she *saw* him drown; with Eva's challenge she acknowledges to herself that she *watched* and even experienced a secret excitement. (Following Nel's example, Sula had watched her mother Hannah burn to death.)

> All these years she had been secretly proud of her calm, controlled behavior when Sula was uncontrollable, her compassion for Sula's frightened and shamed eyes. Now it seemed that what she had thought was maturity, serenity and compassion was only the tranquillity that follows a joyful stimulation. Just as the water closed peacefully over the turbulence of Chicken Little's body, so had contentment washed over her enjoyment.   (p. 146)

Able for the first time to identify with her friend, Nel admits her own capacity for evil, learning finally Sula's disturbing early lessons of human untrustworthiness. Nel had judged Sula harshly and prolonged their estrangement because of her own failure to confront her dark impulses. Her new recognition of her psychological kinship with Sula unlocks Nel's depths of long pent-up emotion. She comes to an anguished realization: It is not Jude after all, but Sula, her childhood companion, that she misses so painfully. She pours out her grief, releasing feelings she has long denied. In her mourning for Sula, twenty-four years after her friend's death, Nel at last weeps. With her new willingness to face suppressed feelings comes relief from another longstanding malaise, an imaginary dread. As she weeps by Sula's grave, a vague terror breaks and scatters like dandelion seeds, her ominous fears exorcised (p. 149). She has been the villain of the novel, but her tears are a cleansing baptism.[9]

According to Carl F. Keppler, the second self in literature (here, Sula) is the darker, mysterious, more aware one. Often in conflict, the two parties to this relationship represent for each other their own unacknowledged potentials, simultaneously fascinating and frightening. The symbol of the second self signifies the human desire to become whole through complete development of the total range of possible selfhood. Tensions between the two may lead to destruction, but, says Keppler, the process "strips away all masks of self-enlargement."[10] In this way, Nel and Sula grow in self-knowledge and understanding through their links to each other.

In the novel Sula learns what she does of the meaning of human relatedness and of the human admixture of good and evil in her link to Nel. As the second self, Sula experiments with freedom and honesty beyond the limits allowable within the social order and lives the life of adventure Nel dreamed of but denied herself. Nel, on the other hand, expands her imaginative and emotional capacity through her association with Sula. It is her continuing love for Sula that makes possible her most cogent insight into her own motivation and her deepest emotional response. When she weeps for Sula, she is freed from old constraints and misconceptions, stripped of her false moral pride and smugness. Through this mourning for her dead friend/self at Sula's graveside, Nel is symbolically reborn as the surviving self, continuing the process of growth and self-awareness that Sula began.

Nel's moment of insight, however, is not couched in the glowing redemptive images associated with the epic realizations of most heroes, but in more ironic, more limited terms. The book ends with her lamentation: "It was a fine cry—loud and long—but it had no bottom and it had no top, just circles and circles of sorrow" (p. 149). In the novel's vision, the ability to survive in the face of a hostile world and to accept one's fate in full self-knowledge constitutes the real nobility left to the hero. The truest heroism lies not in external battle, as in the wars which destroy the novel's men, but in confrontation with the self. Nel, who never left home, makes the terrifying journey into the depths of her soul. By admitting the guilt she had tried to deny, and recognizing her failure of sympathy for her friend, Nel comes to terms with herself and frees her emotional capacity. Thus, Nel, the cautious, conventional woman, learns the meaning of Sula's life, and survives.

Notes

[1] For a discussion of the irony in *Sula*, see Chikwenye Okonjo Ogunyemi, "*Sula*: 'A Nigger Joke.'" *Black American Literature Forum* 13 (1979): 130-133.

[2] For a discussion of multiple perspectives in *Sula*, see Barbara Lounsberry and Grace Ann Hovet, "Principles of Perception in Toni Morrison's *Sula*." *Black American Literature Forum* 13 (1979): 126-129.

[3] This point is made by Odette C. Martin in "*Sula*." *First World*, Winter 1977, pp. 35-44.

[4] See Annis Pratt's *Archetypal Patterns in Women's Fiction* (Bloomington: Indiana University Press, 1981), esp. pp. 9-37.

[5] See Lavinia Chase, "The Willing Victim," diss. University of Connecticut 1978, pp. 125-126; Lounsberry and Hovet, p. 128; and Ogunyemi, p. 132.

[6] *Sula* (1973; rpt. New York: Bantam Books, 1975), p. 3. Future references will be to this edition and will occur parenthetically in the text.

[7] Simone de Beauvoir, *Pour une Morale de l'Ambiguité* (Paris: Gallimard, 1965).

[8] See Jane Bakerman's "The Seams Can't Show: An Interview with Toni Morrison." *Black American Literature Forum* 12 (1978): 60.

[9] In his article, Ogunyemi analyzes the reversal of Nel from hero to villain in greater detail, but he fails to note her redemption and subsequent attainment of true heroic stature.

[10] *The Literature of the Second Self* (Tucson: University of Arizona Press, 1972), pp. 194-195.

The Telling of *Beloved*

Eusebio L. Rodrigues

Beloved is a triumph of storytelling. Toni Morrison fuses arts that belong to black oral folk tradition with strategies that are sophisticatedly modern in order to create the blues mode in fiction, and tell a tale thick in texture and richly complex in meaning. The reader has to be a hearer too. For the printed words leap into sound to enter a consciousness that has to suspend disbelief willingly and become that of a child again, open to magic and wonder.

"124 was spiteful": thus the narrative shock tactics begin.[1] Here is no fairy tale opening but an entrance (124 is not a number but a house as the last sentence of the first paragraph will confirm) into a real unreal world. Toni Morrison's narrator—it is a woman's voice, deep, daring, folkwise—has full faith in her listeners (curious males have gathered around her) and in their ability to absorb multiple meanings. She plunges into *medias res* and begins her tale with the arrival of Paul D.

Paul's arrival sets the story in motion. Outraged by the spiteful persecution of a "haunt" that resents his sudden irruption into a house it has taken possession of, Paul attacks it and drives it out. The incident has a tremendous impact—on Paul, on Sethe, who has resigned herself to a certain way of life, on Denver, who feels deprived of the only companion she ever had, and especially on the listener, who is bewildered, utterly disoriented. For he is flung into a dark fictional world without any bearings or explanations. He has to be patient and wait for light to filter in through cracks in the thick darkness. Exhalations from the dim past arise—a baby is furious at having its throat cut, a grandmother's name is Baby Suggs, a baby is born in 1855, Sethe's milk is taken—but they lack meaning and cannot,

yet, be chronologically aligned or connected with the events of
the present, the year 1873.

Toni Morrison begins the slow process of conjuring up a
world that has receded into the past. Here is no extended Prous-
tian act of remembering a lost world with the help of a
madeleine dipped in tea. For the past, racial and personal, seared
into the being of her characters, has to be exorcized by "rememory." Unspeakable, it emerges reluctantly. The major characters,
Sethe and Paul, have to tear the terrible past, bit by painful bit,
out of their being so that they, and Denver, can confront it and
be healed. Toni Morrison's narrator will stage an extended blues
performance, controlling the release of these memories, synco-
pating the accompanying stories of Sixo, Stamp Paid and
Grandmother Suggs, making rhythms clash, turning beats into
offbeats and crossbeats, introducing blue notes of loneliness and
injustice and despair, generating, at the end, meanings that hit
her listeners in the heart, that region below the intellect where
knowledge deepens into understanding.

The structural ordering of this "aural" novel is not spatial
but musical.[2] It consists of a title, a dedication to Sixty Million
and more, an epigraph from an obscure Biblical passage, and
three unequal parts. Part I, of eighteen sections, appears to be
lopsidedly long, a stretch of 163 pages; Part II, with its seven sections, goes on for 70 pages; Part Ill, of 3 sections and only 38
pages, ends with a word that is an isolate, at once a re-dedication
and a whispered prayer, Beloved.

Part I takes its time in order to establish the many modes
Toni Morrison uses to create a world. Her narrator begins the
tale, and immediately allows an interplay of voices to begin.
Torn fragments of the past float out of Sethe and Paul, who have
met again after eighteen long years. Their voices join those of
Baby Suggs, dead for eight years, and of Denver, for whom only
the present matters. The voices set a world spinning, the world
of slaves and slavery whose horrors can no longer be visualized
today but whose sounds of pain and suffering still linger on.
They issue out of the shared stories of Sethe and Paul D set in
two focal regions: in Sweet Home, a farm in Kentucky, where
events lake place that project and compress rural slave life before
1865; and in 124 Bluestone Road on the outskirts of Cincinnati,
Ohio, an urban setting that highlights the painful consequences
of post Civil War freedom. The narrator transforms the interlinked stories of Sethe and Paul into a paradigm of what it

meant to be a slave, especially a woman slave in America.

History, however, is not treated as mere documentary. For that readers could turn to slave narratives. Toni Morrison makes history integral to her novel. In musical terms her narrative melodies are sung against the groundbeat of historical detail. The details are thrown in casually, understated, as in the true blues idiom, to intensify the horror. Baby Suggs' eight children had six fathers. Men were put out to stud, slave women were sold suddenly, children vanished into the unknown. After the war there was chaos, black human blood cooked in a lynch fire stank (180), there was madness, segregation, the South was "infected by the Klan" (66). Before the war hangings were common (Sethe saw her mother's unrecognizable corpse cut down), slaves were branded (Sethe's mother's identification mark was a cross and circle burnt into the skin under her breast), and an iron bit was thrust into the mouth for days as punishment (Paul complained not about sucking iron but about his intense need to spit). What happened before the slaves got to America was, for them, only a dim memory. At times Sethe remembers her mother dancing the antelope (there is no such animal in America) and remembers, at times, faintly, the ghostly voice of Nan, her mother's friend, speaking about a sea voyage in a language Sethe knew but has now forgotten (62). The memories of the other characters do not extend to the African past. The narrator will devise a way to resurrect this past.

But before this past can spring to life for the community of listeners (women, their work done, have joined the semi-circle now), the present has to be made alive and exciting. The telling therefore does not begin from a point fixed in time. Nor will the narrator use symbolism (an overused mode), or channel her stories through points of view (too thin, too limited), or through a consciousness that flows like a stream. The words will not have a Hemingway translucence but a Faulknerian density, for the language, slow moving, will be thick with history. Tenses will shift when needed to quicken pace. The oral-aural mode will use repetition to intensify the experience. Words will be repeated; phrases and images will be used over and over again to generate rhythmic meanings; fragments of a story will recur, embedded in other fragments of other stories. A born bard, the narrator, a blueswoman, will cast a spell on her audience so that fragments, phrases, words accelerate and work together to create a mythic tale.

The words repeated are simple but vibrant. Plans, re-peated to warn slaves not to make any, for they have no future, anything could happen any time. Interlinked words, pieces, parts, sections, warn a slave about the lack of a unitary self. The slave is a bundle of pieces, of names, food, shelter provided by changing masters; a collection of fractured parts, outer and inner, that have been defiled. Sethe knows she could easily break into pieces. That is why Baby Suggs bathed the rescued Sethe in sec-tions; that is why Paul D will have to wash off Sethe's defile-ment part by piece by section at the end, before his love (like that of Sixo's woman) can make the pieces come together. Beloved, it becomes clear, is afraid of breaking up into pieces, an indica-tion that she is a composite of slave pieces of the past.

Smile/smiling: these word-forms, tossed out casually at first (7, 50), begin to resound when associated with Beloved, who emerges from the water smiling mysteriously, fascinating Den-ver. They gather more resonance when Sethe connects the smile with her mother's smile, and realizes that her mother "had smiled when she did not smile" (203), realizes further that it was the iron bit clamped on the tongue that had produced that perpetual smile. It was the same smile worn by the Saturday prostitutes who worked the slaughterhouse yard on pay day. Sethe's own smile, as she makes these connections, is one of knowledge. Paul D, during the telling of his story to Sethe, can understand why, when he was led away, iron bit in the mouth, his hatred had focused on Mister, "the smiling boss of roosters" (106). What Paul saw on the rooster was a white smile of supreme contempt and arrogance, a looking down on one less than a chicken. In Part III the full force of the word-forms rings loud and clear. Beloved smiles dazzingly before she explodes out of existence. What remains at the end is the scar on her handsawed throat, the "smile under the chin" (275), the memory for Sethe of "the little shadow of a smile" (239). Smiling, the lis-tener realizes, is a silent statement of endurance. To smile is to know the horror of what it means to be a slave.

The narrator makes words function as musical notes. She also makes use of musical phrases together with chordal accom-paniments to produce assonance, consonance, dissonance. "Wear her out" (13): associated at first with the young Denver, who is always tired, this phrase is applied to Sethe and then modulated and amplified when linked with Baby Suggs and Stamp Paid. Stamp Paid himself feels bone tired (176) towards the end; only then does he understand the marrow weariness that made Baby Suggs give up the struggle, and get into bed to die. "Lay it all down" (174), she advises Sethe and Denver, echoing a line out of a spiritual. Sword and shield, lay it all down; she urges resignation, it's useless to fight, one cannot ever defend oneself. The phrase becomes a refrain, a burden (in both senses), that insists on the unbearable weight of racial suffering and injustice.

Images and metaphors of food intensify this suffering. "The stone had eaten the sun's rays" (40): a mere trick of style, did the verb not compel listener and reader to pause, for "eaten" springs out of the consciousness of the famished Sethe. Sethe is constantly chewing and swallowing; she keeps "gnawing" (162) at the past. The narrator uses the language of hunger lest her listeners forget essential truths, that all food was decided and provided by the masters, and that hunger was yet another burden of slave life. Sugar was never provided; that's why Denver and Beloved crave sweet things. The only food the slave mother could provide her babies was her own milk. "All I ever had," Sethe tells Paul (159). That's why she felt outraged when the two white boys stole her nursing milk. That is why she was ready to bite out the eyes, to gnaw the cheek of anyone who would stop her from getting to her starving baby. That's what drove her on from Kentucky to Ohio.

Milk, more than just food, was the flow of love Sethe wanted to release into her babies. Denver, sucking on a bloody nipple, took in Sethe's milk with her sister's blood. The baby sister never did get enough of Sethe's milk. That is why, when she returns as Beloved, she has a "hungry" face. Sethe, says the narrator, "was licked, tasted, eaten by Beloved's eyes" (57). Beloved was "greedy" to hear Sethe talk, and Sethe "feeds" her with stories of the past it always hurt her to tell others, even Denver. The narrator's language becomes thick with insistent references to and images and metaphors of food and hunger, so that listener and reader become aware of many slave hungers—for food, for things sweet, for an understanding of the past, for communion, for community, and, above all, for a form of sustenance slaves were deprived of, love. It was dangerous to love, for the beloved could be torn away at any time. Beloved, as name, title and emanation, now gathers significance but the meanings do not come together yet. Nor can the hearers grasp the connections between food and religion—"the berries that tasted like church" (136), the Biblical references to "loaves and fishes" (137), the setting-up of the food after Baby Suggs' funeral. All connections and meanings, all notes and musical phrases, will be made to converge and resonate in Parts II and III.

Before such a convergence can occur there has to be an awareness of the magical sounds of the language through which meanings flow. Toni Morrison undermines the heaviness of print by turning word-shapes into word-sounds in order to allow her narrator to chant, to sing, to exploit sound effects. ". . . No. No. Nono. Nonono" (163): these staccato drumbeats—single, double, triple—translate Sethe's fears of the threatening white world into ominous sounds. Word-sounds enact the rhythmic steps of a dance: "A little two-step, two-step, make-a-new-step, slide, slide and strut on down" (74). A page presents consecutive paragraphs that have a one-word beginning, "but" with a period (223). The reader can see the pattern the buts make; the listener hears the repeated thuds that drive in the utter futility of slaves making plans to escape. At one point the narrator refers to Sethe's "bedding" dress made up of pieces Sethe put together— two pillow cases, a dresser scarf with a hole in it, an old sash, mosquito netting (59). The strange adjective is used to trigger an ironic rhyme-echo, for a slave woman could never have a "wedding" with a ceremony and a preacher, but only a coupling. Sad, but full of admiration and affection for Sethe, the narrator herself turns celebrant, the music of her language transforming the mating into a unique fertility rite in a tiny cornfield, wit-nessed by their friends who partake of the young corn. Four-teen-year-old Sethe's virgin surrender to Halle, her moments of pain and joy, have as accompaniments the dance of the corn-stalks, the husk, the cornsilk hair, the pulling down of the tight sheath, the ripping sound, the juice, the loose silk, the jailed-up flavor running free, the joy (27). Light monosyllabic sounds bring this epithalamium to a close: "How loose the silk. How fine and loose and free."

Beloved makes many aural demands for its musical pat-terns are many. Toni Morrison turns her narrator into a Bakhtinian ventriloquist who throws her voice into Baby Suggs. Oh my people, cries Baby Suggs, that preacher without a church, calling out to her congregation in the Clearing, repeating the words "here" and "yonder," and "flesh" and "heart" and "love," exhorting her people to love their unloved flesh, their beating hearts, so moving them that they make music for her dance (89).

By using repetition for emphasis, participles for movement, internal rhyme and alliteration, the narrator heightens the voice and the word-patterns of Paul D (who cannot read) to translate into thudbeats the unspeakable fears and cravings of forty-six chain-linked chain-dancing men pounding away at rocks with their sledge hammers:

> They sang it out and beat it up, garbling the words so
> they could not be understood; tricking the words so their
> syllables yielded up other meanings. They sang the
> women they knew; the children they had been; the an-
> imals they had tamed themselves or seen others tame.
> They sang of bosses and masters and misses; of mules
> and dogs and the shamelessness of life. They sang lov-
> ingly of graveyards and sisters long gone. Of pork in
> the woods; meal in the pan; fish on the line; cane, rain,
> and rocking chairs.   (108)

Toni Morrison endows her narrator with a voice that has both range and energy, without being artificial or literary. It is a human voice, warm and friendly, not detached or distant, a voice that reaches out to touch the whole village community now gathered around her. She is, after all, their bard; she knows their language and can speak the vernacular. There is no need, therefore, for any comments, or for the language of explanations; only the need for a heightening of the black idiom in order to summon up a world buried in their racial memory.

Hence the language intensification. "Knees wide open as the grave" (5): this startling simile erupts as Sethe remembers rutting among the headstones to get the seven letters of "Beloved" chiseled for free. A flirtation "so subtle you had to scratch for it" (7): Sethe's verb springs out of her world; the implied image is that of hens in a farmyard. A memory of something shameful seeps "into a slit" in Sethe's mind (61); she is poised on the "the lip" of sleep (85); Beloved has "rinsed" certain memories out of her mind, explains Sethe to Denver (119). The language becomes intensely vibrant at times, as when Paul D suddenly realizes he was completely wrong about Sethe:

> This here Sethe was new. The ghost in her house didn't
> bother her for the very same reason a room-and-board
> witch with new shoes was welcome. This here Sethe
> talked about love like any other woman; talked about
> baby clothes like any other woman, but what she meant

> could cleave the bone. This here Sethe talked about
> safety with a handsaw. This here new Sethe didn't
> know where she stopped and the world began.   (164)

The verbal phrase, "cleave the bone," the repetition of "talked,"
of "like any other woman," the repetition of thematic words
used earlier in the story, "love," "safety," "world," the insertion
of "here" between "this" and "Sethe" to colloquialize the phrase,
its repetition three times, and then the modulation into a four
beat phrase "this here new Sethe"—all work together to produce
the thick flow of Paul's realization.

Toni Morrison's ability to charge the vernacular with
power and sound enables her to give a mythic form to the story
of her people, the Afro-Americans. Oh my people, cries Toni
Morrison, hear the voice of the bard. This bard is a Blakean *griot*
in whom the ancestral experience is stored and who can see and
sing the past, present, and future. She sings an ongoing story of
the savage uprooting of sixty million and more, of a sea passage
from Africa to America, of selves fractured and reduced to things
lower than animals, of freedom imposed by others from the outside, and then the painful process of healing, of the achieving of
inner freedom, and of slowly discovering themselves as human
beings in a new world. It is a story of generations, of two hun-
dred years and more compressed in time and channeled through
a few individuals. The telling is a teaching, too, directed to the
generations yet to come, lest they forget. History had to be transformed into myth.

Toni Morrison has her narrator employ the technique of
circling round and round the subject that Sethe, her central
character, uses for telling the essentials of her story to Paul D:
"Circling, circling, now she was gnawing something else instead
of getting to the point" (162). All the stories—that of Sethe and
Paul D, of Baby Suggs and Stamp Paid, of Beloved and Denver,
and of Sixo—have their chronologies fractured and the "pieces"
made to spin together to form one story, monstrous and heroic.
The fragments keep sliding into and out of each other for they
cannot be separated. Their love for each other makes Sethe's
story Paul's too. The stories of Baby Suggs and Stamp Paid tell of
an earlier generation. The stories of Sixo and the Cherokee Indians present yet another account of suffering and injustice. Denver's story leads into the future, while Beloved's reaches to the
past. Sure her people will slowly understand the story of their
own past, the narrator begins with Sethe.

Sethe, in 1873, has resigned herself to her situation. Isolated from the Bluestone community, terrified of the exhalations of the past she kept buried within her damaged being, Sethe needs healing. The re-entry of Paul D and of Beloved into her life begins the slow process that leads her to understanding, love and community. Sethe is compelled to re-live two ordeals, the birth of Denver and the killing of her third child.

The story of Sethe's harrowing escape and of Denver's miraculous birth takes eight sections of Part I (up to p. 85) to be told, but the narrator does not release all its meanings. Certain clues are offered; the listener gets accustomed to a mode of telling that involves delay, repetition, and a slow but controlled release of information. Sethe casually mentions "that girl looking for velvet" (8) to Paul D. Only later (32) is her name, Amy, revealed (the first clue, the name, from Old French, means *beloved*). The story is relayed through dialogue, recall and narration. Sethe begins the narrative; Denver remembers parts that Sethe told her, and, as if under a spell, she "steps into the told story" (29) to recreate it for Beloved. The narrator takes over and finishes the telling which is exciting, full of horror and pathos and beauty. She smuggles in significant truths through the words of Amy—that anything dead coming back to life hurts (35), that nothing can heal without pain (78)—that she hopes some of her listeners will ponder. The unexpected aria that bursts out of the narrator towards the end, just after the birth of Denver, is a musical celebration the audience can respond to but cannot understand, yet:

> Spores of bluefern growing in the hollows along the riverbank float toward the water in silver-blue lines hard to see unless you are in or near them, lying right at the river's edge when the sunshots are low and drained. Often they are mistook for insects—but they are seeds in which the whole generation sleeps confident of a future. And for a moment it is easy to believe each one has one—will become all of what is contained in the spore: will live out its days as planned. This moment of certainty lasts no longer than that; longer, perhaps, than the spore itself. (84)

The story of Sethe's other ordeal is told in "pieces" that are scattered through all 18 sections of Part I, and that have to be put together. The focus is on consecutive days, four weeks after Sethe's arrival at 124. On the first day the whole community is invited to a feast, a communion, a ritual "celebration of black-berries that put Christmas to shame" (147). The second day is one of foreboding for Baby Suggs, who smells two odors, one of disapproval, the other of a "dark and coming thing." What happens in the shed appears to be both a killing and a ritual sacrifice, the red blood spurting out of the cut throat of the baby held against the mother's chest.

The horror is not immediate, nor are the details graphic. The scene has a stabbing intensity, for it is a chill horror that takes time to penetrate and implode. The narrative tactics shift; the temperature of the language drops. The scene (section 16 of Part I, 148-153) is relayed through four voices that slide one into the other to form a "white" composite. That of the slave catcher presents a hunter calculating his profit: "Unlike a snake or a bear, a dead nigger could not be skinned for profit and was not worth his own dead weight in coin" (148). The nephew simply cannot understand why and how a mere beating could cause such a reaction. The schoolteacher presents a doleful view of "creatures God has given you the responsibility of" (150). The sheriff sees before him a proof that freedom should not have been imposed so soon on these poor savages. The language of all four voices is cold, aloof, detached, clinical. After all these are creatures and cannibals, aren't they, what else can one expect. Drenched in savage irony the scene becomes almost unbearable. Mercifully the narrator takes over; the ironic mode loses its edge but still continues with the sudden entry (as in a Hitchcock movie) of two white children, one bearing shoes for Baby Suggs to repair. The unmentioned color emits a tiny scream as the narrator's voice drops into silence at the end: "The hot sun dried Sethe's dress, stiff as rigor mortis" (153).

The story of Sethe and her ordeals forms the spinning center around which the other stories of collapse spin. The outer circle is made up of the stories of the Cherokee (yet another people decimated, and uprooted from the lands they owned) and of Sixo the Indian, Paul's "brother," who laughs when his feet are roasted and sings "Seven-O!, Seven-O!" before he is shot. Then the story of Baby Suggs, seventy years old, who had proclaimed the gospel of love after she got her freedom. She realizes that she had preached a lie, and that it was all useless. White folks came into my yard, she says, using the language of understatement. She "lays down" in bed to die there. Two sentences sum up the slave life of Paul, whose heart has become a rusty tobacco tin into which he has stuffed his experiences: "It was some time before he could put Alfred, Georgia, Sixo, Halle, his brothers, Sethe, Mister, the taste of iron, the sight of butter, the smell of hickory, notebook paper, one by one, into the tobacco tin lodged in his chest. By the time he got to 124 nothing in this world could pry it open" (113). How much is a nigger supposed to take, he asks. All he can, Stamp Paid replies, and Paul can only repeat why why why why why. The Stamp Paid story is of one who had dedicated his entire life to the rescue and service of his people. He finds himself in a state of despair in 1874, nine years after his people were set free. He had found in his boat a tiny red ribbon that smelt of skin and embodied for him all the lynchings and the burnings that his people still had to endure. "What *are* these people? You tell me, Jesus. What *are* they?" (180) he asks.

The narrator is confident that this question to Jesus will direct her audience (some white people have drifted into the group now) to the Christian dimensions of her tale. After all, they also have been sustained and comforted by their Christian faith and by the Bible. They would pick up the Biblical references to "loaves and fishes" during the celebratory feast, to Stamp Paid's real name, Joshua (the successor to Moses), and to the origins in Genesis of Sethe's name. They would realize that Baby Suggs had lost faith in the God she once believed in; that Stamp Paid, who had relied on the Word and who had believed that "these things too will pass" (179), abandoned his efforts to rescue the inhabitants of 124 menacingly "ringed with voices like a noose" (183). And they would sense that additional help was needed from other sources to deal with things "older, but not stronger, than He Himself was" (172).

Listeners (aware of African religious beliefs) and readers (familiar with books by Janheinz Jahn and Geoffrey Parrinder, and with the Indic tradition) slowly begin to realize that Beloved has sprung out of pre-Christian sources. A complex creation, Beloved is made up of "pieces" that Toni Morrison has spun into being so skillfully that it is difficult to isolate their sources. Some elements derive from the Afro-American belief, shared by the Bluestone community, that the unfulfilled dead can return to the scene of their former existence. According to Baby Suggs almost every house is "packed to its rafters with some dead Negro's grief" (5). Other elements spring from the belief, purely African, that "the departed are spiritual forces which can influ-

ence their living descendants. In this their only purpose is to increase the life force of their descendants.[3] Toni Morrison fuses
these elements with others of her own invention in order to intensify her tale and raise it to the level of myth. She makes her
narrator control the pace of the telling, releasing the story slowly
so that listener and reader are persuaded to accept Beloved as a
"presence," allowing a number of meanings to accumulate so
that, at the end, it becomes a story of haunting significance.

In the beginning the baby ghost is merely a disturbance,
mysterious not to Sethe and Denver but to the listeners, exciting
their interest in a good story. Only after the Thursday carnival,[4]
after Beloved returns from the other side of the grave, does the
tale become more than a ghost story. Toni Morrison set herself
two fictional problems. She had to delay Sethe's recognition of
Beloved as her baby daughter, while allowing Denver to be
aware that Beloved is her sister almost from the beginning. The
second problem was to provide Beloved with a voice and a language. Toni Morrison carefully controls the release of details
about Beloved. That Beloved is a nineteen-year-old (the age she
would have been had she lived) who acts like a baby in the beginning is clear (though not to Sethe who is distracted by her
love of Paul D): Beloved has sleepy eyes, her hands and feet are
soft, her skin is flawless, she cannot hold her bead up, she is in-
continent. She "grows" up in the course of a few days because
Sethe "feeds" her with stories of her own past. This "feeding," a
form of narrative strategy, allows the novelist to evoke Sethe's
past for her readers, and it allows Sethe to exorcize what she had
kept buried within herself. Sethe's rememory pours out of her
in response to the many questions Beloved keeps asking, using a
strange, raspy voice. It takes over four weeks for Beloved's
"gravelly" voice, with its African cadence, to shift unobtrusively
into the rhythms of Afro-American speech.

The talks with Sethe establish the reality of Beloved as a
human being. The scenes with Denver and with Paul suggest
that Beloved is also a catalytic life force. The shed behind 124 becomes the locale where the racial past is reenacted. Beloved
"moves" Paul D (the way slaves were moved from place to place;
there was nothing they or Paul could do about it), "like a rag
doll" (126, 221), out of Sethe's bed and into the dark shed where
she forces him, much against his will, to have sex with her, and
to call her by her true name, Beloved, not the one the "ghosts
without skin" called her in the daylight, bitch (241). Paul turns

into a version of Seth, the black man on the slave ship whom Sethe's mother loved and after whom Sethe was named. The dark shed becomes the ship's hold as Beloved forces Denver to re-live the experience of panic, suffocation and thick darkness (with cracks of daylight) where the self is reduced to nothing. These painful experiences will be healing (as Amy had said). Denver, who belongs to the future, lives through a racial past without whose knowledge she would not be complete. Paul's rusty tobacco tin, which "nothing *in this world* could pry open" (my italics), opens up into a red, warm heart.

Before presenting Sethe's sorrows and sufferings the narrator halts the recitative and turns into a blueswoman, making a trio of voices sing "unspeakable thoughts, unspoken" (199). The timing of this musical interlude sung by a mother and her two daughters is exactly right: Paul D has been made to leave 124; Sethe knows that her baby has come back from the other side; and the past has been disinterred. The interlude of four sections (200-217) provides a time of rest and slowdown before the final narrative outburst.

The first two sections (200-209) open with the voiced thoughts of Sethe and of Denver, recapitulating, in fragments, the significant moments of their past. The third section (210-213) begins in the present with "I am Beloved and she is mine." Then the I swells into a collective choric I that comes as if from a distant time and place, as though sixty million and more voices had been compressed into one. Toni Morrison could use only a few typographical devices to activate print into tempo.[5] All punctuation is banished (except for the period that ends the opening sentence). There is quadruple spacing between sentences and there are double gaps between paragraphs. These pauses slow down the voice and make it resonate, so that a lamentation fills the air as the African beginnings of the horror are enacted. Visual details blur and dissolve: women crouch in the jungle picking flowers in baskets, there is gunsmoke during the hunt for slaves, the men are crammed into the ship's hold,[6] children and women, naked, crouch on the deck and on the bridge, storms at sea force men and women to be packed together, there is the sweet rotten smell of death, corpses are stacked in piles on the deck and then pushed out into the sea with poles, suicide by jumping into the sea and rapes are common.

Out of such visual horror arise cries of anguish as beloved

is torn from beloved, women from their children, mothers from their daughters. The anguish is never ending, for "all of it is now it is all new" (210). The past is still present, as those who have listened to the tale so far knew. Beloved becomes the embodiment of all slave daughters; Sethe stands for generations of slave mothers. Denver experiences something worse than death, the utter lack of self in the shed (123); Paul trembles uncontrollably in Georgia (106) like the man in the hold packed so tight he had no room even to tremble in order to die (211); Sethe experiences choking (96) to make her know what it felt like to wear an iron circle around her neck (213); Beloved gazes in tears at the turtles in the stream behind 124 (105), as if her earlier self were looking for her Seth who had leapt from the bridge of the slave ship. All experiences repeat or parallel each other. The fourth section returns the listeners to the present where the trio of voices chant a dirge in liturgical fashion as the interlude ends.

The narrator then takes up again the story of Sethe, who lavishes all her love on her baby daughter, excluding Denver and feeding the uncomprehending Beloved with explanations, telling her that she had to kill her in order to save her. Beloved grows monstrously fat devouring Sethe's love while Sethe wastes away. Denver, through whom most of Part III is channeled, does not understand what is happening but is afraid there could be another killing.

Both reader and listener have to understand why Beloved and Sethe behave in this unnatural manner. Sethe does not realize that Beloved's demands are not those of a human being, but of an impersonal life force that has got what it wanted, but cannot stop its blind, unreasonable demands for more. The narrator calls her "wild game" (242). The Bluestone community refers to her as an "it" that will destroy Sethe, who has committed a crime. Sethe, on the other hand, believes that "what she had done was right because it came from true love" (251).

Toni Morrison does not judge Sethe. Neither does her narrator allow her listeners to pass judgment on Sethe. The Bluestone community cannot forgive what they regard as an act of senseless murder. Even Baby Suggs was horrified on that day, and fell on her knees begging God's pardon for Sethe (152-153, 203). Denver, who is afraid of her mother even though she loves her (102), has an inkling of what it was that drove Sethe on: it was a "something" in her mother that made it all right to "kill her own" (205). The thing was "coiled" up in her, too, for

Denver felt it leap within her at certain moments (102, 104).

What the "thing" is is never made clear. But Sethe's story provides some clues. The process begins at edenic Sweet Home, that "cradle" (219) of innocence, at the moment when Sethe's knowledge of evil begins, the knowledge that the white world, in the person of schoolteacher, considered her part animal. He had told his nephews to categorize Sethe by setting down her animal characteristics on the right, her human ones on the left (193). Overhearing these words, Sethe feels her head itch as if somebody were sticking fine needles in her scalp (193).[7] During the escape, before the meeting with Amy, Sethe senses a "*something*" that came out of the earth into her and impelled her to attack: "like a snake. All jaws and hungry" (31).

It was this "something," a blind animal force perhaps, that leapt within Sethe just before the killing. At the sight of schoolteacher's hat she heard wings: "Little hummingbirds stuck their needle beaks right through her headcloth into her hair and beat their wings" (163). Stamp Paid, who was present, saw a dramatic change in Sethe, whose face "beaked"[8] and whose hands worked like claws before she snatched up her children "like a hawk on the wing," and dragged them into the shed (157).

Stamp Paid tries to tell Paul D that love drove Sethe to "outhurt the hurter" (234). Paul cannot understand such love. Too thick (164), he tells Sethe, adding that Sethe bad two legs not four, implying that she was not an animal but a human being (165). A "forest" sprang up between them, adds the narrator who, reluctant to explain anything to listener or reader, compels them to ponder the image of the forest.

Yet another clue bad been provided earlier when, asked by Paul to have his baby. Sethe thought: "Unless carefree, mother love was a killer" (132). Paul D had observed that, for a slave, any form of love was fraught with danger, and that human love needed freedom. One can only speculate that mother love, when not allowed free expression and growth in human society, remains a primal instinct. Fiercely possessive and predatory, it kills to protect the young from the enemy. That explains perhaps why there are so many animal references. Slaves were regarded as property, as possessions, as animals.

In this light Sethe's act of murder transforms itself from a mere killing into a ritual sacrifice of the beloved, an expression of the helpless rage and outrage of many slave mothers who either wanted to or did kill their young to deliver them from slavery.[9] But one sin cannot cancel out another. 124 with its shed is more than a gray and white house: it becomes the arena where the resurrected past demands vengeance and threatens to overwhelm the present. A ritual atonement is needed. Denver, the future, has to step out of this dark world to seek help. She goes to the community.

With a few deft touches all through Parts I & II, the narrator has established the reality of the Bluestone community, a loosely knit group of colored folks living at the city's edge. They are a good bunch, Stamp Paid tells Paul D, a little proud and mean at times, but ready to help anyone in need. They had two meeting centers: the Church of the Holy Redeemer with Reverend Pike as preacher, and the Clearing in the woods where that unchurched preacher, Baby Suggs, holy, restored their faith in themselves and in their bodies. 124, at that time, had been a "cheerful, buzzing house" (86), a way station and a place of refuge fur runaways, where Baby Suggs provided food, comfort and help. What led to the estrangement between 124 and the community is not quite clear, but the narrator is confident that her listeners (their circle has now expanded into a vast human congregation) will understand and forgive human failings.

A few listeners might be aware of the term *hubris*, but all would know that pride and arrogance were sins that could lead to misunderstanding. Baby Suggs knew that she had been guilty of pride on the day of the celebration, knew that she had "offended them by excess" (138). That is why, on the next day, she could smell the disapproval of the community. The ninety friends and neighbors were guilty too, of enjoying the feast of "loaves and fishes" and then displaying anger, envy and resentment towards the provider. Sethe, too, is guilty, of arrogantly isolating herself and not going to the community for help, even after the death of Baby Suggs. The setting-up after the funeral did not lead to communion. Sethe did not eat of their food, and they would not eat what she provided. It is Stamp Paid, that Soldier of Christ (171), who tries to help. Driven by a sense of guilt and by the memory of his friend, Baby Suggs, he tries to pass through two barriers: the circle of nightmarish voices, and the door that remains locked despite his knocking. He abandons his efforts to reach the inhabitants of 124.

Having made her listeners fully aware of the many meanings of 124, the narrator now quickens the pace of the telling. The tempo increases, the sound effects grow intense. "124 was loud," the opening of Part II (169), echoes the opening of Part I, "124 was spiteful," and there is a re-echo in the opening of Part III, "124 was quiet" (239). Quiet because its inhabitants, locked in a meaningless love, were starving and would die of hunger. Denver is afraid of stepping off the porch of this prison:

> *Out there where* small things scratched and sometimes touched. *Where* words could be spoken that would close your ears shut. *Where*, if you *were* alone, feeling could overtake you and stick to you like a shadow. *Out there where there were* places in which things so bad had happened that when you *were* near them it would happen again. Like Sweet Home *where* time didn't pass and *where*, like her mother said, the bad was waiting for her as well. How would she know these places? What was more—much more—*out there were* white people and how could you tell about them?
>
> (244-245; italics mine)

The listener can easily respond to the reference to Sweet Home as a place where time had stopped, to the rhyme-echoes and repetition (with variation) of "out there," "where," and "were" that enact Denver's fears and hesitations, and trigger Denver's re-memory of the rats in prison and her sudden deafness.

Neither Sethe nor Denver can hear the loud voices that menace 124. Only Stamp Paid, that witness of his peoples sufferings, listens and can recognize the sets of voices: the roaring of all the slaves who were lynched and burned; and the terrified mutterings, near the porch, of whites (like the schoolteacher who had created a "jungle" in Sethe) in whom the jungle of hate and terror had entered. The pack of haunts is ready to pounce.

The listeners can tell the end is near. The narrator summons up techniques that tellers of tales use to create suspense—tantalizing pauses, breaks in the narrative, switches and cross-telling (like cross-cutting in film). It is an ominous Friday, three in the afternoon, a steaming tropical day reeking with foul odors. Three narrative movements converge: Bluestone women, thirty of them, led by Ella, make their way to 124 to rescue Sethe from the devil child; Mr. Bodwin, who had helped in the defense of Sethe, is on his way to 124 (where he had been born), to fetch Denver, who is waiting for him on the porch; Sethe, inside 124, uses an ice pick to break some ice for the sweating Beloved.

To amplify her story the narrator now summons her co-

tellers, the blueswoman and the bard. The blueswoman vocal-
izes the rhythms of the approaching mumbling chorus of thirty
women (significantly, no man, not even Stamp Paid, is present).
Some of them kneel outside the yard, as though in church, and
begin a series of responses to a prayer call: "Yes, yes, yes, oh yes.
Hear me. Hear me. Do it, maker, do it. Yes" (258). Then Ella
begins to holler,[10] an elemental cry that sweeps all the women to
the very beginning, of time perhaps, even before the Christian
Word. "In the beginning was the sound," the blueswoman announces (259).

The narrative pauses, then the narrator switches to Edward Bodwin, driving a cart to 124, haunted by time and by the
recent wars and the fight over abolition that made him lose faith
in what his father had told him, that human life is holy. The
narrative breaks again to Sethe and Beloved standing on the
porch of 124. The three movements converge and combine.

The blueswoman becomes one with the community of
women out of whose being sounds explode, and rise to a
crescendo of pure sound. More than a speech act, it is a *mantra*-
like utterance that rises from the creative female depths of their
self, an act of exorcism:[11] "Building voice upon voice until they
found it, and when they did it was a wave of sound wide enough
to sound deep water and knock the pods off chestnut trees. It
broke over Sethe and she trembled like the baptized in its wash"
(261). The reference to water, the word "sound" used as a verb
and noun, the allusion to Baby Suggs and to her powers associated with nature, "tremble," the word linked with Paul D, the
double implication of "wash," all insist that this unpremeditated
rite combines a pre-Christian archetypal cleansing with Christian
baptism. Beloved's dazzling smile suggests that she does "understand" what has happened. But the listeners are puzzled.

It is the bard who knows what has been exorcized and begins to chant, switching from the past to the present tense because "all is now." The events of the past are once again made
present. The words used earlier for what happened in 1855 (the
definite green of the leaves, the staccato drumbeats of Sethe's
fears) are repeated and relayed through Sethe's rememory. But
this time, ice pick in hand, Sethe (after she sees Edward Bodwin's hat) attacks not her beloved but the "schoolteacher" at-
tacker, a normal human reaction for the "thing" has been exorcised out of her. Denver and the women move in to stop her.
The words used in the interlude (pile, faces, people, the man

without skin) are also repeated to summon back from the remote past Beloved's ordeals on the slave ship. Then Beloved, her belly swollen with the past, vanishes. But this monstrous African past cannot be completely exorcized. It will linger on, wanting to be at least remembered.

The listeners, held spellbound by these events, experience catharsis. The tale has reached into their hearts and touched basic human emotions. It moves them, but not to action. For Toni Morrison is an artist, not a sociologist or a politician. Like Conrad, who wanted, before all, to make his readers *see*, Toni Morrison wants to make her people *listen* and, like the spirit of Baby Suggs urging Denver (244), know the truth about themselves and their "roots." Like Conrad, too, Toni Morrison feels compelled to "render the highest kind of justice to the visible universe."[12] The institution of slavery is condemned, but all white people are not. The listeners remember Amy (a "slave" herself who, significantly, is on her pilgrim way to Boston), the Garners (Sethe looked upon Mrs. Garner as if she was her mother), the Bodwins, even the sheriff (who had looked away when Sethe nursed Denver). But Toni Morrison insists that true freedom is essential and that equality between peoples is of absolute necessity. That is why the goodness of the Garners and the Bodwins is somehow flawed: on a shelf in the Bodwin house Denver sees a black boy figurine kneeling on a pedestal that reads: "At Yo Service" (255).

Toni Morrison's sense of justice and compassion leads her to introduce notes of hope. The many Christian references suggest such a possibility, especially the name of the community church, and the redemptive tree of suffering that Sethe carries on her back and will carry for a lifetime. Paul's love will heal Sethe, rescue her from the fate that befell Baby Suggs, and put her pieces together. In the tableau at the end Paul touches Sethe's face as he whispers his tribute to her: "You your best thing, Sethe. You are" (273). The story of Sethe and Paul will gradually recede into the past. Denver is the future. She is the child of the race, "my heart," Stamp Paid tells Paul D (265). Lady Jones can see "everybody's child" in her face (246). Clever and intelligent, she will go to Oberlin. Denver is like Seven-O, which is not just a cry of warning to his woman, but a continuation of Sixo, the name of his "seed" which she bears away with her. Denver needs no tribute, for the narrator has already sung an aria to celebrate her birth; she is the seed "in which the whole generation sleeps confident of the future" (84).

With the stories of Sethe, Paul, and Denver told, the narrator and the bard know that the telling has to come to a stop. Their listeners have been rapt into a mythic world. But humankind cannot live there for long. The account of what happened to Paul D, which balances the story of Sethe, allows the listeners to return to ordinary human reality. When Paul D and Stamp Paid talk about what happened at 124, a strange laughter, like Sixo's, erupts out of them. "To keep from cryin' I open my mouth an' laughs," as Langston Hughes puts it.[13] Narrator and bard have finished their tasks, but something remains to be done. The blueswoman takes over.

She begins to keen, as though at a wake, a ceremony held in order to remember, to celebrate, and then to forget. But the lament soon changes into the sound of a biblical voice from on high (sounded in the epigraph), that summons an alien people unto itself and calls them beloved.[14] The community remembers what Sethe rememoried, the voice of the preacher at the baby's funeral telling them who they are, addressing them all as Dearly Beloved. The voice of the blueswoman now develops a powerful hum, for she expresses, as in basic blues, not her own feelings but those of all her people. It uses not the minor (though it sounds plaintive) but the major mode of the classical blues. The words are unimportant for they all have been heard before, except the twice repeated, two-word word, "disremembered," which associates memory with pieces.[15] The blueswoman and the community know that the past can linger on but has to be laid to rest. As in a blues ending they announce, then repeat, then repeat again, mixing the past and present tenses, that it was/is "not a story to pass on." Till, finally, the blueswoman allows her voice to sink into silence after a whispered prayer, Beloved.

Notes

[1] Toni Morrison, *Beloved* (New York: New American Library, 1987) 3. Hereafter page references will be cited in the text. Other page references will help the reader to locate specific moments in this complex novel. Toni Morrison calls attention to the significance of the opening sentence of *Beloved* in "Unspeakable Things Unspoken: The Afro-American Presence in American Literature," *Michigan Quarterly Review* Winter 1989: 31-32.

[2] Toni Morrison comments on the oral-aural qualities of her fiction in an interview: "Ah well, that may mean that my efforts to make aural literature— A-U-R-A-L—work because I do hear it. It has to be read in silence and that's just one phase of the work but it also has to *sound* and if it doesn't *sound* right. . . . Even though I don't speak it when I'm writing it, I have this interior piece, I guess, in my bead that reads, so that the way I hear it is the way I write it and I guess that's the way I would read it aloud. The point is not to need the adverbs to say how it sounds but to have the sound of it in the sentence, and if it needs a lot of footnotes or editorial remarks or description in order to say how it sounded, then there's something wrong with it." (Christina Davis, "Interview with Toni Morrison," *Présence Africaine* 145, 1st Quarterly 1988: 148).

[3] Janheinz Jahn, *Muntu* (New York: Grove Press, Inc., 1961) 110. A. K. Forbes (*Ras Mala: Hindu Annals of Western India* [New Delhi, India: Heritage Publications, 1973] 674) refers to spirits called bhoots: "Bhoots are . . . daimons—spirits of men or women deceased . . . still unhappily entangled in human passions, desires, or anxieties . . . seeking to inflict pain, to practice delusion, or to enjoy pleasure through the instrumentality of a living human body, of which they take temporary possession."

[4] That was a bad sign according to Stamp Paid (235). Geoffrey Parrinder (*African Traditional Religion* [London: Sheldon Press, 1974]) has a chapter on Nature Gods (pp. 43-54). He refers to a grave-digging ceremony that uses a prayer that begins: "Earth, whose day is Thursday. . . ." The references to water gods and to the snake cult could help in explaining some elements in the novel. Toni Morrison also makes references to directional signs, left and right, which are significant in Indic culture.

[5] Faulkner experimented with italics and other devices to project mind-voice in some of his novels, especially in *Light in August*. He wanted his publishers to use different colored inks for the Benjy section of *The Sound and the Fury*.

[6] In the *Time* interview (May 22, 1989, p. 120) Toni Morrison refers to "travel accounts of people who were in the Congo—that's a wide river—saying, 'We could not get the boat through the river, it was choked with bodies.' That's like a logjam. A lot of people died. Half of them died in those ships." In his introduction to *Adventures of an African Slaver* by Captain Theodore Canot (New York: Dover Publications Inc., 1969) Malcolm Cowley mentions a strange phenomenon: that "in Bonny River . . . the bodies of slaves washed backwards and forwards with the tide, the women floating, it is said, face downwards; the men on their backs, staring into perpetual clouds which were almost the color of their eyes" (IX). In the slaveship's hold "the slaves were packed as tightly as cases of whisky. . . . The slaves were laid on their sides, spoon-fashion, the bent knees of one fitting into the hamstrings of his neighbor. On some vessels they could not even lie down; they spent the voyage sitting on each other's laps" (XII). Beloved demonstrates this position to Denver in the shed when she "bends over, curls up and rocks" (124).

[7] There are two other references to birds in Sethe's hair (188). Mrs. Garner thinks Sethe has lice in her hair (195).

[8] That is why Paul D keeps repeating to Stamp Paid (154-158) that the mouth shown on the newspaper clipping wasn't Sethe's.

9 No statistics on slave infanticide are available. Deborah Gray White (*Ar'n't I a Woman?* [New York: W. W. Norton and Co., 1985] 88) writes: "In 1830 a North Carolina slave woman was convicted of murdering her own child. A year later a Missouri slave was accused of poisoning and smothering her infant, and in 1834, Elizabeth, one of James Polk's slaves, was said to have smothered her newborn. No one will ever know what drove these women to kill their infants, if they did. Some whites thought slave women lacked maternal feeling, yet a few women who killed their children claimed to have done so because of their intense concern for their offspring."

10 The holler was a call or a cry used in the fields in the south. According to Tilford Brooks (*America's Black Heritage* [New Jersey: Prentice-Hall Inc., 1984] 52), "the holler is perhaps the most important single element in the blues, partly by virtue of the intensity of its personal expression."

11 *Mantra* is a Sanskrit term difficult to translate and impossible to define. The most recent book on the subject is a collection of essays edited by Harvey P. Alper, *MANTRA* (State University of New York Press, 1989). According to Fritz Staal, mantras "are used in ritual or meditation to bring about effects that are stated to he 'ineffable' and 'beyond language.'" They represent rudiments of something that existed before language. André Padoux quotes from Abhinavagupta who describes the hissing sounds/vibrations that appear in the throat of a woman at the moment of orgasm: "In this context, such a sound, since it issues spontaneously from the depths of the self, goes beyond the bounds of ordinary human existence. It is felt as going back to the source of life . . ." (304). These quotations may help in the understanding of *Beloved*. Those interested in knowing about the Indic tradition should read a recent book of essays edited by Alf Hiltebeital, *Criminal Gods and Demon Devotees* (State University of New York Press, 1989), especially the essay by David M. Knipe, "Night of the Growing Dead: A Cult of Virabhadra in Coastal Andhra," 123-156.

12 Joseph Conrad, *The Nigger of the Narcissus*, ed. R. Kimborough. W. W. Norton & Co., 1979, 145.

13 Used by Janheinz Jahn as an epigraph to his chapter on the blues, p. 217.

14 The passage from Romans 9:25 is a modified quotation from Hosea 2:23, which implies that God looks forward to the day when his people will once more be his people. According to F. F. Bruce (*The Letter of Paul to the Romans* [Michigan: W. B. Eerdman's Publishing Co., 1985] 185), "what Paul does here is to take this promise, which referred to a situation within the frontiers of the chosen people, and extract from it a principle of divine action which in his day was reproducing itself on a world-wide scale."

15 Deborah Horvitz, in her insightful, pioneering essay on *Beloved* ("Nameless Ghosts: Possession and Dispossession in *Beloved*," *Studies in American Fiction* 17, no. 2, Autumn 1989: 157-167) offers an analysis of this word.

Toni Morrison's *Beloved*:
History, "Rememory," and a "Clamor for a Kiss"

Caroline Rody

> *i am accused of tending to the past*
> *as if i made it,*
> *as if i sculpted it*
> *with my own hands. i did not.*
> *the past was waiting for me*
> *when i came,*
> *a monstrous unnamed baby,*
> *and i with my mother's itch*
> *took it to breast*
> *and named it*
> *History.*
> *she is more human now,*
> *learning language everyday,*
> *remembering faces, names and dates.*
> *when she is strong enough to travel*
> *on her own, beware, she will.*
>
> **Lucille Clifton,**
> **"i am accused of tending to the past. . . ."**

> *momma*
> *help me*
> *turn the face of history*
> to your face.
>
> **June Jordan,**
> **"Gettin Down to Get Over"**

> *You came right on back like a good girl,*
> *like a daughter. . . .*
>
> **Toni Morrison,** *Beloved*

On the back of the New American Library edition of Toni Morrison's *Beloved*, reviewer John Leonard proclaims, "I can't imagine American literature without it." Evidently intended as consummate praise, this remark would seem to congratulate Morrison for having written into the incomplete canon of American literature the very chapter of American history it had long lacked: the story of the African Americans who survived slavery. In an important sense, *Beloved* is manifestly about the filling of historical gaps. "Sixty million and more," reads Morrison's dedication, simply, suggesting at once the numerous ancestors the novel attempts to memorialize and a vast absence its words could never fill.[1]

Yet how odd it is that we should now be unable to "imagine American literature" without the strange, idiosyncratic imaginative world of *Beloved*. A reading of the novel as a recuperation of unrepresented history does not begin to account for its cultivation of the bizarre and uncanny; its revival of gothic conventions—the haunted house, the bloody secret, the sexually alluring ghost; its obsessive, claustrophobic plot focus; and an emotional climate that changes from pained repression to volcanic fury to a suspended lovers' swoon. All of this seems somehow excessive to the requirements of a historical novel that would recuperate the story of African-American slavery and survival.

Beloved is, however, a historical novel; Morrison rewrites the life of the historical figure Margaret Garner, who killed her child to prevent her recapture into slavery, and sets this story as the focus of an epic-scale recreation of African-American life under slavery and in its aftermath.[2] What are we to make of the shape of this "history"? Why focus on an astonishing act of violence committed not *upon* but *by* a slave woman? Why should this slave story be central for Morrison, and why should we be brought to reimagine this chapter of American history through the prism of a haunting, passionate, violent, and ultimately unresolved relationship between a mother and daughter?

The peculiarity of this "history" suggests a design different from those described by most theories of the historical novel. Certainly Morrison's slavery novel achieves the realist portrayal of great "social trends and historical forces" that Georg Lukács endorses, in the classic historical novels, as offering a "prehistory of the present" (34, 337). The plot of the ghost girl can also be seen to draw upon the modes of historical romance and supernatural tale, which have traditionally served to "[transform] black history into mythic fiction" (Campbell xvii). *Beloved* further suggests the influence on African-American historical fiction of magic realism, read in recent Latin American and third world fictional "histories" as a revisionary postcolonial narrative mode, mediating the cultural and epistemological clashes of colonial history (Slemon 20-21). Yet while we can read revisionary mythification in Morrison's history, we still have not accounted for its interest in a murderous mother and ghostly daughter.

Poststructuralist critics of African-American historical fiction would have us read *Beloved* as less a mimetic or mythic recreation of the real than an entrant into ongoing historiographic discourse, inescapably about the problem of writing history in the complicated moment in which we tell the past (see Gates xi; McDowell, "Negotiating" 144-147). Though touched by the prevailing postmodern irony toward questions of truth and representation, fiction and history, *Beloved* and most contemporary novels of slavery are not "historiographic metafictions" denying the possibility of historical "Truth" (Hutcheon 109, 113). For these novels, much as for abolitionist slave narratives, the burden of communicating an authentic truth remains, and the inherited conviction of slavery's evil renders the word of fictional slaves true in a sense not solely epistemological or even political but moral. Postmodern fictions with battles still to fight, today's African-American slave "histories," though they may center upon questions of memory, knowledge, and identity, share with many ethnic, feminist, and postcolonial texts the impulse "to create an authoritative voice, not to undermine an already existing one" (Zimmerman 176). Thus Morrison calls on writers to de-emphasize the institution of slavery and put the "authority back into the hands of the slave" (qtd. in McDowell, "Negotiating" 160).

But this remark gathers irony when we return to the difficulty of interpreting *Beloved* as historical text: namely, the awesome authority Morrison puts into the hands of her slave-heroine. Surely we can read *Beloved* as a historiographic intervention, a strategic recentering of American history in the lives of the historically dispossessed. But by what logic does the plot of child murder serve any late twentieth-century ideological interest? In what sense does this plot assert the historiographic authority of an African-American woman's hands? If these theoretical approaches do not greatly illuminate the historicity of the ghost story without which our literature was incomplete, it may be because they view historical writing solely in terms of ideologies of representation, without considering the affective aspect of history writing, insofar as the historiographic project enacts a relationship of desire, an emotional implication of present and past. While *Beloved* is evidently a politically engaged novel, it is also a novel of extraordinary psychological reach. I suggest that to account for *Beloved* we integrate an ideological reading of historical fiction with a reading of the inscribed psychological project of reimagining an inherited past.

1

In contemporary black "histories," we may, indeed, have difficulty separating the political, the psychological, and the ethnic. Discussing the recent "flood" of African-American novels about slavery, Deborah McDowell muses, "Why the compulsion to repeat the massive story of slavery in the contemporary Afro-American novel? . . ." ("Negotiating" 144). This hint at a collective psychological source of the trend, if dropped somewhat playfully, probably confirms our vague sense that larger processes in African-American history and culture are at work here, that the slavery novels of our moment mark the arrival of African-American literature at a juncture of particularly profound cultural reckoning.

For the group of black writers who have attained unprecedented literary authority and audience in an era of intensifying social crisis for the African-American community, the return to the subject of slavery would seem to articulate an ironic coming-of-age. Time and success have brought black literature to a place where the vista seems to be all of memory and return. When Hazel Carby asked in the late 1980s why relatively few African-American novels had focused on slavery, it seems she merely spoke too soon (125). By 1993 the roster of such texts has grown long, and we are looking at a genre in full swing, exhibiting an astonishing diversity and range.[3] Today's most celebrated black writers, engaged in the profound mythopoetic enterprise of identification with slave ancestors, return African-American literary culture to its "roots," reviving with new dignity the foundational genre of this literature: the slave narrative (Gates xxxiii).

Following Margaret Walker's epic *Jubilee* (1966) and gaining greatest popular notice with the phenomenon of Alex Haley's *Roots* (1976), African-American writers have undertaken a collective return to the story of slavery unimaginable in preceding decades. The reasons for the long deferral of this project are complex, but the return itself has a resonance that is unmistakable (see Campbell xiv, 112, 158; Christian 326, 330-332, 334-338; Carby 125-127). In the surge of African-American cultural production that followed the civil rights era, amidst an overriding concern with new articulations of racial identity, a moment arrived when it became possible—and, apparently, crucial—for writers to take on the fictional persona of a slave. As nations when they rise, for good or ill, look back and reexplain to the world the past that produced their emergence in strength, so Afro-America in the 1970s, 1980s, and 1990s has returned to the scriptural endeavor of rewriting the texts of its own genesis.[4] Having attained a certain measure of power, perhaps a certain measure of safety, of distance from the slave past sufficient to risk intimacy, along with increased access to publication and a growing mainstream audience, black writers began to speak with the tongue of the ancestor, claiming their place in American culture and letters upon the same ground—in history's spiral—as that upon which the slave's voice first emerged. They thus invoke a heritage not only of suffering and resistance but also of self-definition in the face of racist ideologies of literary authority.[5]

A devotee of slave narratives, Morrison long anticipated their literary resurgence. As a Random House editor in 1976, Morrison told an interviewer:

> You know . . . just for sustenance, I read those slave narratives—there are sometimes three or four sentences or half a page, each one of which could be developed in an art form, marvelous. Just to figure out how to—you mean to tell me she beat the dogs and the man and pulled a stump out of the ground? Who is she, you know? Who is she? It's just incredible. And all of that will surface, it *will surface*, and my *huge* joy is thinking that I am in some way part of that when I sit here in this office. . . .   ("Intimate" 229)

In this remark the gender of slave narrators who most fascinate Morrison ("Who is she? . . . Who is she?") is explicit and somewhat remarkable, given that fewer than 12 percent of published slave narratives were written by women (Blassingame 83) and that the popular image of the slave has been male from abolition days to the present (see McDowell, "In the First Place"). Recent feminist scholarship on female slaves has been revising the gendering of this genre, and the large proportion of today's fictional "neoslave narratives" (Bell 289) to reimagine slavery from a black female point of view constitutes a collective symbolic reauthorization of the voice of the female slave, part of the recuperation of "herstory" ongoing in the post-1960s black women's literary "renaissance."[6]

Though the rise in historical novels by black writers testifies to a sociopolitical rise to the authority and the desire to represent the genesis of their people, this aura of ascent should not obscure the psychological descent, the paradoxical willingness to hit psychic bottom that distinguishes today's African-American literary triumphs. The stories these novels recuperate are, after all, about deprivation and suffering often literally unspeakable. Morrison notes that slave narrators, "shaping the experience to make it palatable" for white readers, dropped a "veil" over "their interior life" ("Site" 110). Whether we view her attempt to unveil that "interior" in a novel as homage or audacity, the "anxiety of influence" operative in her retelling is shaped by a distinctive sense of interiority, an "ethnic," "familial" relationship to an inherited, traumatic story. For an African-American writer, slavery is a story known in the bones and yet not at all. "How could she bear witness to what she never lived?" asks Gayl Jones's *Corregidora* (103), crystallizing the paradox of contemporary black rewritings of slavery. Writing that bears witness to an inherited tragedy approaches the past with an interest much more urgent than historical curiosity or even political revisionism. Inserting authorial consciousness into the very processes of history that accomplished the racial "othering" of the self, novels of slavery make their claims to knowledge and power face-to-face with destruction. We might think of such fictions as structures of historiographic desire, attempts to span a vast gap of time, loss, and ignorance to achieve an intimate bond, a bridge of restitution or healing, between the authorial present and the ancestral past.

Years before *Beloved* Morrison spoke of her fiction in terms of the transmission of cultural inheritance: because black people no longer live in places where parents "sit around and tell their children those . . . archetypal stories," the novel must take up the traditional "healing" function of African-American folk music and tales ("Rootedness" 340). The culture-bearing impulse generates in Morrison's novels characters of mythic stature, with tale-telling names and marked bodies,[7] along with the voice of a communal chorus and a narrative voice of an "oral quality" ("An Interview" 409) modeled on "a black preacher [who] requires his congregation to . . . join him in the sermon"; "not the separate, isolated ivory tower voice of a very different kind of person but an implied 'we' in narration" ("Rootedness" 341-343).[8] Aspiring to a voice that sounds like "we," Morrison attempts a communal textuality: "If anything I do, in the way of writing novels . . . isn't about the village or the community or about you, then it is not about anything" ("Rootedness" 344). Upon finishing a book, she has said, "I feel a little lonely, as though I've lost touch . . . with some collective memory" ("Toni Morrison" 131). Writing that contacts collective memory conflates the personal and the communal, works to open the "interior life" of the individual into the "anterior life" of the people (Clemons 75), what Morrison has referred to as "the life of that organism to which I belong which is black people in this country" ("Interview" 413).

  In writing *Beloved* Morrison's Whitmanesque will to communal subjectivity confronts its antithesis and perhaps its deepest source—the catastrophic destruction of community under slavery. With a capacity for pain and a sustained focus on the dead unprecedented in the African-American novel, *Beloved* includes in the storytelling "we" numberless lost forebears. More than a "history," *Beloved* serves for its author as a substitute:

> There is no place here where I can go, or where you can go, and think about, or not think about, or summon the presences of, or recollect the absences of—slaves. . . . Something that reminds us of the ones who made the journey, and those who did not make it. There is no suitable memorial—or plaque, or wreath, or wall, or park, or skyscraper lobby. There's no three hundred foot tower. . . . And because such a place doesn't exist that *I* know of, the book had to. (Lecture)

Reconceiving the historical novel as memorial, Morrison illuminates the psychological structure of ethnic historical fiction. Like all memorials, *Beloved* is not a "place" of the dead but a place where survivors can go to "summon" and "recollect," to look upon the sculpted shape of their own sorrow. *Beloved* cannot recover the "interior life" of slaves, but by dramatizing the psychological legacy of slavery, it portrays that "interior" place in the African-American psyche where a slave's face still haunts.

When first conceiving her rewriting of Margaret Garner's life, Morrison has said, "It was an era I didn't want to get into—going back into and through grief" ("It's OK" 45). This "grief" seems almost a palpable atmosphere; in the personal psychological return required to write *Beloved*, it was not history Morrison had to go "back into and through" but an intensity of hovering emotion attributed neither to the ancestors nor to herself but filling the space between them. Merging the psychological, the communal, and the historical, Morrison's novel goes "back into and through" time and pain together. Returning to the surface, it brings to the present an archetypal figure for the emotional labor of its own recuperative writing: the return of a dead ancestor. I read the haunting, resurrection, and exorcism of the beloved ghost as the inscription of the writer's haunted negotiations with her people's past. Setting a metahistorical struggle between mother and ghostly daughter at the center of an epic reimagining of an entire ancestry, Morrison's history centrally dramatizes the problem of imagining, writing, and publishing—"witnessing"—a story about her own daughterly heritage. And, as I shall argue, the ghost Beloved, who gives a body and face to that which is in excess of African-American history—the absences at that history's core—also functions, in a dramatic reversal, as a marvelous figure for the struggle of daughterly historiographic desire itself.

2

In the "village" of *Beloved*, the multigenerational, culture-bearing black community of Morrison's ideal appears in devastated form, in the persons of a few traumatized survivors, eking out an existence in the aftermath of slavery. Foregrounded in the novel, the telling of stories becomes memory's struggle with catastrophe and loss. For Morrison's characters, as for the novel in its contemporary moment, cultural transmission requires the retrieval of traumatic memories. This "history" thus acquires the function of communal "talking cure": its characters, author, and readers delve into the past, repeating painful stories to work toward the health of fuller awareness.

Beloved opens upon the haunted house where, shunned by the neighborhood, Morrison's heroine Sethe is raising her daughter Denver in an atmosphere of stagnant grief. Together they have come to accept what drove two sons away from home: the "spiteful" baby ghost (3) who makes herself known by clashings of pots and furniture, pools of red light by the doorway, tiny hand prints in the cake. Into this scene walks Paul D, that rare "kind of man who could walk into a house and make the women cry" (17). His arrival changes the climate of repression: he chases the invisible haunter from the house and sparks in Sethe "the temptation to trust and remember," "to go ahead and feel" (30), for the first time in years. His past, too, has required profound repression: he has a "tobacco tin buried in his chest where a red heart used to be. Its lid rusted shut" (72-73). Together, Sethe and Paul D begin a mutual talking cure that promises a mutual future. As their halting, gradual storytelling is taken up by other characters, the novel's present unfolds entwined in multiple strands of time, voice, incident, and perspective.

Storytelling becomes the text's self-conscious task; many scenes present a character narrating his or her life to a listener. The novel's distinctive tone arises from the very difficulty of telling for those recovering from the traumas of slavery—witnessing the murder, torture, or sale of family and friends; being whipped, chained, led with an iron bit in the mouth, and housed in an underground "box"; being examined and catalogued in terms of "human" and "animal" characteristics, or forcibly "nursed" by white boys when one's breasts held milk for a baby. These experiences fragment and block the memories of Morrison's ex-slaves, whose stories are revealed in bits, out of sequence, in a painful eking out and holding back often rendered in spare synecdoche: "Paul D had only begun . . . when her fingers on his knee, soft and reassuring, stopped him. . . . Saying more might push them both to a place they couldn't get back from. Sethe rubbed and rubbed. . . . She hoped it calmed him as it did her. Like kneading bread . . . working dough. Nothing bet-

ter than that to start the day's serious work of beating back the
past" (73).

As the narrative loops around events, dramatizing pain's
effect on memory, it also suggests a hesitance to force the past
out of characters whose memories stand in for the suffering of
innumerable unknown people. Any recuperations are performed against a blank background of storylessness, symbolic of
our historical knowledge of African Americans and of their representation in our literature. Morrison chooses just one family's
haunted house to explicate, but as Grandma Baby Suggs says,
"Not a house in the country ain't packed to the rafters with
some dead Negro's grief" (5). Every American house is a
haunted house. As *Beloved* revives the past in the modes of
haunting, memory, and storytelling, it becomes an exercise in
the poetics of absence.

Morrison's prose inventively represents the multiple
shades of loss and absence known to slaves: "Anybody Baby
Suggs knew, let alone loved, who hadn't run off or been hanged,
got rented out, loaned out, bought up, brought back, stored up,
mortgaged, won, stolen, or seized" (23). Characters tend to
gather around them clusters of the lost. "Did Patty lose her
lisp?" Baby Suggs wonders about the children sold from her;
"what color did Famous' skin finally take?" (139). On his post-
war trek north, Paul D saw "twelve dead blacks in the first eighteen miles," and "by the time he got to Mobile, he had seen more
dead people than living ones" (269). A traveling man, Paul D
brings to the text a voice of tribal griot-cum-historical eyewitness:
"During, before, and after the war he had seen Negroes so
stunned, or hungry, or tired or bereft it was a wonder they re-
called or said anything. Who, like him, had hidden in caves and
fought owls for food . . . stole from pigs . . . slept in trees in the
day and walked by night. . . . Once he met a Negro about four-
teen years old who lived by himself in the woods and said he
couldn't remember living anywhere else. He saw a witless colored woman jailed and hanged for stealing ducks she believed
were her own babies" (66). Passages like this bring to the novel
cinematic visions of an entire struggling people, among whom
Morrison names a precious few characters for detailed narration.
The reader learns, like Ella as she aids escaping slaves, to listen
"for the holes—the things the fugitives did not say, the questions they did not ask . . . the unnamed, unmentioned people
left behind" (92). To demarcate the "holes" Morrison has charac-

ters repeat isolated remembered details, metonymies for unre-
countable emotional experiences, the more poignant for their
banality. Baby Suggs recalls, "My first-born. All I can remember
of her is how she loved the burned bottom of bread. Can you
beat that? Eight children and that's all I remember" (5).

"That's all you let yourself remember," Sethe replies. In
this landscape of loss it is Morrison's pensive heroine, the
"queenly woman" (12) with blood on her hands and a "tree"
scarred into her back, who articulates the novel's theory of
memory and repression in a distinctive, neologistic vocabulary.
To the girl who arrives at the door from nowhere and claims to
have no past, Sethe says, "You disremember everything? I
never knew my mother neither, but I saw her a couple of times.
Did you never see yours?" (118-119). The suggestive verb "disremember" is complemented in Sethe's usage by the idiosyncratic "rememory," which works as both noun and verb: "I don't
'spect you rememory this, but . . ." (160). The repetition of "rememory" underscores the text's preoccupation with the problematics of the mind in time. Sethe explains her experience of
time and "rememory": "If a house burns down, it's gone, but the
place—the picture of it—stays, and not just in my rememory, but
out there, in the world. . . . Some day you be walking down the
road and you hear something or see something going on. So
clear. And you think it's you thinking it up. . . . But no. It's
when you bump into a rememory that belongs to somebody else
. . ." (35-36). For Sethe a "rememory" (an individual experience)
hangs around as a "picture" that can enter another's "rememory" (the part of the brain that "rememories") and complicate
consciousness and identity. "Rememory" as trope postulates the
interconnectedness of minds, past and present, and thus neatly
conjoins the novel's supernatural vision with its aspiration to
communal epic, realizing the "collective memory" of which
Morrison speaks. For while the prefix "re" (normally used for
the act, not the property of consciousness) suggests that "rememory" is an active, creative mental function, Sethe's explanation describes a natural—or a supernatural—phenomenon. For
Sethe as for her author, then, to "rememory" is to use one's
imaginative power to realize a latent, abiding connection to the
past.

"Rememory" thus functions in Morrison's "history" as a
trope for the problem of reimagining one's heritage. The novel's entire poetics of memory, all of Sethe and Paul D's troubles

with remembering, can be seen to figure the problem not of Morrison's own memory, of course, but of her imagination as it encounters her people's past. The characters who do not want to or can not remember their stories reverse the desire of the writer who wants to know and tell a communal history. She must work to "rememory" these ancestors who wish they could forget. In the absence of their particular faces, she must create the characters she wants to mourn. The elevation of memory to a supernatural power that connects all minds, making it possible to "bump into a rememory that belongs to somebody else," is generated by authorial desire to write like a "we" about unknown ancestors. "Rememory" transforms memory into a property of consciousness with the heightened imaginative power sufficient to the ethnic historical novel's claim to represent the past.

Along with this heightened notion of memory, the text's inscription of the psychological project of ethnic historical recuperation relies upon heightened tropes of naming and love. Morrison's epigraph, a passage from Romans 9.25, combines these: "I will call them my people, / which were not my people; / and her beloved, / which was not beloved." Suggesting that the naming function of the text be read as an offering of narrative love, the epigraph proposes a kind of history-telling that can turn estrangement into intimacy. "Beloved," Morrison names the lost past, and "Beloved" is the novel's final word. This implied function of narrative love seeks to repair the violation of love wreaked upon Morrison's characters by slavery, separation, and death. Considering newborn Denver's chances of survival, Ella tells Sethe, "If anybody was to ask me I'd say, 'Don't love nothing'" (92). Like memory, love must defend itself against history. For Paul D in the prison camp, survival meant "you protected yourself and loved small": "Picked the tiniest stars out of the sky to own. . . . Grass blades, salamanders. . . . Anything bigger wouldn't do. A woman, a child, a brother—a big love like that would split you wide open . . . to get to a place where you could love anything you chose—not to need permission for desire—well now, *that* was freedom" (162). Equating "freedom"— a consummate signifier in African-American literature and culture—with the right to love as one chooses, Morrison's text exercises its freedom to cast "long-distance love" (95) backward in time and bestow names upon—thus "freeing"—some of the African Americans history forgot. In the dialectic between the lost past and the rememorying function of narrative love,

Beloved reconceives the historical text as a transformative space: a space in which the present takes the past in a new and transforming embrace, constructed for mutual healing.

The transforming power of narrative is underscored in *Beloved* by the many inset scenes of storytelling; the familial or communal contexts of these story "exchanges," in Ross Chambers's terms (8), dramatize the power of cultural transmission to transform family relationships.[9] For example, at the novel's mythological core is the story Sethe often tells Denver of her birth under horrid conditions while her mother ran from slavery. This story—a significant feminization of the archetypal slave escape narrative—is "exchanged" in the understanding that the hardships endured by the mother should contribute to the child's sense of self. Denver is the daughter who emerges from the storytelling a woman, embraces her community, learns to read and write, and even plans to go to college.[10] This storytelling exchange is a model for the intergenerational transmission of African-American oral culture; it is Denver who actually retells the escape-childbirth story in the novel. Born in a canoe on the Ohio River, between slavery and freedom, Denver the survivor and story-inheritor becomes a proto-Morrison, bearer of the family exodus saga into literate American culture.[11]

The storytelling transaction between Sethe and Paul D is different: the lovers engage in a mutual unburdening of the past in the hopes of a mutual healing and of a future together. "He wants to put his story next to hers," Morrison concludes their protracted and arduous romance (273). The reconciliation of the sexes resulting from this story exchange is a particularly notable transformation, given recent controversy about the representation of black men in black women's texts (see McDowell, "Reading"). Morrison, who has consistently written complex and nuanced black male characters (for example, Cholly Breedlove, Shadrack, Milkman Dead, Son, and Joe Trace), here creates a man whose entry into the house of fiction starts a rush not just of female tears but of female autobiography. A muse to the storytelling Sethe—or to Morrison—Paul D also offers hope of futurity at the telling's end: "Sethe," he says, "me and you, we got more yesterday than anybody. We need some kind of tomorrow" (273). The exchange between these two, developing from shared confessions to an actual romantic ending, gestures at a further transformation: the reconstitution of the black family after a time of devastation. When Paul D announces that the traumatic story has run its course and suggests its resolution in a vague futurity, his words manage the interface of this "history" and its crises with those of the present.

While most of the text's narrative exchanges can be read in terms of cultural transmission, the retrieval of stories to strengthen identity and community, this explanation cannot account for the tellings involving the ghost Beloved, which do not strengthen community but threaten Sethe's relationships and even her life.   To understand the story transactions with Beloved—and the text's transactions with the past—we must examine the strange character at the novel's heart.

The mysterious, beautiful woman who emerges fully dressed from the stream behind Morrison's haunted house, remembering little besides crouching in the dark, longing for a certain woman's face, and crossing a bridge, turns out to be the resurrected baby Sethe murdered 18 years earlier. She wants her mother with all the intensity of an abandoned two-year-old. In this rememory of Margaret Garner and her daughter, however, the ghost comes to embody much "more," as Denver puts it (266). Morrison gives her the distinctive name everyone privately gives to their most beloved; it expresses at once the greatest anonymity and the dearest specificity. It is her name because she died still unnamed, and when Sethe heard the preacher speak the word *beloved* at her burial, she had it cut on her baby daughter's tombstone. But when the preacher said "Dearly Beloved," he must have been addressing the living assembled there and not, as the grieving Sethe thought, the dead child. "Beloved" names everyone, in the official, impersonal rhetoric of the church and names everyone who is intimately loved, but does not name the forgotten. Morrison has the name perform precisely this last function; the novel's defining conceit is to call the unnamed "beloved." Part of Beloved's strangeness derives, then, from the emotional burden she carries as a symbolic compression of innumerable forgotten people into one miraculously resurrected personality, the remembering of the "sixty million" in one youthful body.[12] Another part is just the weirdness of a ghost: like all the ghosts in literature, she embodies a fearful claim of the past upon the present, the past's desire to be recognized by, and even possess, the living.

Yet to write history as a ghost story, to cast the past as longing for *us*, instead of the other way around, is to inscribe a reversal of desire that informs this text's structure—and the structure of all ghost tales—on a deep level. Indeed, in imagining the longing of the murdered child for the mother, Morrison reverses the usual direction of grief, in which the living mourn the dead; the child or descendent mourns the mother or ancestor. The novel's emblematic figure of the mourning baby girl, embodying this reversal of desire, can thus function to figure both the lost past and the mourning author—the "daughter" of this lost ancestry, desiring the face of the mother from whom time has separated her. This is to say that the historical project of the novel is in a profound sense a mother-quest, an African-American feminist "herstory" that posits a kind of "mother of history" and sends a surrogate, time-traveling daughter to enact its demonic errand of love or revenge: seeking to regain her, to heal historical separation, to know the story of the mother history forgot. Morrison spares no expense in articulating Beloved's primal, pre-Oedipal craving for her mother's face: "I am not separate from her . . . her face is my own and I want to be there in the place where her face is. . . . I want to be the two of us. I want the join . . ." (210-213). Embodying an insatiable, childish, jealous desire for the absent mother's face, to see and be seen, to commune and kiss and know and be known, Beloved is a marvelous figuration of the woman writer's struggle with and desire for the face of the absent past, for her matrilineage, for the lost mothers she would rewrite.

In the return of Beloved, Morrison's "rememory" of the murderer-mother thus demonstrates the psychological structure of a daughter's desire.[13] "How could she do that?" Morrison wondered about Margaret Garner, and "because I could not answer that question," she has said, "I introduced into the book one who had the right to the answer, her dead daughter" ("African-Americans"). That the dead daughter of *Beloved* functions as a surrogate self becomes startlingly clear in Morrison's 1985 "Conversation" with Gloria Naylor on the evolution of her oeuvre. Discussing the imaginative project that impelled her first novel, *The Bluest Eye*, Morrison speaks of the recovery of a "dead girl" who was a lost aspect of herself: "I remembered being a person who did belong in this earth . . . [but] there was no me in this world. And I was looking for that dead girl and I thought I might talk about that dead girl . . ." ("Conversation" 198-199). Years later, developing the psychological world of *Beloved*, Morrison imaginatively conceived the "self" as a separate entity, like "a *twin* or a thirst or a friend or something that sits right next to

you and watches you"; "I . . . just projected her out into the
earth," she explains, "[as] the girl that Margaret Garner killed"
(208).[14] After years of sustained creative work, Morrison concludes, "[the girl] comes running when called—walks freely
around the house. . . . She is here now, alive" (217). Thus personifying her developing oeuvre as a gradually resurrected girl-
self, Morrison creates an emblematic figure for the contemporary
black women's "renaissance."[15]

Shaping that gift into the ghost Beloved, Morrison dramatizes the black literary daughter's imaginative return to maternal
history. Though *Beloved* began as an inquiry into the motives
of the mother, the energy of desire in the text is embodied in the
phantom daughter, who returns through time to question the
mother. And though the plot turns upon the loss of a child, this
history-as-daughter's-rememory is pervaded with grief for lost
mothers: Beloved's aching desire for Sethe; Sethe's mourning
for Baby Suggs, the mother-in-law almost as present in memory
after her death as is her ghostly granddaughter; and Sethe's loss
of her own mother, remembered in excruciating fragments: a hat
in the rice fields, a scar under her breast (61). This multiple
mourning for mothers inscribes in our literature the tragic experience of African-American children and women under slavery,
systematically denied mothers and denied the mother-right by
the pitiless traffic in human labor and by enforced wet-nursing.
Her mother sent to the fields, Sethe was suckled by the plantation nurse: "The little whitebabies got it first and I got what was
left. Or none. There was no nursing milk to call my own. I
know what it is to be without the milk that belongs to you . . ."
(200). Echoing through this "history" is a cry for mother's milk,
fusing a mass-scale historical deprivation with that of the thirst-
ing self, the daughter deprived of her "disremembered" matrilineage.

The welling-up of mother-daughter longing reaches a
climax at the moment when Sethe realizes Beloved is her
daughter returned from death; in this moment of perfect restitution, though she holds a cup in her hand, "no milk spilled." A
rush of mothers' voices is unleashed, recalling lost daughters or
urging remembrance on them:

> From where she sat Sethe could not examine it, not the
> hairline, nor the eyebrows, the lips, nor. . . .
> 'All I remember,' Baby Suggs had said, 'is how she
> loved the burned bottom of bread. Her little hands I

wouldn't know em if they slapped me.'
. . . the birthmark, nor the color of the gums, the shape
of her ears, nor. . . .
'Here. Look here. This is your ma'am. If you can't tell
me by my face, look here.'   (175)

Set amid the echoes of so many separations, the miraculous reunion of Beloved and Sethe gathers emotional force: one child
restored, one grieving mother's wish come true.[16]

The mother-daughter dialectic that shapes this "history"
generates intensely relational forms of identity among female
characters. Morrison's women are linked by a three-generation
chain of scars, marking both bond and breach: Sethe's mother
urges her daughter to recognize her body in death by the scar
under her breast, and Sethe's resurrected daughter bears on her
neck the mark of her mother's handsaw. Between them, Sethe
has "a chokecherry tree" on her back, the scar of a brutal whipping. Schoolteacher's nephews whip Sethe for reporting their
first act of violence against her—the one which looms much
larger in her memory: forcibly "nursing" her breast milk. The
tree is thus associated with Sethe's violated motherhood, the
visible sign of the crime she repeatedly laments: "they took my
milk!" (17). In this novel of mother-quest, Morrison replaces the
prototypical white master's crime against black slave women—
rape—with a virtual rape of Sethe's motherhood.[17] The tree is a
cruciform emblem of her suffering but also an emblem of her
place in generation; as the second of three links—a "trunk" with
roots and with "branches," "leaves," and "blossoms" (79)—Sethe
carries the family tree on her back.[18] As a child, she misunderstood the pain such scars record, and when her mother said,
"you can know me by this mark," Sethe replied, "but how will
you know me? . . . Mark the mark on me, too" (61). Though
Sethe's mother slapped her, Morrison's portrayal of the lost
mothers of African-American history inscribes, indelibly, the
daughter's reckless willingness to bear the mark of the mother's
pain.

The mother-daughter structure also surfaces in a surprising interchangeability of generational positions among female
characters. This occurs not only in the ominous passage in
which Beloved grows into the mother and Sethe shrinks into
the child (250) but also in a curious play on the word "baby,"
most striking in the name of the matriarch Baby Suggs.
"Grandma Baby," as she is oxymoronically called in her old age,

got her name from an affectionate husband; the "baby ghost" returns as an infantile young woman; and Denver too is called
"baby" at the moment in her eighteenth year when she leaves
her mother's house and enters the community to seek work and
food for her family: "'Oh baby,' said Mrs. Jones. 'Oh, baby,'" and
Denver "did not know it then, but it was the word 'baby,' said
softly and with such kindness, that inaugurated her life in the
world as a woman" (248).   The circulation of female identity
through the positions "baby," "daughter," "woman," "mother,"
and "grandmother" links Morrison's female characters in an
imaginative fusion that reflects the daughter-mother psychic dialectic of this "history," a time-transcending structure in which
the novel of history meets the poetics of motherlove: "Grown
don't mean nothing to a mother," Sethe says; "they get bigger,
older, but grown? . . . In my heart it don't mean a thing" (45).
Thinking back like a mother, to misquote Virginia Woolf, Morrison's history adds a motherlove to its repertoire of tropes for
the conquest of time.[19]
        If the ghostly daughter can figure both the return of the
past and the desire of the past-questing writer, the obsessive
mother-daughter dialectics of *Beloved* also make sense as a
structure of literary inheritance.   The search for the lost
"mother" of history might be read as an agnostic struggle—or
better, an ambivalent "female affiliation complex" (Gilbert and
Gubar 168-171)—with the literary foremothers whose influence
and whose loss to history Morrison feels so intensely ("Who is
she? . . . Who is she?"): the writers of the slave narratives.
Vital and impressive in their escape tales, these earliest African-
American women writers represent for Morrison a culturally
originary moment and a rich, barely tapped literary inheritance.
Yet though their existence is foundational to Morrison's sense of
authorship, as chosen antecedents they elude authorial desire,
veiling in their near-anonymity much more than they reveal.
These foremothers can be glimpsed today, usually, only in brief
texts published under names recorded nowhere else, collected in
volumes holding myriad variations on the same protean plot.
In their day the slave narrators had much less literary authority
than does the best-selling Morrison and even today the truth-sta-
tus of their tales is debated. Still, the historical value of the narratives far surpasses that of a belated "neoslave narrative" that
reimagines historical truth. Though it is Morrison's *huge* joy"
to help slave authors to "surface" in contemporary writing

("Intimate" 229), it is also her lot to view them from across a great divide and see in them the dim faces of origin she will never fully capture. In the jealous longing of the abandoned daughter, the novel figures its relationship to the unknown ancestress-muse of the African-American women's literary renaissance.[20]

Just as the ghost daughter's return to the mother can be read as a reversal of authorial historiographic desire, the daughter also reverses the structure of narrative seduction identified by Chambers: rather than seduce a listener, Beloved seduces Sethe into telling her story. Coming from the place of the dead, this ghost begs to have history told to her. The novel's normative story-exchange between mother and child, carried out by Sethe and Denver in the daylight realm of the present, transacts the inheritance of a real daughter and promises real-world continuity; the exchange between Sethe and Beloved, however, is symbolic of the deep workings of the psyche in struggle with the past, involving guilt, longing, and fury, threatening disintegration and death. From the moment she arrives her strange appeal works on Sethe, who accepts her into the household, accepts her increasing physical intimacy, and finally recognizes her as her lost daughter. All the while, Beloved coaxes information from Sethe, stories she had never wanted to tell before but which now flow out of her. Toward the novel's emotional climax, Denver is excluded from the central drama, and Beloved has Sethe all to herself. The relationship intensifies to a frenzy; standing outside the house the old man Stamp Paid hears "a conflagration of hasty voices," among which "all he could make out was the word *mine*" (172): "[H]e kept on through the voices, and tried once more to knock on the door of 124. This time, although he couldn't cipher but one word, he believed he knew who spoke them. The people of the broken necks, of fire-cooked blood and black girls who had lost their ribbons. What a roaring" (181).

In this mother-daughter struggle Stamp hears the concentrated agony of the entire people.[21] The reunion of Sethe and Beloved crystallizes the vast problem of facing and reclaiming African-American history in a terrible mother-daughter seduction-struggle for the story. Morrison's desire to represent Margaret Garner and her generation and to write a story that could lie "next to hers," so to speak, generates the bodily form of a ghostly child who floats through time, finds the mother for whom she longs, wins her embrace, and nearly strangles her to death. The mother's murder of her daughter, the daughter's resurrection, and all the novel's gothic horror seem excessive to history in the sense of an objective "prehistory of the present" because they illustrate quite a different sense of history: the subjective, ethnic possession of history understood as the prehistory of the self. Encountering the story of Margaret Garner, Morrison could not get it out of her mind, and her return to embrace this impossible mother-figure in fiction suggests the impossibility and the urgency of embracing one's inheritance of such a history, one's living relationship to so much death. In a moment when a black woman writer at last possesses the authority to take her history into her own hands, Morrison risks—and confirms—that authority with the figure of a fearsome foremother, thereby revealing a daughter's vulnerability to her history, its haunting, violent grip on the mind, the dangerous pull of love that draws her back. If our literature was incomplete without *Beloved*, it was because we had not been told the story of slavery by a writer willing to undertake the life-and-death story of the surviving self.

3

We can read in the obsessive relationship at the center of this text the figuration of authorial desire/grief for a lost mother-of-history, the active principle in Morrison's reimagining of her ancestral community. Our account is incomplete, however, without attention to the implications of the gendering and sexuality of the ghost: Beloved's haunting is a metaphoric return of the past in the form of an excess of female desire. Figuring the disremembered past as "the girl who waited to be loved" (274), Morrison conflates the problematics of time, loss, and representation with a drama of inconsumable female desire. Calling the past "Beloved" and remembering it in a female body, the text gives one name to the lost of history and buried female desire, and it stages the simultaneous resurrection of both.

When the lost past returns in *Beloved*, it demonstrates a startling sexuality. Susan Willis has argued that Morrison tends to figure history, particularly "the loss of history and culture" resulting from the African-American northern and urban migrations in "sexual terms"; sexuality erupts in her novels to evoke earlier, more vital modes of black life (35). When the bourgeois black women in *The Bluest Eye* maintain vigilance against "eruptions of funk" (68), Willis claims, "funk" signifies "the intrusion of the past in the present" (41). The "funk" in Morrison's earlier novels suggests, then, a distinctively black female sexuality inseparable from a sense of historical continuity. Yet the ghost Beloved is an eruption of powerful, physical female desire that radically threatens the distinction between past and present as well as the household and the throats of the living. The disruptive sexuality of a murdered girl returned from the dead is a funky nightmare, an agony of limitless sexual desire expressive of the lot of the disremembered in time.

Strikingly, this ghostly longing does not restrict its objects by gender. Beloved seduces Paul D but cannot "take her eyes off Sethe": "Stooping to shake the damper, or snapping sticks for kindlin, Sethe was licked, tasted, eaten by Beloved's eyes . . . she felt Beloved touch her. A touch no heavier than a feather but loaded . . . with desire. Sethe stirred and looked . . . into her eyes. The longing she saw there was bottomless" (57-58). When one day Beloved's massaging strokes turn to "lips that kept on kissing," Sethe startles, saying, "You too old for that" (97-98). If this moment can be explained as just the cognitive clash produced by the returned baby-ghost plot, a central section of the book is even more substantially homoerotic in content and structure.

When Sethe discovers Beloved's identity, she interprets her reappearance as a sign of forgiveness, and in immense relief she turns her back on the world and devotes herself to loving Beloved. The novel then embarks upon 18 pages of "unspeakable thoughts, unspoken" (199) by Sethe and her two daughters, now an isolated and passionate trio, who, having locked the door, enter a communion of love, outside time. Echoing the *Song of Songs*, each speaks a monologue in turn: "Beloved, she my daughter. She mine"; "Beloved is my sister"; "I am Beloved and she is mine" (200-210). Their voices then join in a fugue of woman-woman love: "You are my sister / You are my daughter / You are my face; you are me"; "I have your milk / I have your smile / I will take care of you"; "You are mine / You are mine / You are mine" (216-217).

In this fantasy of fulfilled female desire, the text seems to find its heart. When Beloved's "lesbian" desire first disrupts Sethe's household, it is one with the volcanic return of the repressed past she brings with her, out of the closet, as it were, and into the house of the present. But when Sethe locks her house against the world—in particular the male world of Stamp Paid and Paul D—lesbian desire is no longer disturbing; rather, the *jouissant* communion that ensues seems a momentary utopian resolution of the war between present and past. If the fluctuations of sexuality in Morrison can be seen to encode historical process, this "lesbian" section of *Beloved* might constitute a momentary "separatist" resolution of historical tensions, in a realm "free at last," as Morrison suggestively puts it (199), of male interpretation or authority—free, in fact, of history. But if, as I have argued, Beloved figures both the lost past and the desiring present, her desire for Sethe suggests a "matrisexual" narrative desire.[22] The seduction of the ancestress for her story, which Beloved undertakes for Morrison, here rests in an ahistorical, pre-Oedipal fantasy that unites "mother" and "child" as lovers. As the form joins their separate voices in ritualized call and response, female historiographic agon is, for a moment, perfectly resolved.[23]

The perfect, timeless moment passes, however; Sethe has left her job, and when the food runs out, Denver goes into the world to find some and begins to bring her haunted family back into its community and into time. At home the love-feast has passed the satiation point; Beloved demands more and more from Sethe, while accusing her of desertion. Slowly she begins to grow bigger, while Sethe diminishes, so that it seems to Denver that "the thing was done": "Beloved bending over Sethe looked the mother, Sethe the teething child. . . . Beloved ate up her life, took it, swelled up with it. . . . And the older woman yielded it up without a murmur" (250). The murdered baby turned lesbian ghost has become a vampire. A difficult emotional crossing is made when the text acknowledges that the murdered innocent, the forgotten past, can become, if allowed to return and take over our present-day households, a killer. When the women of the town hear that Sethe's murdered baby has returned, they overcome their longtime disgust and decide that "nobody got that coming" (256). Thirty-strong, they march to the house and perform a collective exorcism; Beloved vanishes. Paul D then returns to bring Sethe out of a traumatic withdrawal, and into "some kind of tomorrow."

Having shaken the fictional present of Sethe's life free of the burden of its past, Morrison ends her story. She then closes the text with a two-page coda that leaves Sethe's living family behind and meditates only on Beloved and her meaning for our present moment.   There is a recognition here that, like the ghost-vampire of Sethe's past, writing, too, can feed on the historical mother, grow larger than her, potentially kill her; and "when you kill the ancestor," Morrison has said, "you kill yourself" ("Rootedness" 344).   Taking leave of history, the novel leaves the slave mother to her own moment, to herself—whoever she was.   When she reads a slave woman's narrative, Morrison wonders, "Who is she? . . . Who is she?"   But at her slave novel's end, she lets the foremother question herself: "Me? Me?"   Sethe asks, her story's final words and her reply when Paul D tells her "You your best thing, Sethe" (273).   *Beloved* ultimately leaves the mother of history to possess herself, stops haunting her with the losses of the past or with our present longing.

Yet the text does not give up Beloved.   She is a possession rescued from the past, a mirror-image of the daughter who searches backwards in time.   In the final two pages Morrison diminishes Beloved's body once again to a haunting, carrying the losses of history as "a loneliness" that we banish from thought as we banish denied desire (274).   Having told history as the painful remembering of the forgotten, *Beloved* ends by "witnessing" the process of dis(re)memberment, as "the girl who waited to be loved and cry shame erupts into her separate parts, to make it easy for the chewing laughter to swallow her all away" (274).   The coda depicts human collusion with passing time—the general hunger to reabsorb and repress loss that afflicts the storytelling village: "Disremembered and unaccounted for, she cannot be lost because no one is looking for her. . . . They forgot her like a bad dream. . . . Sometimes the photograph of a close friend or relative—looked at too long—shifts, and something more familiar than the dear face itself moves there.   They can touch it if they like, but don't . . ." (274-275).

The meditations of this prose-poem, "transfiguring and disseminating the haunting" (Lecture), bring history to an unclosed closure and the haunt to our own houses.   Morrison seems to unravel the illusion of historical mimesis created in the preceding fiction and to describe the text's history-telling as the inverse of cultural transmission, the shadowy underside of family inheritance, a romance with the painfully reanimated body of loss.   The text repeats three times in closing that this is "not a story to pass on," a statement best read not as a warning against repetition but as a description by negation. *Beloved* is not a story of presence and continuity but one that delineates the place of absence: "By and by all trace is gone. . . . The rest is weather. Not the breath of the disremembered and unaccounted for, but wind in the caves, or spring ice thawing too quickly. Just weather. Certainly no clamor for a kiss. Beloved" (275). Speaking in negatives, Morrison makes absence exquisitely tangible; the lost past is "not the breath of the disremembered and unaccounted for" but "just weather"; the lovely nonsubstance "just weather" rolls away before the stunning silence, "certainly no clamor for a kiss." For us of course, closing the book, there is nothing but weather. The past does not exist unless we choose to hear its clamor. Morrison stages an encounter with the past in a drama of such clamorous desire that she does make us seem to hear loss clamor back. And in ending, having once again hushed the obscure absences and denied desires that her fiction aroused, she seals our relationship to the lost past with the offering of a name: "Beloved." Thus her history achieves its embrace.

Notes

[1] Morrison explains the "sixty million" as "the best educated guess at the number of black Africans who never even made it into slavery—those who died either as captives in Africa or on slave ships" (Clemons 75).

[2] For Margaret Garner's story see Harris, which reprints an 1856 newspaper account of the incident (10). Morrison first encountered the story when working on Harris's book as an editor at Random House. For a fuller account of Garner's story, see Lerner 60-63.

[3] Carby examines Arna Bontemps's *Black Thunder* (1936) and Margaret Walker's *Jubilee* (1966) and mentions Ishmael Reed's *Flight to Canada* (1976), David Bradley's *The Chaneysville Incident* (1981), Sherley Anne Williams's *Dessa Rose* (1986), and Toni Morrison's *Beloved* (1987). To this list we might add Ernest Gaines's *The Autobiography of Miss Jane Pittman* (1971), Gayl Jones's *Corregidora* (1975), Alex Haley's *Roots* (1976), Barbara Chase-Riboud's *Sally Hemings* (1979), Octavia Butler's *Kindred* (1979), Charles Johnson's *Oxherding Tale* (1982) and *Middle Passage* (1990), Jewelle Gomez's *The Gilda Stories* (1991), J. California Cooper's *Family* (1991), and new novels of Caribbean slavery, including Maryse Conde's *I, Tituba: Black Witch of Salem* (1992) and Caryl Phillips's *Cambridge* (1992).

[4] The historical novel as genre tends to be intimately connected to group identity, to a group's development of the authority or cultural need to

represent its history. The connection between historical fiction and nationalism is central, for example, to Lukács's reading of Walter Scott (30-63). Notably, the rise of black women to historiographic authority follows the post-civil rights and women's movement booms in black and women's literatures and leads the surge in new feminist historical texts across the spectrum of ethnic and postcolonial women's literatures.

5 The original slave narrative, Gates argues, "represents the attempts of blacks to *write themselves into being*" (xxiii), though ex-slaves generally could publish only with extensive supporting documentation by whites, testifying to their authorship, their literacy and their very existence.

6 Particularly important to recent feminist scholarship has been the authentication by Yellin of Harriet Jacobs's previously discredited narrative *Incidents in the Life of a Slave Girl*. See also Braxton.

7 Such characters include Pilate, First Corinthians, and Milkman in *Song of Solomon*; Sula, Eva Peace, and the three Deweys in *Sula*; and besides the ghost Beloved herself, Baby Suggs, Sethe, Stamp Paid, and the three Pauls in *Beloved*.

8 A communal chorus can be heard in the grieving women at Chicken Little's funeral in *Sula*, the various female spirits in *Tar Baby*, and the exorcising women in *Beloved*. An imaginative conflation of "I" and "we," self and community, recurs in Morrison's recorded remarks. "When I view the world, perceive it and write about it," she told Claudia Tate, "it's the world of black people" ("Toni Morrison" 118). "I write for black women," she said to Sandi Russell; "we are not addressing the men, as some white female writers do" ("It's OK" 46). To Tate again, "My audience is always the people in the book I'm writing at the time. I don't think of an extended audience." And in the same interview, "I wrote *Sula* and *The Bluest Eye* because they were the books I wanted to read. No one had written them yet, so I wrote them" (122). For Morrison, evidently, writing activates communion—among readers, other writers, a community, an ancestry, fictional characters, and the self.

9 Chambers argues that narrative is always a transaction based on "an initial *contract*, an understanding between the participants in the exchange as to the purposes served by the narrative function, its 'point'" (8). The "point" of a given narrative is suggested internally by "specific indications of the narrative situation appropriate to it," such as an inset seduction of a listener, an exchange with the power to "change relationships" (4, 9).

10 Denver's character inhabits less the folkloric and more the realist narrative world. Unlike Sethe, Beloved, and other Morrison women, she has no emblematic scar. Yet Sethe calls her a "charmed child" (41); her character figures African-American survival, the unlegendary descendants who have put the memory of such as Beloved behind them. Standing in for the reader as belated receiver of the story of slavery, Denver is sometimes alienated and annoyed: "How come everybody run off from Sweet Home can't stop talking about it?" (13), and often tormented by a story-inheritor's mixed emotions: "She loved it because it was all about herself; but she hated it too because it made her feel like a bill was owing somewhere and she, Denver, had to pay it" (77). And like her author, Denver cannot know, but only "rememory" her family's stories: she tells her birth story to Beloved "seeing it . . . and feeling how it must have felt to her mother"; together "the two did the best they could to create what really

happened" (78).

[11] Notably, Denver also brings the family story into dialogue with whites. Named for the white girl Amy Denver, who assists at her birth, Denver has a white "mother" along with her black one. A white female teacher who prepares her for Oberlin seals Denver's connection to white culture. The role of white female characters in the birth and nurturance of this fictional daughter seems to cast white women in a supporting relationship to the fictional project itself. Further, the dramatic encounter of Sethe and Amy in the American wilderness, bonding over the archetypal female experiences of giving birth and fleeing male violence, can be read as a female reimagination of the Huck-and-Jim interracial duos of American fiction and popular culture. With a name that suggests the Wild West and a quest for Boston, Amy evokes a continent of nineteenth-century white American female existence, interestingly represented as earthy and independent, bucking the tide by leaving home, moving eastward, and aiding a slave woman on the run. In the light of Sherley Anne Williams's *Dessa Rose* (1986), which also represents a relationship between a pregnant, escaping slave woman and a sympathetic white woman, we might trace the formation of a significant myth of American female interracial bonding.

[12] Beloved's monologue (210-214) suggests that she recalls the Middle Passage, that she carries a vast ancestral memory, and thus is the ghost of many more than one lost soul.

[13] This assertion does not contradict Hirsch's claim that in *Beloved* Morrison tells the mother's story and thus "[opens] the space for maternal narrative in feminist fiction" (198) or Liscio's related claim that in *Beloved* Morrison is "Writing Mother's Milk." Rather, I would argue, *Beloved* turns the "daughterly" feminist plot, in Hirsch's terms, into a project of daughterly return to the mother. Recuperating both the (historical) mother's story and "the black mother-infant daughter bond" (Liscio 39), *Beloved* aims to reunite the daughter's and the mother's voices in dialogue.

[14] Describing this precursor of Beloved, the dead girl brought back to the world, as a figure for her imaginative work, Morrison uses what would become the language of the coda to *Beloved* (in reverse form): writing *The Bluest Eye* Morrison began the process of "bit by bit . . . rescuing her from the grave of time and inattention," recovering "[h]er fingernails maybe in the first book; face and legs, perhaps, the second time," so that "[s]he is here now, alive" ("Conversation" 217). The coda to *Beloved*, by contrast, fragments and dissolves the dead girl back into "time and inattention."

[15] Morrison's description of the "dead girl" is remarkably like her descriptions of the new "renaissance" generation of black women writers (see "Conversation" 217; "Interview" 418). Indeed, the fantastic figure of a reborn, resurrected, time-traveling, or otherwise magical black daughter that now proliferates in African-American women's historical fictions seems the embodied "spirit" of the black women's "renaissance." The recurrent plot of the marvelous time-traveling daughter who returns to the mother-of-history is an allegory of the desire—and the newly acquired literary authority—to reimagine the genesis of the black female self, that is, of the power of black feminist reimagination. I elaborate this argument in a work in progress, tentatively entitled "The Daughter's Return: Revisions of History in Contemporary African-

American and Caribbean Women's Fiction."

[16] Locating history in a mother-daughter relationship and foregrounding scenes of childbirth and nursing, Morrison joins many contemporary women writers of female-centered historical fictions in recovering childbirth as the site of history-in-the-making. Childbirth becomes the definitive female trope for historical origins and normative, healthy inheritance in recent women's fiction. But if history is an ordinary woman giving birth, distortions of the normal birth plot reflect the impact of bad history on ordinary women. Scenes of childbirth-gone-wrong—occurring in strange or dangerous circumstances, resulting in the death of mother or child or in their subsequent separation—become emblematic of historical trauma. In the slave mother's murder of her daughter, Morrison gives us a female image for demonic history. Finally, in scenes of mother-daughter reunion, Morrison and others figure their own work of daughterly historical return, of recuperation of the mother-of-history.

[17] *Beloved* in effect rewrites black wet-nursing as institutionalized rape. When her daughter is restored to her, Sethe's remarks fuse the resentment of a wet nurse and a rape survivor: "Nobody will ever get my milk no more except my own children. I never had to give it to nobody else—and the one time I did it was took from me—they held me down and took it. Milk that belonged to my baby" (200).

[18] All three scars form crosses, for the mother has "a circle and a cross burnt right in the skin" (61), and Beloved has a horizontal line across her neck; the inheritance of slavery is, allegorically, these women's cross to bear.

[19] Motherlove in *Beloved* is a force stronger than death: "For a baby," Denver says of the ghost, "she throws a powerful spell." "No more powerful than the way I loved her," Sethe replies (4), asserting later in her monologue, "Beloved, she my daughter . . . my love was tough and she back now." Beyond the grave powerful foremothers hold sway: "My plan was to take us all to the other side where my own ma'am is," Sethe says of her attempt to kill her children and herself, and when Beloved returns she thinks, "I bet you Baby Suggs, on the other side, helped" (200-203).

[20] In reviving the slave mother figure, Morrison reproduces neither the titillating rape scenes predominant in the portraits of slave women in men's narratives (see Foster) nor the archetypal "outraged mother" described by Braxton. Though the pregnant Sethe prepares to devour an assailant, and though she gives birth when nearly dead herself, and rages against the theft of her milk, when she kills her child the archetype is shattered. Morrison's willingness to create heroines who break the rules for "positive" representation of the race (see McDowell, "'The Self and the Other'"; Spillers) here produces the absolute antitype of the good black mother and of the good daughter while insisting on our sympathy for both. *Beloved*'s ambiguous treatment of the slave woman creates a certain alienation effect; the experience of sympathizing with the slave mother who kills her child may cause readers to feel (as many of my students have felt) that they have begun to realize the full horror of slavery for the first time.

[21] Rigney persuasively reads this conflagration of voices as an evocation of "the mother tongue," "a semiotic jungle in which language itself defies convention and the laws of logic," and more specifically, "a black *woman's* jungle" (17-18).

[22] Chodorow uses this term to describe the original sexuality of children (95).

[23] A "lesbian" reading of *Beloved* would probably be rejected by Morrison, who has denied she wrote a lesbian novel in *Sula*, insisting it depicts the close female friendship historically characteristic of black women ("It's OK" 45). Certainly the many strong, close female bonds in Morrison's novels—particularly the recurring three-woman households—strike us as affirmations of women's love and culture, and of a feminist aesthetic, without necessarily implying lesbianism. But it is interesting that after rejecting such readings of *Sula* Morrison would write a novel that lends itself even more to reading as a "lesbian" text. Morrison's figuration of human relationships tends to blur all the "kinds" of love, the distinctions between emotions, as when Sethe, upon realizing her daughter has returned to her, "ascended the lily-white stairs like a bride" (176) or when speaking "unspoken" thoughts to Beloved, she says that Paul D "found out about me and you in the shed" (202-203), and unwittingly connects motherly murder to clandestine love-making. "Love is or it ain't," Sethe tells Paul D (164). Clearly female homoerotics remains a vital element in Morrison's vocabulary of interchangeable tropes for love.

Works Cited

Bell, Bernard W. *The Afro-American Novel and Its Tradition.* Amherst: University of Massachusetts Press, 1987.

Blassingame, John. "Using the Testimony of Ex-Slaves: Approaches and Problems." Davis and Gates, 78-98.

Braxton, Joanne M. "Harriet Jacobs' *Incidents in the Life of a Slave Girl*: The Re-definition of the Slave Narrative Genre." *Massachusetts Review* 27 (1986): 379-387.

Campbell, Jane. *Mythic Black Fiction: The Transformation of History.* Knoxville: University of Tennessee Press, 1986.

Carby, Hazel V. "Ideologies of Black Folk: The Historical Novel of Slavery." McDowell and Rampersad, 125-143.

Chambers, Ross. *Story and Situation: Narrative Seduction and the Power of Fiction.* Minneapolis: University of Minnesota Press, 1984.

Chodorow, Nancy. *The Reproduction of Mothering: Psychoanalysis and the Sociology of Gender.* Berkeley: University of California Press, 1978.

Christian, Barbara. "Somebody Forgot to Tell Somebody Something: African-American Women's Historical Novels." *Wild Women in the Whirlwind: Afra-American Culture and the Contemporary Literary Renaissance.* Ed. Joanne M. Braxton and Andree Nicola McLaughlin. New Brunswick, New Jersey: Rutgers University Press, 1990. 326-341.

Clemons, Walter. "A Gravestone of Memories." *Newsweek* 28 September 1989: 74-75.

Davis, Charles T. and Henry Louis Gates, Jr., eds. *The Slave's Narrative.* Oxford: Oxford University Press, 1985.

Foster, Frances. "'In Respect to Females . . .': Differences in the Portrayals of Women by Male and Female Narrators." *Black American Literature Forum* 15 (1981): 66-70.

Gates, Henry Louis, Jr. "The Language of Slavery." Davis and Gates, xi-xxiv.

Gates, Henry Louis, Jr. and K. A. Appiah, eds. *Toni Morrison: Critical Perspectives Past and Present*. New York: Amistad, 1993.

Gilbert, Sandra and Susan Gubar. *The War of the Words*. New Haven: Yale University Press, 1988. Vol. 1 of *No Man's Land: The Place of the Woman Writer in the Twentieth Century*. 3 Vols. 1988-1994.

Harris, Middleton A. *The Black Book*. New York: Random, 1974.

Hirsch, Marianne. *The Mother/Daughter Plot: Narrative, Psychoanalysis, Feminism*. Bloomington: Indiana University Press, 1989.

Hutcheon, Linda. *A Poetics of Post-modernism: History, Theory, Fiction*. London: Routledge, 1988.

Lerner, Gayl. *Corregidora*. 1975. Boston: Beacon, 1986.

Lerner, Gerda, ed. *Black Women in White America: A Documentary History*. 1972. New York: Vintage, 1973.

Liscio, Lorraine. "*Beloved*'s Narrative: Writing Mother's Milk." *Tulsa Studies in Women's Literature* 11 (1992): 31-46.

Lukács, Georg. *The Historical Novel*. Trans. Hannah Mitchell and Stanley Mitchell. 1962. Atlantic Highlands: Humanities, 1978.

McDowell, Deborah E. "In the First Place: Making Frederick Douglass and the Afro-American Narrative Tradition." *Critical Essays on Frederick Douglass*. Ed. William Andrews. Boston: Hall, 1991. 192-214.

—. "Negotiating Between Tenses: Witnessing Slavery after Freedom—*Dessa Rose*." McDowell and Rampersad. 144-163.

—. "Reading Family Matters." *Changing Our Own Words: Essays on Criticism, Theory, and Writing by Black Women*. Ed. Cheryl A. Wall. New Brunswick: Rutgers University Press, 1989. 75-97.

—. "'The Self and the Other': Reading Toni Morrison's *Sula* and the Black Female Text." *Critical Essays on Toni Morrison*. Ed. Nellie Y. McKay. Boston: Hall, 1988. 77-90.

McDowell, Deborah E. and Arnold Rampersad. *Slavery and the Literary Imagination*. Selected Papers from the English Institute, New Series 13. Baltimore: Johns Hopkins University Press, 1989.

Morrison, Toni. "African-Americans, Part III: Toni Morrison and Trudier Harris." *Soundings*. WTJU, Charlottesville, Virginia, 20 February 1991.

—. *Beloved*. New York: Plume-NAL, 1987.

—. "A Conversation: Gloria Naylor and Toni Morrison." With Naylor. *Southern Review* 21 (1985): 567-593. Rptd. in *Conversations with Toni Morrison*. Ed. Danille Taylor-Guthrie. Jackson: University Press of Mississippi, 1994. 188-217.

—. *The Bluest Eye: A Novel*. New York: Holt, 1970.

—. "An Interview with Toni Morrison." With Nellie McKay. Gates and Appiah. 396-411.

—. "Interview with Toni Morrison." With Christina Davis. Gates and Appiah. 412-420.

—. "Intimate Things in Place: A Conversation with Toni Morrison." With Robert B. Stepto. *Chant of Saints*. Ed. Michael S. Harper and Stepto. Urbana: University of Illinois Press, 1979. 213-229.

—. "It's OK to Say OK." With Sandi Russell. *Critical Essays on Toni Morrison*. Ed. Nellie Y. McKay. Boston: Hall, 1988. 43-54.

—. Lecture. Frederick G. Melcher Book Award. Unitarian Universalist Association. Cambridge, Massachusetts, 12 October 1988. *Cambridge Forum*. WVTF, Roanoke, Virginia. 5 April 1991.

—. "Rootedness: The Ancestor as Foundation." With Mari Evans. *Black Women Writers (1950-1980): A Critical Evaluation*. Ed. Evans. Garden City: Anchor-Doubleday, 1984. 339-345.

—. "The Site of Memory." Inventing the Truth: The Art and Craft of Memoir. Ed. William Zinsser. Boston: Houghton, 1987. 101-124.

—. "Toni Morrison." With Claudia Tate. *Black Women Writers at Work*. Ed. Claudia Tate. New York: Continuum, 1983. 117-131.

Rigney, Barbara Hill. *The Voices of Toni Morrison*. Columbus: Ohio State University Press, 1991.

Slemon, Stephen. "Magic Realism as Post-Colonial Discourse." *Canadian Literature* 116 (1988): 9-24.

Spillers, Hortense J. "A Hateful Passion, a Lost Love." *Toni Morrison*. Ed. Harold Bloom. Modern Critical Views Series. New York: Chelsea House, 1990. 27-53.

Willis, Susan. "Eruptions of Funk: Historicizing Toni Morrison." *Black American Literature Forum* 16 (1982): 34-42.

Yellin, Jean Fagin. "Text and Context of Harriet Jacobs' *Incidents in the Life of a Slave Girl: Written by Herself*." Davis and Gates. 262-282.

Zimmerman, Bonnie. "Feminist Fiction and the Postmodern Challenge." *Postmodern Fiction: A Bio-Bibliographical Guide*. Ed. Larry McCaffery. Westport: Greenwood, 1986. 175-188.

Belonging and Freedom in Morrison's *Beloved*: Slavery, Sentimentality, and the Evolution of Consciousness

Howard W. Fulweiler

I.

For over a century readers have scratched their heads over the puzzling conclusion of Mark Twain's *Huckleberry Finn*.[1] How could a book some readers judge to be the great American novel end in a ludicrous farce? An escaped slave of dignity, intelligence, and moral insight is needlessly imprisoned and persuaded to take part in a burlesque parody of the sentimental literary themes of the nineteenth-century, epitomized by the complaint Tom Sawyer manufactures for Jim: "a captive heart busted."[2]

It is even more puzzling that 130 years after emancipation contemporary histories of slavery suffer from analogous ambiguity. We learn that African slavery in America was a brutal exploitation, *but* the paternalism of the planters sometimes instilled a sense of humanity in the exploited slaves. The slaves themselves desired freedom above all else, *but* many yearned for some aspects of familiar "slavery times." Slaveowners suffered hurt feelings as well as financial loss when "their Negroes" left the plantations after abolition or the end of the war. Freedom, the central goal and hope of slaves, was nonetheless often seen as antagonistic to "family values" by both races.[3]

The Biblical resonances of Violet Gunthorpe, an elderly former slave interviewed during the Federal Writing Project of the 1930s, express the conflict very well:

> Us had no education, no land, no mule, no cow, not a pig,
> nor a chicken, to set up housekeeping. The birds had
> nests in the air, the foxes had holes in the ground, and
> the fishes had beds under the great falls, but us colored
> folks was left without any place to lay our heads. (96)

When the Union Army took away all the food, livestock, and crops, she concluded, "all us had to thank them for, was a hungry belly, and Freedom" (96). In Violet Gunthorpe's remembered dilemma lies a clue to American ambivalence towards slavery: human anxiety at the choice between a more secure "belonging"—even at the cost of slavery—and a desired but dangerous freedom—even at the cost of life itself. This conflict—especially challenging for nineteenth-century African-Americans—also has relevance for the general evolution of Western consciousness as a whole, in which the enslavement of Africans by Europeans has played a major role in modern times. This essay will attempt to show how Toni Morrison's novel *Beloved*, a fictional re-creation of the slave experience from within, illuminates both the experience of the slaves themselves and the larger consciousness of which it is a part. First, however, I must explain the phrase, "evolution of consciousness." To say that human consciousness evolves is to say that the basic human mode of experiencing reality is not unchanging.[4] Its constant evolution is more than a matter of human beings of different times and different cultures seeing the same "reality" and coming to different conclusions about it. Since the "real world" for human perception is necessarily limited to the phenomenal world (whatever it might be in actuality), an evolution of consciousness implies further that the real world, the familiar or common-sense world of any given culture, must be in part the product of the consciousness of its members and thus itself subject to change. The world must evolve in organic connection with the consciousness which experiences it. The history of language and the history of science have had much to reveal about this historical and epistemological state of affairs.[5] Much philosophy since Kant has emphasized the participation of the human mind in the creation, or evocation, of these phenomena. This emphasis has been shared by historical theorists such as R. G. Collingwood, Thomas Kuhn, and Michele Foucault.[6]

Working from these general assumptions, Owen Barfield has argued in various works that there has been a progressive development in the human race from an earlier "universal or

generalized consciousness, which embraced both man and nature," to the more "individualized and alienated self-conscious-
ness" that characterizes modern times.[7] A key term in Barfield's
account, borrowed from anthropologists like Durkheim, Lévy-
Bruhl, and others, is "participation." Barfield's argument, however, is not so much sociological as, say, Durkheim's, but is historical, philosophical, and linguistic, suggesting that pre-scien-
tific people do not assume that the phenomena of the world
which they perceive are totally separate from themselves as
moderns do. "In the act of perception, they are not detached, as
we are, from the representations. For us the only connection *of
which we are conscious* is the external one through the senses.
Not so for them" (*Saving the Appearances* 31). The term "participation," therefore, is a broad epistemological description which
refers to the necessary relationship between human beings and
the phenomenal world. It is the "extra-sensory link between
man and the phenomena," the non-material connection between human beings and the nature they perceive (40).

The evolution of consciousness of Western men and
women may be understood in the light of their gradual development away from what Barfield calls "original participation,"
the immediately experienced sense of belonging observed in
primitive people.[8] In achieving the logical thought patterns
upon which modern Western civilization is based, human beings have suppressed the more active experience of participation
in their phenomena characteristic of earlier cultures. As a usable
fiction they have come to regard phenomena simply as facts, totally independent of human consciousness. Although participation of some sort must be admitted as a logical necessity, it has
simply been repressed from modern consciousness, much as
Freud claimed sexual materials were repressed from Victorian
bourgeois consciousness. Although Morrison has not discussed
these matters directly, the concept of consciousness evolving in
relationship with the nature of which it is conscious has been
very much a part of her fictional world. In *Tar Baby*, for example, the Black male protagonist, Son, is warned against the modern, urbanized black woman Jadine, because she has separated
herself from nature and the past: "Forget her. There is nothing
in her parts for you. She has forgotten her ancient properties."
A similar assumption of human spiritual connection to the environment is central to *Song of Solomon* as well as *Beloved*.

The consequences of the suppression of the awareness of

participation have been enormous. As noted above it is an important cause or modern loneliness and alienation. It is also a central cause of sentimentality—the mirror image of loneliness and alienation—and the habit of the heart which so concerned Mark Twain. The advent of sentimentality in modern times—the late seventeenth-century to the present—especially concerns us here. As the last of original participation began to slip away from European consciousness, thinkers and writers attempted more and more desperately to recover whatever vestiges of it they could. Sensitive Victorians, for instance, felt themselves increasingly isolated, increasingly bereft of the sense of belonging, not only to an organic Church or State, or an extended family, but to nature as well. Darwin accelerated the psychic transformation of his contemporaries. Once assuming that they were children of nature, now they were led to the more mechanical notion that they were objects in it. This change of perception engendered a search for the remnants of belonging, for the links that might still connect human beings to nature and to the past. A strident new insistence on a reified notion or idea of what had formerly been an immediate experience, is the characteristic manifestation of modern sentimentality.[9]

The search for participating links to cling to evoke responses such as the rise of nationalism, the anxious revival of religious orthodoxy, and the intense interest in the non-material significance of nature characterized by the Romantic Movement. The greatest area of feared loss in which Victorians on both sides of the Atlantic attempted to make restorations was that of family, children, and especially women. The felt loss of connection in all of these areas was valid, but the sometimes frantic responses were very much vulnerable to sentimentality.

The fiction of Mark Twain highlighted the link between this wide-spread sentimentality and the issue that finally shook the United States to its foundation in the middle of the nineteenth-century: the relationship of the European immigrants to America and the Africans whom they had enslaved in the new land of freedom. It was Twain's opinion that a Southern fixation on the sentimentality of Sir Walter Scott helped to bring on the Civil War. The silly sentimentality of Emmeline Grangerford in *Huckleberry Finn* has a dark underside in the homicidal mania of the Grangerfords and the Shepherdsons feuding over family honor. An important aspect of this sinister side to the Grangerford-Shepherdson sentimentality is its connection with the injustice of the institution of slavery.

What Mark Twain described in fiction has been an often recorded historical phenomenon.[10]   Sentimental racism attributed special religious sensitivity to the African slave. The picture of the Negro as a "natural Christian" was popularized throughout America in the figure of Uncle Tom in Harriet Beecher Stowe's *Uncle Tom's Cabin*. Tom, like Little Eva or the many dying female children of Victorian sentimental fiction, speaks for an evangelical "religion of the heart." Among "romantic racialists" there was a widespread opinion that women and Negroes had much in common, which in George M. Frederickson's acid comment "often revealed a mixture of cant, condescension, and sentimentality, not unlike the popular, nineteenth-century view of womanly virtue, which it so closely resembled" (110-115, 125).

The response of slaveholding white America to the evolution of consciousness discussed earlier was on the one hand a cold laissez-faire calculation which saw the advantage of using slaves in an industrial world—much as did the rulers of Nazi Germany during World War II. On the other hand the slaveholders developed a sentimental myth of "family" and the supposed childlike closeness to nature of the slaves in order to repress awareness of the actual harshness and cold mechanism of the world they had created. In this "double consciousness," they very much paralleled the frame of mind of Victorian England with its brutal factory system yoked with a saccharine domestic sentimentality.

We thus observe a battle in the general Western consciousness between two forces. The Enlightenment had convincingly pointed to a new order—the substitution of a more rational civilization for an older participative one which seemed outdated. The fear engendered by the prospect of total change, however, evoked a powerful opposing desire for continuation rather than substitution. English Victorian culture suffered an inner conflict between a cold rationalistic spirit of innovation, shorn of tradition and entangling relationship, and a warm, yearning need for relationship, for things to stay the same in a kind of timeless childhood. American culture was divided in a similar way, not only between the industrial North and the agrarian South, but in the slaveholding South itself there was a compulsion to create a sentimental Sambo to mitigate the industrial model of slave oppression.

In *Beloved*, Morrison considers these larger issues as they occur not in European or white American consciousness, but in African-American consciousness during slavery and its aftermath. How were *black* people to be liberated from slavery, yet maintain a sense of belonging? of family and community? How were *they* to overcome loneliness and isolation, and yet achieve freedom? This dilemma is not unrelated to Western consciousness as a whole.

II.

In the light of the general development of Western consciousness it is not surprising that *Beloved*, despite its serious attempt to re-create the reality of nineteenth-century American history, makes use of all the tropes of nineteenth-century sentimental fiction, crowded as it was with struggling families, suffering orphans, and saintly females. The central event of *Beloved* is also the central icon of Victorian sentimentality on both sides of the Atlantic: the death of a female child. Stowe's Little Eva and Dickens's little Nell are popular examples at the head of a long list. Suffering women are the leading characters of *Beloved*: Sethe, the self-sacrificing mother; Baby Suggs, the sibyl-like grandmother; Denver, born during the trauma of her mother's escape from slavery; Beloved, the murdered child who returns as a vengeful ghost; Amy Denver, the orphaned "white-girl"; even the ineffectual Mrs. Garner, the kindly but mortally ill slave owner. These women take their place in the nineteenth-century literary tradition of oppressed females: Browning's Pompilia, Hawthorne's Hester Prynne, Dickens's Lizzie Hexam and Esther Summerson, George Eliot's Maggie Tulliver, Bronté's Jane Eyre, James's Isabel Archer, Hardy's Tess. In the theatre there is not only the ubiquitous appearance of Little Eva, but of little Mary Morgan in William Pratt's *Ten Nights in a Bar-Room* or Zoe in Boucicault's *The Octoroon*. The real-life idolization of dead women by nineteenth-century writers is well known: Dickens's Mary Hogarth, James's Minny Temple, Browning's Elizabeth Barrett, Mill's Harriet Taylor, and Twain's Susy.

Beloved begins in an Edenic rural setting, Sweet Home farm, owned by kindly Kentuckians. This ironically named par-

adise of belonging and early harmony is created to expose its illusory nature, a strategy common in Victorian fiction as well.
Although Emily Brontë's Thrushcross Grange harbors a presumably civilized atmosphere for childhood when contrasted to
the dark cruelties of Wuthering Heights, it is nonetheless filled
with self-centered quarreling, tantrums, and mistreated animals.
David Copperfield's idyllic childhood home, Blunderstone
Rookery, becomes a dark prison with the advent of the Murd-
stones after his father's death.

In polar relationship to the common representations of
ideal childhood is the ironic fact that nineteenth-century fiction
could hardly exist without orphans. These emblems of the loss
of connection embody the anxiety of their age, its alienation and
its loneliness. Oliver Twist, Pip, Jane Eyre, Becky Sharpe, Tom
Sawyer, and Huck Finn represent the mainstream of nineteenth-
century fiction. Except for Sethe's two daughters and her disap-
pearing husband Halle, all the major characters of *Beloved* are
orphans. The conditions of slavery have destroyed the possibility of stable families. The Sweet Home "men" have no contact
with their parents. Sethe's mother was hanged; she doesn't
know who her father was. Amy Denver, the "whitegirl" who
helps Sethe deliver her baby, is an orphan, serving like Huck
Finn as a naïve commentator on a society founded upon black
slavery and the exploitation of poor whites. On her pathetic and
quixotic journey to Boston to find velvet, she wistfully sings a
remembered lullaby of her mother to Sethe, another orphan.
Paul D demonstrates the insatiable thirst of the orphan for connection during his lonely wandering after the Civil War: "each
time he discovered large families of black people he made them
identify over and over who each was, what relation, who, in fact,
belonged to who" (219).

One of the most common themes in nineteenth-century
literature and graphic art is the human connection to nature,
coupled with anxiety that the connection had been broken. This
issue was the motive for both the Romantic Movement and the
following rise of domestic sentimentality. Morrison again follows nineteenth-century tradition in placing considerable emphasis on the role of nature in all her novels. This is an interesting characteristic in light of the remark of Arnold Rampersad
that "Very few black writers, if any, have been teased by the great
question of Nature and its relationship to humanity" (223). It
has been suggested that Morrison's particular interest in nature

is an attempt to link her characters to Africa and to an African past presumably more intimately in touch with nature.[11]

The importance of spiritual links to nature which have been threatened appears everywhere in *Beloved*. Not only is it evident in the plight of the dislocated Africans, but also in the lives of the dispossessed Cherokee who aid Paul D in his escape from Alfred, Georgia, and in the reverence of Sixo for the "Redmen's Presence" in a lodge they had used "when they thought the land was theirs" (24). Paul D hears the ghosts of the dead Miami (155). The spiritual power of the natural Clearing in which Baby Suggs preaches her gospel of the love of nature and humanity provides a conduit between the African-Americans of Cincinnati and both nature and the past (87-89).

The most devastating damage done to the slaves of Sweet Home after the death of the kindly Mr. Garner results from the continuing attack on their status as natural beings. The Sweet Home men are stripped of their essential manhood: "schoolteacher broke into children what Garner had raised into men" (220). Paul D leaves the farm with a bit in his mouth, emasculated beneath the status even of the rooster, "Mister." More emblematic is the kind of rape perpetrated on Sethe, as the nephews take her mother's milk from her. In its bizarre horror—schoolteacher has bidden his students to take notes—it is not just an assault on Sethe, but on nature itself as embodied in motherhood. The crime not only robs Sethe of her human dignity, but aims at the very origins of humanity. An unnatural act, it is ultimately responsible for Sethe's "unnatural" murder of her child. It reduces the organic human relation to nature to a soulless mechanical one.

In its attack on motherhood and the spiritual origins of humankind this incident is closely related to common themes of Victorian fiction. The brutal utilitarian industrialist, Josiah Bounderby, symbolically rejects his mother in Dickens's *Hard Times*. In a similar gesture Michael Henchard sells his wife in Hardy's *The Mayor of Casterbridge*. The literary picture most indelibly imprinted on the nineteenth-century American mind comes from *Uncle Tom's Cabin*, both novel and play. Eliza Harris, clutching her baby as she crosses the Ohio River over the ice with the slave catchers in pursuit, is perhaps the most widely known scene in American literature. The analogy with Sethe's flight across the Ohio to save her children is apparent.

Many critics, of course, have argued for the special origi-

nality of African-American literature in general and of Morrison's work in particular. Some years ago Houston A. Baker, Jr.
wrote that

> Black folklore and the black American literary tradi-
> tion that grew out of it reflect a culture that is distinc-
> tive both of white American and of African culture, and
> therefore neither can provide valid standards by
> which black American folklore and literature may be
> judged.   (14)

This statement is correct if by it one means that African-American literature should not be judged as an imperfect clone of
other traditions. The first step in criticism is to *distinguish* one
literature from another. The critical work of distinction, however, should not mean a total separation of each from all the
rest. Morrison's work has developed from the literary tradition
of Europe as well as from those of Africa and America.

Morrison has made use of the materials of Victorian fiction in creating her novel—especially those materials most often
sentimentalized by Victorian writers. Yet *Beloved* is very different from *Uncle Tom's Cabin* or *Oliver Twist*—books of great
power and also of great sentimentality. Despite its affinity with
earlier sentimental fiction, few would charge *Beloved* with sentimentality. Why not?

III.

Although Morrison was a student of classical literature in
college, this fact is less important than her continuing effort to
place her narrative in a larger context. Like Matthew Arnold in
the nineteenth-century, she has searched for a stability and a
universality to balance the sentimentality and narcissistic individuality of modern times. Despite its reliance on the *materials*
of Victorian sentimental fiction, *Beloved* reaches to an earlier
time for its literary forms. It makes use of the classical genres,
and in fact the *mentalité* of a time *before* the loss of participation
and the concomitant rise of literary sentimentality. Its deepest
structures are in sympathy with epic, with tragedy, and with the
rhythms of Scripture.

Beloved fulfills many of the formal requirements of the

epic. It purports to be the story of a whole people—the "Sixty Million" Africans killed by slavery. There is a supernatural machinery which affects the outcome. There is an epic feast and games. Against a background of war and struggle there are two featured epic journeys, Sethe's flight to freedom from Sweet Home to Cincinnati and Paul D's eighteen-year wandering before his arrival at Bluestone Road. Both journeys—like that of the *Aeneid*—move from catastrophe and the destruction of home and family to a new locality and a new life. Both Sethe and Paul D, again like Aeneas, are haunted by ghosts of the past. There is also a hint of the traditional return motif as it appears in *The Odyssey*. When Paul D finally comes back to Sethe at Bluestone Road, he finds the ancient dog, Here Boy, now feeble, as Odysseus finds his dog on his return to Ithaca.

The atmosphere of *Beloved* is quite different from conventional nineteenth- or twentieth-century fiction. It appeals to the traditional tragic sense. Sethe is neither a sentimental oppressed heroine nor the pathetic object of forces beyond her control. Although Sethe is a victim of slavery and racism, she is also the responsible author of her acts. The murder of her child isolates her from her community. The crime is considered more reprehensible by her black neighbors than by the whites. Although infanticide sometimes occurred during slavery, slaves for the most part recognized it as murder as do the African-Americans of Cincinnati (Genovese 497). Sethe is culpable despite the powerful forces which lead her to her crime. She moves in the same world with Oedipus, who says at the end of *Oedipus Rex*:

> It was Apollo, friends, Apollo,
> that brought this bitter bitterness, my sorrows to
> completion.
> But the hand that struck me
> was none but my own.   (II. 1329-1332)

In her isolation and in her pride Sethe transcends the sentimental literary tradition from which she comes and the sentimental image of African-Americans invented by slave holders and still popular among many white Americans.

The Furies pursue Sethe and her family in the form of an infant ghost. "Who would have thought a little old baby could harbor so much rage?" (5). The devastating effects of slavery which envelop the entire African community do not constitute

an excuse for the individual transgressor. When Sethe suggests
moving from their haunted house Baby Suggs's response has
the finality of Nemesis: "What'd be the point? . . . Not a house
in the country ain't packed to the rafters with some dead Negro's
grief" (5). The tragic consequences of Sethe's murder of her
child are apparent on the opening page of the novel. Sethe and
Denver are the only family members left to suffer the haunting.

> The grandmother, Baby Suggs, was dead, and the sons,
> Howard and Buglar, had run away by the time they
> were thirteen years old—as soon as merely looking in a
> mirror shattered it (that was the signal for Buglar); as
> soon as two tiny hand prints appeared in the cake (that
> was it for Howard).   (3)

Late in the novel, Sethe's moving interior monologue on
the apparent return of Beloved evokes sympathy and yet reveals
her possessive fixation on her supposed daughter. The soliloquy
opens with the sentences, "Beloved, she my daughter. She
mine. She come back to me of her own free will and I don't
have to explain a thing" (200). It concludes with her memory of
despair, now overcome by the return of her daughter. "I could-
n't lay down nowhere in peace, back then. Now I can. I can
sleep like the drowned, have mercy. She come back to me, my
daughter, and she is mine" (204).

The mysterious adult Beloved who returns serves as a
kind of illusory self-justification to assuage Sethe's sense of guilt,
but also as a trigger for neurotic responses from both Sethe and
Denver, as well as a sexual response from Paul D. Denver's interior monologue is an ironic commentary on her mother's. The
neuroticism of Denver's monologue, as well as its ironic relation to Sethe's, appears in the last words: "She's mine, Beloved.
She's mine" (209).

Denver's matter-of-fact fear of her mother informs her
monologue and adds further irony to her mother's self-absorbed
soliloquy which precedes it.

> I love my mother but I know she killed one of her own
> daughters, and tender as she is with me, I'm scared of
> her because of it. She missed killing my brothers and
> they knew it . . . there sure is something in her that
> makes it all right to kill her own.   (205)

Sethe's act takes on greater significance when seen through the eyes of the other human beings involved—in this case the tragic chorus of Denver, Buglar, Howard, and ultimately the entire African community. Morrison's subtle control of narrative point of view through Joycean stream-of-consciousness soliloquies does not lead to a modernist sensibility, but to the older world of tragedy. Sethe is more like Medea than Molly Bloom. As Morrison has said "she has stepped across the line, so to speak. It's understandable but excessive." The black townspeople of Cincinnati "abandon her because of what they felt was her pride" (*Conversations* 252). The extraordinary difficulty of Sethe's situation brings about its genuinely tragic resonances: "It was the right thing to do, but she had no right to do it" (272).

Sethe describes her love as "tough" in her soliloquy, but Paul D has said in reference to the killing, "Your love is too thick" (200, 164). He denies the simple determinist excuse that Sethe was not responsible for her act: "You got two feet, Sethe, not four" (165). At this point Morrison portrays Paul D as a tragic protagonist as well as Sethe. His accusation, true as it may be, is untimely and empty from one who has himself secretly fornicated with the returned Beloved. Later he recognizes his hypocrisy: "How fast he had moved from his shame to hers. From his cold-house secret straight to her too-thick love" (165).

Although Sethe's murder of her child is the central tragic act of the novel, the consequences of the crime do not affect Sethe alone, but are apparent in the obsessive behavior of Denver and Paul D, as well as Sethe, towards the returned Beloved who now haunts all three. The power of the dead to affect the living is perhaps the most common theme of traditional tragedy. This power is extended far beyond Sethe, Denver, and Paul D to the entire African-American community, which is affected by the ghost of a child, just as Scotland is affected by the ghost of Banquo, Denmark by Prince Hamlet's murdered father, or Thebes by the blood of the wronged Laios.

* * *

Although *Beloved* has clear affinities with classical tragedy, it is even more closely related to the Bible. It is an historical commonplace that Christianity and its interpretation of world history in the Scriptures formed a psychic shield and an intellectual explanation for the Africans kidnapped from their homes and reduced to bondage in a strange land. The influence of the Biblical narratives gives further dignity to the lives of Morrison's fictional characters as well.

The key narrative is the Genesis account of the Fall, an explanatory metaphor for the rest of the Bible and especially appropriate in setting the theme of *Beloved*. Sweet Home farm is the site of an Edenic existence from which the slaves are ejected—not as a result of their sins, but of the crimes of schoolteacher and the nephews. Although they live at Sweet Home and belong initially to a kind master, they are nonetheless enslaved. Like Adam and Eve in the garden, they lack adult consciousness. Their lives are characterized by deprivations of all kinds, including a limited sense of self and self-worth. One of the more moving scenes in the book is Baby Suggs's achievement of self consciousness when her son buys her freedom.

> She didn't know what she looked like and was not curious. But suddenly she saw her hands and thought with a clarity as simple as it was dazzling, 'These hands belong to me. These my hands.' Next she felt a knocking in her chest and discovered something else new; her own heartbeat. Had it been there all along?   (141)

As in the larger pattern of the Bible, there is a continuation of the initial conflict between a world of childlike participation where only obedience is required and a new world of consciousness, freedom, and the possibility of moral failure. The struggles of Sethe and Paul D have resonances with those of Moses and the children of Israel, an analogy widely recognized by nineteenth-century African slaves. The Biblical theme of Belonging (as in the Israelites' nostalgia for the fleshpots of Egypt) versus Freedom (the dangerous wandering in the wilderness) is further related to the conflict between a coercive community and an alienated individualism among the emancipated African-Americans of Cincinnati, Ohio.

The Scriptural imagery of the novel continues as Sethe and her children are led across the Ohio River by a wise boatman named Stamp Paid, a name suggesting independence and responsibility. Although we learn that Stamp Paid named himself, he mentions that he was once called Joshua, a name which suggests his salvific role in leading the whole community into the Promised Land (233). Like Joshua he is not only a type of Christ allegorically, but he in fact tries to be a "high-minded Soldier of Christ," despite his self-doubt.

New Testament allusions permeate the novel. A recurrent image is that of washing or massaging feet: Amy Denver massages Sethe's swollen feet (35); Sethe offers to soak Paul D's feet after his travels (8); Baby Suggs washes Sethe's feet (93); Paul D returns to the isolated Sethe at the end of the novel and asks permission to heat up water to "rub your feet" (272). These reciprocal acts of humility and service are related to Christ's washing the feet of the disciples at the Last Supper: "If I then, your Lord and Teacher, have washed your feet, you also ought to wash one another's feet" (John 13:14).

The list of allusions is long. The miraculous feast, beginning with Stamp Paid's blackberries and growing under the supervision of Baby Suggs echoes the feeding of the five thousand from the fourth gospel.

> Now to take two buckets of blackberries and make ten, maybe twelve pies; to have turkey enough for the whole town pretty near, new peas in September, fresh cream but no cow, ice and sugar, batter bread, bread pudding, raised bread, shortbread—it made them mad. Loaves and fishes were His powers—they did not belong to an ex-slave who had probably never carried one hundred pounds to the scale, or picked okra with a baby on her back.   (137)

The heavy emphasis on bread in this passage coupled with the envy of the feasters at 124 Bluestone Road parallels the resentful murmuring among Christ's followers at His claim to be the "bread of heaven": "The Jews then murmured at him. . . . They said, 'Is not this Jesus, the son of Joseph, whose father and mother we know?'" (John 6:41-42). Both incidents anticipate the catastrophe to come in their respective narratives: Sethe's murder of her child and the crucifixion of Christ.

The connection of the human suffering of the characters and the sacrifice of Christ is hinted at throughout the novel. Perhaps the most powerful and most significant example is Amy Denver's description of Sethe's torn back after her whipping by the nephews. The "tree" to which Amy refers is a multivalent symbol which relates the brutal mutilation both to the expiatory suffering of Christ on the cross and to the redemptive power of the natural world. Like Huck Finn, Amy is an unconscious theologian:

> It's a tree, Lu. A chokecherry tree. See, here's the
> trunk—it's red and split open, full of sap, and this
> here's the parting for the branches. You got a mighty
> lot of branches. Leaves, too, look like, and dern if these
> ain't blossoms, tiny little cherry blossoms, just as white.
> Your back got a whole tree on it. In bloom. What God
> have in mind, I wonder.   (79)

The tension between belonging and freedom, community
and independence, as it becomes enmeshed in a bizarre mixture
of guilt and possessive love, grows into what amounts to an allegorical cartoon in the final neurotic relationship of Sethe and
Beloved, a relationship from which Denver is excluded.
Beloved's psychic dominance over Sethe echoes the grotesque
emblems of similar obsessed bondage in allegorical works such
as *The Faerie Queene*, *Pilgrim's Progress*, or *Paradise Lost*.

> Beloved bending over Sethe looked the mother, Sethe
> the teething child. . . . The bigger Beloved got, the
> smaller Sethe became, the brighter Beloved's eyes, the
> more those eyes that used never to look away became
> slits of sleeplessness. Sethe no longer combed her hair
> or splashed her face with water. She sat in the chair
> licking her lips like a chastised child, while Beloved
> ate up her life, took it, swelled up with it, grew taller
> on it. And the older woman yielded it up without a
> murmur.   (250)

Karen Carmean has written that Morrison intended the
revenant Beloved to be a kind of "mirror" to reflect the inner
lives of the other characters (85). Thus the emblem of her
swelling pregnancy reflects her domination over Sethe's mind
and her seduction of Paul D's body. As an allegorical figure she
is analogous to Satan's pregnant daughter, Sin, in *Paradise Lost*.
In the climactic scene of the community exorcism she is
described as naked and pregnant with "vines of hair twisted
all over her head" (261), reminiscent of a Dionysian Maenad
or possibly the dangerous Medusa who was killed while
pregnant.

Trudier Harris has remarked perceptively that "by denying to Sethe the power to support herself, Beloved initially attacks Sethe's spirit of independence" (159). It is ironic that a figure so damaged by slavery—whether she is the ghost of the
murdered child, the escaped concubine of a "whiteman over by
Deer Creek" (235), or the representative of all the sufferers of the

Middle Passage—should be instrumental in returning Sethe to bondage.

The image of Sethe and Beloved locked tightly in an obsessed relationship, a fixation which also extends to Denver and Paul D, has significance beyond the particular psychology of the four characters.   The haunting presence of slavery and of wronged Africans in the America beyond Bluestone Road suggests a larger analogy. The relationship between white people and black people since the Civil War has also been obsessed and imprisoned. Beloved returned is not only a mirror for the other fictional characters, but for actual white Americans as well. Frederickson has made the fairly obvious suggestion that obsessive white fears of African-Americans may be a "projection of unacknowledged guilt feelings derived from their own brutality toward blacks" (282).

While this interpretation is undoubtedly true, it has been the goal of this essay to explain this psychological phenomenon not only in terms of repressed guilt, but as the unconscious repression of the participating portion of the human self. When the modern Western consciousness in its drive towards freedom and independence rejected its roots and its spiritual connections, it set about, ironically, to enslave those who seemed to represent those old links and in doing so entered into a psychic bondage of mutual disaster.   This historical moment in the evolution of Western consciousness is marked by Stamp Paid on the first day he sees "the two backs" of Sethe and Beloved together through the window. Sensing a supernatural presence, he meditates profoundly on the reciprocal relation of whites and blacks:

> Whitepeople believed that whatever the manners, under every dark skin was a jungle. Swift unnavigable waters, swinging screaming baboons, sleeping snakes, red gums ready for their sweet white blood. . . . The more colored people spent their strength trying to convince them how gentle they were, how clever and loving, how human . . . the deeper and more tangled the jungle grew inside. But it wasn't the jungle blacks brought with them to this place. . . . It was the jungle whitefolks planted in them. And it grew. It spread. In, through and after life, it spread, until it invaded the whites who had made it. Touched them every one. Changed and altered them. Made them bloody, silly, worse than even they wanted to be, so scared were they of the jungle they had made. The screaming baboon

lived under their own white skin; the red gums were
their own.   (198-199)

This image of two races locked in a reciprocal psychic
paralysis is also the emblem of the evolving Western consciousness as a whole, which having forgotten its "ancient properties,"
suffers the punishment of a freedom which has turned to lonely
alienation and self-hatred.

IV.

Although *Beloved* is about the particular experience of
the slaves of Sweet Home plantation in Kentucky and their lives
in Cincinnati after emancipation, it relates their experience not
only to the more universal evolution of consciousness recorded
in the classical literary genres but also to one of the most important episodes in American and European history, the systematic
enslavement of people of color from the seventeenth to the late
nineteenth-century.   It is, finally, impossible to talk about the
developing consciousness of black people in America without
considering that of whites.   Although the external events are
known, their significance for Western consciousness requires
further investigation and understanding.
      Over ninety years ago W. E. B. Du Bois identified the prob-
lem of the twentieth-century as "the problem of the color-line"
(10).   Although it existed before the twentieth-century, the problem is especially one of modern times, becoming clearly visible
only at the end of the seventeenth-century.   Although there was
plenty of slavery and oppression in antiquity, it does not appear
to have been racially based.   The Crusades were conducted by Europeans against Arabs, but the issues seem to have been religious
rather than racial, as was apparently the struggle between the
Christians and the Moors in Spain.
      Looking at the relation of the races in the light of the evo-
lution of Western consciousness discussed above is revealing.
As we saw, the development of intense individualism and the
rejection of the earlier participating sense of reality gave birth to
a countervailing force, sentimentality, in a clandestine and often
inauthentic attempt to recover the spiritual sense of connection
which was lost.   There was a struggle between the Enlighten-

ment and the cult of Sensibility during the eighteenth-century, and between the Industrial Revolution and domestic sentimentality in the nineteenth.

Little noticed, however, has been the intriguing coincidence that the enslavement of Africans by Europeans paralleled this struggle and the rise of sentimentality. In fact the enormous long-term conflict between the two peoples is analogous to the psychomachia within the mind of Europe. The historic meeting of Europeans with Africans and Native Americans is the story of the newly non-participating consciousness repressing an older participating consciousness wherever it found it: one people technically free, but rootless servants of what Coleridge termed the "mechanical understanding";[12] the other people maintaining the sense of human belonging and connection, but unfree, both psychologically and politically.

This divided stream has been central to the development of Western consciousness in recent times. As Morrison has said of the Enlightenment, "The concept of freedom did not emerge in a vacuum. Nothing highlighted freedom—if it did not in fact create it—like slavery." In the "construction of blackness *and* enslavement could be found not only the not-free, but also, with the dramatic polarity created by skin color, the projection of the not-me." Criticism needs to consider how "the image of reined-in, bound, suppressed, and repressed darkness became objectified in American literature as an Africanist persona" (*Playing* 38-39).

Racism has had an evolutionary development in America. Although racism appeared as a concomitant of slavery as early as the seventeen-century it appears not to have become central to the American psyche until the nineteenth-century. Frederickson has argued that it did not reach "full ideological consciousness" until given shape and form by contemporary movements in both social and scientific thought (xl, 321-322). There came to be increased stress in literature and historical writing in both America and Britain on the special tendencies of particular "races," a kind of romantic racism, as an explanation of society and culture (97). One thinks of Carlyle, the Germanophile and stern critic of laxity towards the Blacks of the West Indies, or Matthew Arnold's cultural theories based on Hellenism, Hebraism, Celtic magic or French rationality. More ominous were the supposedly scientific racial opinions of Darwin and Huxley.

Frederickson has identified two opposite attitudes towards Negroes in mid-nineteenth-century American thought. The first is a kind of "hard racism" that in its extreme version created the "Negro as beast" (58). This kind of thought was especially common in the North where racial prejudice grew not only in popular opposition to abolition but perhaps because "the rise of egalitarianism and competitive individualism resulted, as Tocqueville had suggested, in an increase of status anxiety among whites" (41). As intimated by Morrison, there was a connection between egalitarian democracy and Negrophobia. In this nineteenth-century political alliance, American society, like that of South Africa in recent history, was to be organized by an egalitarian Herrenvolk who would rule the inferior race according to scientific principles, while maintaining equality among themselves.

This so-called "hard racism" contested "for supremacy in Southern propaganda with the 'soft' image of the black slave as beloved child" (58). Brutal exploitation could be masked by the racial sentimentality of the patriarchal, aristocratic theory of slavery, with its sentimental picture of the slaves themselves: the Africans who preferred the master's children to their own; the natural Christians in simplicity and loyalty; the lovable, though irresponsible children.

Herman Melville focused sharply on this soft racism in the naive sentimentality of Amasa Delano, who imagines in *Benito Cereno* that the murderous mutineer, Babo, slyly pretending to be under Don Benito's control, is performing his duties "with that affectionate zeal . . . which has gained for the Negro the repute of making the most pleasing body-servant in the world." Captain Delano, we are told ironically, "took to Negroes, not philanthropically, but genially, just as other men to Newfoundland dogs" (219, 258).

Although some white slave owners tried to avoid both sentimentality and cruelty, and to treat their slaves as human beings, societal forces nearly always doomed such attempts. In *Beloved*, for instance, Mr. Garner attempts a kindly paternalism, recognizing the humanity and worth of his slaves. Although he refers to them as "men" rather than boys, his good intentions are illusory. The slaves "were only Sweet Home men at Sweet Home. One step off that ground and they were trespassers among the human race. Watchdogs without teeth; steer bulls without horns; gelded workhorses whose neigh and whinny could not be translated into a language responsible humans spoke" (125).

As the hidden realities of a bloody slave rebellion behind the bland surface of Melville's story suggest, the two versions of racism, the hard and the soft, were inextricably related and were often expressed at different times by the same person—as they continue to be. The role of race has been of central importance in the more recent stages of the evolution of consciousness I have theorized. To state a complicated development briefly, Western Europeans and their American counterparts repressed their earlier awareness of participation in favor of individualism and supposedly logical thought, only to introduce sentimentality as a bogus replacement for the lost participation. The collision of Europeans and people of color had a devastating impact on the latter, as is well known. The effect on the former was also profound. The Europeans met, it seemed, that part of themselves, their spiritual connection to the world around them, which they were in the process of repressing. One thinks of Conrad's Marlow in *Heart of Darkness* steaming up the Congo, shocked by his sense of kinship with the natives peering at him from the jungle.

The general response of the Europeans to this meeting is well known. As they repressed inwardly their own hidden participating selves, so they repressed externally the still participating people of color around them. The marginalization of the Native American or the African paralleled the suppression of the participating human spirit. As sentimentality characterized one aspect of this process within Western consciousness, so it was applied to people of color as an outward emblem of the inner battle. The notion of the African as "beloved child" or even as "woman" took its place in the general inauthentic attempt to recover what was lost—along with the sentimental Victorian worship of women, orphans, even domestic animals. As we have seen, however, sentimentality always maintains a dark underside. Illusory and harmful opposing images also held the field in the nineteenth-century and since: the Demon vs. the Noble Savage; the Beast vs. the Beloved Child; the Trickster vs. Sambo. Although these terms have been projected by whites upon Native Americans and African-Americans, they are in fact increasingly representative of the conflicts in Western consciousness as a whole in all races. They represent the extraordinary difficulty with which human beings in modern times have attempted to adjust the relation between head and heart, between body and spirit: between belonging in the universe as its cared for children and acting in the universe as responsible adults, free from its darker compulsions.

The devastating chaos that characterized the United States in the aftermath of the Civil War created a terrifying backdrop to the psychological conflict between "belonging," even in its former guise of slavery, and freedom, now represented by rootless anomie. In addition to the massive destruction of property, the social fabric of the slave states was demolished; confused and homeless refugees of both races wandered over a war-ravaged countryside. Although scenes from the latter part of *Gone With the Wind* are part of the popular American understanding of the Reconstruction period, the chaos and confusion were in fact much harder on the former slaves, than on the dispossessed masters. Paul D reflects on the chaos devastating the lives of Black people:

> During, before and after the War he had seen Negroes so stunned, or hungry, or tired or bereft it was a wonder they recalled or said anything. Who, like him, had hidden in caves and fought owls for food; who, like him, stole from pigs; who, like him, slept in trees in the day and walked by night; who, like him, had buried themselves in slop and jumped in wells to avoid regulators, raiders, paterollers, veterans, hill men, posses and merrymakers. (66)

This picture of anomie suggests one of the paradoxical themes of *Beloved*: nineteenth-century African-Americans had the dubious choice of being homeless when free and enslaved when at "sweet home." I have argued that this very real and traumatic historical circumstance for post-war African-Americans is analogous to the conflict within Western consciousness itself. It is this conflict which gave rise to the endemic sentimentality of the nineteenth-century on the one hand and its mechanical atomism on the other, a "freedom" understood as *laissez-faire* capitalism early in the century and as Darwinian science later. As we have seen, both these poles of Victorian behavior are intimately connected with American slavery. Patsy Mitchner, an eighty-four-year-old former slave, looked back bitterly on the consequences of the conflict for black people when she was interviewed in 1937.

> Slavery was a bad thing, and freedom, of the kind we

> got, with nothing to live on, was bad. Two snakes full
> of poison. One lying with his head pointing north, the
> other with his head pointing south. Their names was
> slavery and freedom. The snake called slavery lay
> with his head pointed south, and the snake called
> freedom lay with his head pointed north. Both bit the
> nigger, and they was both bad.   (68-69)

Beloved is the story of people who have a sense of belonging in nature and to each other. They belong to white people
legally, but not naturally or morally. When they deny this ille-
gitimate belonging by flight, their original authentic participation in the world is harshly tested. Yet in their difficult search
for freedom they continue to bring with them the spiritual connections which are their heritage. The central characters of the
novel assume their spiritual connection to the world around
them as a given. Baby Suggs's ultimate despair results from her
belief that the spiritual unity and well being of the community
have been thwarted by her daughter-in-law's desperate act and
even by God Himself.

> Her authority in the pulpit, her dance in the Clearing,
> her powerful Call . . . all that had been mocked and re-
> buked by the bloodspill in her backyard. God puzzled
> her and she was too ashamed of Him to say so.   (177)

Sethe's desire for freedom for herself and her children
even at the cost of the children's lives must be seen in the context of the spiritually interconnected world represented by Baby
Suggs and the African community. Sethe's murder of her child
implies a belief that the child "belongs" to her in a way analogous to the way in which the slaves belonged to their masters.
"Beloved, she my daughter. She mine" (200). Slavery begets
slavery in a dismal chain reaction.

Sethe's desperate act is presented as a blow for freedom,
but also a blow against natural law and the community. As such
it echoes the rebellion of Milton's Satan: "I will not serve." The
ironic depth of the narrative is revealed as Sethe constructs a
self-imposed psychological slavery after escaping the legal slavery of Sweet Home. Her self-absorption creates an atmosphere of
rancor at Baby Suggs's funeral: "So Baby Suggs, holy, having devoted her freed life to harmony, was buried amid a regular dance
of pride, fear, condemnation and spite" (171). Motivated by guilt
and pride Sethe builds a prison of isolation: "Whatever is going

on outside my door ain't for me. The world is in this room.
This here's all there is and all there needs to be" (183).

The novel is organized around related opposites: slavery
and freedom, belonging and independence, love as possession
and love as charity. The relation between slavery and freedom is
resolved in a powerful reconciliation of opposites which seems
paradoxical on the surface: Human freedom is earned and slavery overcome through acts of service freely given. Examples of
this theme are found throughout the narrative. Amy Denver
freely offers help to Sethe in her extremity; Halle works to purchase his mother's freedom; the major characters wash one another's feet; both black and white workers on the Underground
Railroad devote themselves to aiding fugitives; the entire
African-American community offers support for the family at
124 Bluestone Road. "I will serve" opens the road to freedom—
the opposite of Satan's defiance. An important moment in this
transformation of slavery to service occurs when Denver in despair at her dysfunctional and nearly starving family seeks the
help of Lady Jones, asking to work for food.

> '. . . My ma'am, she doesn't feel good.'
> 'Oh, baby,' said Mrs. Jones. 'Oh, baby.'
> Denver looked up at her. She did not know it then, but
> it was the word 'baby,' said softly and with such kind-
> ness, that inaugurated her life as a woman.   (248)

Freely willed service to others is the transforming agent
which changes compulsion to choice. The story of Sethe and her
daughters demonstrates that human beings must belong to nature and to each other, but mature and fully human belonging
requires freedom. Slaves do not belong to masters. Children do
not belong to their parents. This inauthentic belonging, as we
have seen, results in the double headed dragon of cruelty and
sentimentality.

The concluding meeting of Paul D and Sethe is an illustration of appropriate relationship. "He wants to put his story next
to hers." That is, Paul D wants to be united with Sethe in a love
relationship, but not to possess her as property. Sethe is weeping
because Beloved has left her: "She was my best thing." Paul D's
gentle correction suggests a mature relationship of love and independence rather than love as possession.

> 'Sethe,' he says, 'me and you, we got more yester-
> days than anybody. We need some kind of tomorrow.'
> He leans over and takes her hand. With the other
> he touches her face. 'You your best thing, Sethe. You
> are." His holding fingers are holding hers.   (272-273)

The redeeming transformation of forced slavery to free service is summarized by the role of Stamp Paid. He physically leads fugitive slaves to freedom by risking himself to ferry them across the Ohio River, but he also establishes them within the community's network of relationship. He not only arranges for homeless Negroes like Paul D to be taken in, but as a "soldier of Christ" and an enthusiastic supporter of Baby Suggs's "Calling" is a bulwark of the spiritual life of the participating community. As Joshua, or even as an incarnation of St. Christopher the Christ bearer who aids travelers, he stands not only for charity and community, but also for mature independence and personal responsibility, "agent, fisherman, boatman, tracker, savior, spy" (136). He has chosen his own name—Stamp Paid.

V.

W. E. B. Du Bois wrote movingly in *The Souls of Black Folk* of the painful double consciousness of African-Americans.

> One ever feels his twoness,—an American, a Negro;
> two souls, two thoughts, two unreconciled strivings; two
> warring ideals in one dark body, whose dogged strength
> alone keeps it from being torn asunder.
> The history of the American Negro is the history of
> this strife,—this longing to attain self-conscious man-
> hood, to merge his double self into a better and truer self.
> In this merging he wishes neither of the older selves to
> be lost.   (3)

Perhaps Du Bois, the former German university student, had Goethe's famous lines from Faust in mind: "*Zwei Seelen wohnen, Ach! in meiner Brust.*" Whether he was consciously quoting Goethe or not, the connection should become evident to us. These two souls have not been the burden of African-Americans alone but have characterized Western consciousness as a whole in its evolution from the older original participation.

Sensitive thinkers like Du Bois and Morrison have focused on the psychic split as it has affected African-Americans. The tension between clinging to the past and going forward into freedom has been Morrison's topic not only in *Beloved* but in most of her work. The unresolved conflict between Son's yesterday and Jadine's tomorrow in *Tar Baby* is paradigmatic. The first half of this paradigm reveals the human values of the past, the "ancient properties." Alone, it may lead to helpless enslavement and a sentimentality to conceal its real character. The second half alone offers new freedom but an alienated liberty empty of meaning. Human beings cannot grow by cutting off the roots which sustain them. *Beloved* responds to the history of Africans in America not by applying the sentimental nostrums of nineteenth-century white people or by recommending a clean break with the past to choose a free but sterile world without "ancient properties." Instead its characters survive as a result of the spiritual roots the black community—against great odds—has been able to maintain.

I began this essay with the anomaly of the conclusion of *Huckleberry Finn*. It is interesting that Morrison has recently suggested another aspect of the puzzle by pointing to "the way black people ignite critical moments of discovery or change or emphasis in literature not written by them" (*Playing* viii). She has in fact made a penetrating comment about the conclusion of Twain's novel. After discussing the humiliating torment Huck and Tom inflict upon Jim, Morrison turns to what they seem to need from him.

> It is not what Jim seems that warrants inquiry, but what Mark Twain, Huck, and especially Tom need from him that should solicit our attention. In that sense the book may indeed be "great" because in its structure, in the hell it puts its readers through at the end, the frontal debate it forces, it simulates and describes the parasitical nature of white freedom.   (56-57)

Although this insight is accurate, I would wish to enlarge upon it. Freedom is of necessity dependent upon its roots. Historically the notion of "freedom" as a description of the ordinary status of human beings was articulated by slaveholders. They developed the concept of their own autonomy in the context not only of the British monarch whom they rejected but also of the Africans whom they held in bondage. As we have seen—and as

Mark Twain saw—they learned to conceal the moral and intellectual failure of slavery under a bogus sentimentality on the
one hand and an aggressive hostility in defense of their own liberty on the other. Tom and Huck first force the sentimentality
on their helpless friend and then Huck determines "to light out
for the Territory ahead of the rest" in a similarly bogus pose of
freedom (226). This drama—both in history and in fiction—has
been an externalization of the internal drama in the modern
mind between the participation of the past, connected but unfree, and the rootless mechanical freedom which has been one of
the chief "discontents" of modern civilization.

Morrison has remarked that *Uncle Tom's Cabin* was not
written for Uncle Tom to read. Instead, as she came to realize:
"the subject of the dream is the dreamer" (*Playing* 17). In the
same way, *Beloved* was not written for Sethe or Paul D to read.
It is an essay on American history but also a profound meditation on modern consciousness in its internal developments and
its external manifestation. Although it was not written for Sethe
and Paul D, it was written both for their descendants and the descendants of those who enslaved them. It looks forward, finally,
to the transformation of slavery into service, and the growth of
freedom into a recognition of the spiritual roots of humankind.

American literature began with the general complaint
that our country was too new to have an interesting Gothic past.
The yearning for haunted castles was, of course, a sentimental
emotion which concealed the increasing sense of alienated
emptiness in the world of the Enlightenment. This sentimentality was shared by both Europeans and Americans searching for a
meaningful memory of the past.

Toni Morrison's *Beloved* has opened the way for a new
American "rememory" for all races. At the end of the novel
Sethe and Paul D are free, but their lives will continue to be
haunted, just as their house had been. Finally, these nineteenth-
century African-Americans are like all Americans. We all continue to live in a haunted house, haunted by the ghost of the
devastating injustice of slavery—and even more—haunted by
the ghosts of our own unconscious selves struggling to belong
and struggling to be free.

Notes

[1] I wish to thank the Research Council of the University of Missouri-Columbia for a semester's leave granted in 1994 which allowed me the time to complete my research for this essay.

[2] See my *"Here a Captive Heart Busted": Studies in the Sentimental Journey of Modern Literature*, 188-189. Richard C. Moreland has suggested, interestingly, that Morrison's *Beloved* should be read as an analogue to *Huckleberry Finn* in "'He Wants to Put his Story Next to Hers': Putting Twain's Story Next to Hers in Morrison's *Beloved*."

[3] See Eugene D. Genovese, *Roll, Jordan, Roll: The World the Slaves Made*. Stanley Elkins, in *Slavery: A Problem in American Institutional and Intellectual Life*, is especially severe on North American slavery as contrasted to that in the Caribbean and Latin America but also mentions the divided opinion on the subject of slavery (1).

[4] Pertinent discussions are found in Erich Auerbach, *Mimesis: The Representation of Reality in Modern Literature*; Owen Barfield, *Saving the Appearances: A Study in Idolatry*; Ernst Cassirer, *The Philosophy of Symbolic Forms*, vols. 1 and 2; R. G. Collingwood, *The Idea of History*; Michel Foucault, *The History of Sexuality*, vol. 1; Thomas Kuhn, *The Structure of Scientific Revolutions*; Claude Lévi-Strauss, *The Savage Mind*; Erich Neumann, *The Origin and History of Consciousness*.

[5] In language one might begin by consulting Barfield; in anthropology, Lévi-Strauss and Mircea Eliade; in the history of science, writers like Thomas Kuhn, Morris Berman, and Michael Polanyi.

[6] See also my *Captive Heart*, 13-23 and Barfield's *Saving the Appearances*, throughout.

[7] *The Rediscovery of Meaning and Other Essays* 5. See also *History in English Words*; *Poetic Diction*; *Saving the Appearances*; and *Speaker's Meaning*.

[8] There has been much controversy about primitives' relation to the world. Barfield made use of Emile Durkheim and Lucien Lévy-Bruhl. See especially Durkheim's *The Elementary Forms of the Religious Life* and Lévy-Bruhl's *How Natives Think*. Among other works that treat the topic are Robert Redfield, *The Primitive World and Its Transformations*; H. and H. A. Frankfort, et al., *Before Philosophy: The Intellectual Adventure of Ancient Man; An Essay on Speculative Thought in the Ancient Near East*; Mircea Eliade, *Myths, Dreams, and Mysteries* and *The Myth of the Eternal Return*; Clifford Geertz, *The Interpretation of Cultures: Selected Essays*; Claude Lévi-Strauss, *The Savage Mind*; and Victor Turner, *Dramas, Fields, and Metaphors: Symbolic Action in Human Society*. See Turner (183-184) for a Durkheimian interest in collective representations.

[9] See my *Here a Captive Heart Busted* (1-31) for a full discussion of sentimentality.

[10] Genovese comments extensively on the sentimental patriarchalism of the slaveholders. Even the slaves themselves could see the connection between the master's patriarchal attitude towards his wife and children and towards them (74). Citing an analogy between the experience of slavery and of the disorienting and brutal conditions of Nazi concentration camps, Elkins describes

the creation of a "Sambo" character among the Africans—not only in a sentimental projection but to some extent in reality (82).

[11] Karen Carmean, for instance, explains "Morrison's decision to person-
alize nature" by referring to the "African vein" in which "nature is *fully* alive,
meaning that it is not materially separated from human existence" (78). Barbara Rigney points to Morrison's romanticizing the African past but judges her
attitude to be ironic (71).

[12] See Coleridge's discussion in *The Statesman's Manual*, in *The Complete Works of Samuel Taylor Coleridge*, ed. W. G. T. Shedd, 7 vols. (New
York: Harper, 1853), 436-437.

Works Cited

Auerbach, Erich. *Mimesis: The Representation of Reality in Modern Literature.* Trans. Willard R. Trask. Princeton: Princeton University Press, 1953;
rpt. 1974.

Baker, Houston A., Jr. *Long Black Song: Essays in Black American Literature
and Culture.* Charlottesville: University Press of Virginia, 1972, 1990.

Barfield, Owen. *History in English Words.* London: Methuen, 1926. Rev. ed.
Grand Rapids, Michigan: William B. Eerdmans, 1967.

—. *Poetic Diction: A Study in Meaning.* London: Faber and Gwyer, 1928. 3rd ed.
Middletown, Connecticut: Wesleyan University Press, 1973.

—. *The Rediscovery of Meaning and Other Essays.* Middletown: Wesleyan
University Press, 1977.

—. *Saving the Appearances: A Study in Idolatry.* New York: Harcourt Brace,
1957.

—. *Speaker's Meaning.* Middletown, Connecticut: Wesleyan University Press,
1967.

Betman, Michael. *The Reenchantment of the World.* Ithaca: Cornell University Press, 1981.

Carmean, Karen. *Toni Morrison's World of Fiction.* Troy, New York: Whitston
Publishing Co., 1993.

Cassirer, Ernst. *The Philosophy of Symbolic Forms.* Vols. 1 and 2. Trans.
Ralph Manheim. New Haven and London: Yale University Press, 1953,
1955.

Coleridge, S. T. *Biographia Literaria or Biographical Sketches of My Literary
Life and Opinions.* Eds. James Engell and W. Jackson Bate. Princeton:
Princeton University Press, 1983.

—. *The Statesman's Manual* in *The Complete Works of Samuel Taylor Coleridge.* Ed. W. G. T. Shedd. 7 Vols. New York: Harper, 1853.

Collingwood, R. G. *The Idea of History.* New York: Oxford University Press,
1946; rpt. 1954.

Du Bois, W. E. Burghardt. *The Souls of Black Folk: Essays and Sketches.* New
York: Dodd, Mead & Co., 1979 (1903).

Durkheim, Emile. *The Elementary Forms of the Religious Life.* Trans. Joseph
Ward Swain. 1915. New York: Free Press, 1968.

Eliade, Mircea. *The Myth of the Eternal Return*. Trans. Willard R. Trask. Princeton: Princeton University Press, 1954.

—. *Myths, Dreams, and Mysteries*. New York: Harper, 1960.

Elkins, Stanley M. *Slavery: A Problem in American Institutional and Intellectual Life*. 1959. 3rd Ed. Rev. Chicago: University of Chicago Press, 1976.

Foucault, Michel. *The History of Sexuality*. Vol. 1. Trans. Robert Hurley. New York: Vantage, 1980.

Frankfort, H. and H. A., et al. *Before Philosophy: The Intellectual Adventure of Ancient Man; An Essay on Speculative Thought in the Ancient Near East*. Baltimore: Penguin, 1963.

Frederickson, George M. *The Black Image in the White Mind: The Debate on Afro-American Character and Destiny 1817-1914*. New York: Harper and Row, 1971.

Fulweiler, Howard W. *"Here a Captive Heart Busted": Studies in the Sentimental Journey of Modern Literature*. New York: Fordham, 1993.

Geertz, Clifford. *The Interpretation of Cultures: Selected Essays*. New York: Basic Books, 1973.

Genovese, Eugene D. *Roll, Jordan, Roll: The World the Slaves Made*. New York: Basic Books, 1973.

Goethe, Johann Wofgang von. *Faust Part I: A New American Version*. Trans. C. F. MacIntyre. New York: New Directions, 1949.

Gunthorpe, Violet, in Belinda Hurmence, ed. *Before Freedom: 48 Histories of Former North and South Carolina Slaves*. New York: Mentor, 1990.

Harris, Trudier. *Fiction and Folklore: The Novels of Toni Morrison*. Knoxville: University of Tennessee Press, 1991.

Holloway, Karla F. C. and Stephanie A. Demetrakopoulos. *New Dimensions of Spirituality: A Biracial and Bicultural Reading of the Novels of Toni Morrison*. New York: Greenwood Press, 1987.

Hurmence, Belinda, ed. *Before Freedom: 48 Oral Histories of Former North and South Carolina Slaves*. New York: Mentor, 1990.

Kuhn, Thomas. *The Structure of Scientific Revolutions*. Chicago: University of Chicago Press, 1962.

Lévi-Strauss, Claude. *The Savage Mind*. Chicago: University of Chicago Press, 1966.

Lévy-Bruhl, Lucien. *How Natives Think*. Trans. Lilian A. Clare. 1926. Princeton: Princeton University Press, 1985.

Melville, Herman. "Benito Cereno." *Herman Melville*. Ed. and Intro. R. W. B. Lewis. New York: Dell, 1962.

Mitchner, Patsy, in Belinda Hurmence, ed. *Before Freedom*.

Moreland, Richard C. "'He Wants to Put his Story Next to Hers': Putting Twain's Story Next to Hers in Morrison's *Beloved*." *Modern Fiction Studies* 39 (Fall/Winter 1993): 501-525.

Morrison, Toni. *Beloved*. New York: Knopf, 1987. Rpt. New American Library, 1988.

—. *Conversations with Toni Morrison*. Ed. Danille Taylor-Guthrie. Jackson: University Press of Mississippi, 1994.

—. *Playing in the Dark: Whiteness and the Literary Imagination*. Cambridge: Harvard University Press, 1992.

—. *Song of Solomon*. New York: Knopf, 1977; Signet, 1978.

—. *Tar Baby*. New York: Knopf, 1981; Penguin, 1982.

Neumann, Erich. *The Origin and History of Consciousness*. Trans. R. F. C. Hull. New York: Pantheon, 1964.

Polanyi, Michael. *Personal Knowledge: Towards a Post-Critical Philosophy*. Chicago: University of Chicago Press, 1958.

Rampersad, Arnold. "Adventures of *Huckleberry Finn* and Afro-American Literature." *Satire or Evasion? Black Perspectives on* Huckleberry Finn. Eds. James S. Leonard, Thomas A. Tenney and Thadious M. Davis. Durham: Duke University Press, 1992.

Redfield, Robert. *The Primitive World and Its Transformations*. Ithaca: Cornell University Press, 1953.

Rigney, Barbara Hill. *The Voices of Toni Morrison*. Columbus: Ohio State University Press, 1991.

Samuels, Wilfred D. and Clenora Hudson-Weems. *Toni Morrison*. Boston: Twayne, 1990.

Sophocles. *Oedipus the King*. Trans. David Grene. *The Complete Greek Tragedies*. Ed. David Grene and Richmond Lattimore. Vol. 2. Chicago: University of Chicago Press, 1959.

Taylor-Guthrie, Danille, ed. *Conversations with Toni Morrison*. Jackson: University Press of Mississippi, 1994.

Turner, Victor. *Dramas, Fields, and Metaphors: Symbolic Action in Human Society*. Ithaca: Cornell University Press, 1974; rpt. 1978.

Twain, Mark. *Adventures of Huckleberry Finn*. Eds. Sculley Bradley, Richmond Croom Beatty and E. Hudson Long. New York: Norton, 1961, 1962.

"will the parts hold?":
The Journey Toward
a Coherent Self in Beloved

Betty Jane Powell

Toni Morrison's *Beloved* represents a continuum of what
Dorothy H. Lee terms the writer's "vision of the human condition," a "preoccupation with the effect of the community on the
individual's achievement and retention of an integrated, acceptable self" (346). Lee points out that Morrison's earlier novels,
The Bluest Eye, Sula, Song of Solomon, and *Tar Baby* draw upon
the inherent need for individual identity within the context of
community. In *Beloved* Toni Morrison writes about the need
for victimized people to form an integrated self in the face of a
fragmented and unacceptable existence. The obstacles confronting characters while living in the world of slavery ensure
fragmentation of both the body and the mind. An environment
in which "men and women were moved around like checkers"
(23), and given whimsically haphazard names, breaks down the
sense of who one is or where one fits into the scheme of things.
The fact that "anyone white could take your whole self for anything that comes to mind" (251) denies autonomy and renders
the self unrecognizable.

Morrison argues that fiction provides the possibility of
"becoming coherent in the world" (Butler-Evans 7), a method
through which the fractures brought about by enslavement and
alienation from community might be fused. Through the
medium of fiction, Morrison sets about the difficult task of fusing such fractures, thereby initiating the possibility of coherence
and recognition for the characters in *Beloved* through freedom
and alliance with community. But, as Sethe says, "Freeing yourself was one thing; claiming ownership of that freed self was an-

other (95); so that many of the characters remain enslaved to a past that they find unspeakable. In order to claim ownership Sethe and the other characters must face the past, speak the unspeakable, and chase away the shadows. Through the recollection and the retelling of fragmented life stories and by forming them into a coherent whole, the characters of *Beloved* free themselves to yoke together stories and bodies, spirit and flesh, and to begin forging a sense of self that holds the promise of the future.

Morrison's major characters are spiritually and physically fragmented individuals who are disconnected from themselves, from each other, and from community. Such alienation results in an emptiness that overpowers the individual. Baby Suggs carries a sadness "at her center, the desolated center where the self that was no self made its home" (140); Sethe has empty eyes "that did not pick up a flicker of light. They were two wells" that "needed to be covered, lidded, marked with some sign to warn folks of what that emptiness held" (9); Denver cries "because she has no self" (123); Paul D wanders the countryside in search of something tangible on which to grasp, carrying his past in "that tobacco tin buried in his chest where a red heart used to be. Its lid rusted shut" (72-73); and Beloved engages in a never-ending struggle to attain cohesion.

The disintegration of self is so complete in *Beloved* that the characters cannot see or recognize their own bodies, just as they are unable to tell their whole stories. For Morrison the ability to see oneself as physically whole and appreciate the beauty of one's body is an integral part of knowing oneself. It is Baby Suggs's ultimate recognition of her own body that allows for salvation through the gathering together of her neighbors' bodies and stories in freedom. While entrapped in the "special kind of slavery" (140) that the Garners offer, all reflections that might be used for self-definition have been taken from Baby Suggs. As a woman, her value to her various owners has been to breed and to work; as a wife, the inversion of slavery has forced separation from her husband; and, as a mother, she has had all but one child taken from her, as if they were so much chattel. So Baby Suggs has no "map to discover what she was like" (140). Severed from any possible linkages to self, Baby Suggs questions who she is:

> Could she sing? (Was it nice to hear when she did?)
> Was she pretty? Was she a good friend? Could she
> have been a loving mother? A faithful wife? Have I
> got a sister and does she favor me? If my mother knew
> me would she like me? (140)

When she moves across the line of demarcation from slavery into freedom Baby Suggs gains a new look at herself. In freedom she begins to see herself for the first time, but she sees only in fragments:

> She didn't know what she looked like and was not curi-
> ous. But suddenly she saw her hands and thought with
> a clarity as simple as it was dazzling, 'These hands be-
> long to me. These *my* hands.' Next she felt a knocking
> in her chest and discovered something else new: her
> own heartbeat. Had it been there all along? (141)

Drawing on this new discovery, Baby Suggs becomes one of Morrison's vehicles through which bodies and stories merge. In her preaching to her neighbors in the clearing, she encourages them to recognize the parts of their bodies and to love them as a whole:

> Love it hard . . . the skin on your back . . . your hands . . .
> your mouth . . . feet that need to rest and to dance; backs
> that need support; shoulders that need arms . . . your
> neck . . . all your inside parts . . . and the beat and beat-
> ing heart, love that too. (88)

Baby Suggs, then, hinges her physical and spiritual coherence on a connection with community, a connection that, for Morrison, reigns supreme in any journey towards self. Her call for a creative vision that repudiates the traditional norms of responsibility and salvation is parallel to Morrison's vision in the novel (Levy 121): "She did not tell them to clean up their lives or to go and sin no more. She did not tell them they were the blessed of the earth, its inheriting meek or its glory bound pure" (88). Rather, she pleads for self-assertion with communal overtones: "She told them that the only grace they could have was the grace they could imagine" (89). She becomes the matriarch, "Baby Suggs, holy," and acts as the invoker of spirit, the relayer of messages, and the giver of love. While in the embrace of community Baby Suggs and the house at 124 Bluestone thrive, with 124 becoming a "buzzing house where Baby Suggs, holy, loved, cautioned, fed, chastised and soothed" (87). It is with the community's damnation of Baby Suggs for gathering too much self, following the celebratory feast in Sethe's honor, and with the baby's murder, that she decides that "Her past had been like her present—intolerable—and since she knew death was anything but forgetfulness, she used the little energy left her for pondering color" (4). Color represents "life in the raw" (38), an unadulterated and uncorrupted promise of what life could be, a bright contrast to the "dark and muted" (38) grayness of reality. Significantly, Denver offers Baby Suggs's quilt with two orange patches to Beloved, rearranging it "so its cheeriest part was in the sick girl's sight line" (54). While color carries recuperative powers—a suggestion of what life might hold—Morrison warns of delving too deeply into a dream world. Baby Suggs's immersion into the world of color reverses her connection to community and completes her isolation from others, while coincidentally dissolving whatever gains toward self she had appropriated.

Morrison punctuates this tentative and elusive aspect of self by aligning the fragmentation of intellectual autobiography (stories) to the fragmentation of corporeal bodies (Levy 120). The reader receives stories in bits and pieces, products of fragmented memory, while at the same time receiving fragmented descriptions of characters. By allowing the narrative to focus on particular body parts, Morrison reduces characters to their most elemental state, like memory, while preparing the foundation for coherence. Amy Denver comes to us largely as an image of wild, tangled hair and large hands that massage Sethe's dead feet back to life; Halle's face covered in butter surfaces as his most lasting image, and it corresponds with the image of Sethe's breasts having the milk stolen from them; Beloved continually has problems keeping her parts together, always fearing exploding, "she could wake up any day and find herself in pieces" (133); Baby Suggs bathes Sethe "in sections, starting with her face" (93); and when Sethe severs the "crawling already? baby['s]" head from its body, holding "her face so her head would stay on" (251), Morrison underlines the terrible fact that at any moment bodies (and stories, and therefore lives) can splinter into parts.

If splintering occurs, the disconnected parts must struggle toward reunion, ultimately finding a way to cohere. The sharing of stories provides one avenue towards coherence. Because "story-telling is the primary folk process in Toni Morrison's fictional world," the characters in Morrison's novels tell stories for reasons of "self-dramatization, self-justification, ego-action" but most significantly for "self-understanding" (Skerritt 243, qtd. in Levy 116). But, if, as Andrew Levy suggests, "the scar [of slavery] intrudes on the story . . . if history hurts too much—then self-understanding and self-definition are damaged products" (116). Although the results might be damaged, coherence through self-definition in Morrison's works usually stems from the coupling together of the pain from the past and the hope for the future through the art of storytelling. In *Beloved* Morrison underscores the difficulty involved in aligning storytelling and memory. Because excruciating pain accompanies memory, stories are uncovered piecemeal, peeling back one thin layer at a time, until the core wound is exposed. This process is further enhanced by Morrison's invention of "rememory." As Ashraf Rushdy points out, with the term "rememory" Morrison adds a new word to the language, connoting both memory and invention (303). "Rememories" allow characters access to events outside their experience and, therefore, outside their memories. As Sethe explains to Denver, a "rememory" "is a picture floating around out there outside my head. . . . Right in the place where it happened" (36). Sethe goes on to tell Denver: "Someday you be walking down the road and you hear something or see something going on. So clear. And you think it's you thinking it up. A thought picture. But no. It's when you bump into a rememory that belongs to somebody else" (36). The gift of "rememory" allows characters to remember and reinvent not only their own stories, but stories of others as well. It offers a way of sharing and diffusing the pain, lifting the burden of memory when it becomes unbearable.

Remembering the past involves for all the characters both a blessing and a curse—on the one hand it sheds light in the darkness, while on the other it causes pain and threatens to become a dangerous obsession. When Baby Suggs complains that all she can remember of her firstborn "is how she loved the burned bottom of bread. . . . Eight children and that's all I remember" (5), Sethe responds "That's all you let yourself remember" (5). But because "Anything dead coming back to life hurts" (35), as Amy Denver tells Sethe, remembering a past that has been so long repressed becomes painful for Sethe: "every mention of her past life hurt. Everything in it was painful or lost. She and Baby Suggs had agreed without saying so that it was unspeakable" (58).

Beloved's arrival in the form of a corporeal body initiates speakability, as Sethe's stories emerge at first haltingly, because "the hurt was always there—like a tender place in the corner of her mouth that the bit left" (58); but they pick up speed at an increasing rate, reaching a frenzied state as the work progresses. When Beloved asks Sethe to "tell me your diamonds" (58), she not only wants to hear the story of how Mr. Garner gave diamond earrings to Sethe for a wedding present, but she is also offering to turn the dark stories of Sethe's past into something shining and valuable. The very telling of the story brings Sethe pleasure:

> . . . as she began telling about the earrings, she found
> herself wanting to, liking it. Perhaps it was Beloved's
> distance from the events itself, or her thirst for hearing
> it—in any case it was an unexpected pleasure.   (58)

Because Sethe has hidden from the past, working hard "to remember as close to nothing as was safe" (26), she has cut herself off from her life, preferring to "keep the past at bay" (42), while relinquishing the future. But her "devious brain" and her "terrible memory" will not grant her forgetfulness, nor will they allow for coherence. Because her brain and her memory open up and shut down sporadically and unpredictably, and because when stories do come, they come in "short replies or rambling, incomplete reveries" (58), Sethe is rendered a victim of her past. Although Paul D initially seems to open possibilities, with his "smile and . . . up front love" that make "her try" to tell her story (159), Sethe finds that "she could never pin it down for anybody who had to ask. If they didn't get it right off—she could never explain" (163). In addition, Paul D has his own "tobacco tin" filled with secrets, and approaches Sethe with a tentative restraint and a conditional love. Beloved, on the other hand, accepts Sethe for who she is, and, although her love turns malevolent toward the end, the acceptance is unconditional. Beloved's hunger for stories allows Sethe to make peace with her own tortured "rememory" (191); "I don't have to remember nothing. I don't even have to explain. She understands it all" (183). Sethe begins to relive the past and begins to gather together the fragments of her life.

But Sethe's movement toward coherence depends on Beloved's ability to bring spirit and body to a state of cohesion.

Beloved's difficulty, and ultimate failure, in forming and maintaining a self (both physical and spiritual), stems at least in part from her ephemeral characterization in the novel. Who or what is she? Is Beloved the corporeal reincarnation of the unnamed "crawling already? baby"; is she, as Deborah Horvitz argues, "the haunting symbol of the many Beloveds—generations of mothers and daughters—hunted down and stolen from Africa" (157); or is she a flesh and blood human being, yet another slave woman held captive by white men to satiate their own perverted desire, as Elizabeth House postulates? She represents all of these things, as Morrison utilizes Beloved's character in such a way that renders final categorization impossible. As Beloved searches for "a place to be" (75), the various possibilities for her identity urge the narrative along. Morrison invites the reader to suspend disbelief, while Beloved struggles to find and sustain life, thriving on the life stories of those around her.

For Sethe, however, Beloved is the receptacle for her stories, "the one and only person she felt she had to convince" (251), and "Sethe's greatest fear was that Beloved might leave . . . before Sethe could make her understand what it meant" (251). Beloved struggles to maintain corporeal substance, drinking "cup after cup of water" (51), and gorging herself on sweets, "honey as well as the wax it came in, sugar sandwiches, the sludgy molasses gone hard and brutal in the can, lemonade, taffy and any type of dessert Sethe brought home from the restaurant" (55), a glucose-like mixture. Her physical hunger grows more ravenous as the work progresses, as does her hunger for stories, and her body grows in proportion, "her belly protruding like a winning watermelon" (250), pregnant with stories. But Beloved is continually in fear of exploding, falling to pieces, or being chewed up. When Beloved loses a tooth she thinks, "This is it. Next it would be her arms, her hand, a toe. Pieces of her would drop maybe one at a time, maybe all at once" (133)—Morrison's comment on the fragility of the self, and the characters' tenuous grasp on identify.

In a search for self-definition, stories, like corporeal bodies, must be gathered together and eventually lie together, so that both a narrative and a physical intercourse take place. Within the slave system, the merging of bodies is largely brought about by rape, beatings, and the marking of bodies, fostering and reinforcing negative images of self—the very acts that cause the splintering of memory (and therefore stories) in the first place. But in *Beloved* it is the consensual intercourse of bodies and stories that brings the hope for recognition and salvation, however tenuous. Certainly Morrison suggests a flicker of hope for communion between the races with the contact between Amy and Sethe. Morrison reverses the roles here, with the white Amy nurturing and soothing a tortured black Sethe. Amy not only nurtures Sethe physically, but she nurtures her with her story and song as well. Sethe listens to Amy's humming, "a humming she concentrated on" (80), and conjures an image of carmine velvet, while Amy, in her pitiful, but romantic, way, attempts to render something beautiful out of the mark left on Sethe's back by Schoolteacher's boys: "It's a tree, Lu. A chokecherry tree. . . . Your back got a whole tree on it. In bloom" (79). Such instances of affection and symbiosis with others bring moments of cohesion throughout the work. Sethe, Beloved, and Denver merge into a gender reversal of the Trinity— Mother, Daughter(s), and Spirit—while ice skating on a frozen pond. This connection represents the only instance in which the three women cohere without vying for each other's attention: "holding hands, bracing each other, they swirled over the ice," laughing in a microcosm in which "nobody saw them fall" (174). On the frozen pond, divorced from the probing eyes of society, the women are free to see each other and to see themselves without the fear of recrimination.

A similar symbiotic need precipitates Paul D's effort to fill Sethe's emptiness and brings him to recall Sixo's remark about his Thirty-Mile Woman, and how "the pieces I am, she gather them and give them back to me in all the right order" (272-273). Placing parts (bodies and stories) in the right order becomes paramount to recognition of self (just as it does in writing a novel), so that Paul D initiates the merging by wanting "to put his story next to hers" (273). Just as the novel attempts to realign the fragments into an orderly whole, Paul D's act of placing his story next to Sethe's attempts both narrative and physical cohesion. When Paul D "leans over and takes her hand," and "with the other he touches her face," and tells Sethe "You your best thing, Sethe. You are," she answers "Me? Me?" (273). Although her response can be read as "only ambiguously hopeful" (Levy 121), it can also be read as standing on the threshold of enlightenment. Sethe has for the first time had such an idea of self broached to her, and the interrogative suggests an opening up, rather than a shutting down.

    Stories open up all sorts of possibilities throughout
Beloved, and are very often used as a kind of barter in the same
way that bodies are bartered. Just as Sethe exchanges "ten minutes for seven letters" (5) on Beloved's headstone, because her
body is all she has to sell, Denver trades partially manufactured
stories in exchange for Beloved's attention. The unspeakability
of the past at 124 Bluestone has isolated Denver and has denied
her access to autonomy. She, in effect, is rendered a slave to her
mother's and grandmother's past lives—until Beloved's appearance. With Beloved's arrival, Denver becomes her own
narrator of stories, constructing "out of the strings she had heard
all her life a net to hold Beloved" (76). Just as Morrison gives
life to Margaret Garner's story through the writing of *Beloved,*
Denver anticipates Beloved's hunger for detail "by giving blood
to the scraps her mother and grandmother had told her—and a
heartbeat" (79). But because remembering and storytelling entail
the "concept of mental recollection and construction that is
never only personal but always interpersonal" (Rushdy 304),
Morrison places the two women in a conspiracy of reconstruction that feeds the needs of both; "Denver spoke, Beloved listened, and the two did the best they could to create what really
happened, how it really was" (79).
    This sort of sharing is crucial to creating a history and a
sense of self, not only for Denver but for all of Morrison's characters who venture out on a quest for self. Without connection
characters fail in their journeys: Sula (*Sula*) is unable to connect
fruitfully with the external word, becomes a pariah in her own
community and finally dies; Son and Jade (*Tar Baby*) experience
dreams, needs, and desires that are at cross-purposes and that
result in separation and loss (Lee 350, 355). In *Beloved* Morrison
strongly suggests that too much connection with the past can
become obsessive and render people immobile in their ability to
connect with others. During the time in which the bond
between Denver, Beloved, and Sethe holds, Denver remains
complacent with her situation. But with the severing of that
bond, with Denver's exclusion from the Trinity, when the two
women "cut Denver out of their games" (234), she realizes that
"it was she who had to step off the edge of the world and die
because if she didn't, they all would" (239). It is Denver's act of
leaving the world of storytelling, knowing the past, but going on,
that provides her with a sense of self and enables her to save
Sethe. She marvels at the "new thought, having a self to look

out for and preserve" (252). Denver emerges at the end of the work as "a strategist" (121), a young woman with a freshly awakened motivation: "Plotting has changed Denver markedly. Where she was once indolent, resentful of every task, now she is spry, executing" (121). She becomes the most cohesive character, the only character who seems to have a concrete sense of who she is and where she going.

Whereas Denver appears to escape from a past that at once nurtures and possesses, Sethe becomes increasingly mired in it. Beloved's voracious hunger for Sethe's stories consumes Sethe: "The bigger Beloved got, the smaller Sethe became. . . . Beloved ate up her life, took it, swelled up with it, grew taller on it. And the older women yielded it up without a murmur" (250). Sethe regresses into a kind of masochistic remembering in which frenzied storytelling saps her of agency—she becomes Beloved's possession. With Denver out of the house, moving toward connection with community, Sethe and Beloved are left in the clutch of destruction and annihilation. Beloved transforms into the abusive mother, "Sethe the teething child" (251), with Beloved "getting bigger, plumper by the day" and Sethe starving: "the flesh between her . . . forefinger and thumb was as thin as china silk" (239). Once again, salvation springs up from community with others, and once again it comes about as the result of storytelling. Denver trades the story of her mother to Lady Jones, Lady Jones, in turn, tells the story to the community, and the community responds with "gifts of food"—"a sack of white beans . . . a plate of cold rabbit . . . a basket of eggs" (249).

Further cohesion comes in the form of Ella and the other women in the community. Ella, whom Morrison describes as a "practical woman" (256), sees the future as "sunset" and the past as "something to leave behind" (257). Because Ella thinks of the past as something she "might have to stomp out," she does not "like the idea of past errors taking possession of the future" (256). Ella had in the past

> delivered, but would not nurse, a hairy white thing, fathered by the 'lowest yet.' It lasted five days never making a sound. The idea of that pup coming back to whip her too set her jaws working.   (258-259)

She, unlike Sethe, understands the danger of residing too long in the past. Since Beloved represents the corporeal embodiment of the past, Sethe's repository for stories, Ella and the other women rise up to squash her impending threat to subsume not only Sethe, but themselves as well. The women group together in front of 124 Bluestone, at first "whispering and murmuring" (258), but

> Building voice upon voice until they found it, and when they did it was a wave of sound wide enough to sound deep water and knock the pods off chestnut trees. It broke over Sethe and she trembled like the baptized in its wash. (261)

The gathering together of individual voices into a coherent unit expels the past at least to a point that will allow healing and perhaps forgetting. By gathering the women into a unified voice, Morrison empowers that voice to "identify those things in the past that are useful and those that are not" (Butler-Evans 7), a role she delegates to her novels as well. The past, in the form of Beloved, "the girl who waited to be loved and cry shame erupts into her separate parts, to make it easy for the chewing laughter to swallow her all away" (274).

When Beloved exits the work, she carries with her (in her) much of the rage and torment experienced by the various characters, thereby opening some opportunity for cohesion of self. She carries Denver's isolation and fear of "the thing that leapt up" and "coiled around her" (104); she carries with her the contents of Paul D's "tobacco tin"; she carries with her, by extension, the pain and outrage of the community of ex-slaves; and she carries Sethe's darkest "rememories." The past, at least temporarily, has served its purpose. As Beloved "erupts into her separate parts," the other characters connect with one another, as their bodies and stories begin to cohere into intelligible selves. But because it seems an ambivalent coherence, Morrison leaves the reader asking, along with Sethe, "will the parts hold?" (273).

Works Cited

Butler-Evans, Elliot. *Race, Gender, and Desire: Narrative Strategies in the Fiction of Toni Cade Cambara, Toni Morrison, and Alice Walker.* Philadelphia: Temple University Press, 1989.

Horvitz, Deborah. "Nameless Ghosts: Possession and Dispossession in *Beloved.*" *Studies in American Fiction* 17 (Autumn 1989): 157-167.

House, Elizabeth B. "Toni Morrison's Ghost: The Beloved Who Is Not Beloved." *Studies in American Fiction* 18 (Spring 1990): 17-26.

Lee, Dorothy H. "The Quest for Self: Triumph and Failure in the Works of Toni Morrison." *Perspectives on Black Women Writers*. Ed. Barbara Christian. New York: Pergamon Press, 1985, 346-359.

Levy, Andrew. "Telling Beloved." *Texas Studies in Literature and Language* 33 (Spring 1991): 114-123.

Morrison, Toni. *Beloved*. New York: Knopf, 1987.

—. *The Bluest Eye*. Simon and Schuster, 1970.

—. *Song of Solomon*. New York: Knopf, 1975.

—. *Sula*. New York: Knopf, 1973.

—. *Tar Baby*. New York: Knopf, 1981.

Rushdy, Ashraf H. A. "'Rememory': Primal Scenes and Construction in Toni Morrison's Novels." *Contemporary Literature* xxxi.3 (1990): 300-323.

Skerritt, Joseph T., Jr. "Recitation to the *Griot*: Storytelling and Learning in Toni Morrison's *Song of Solomon*." *Conjuring: Black Women, Fiction and Literature*. Ed. Marjorie Pryse and Hortense J. Spillers. Bloomington: Indiana University Press, 1985.

The Bonds of Love
nd the Boundaries of Self in Toni Morrison's
Beloved

Barbara Schapiro

Toni Morrison's *Beloved* penetrates, perhaps more deeply than any historical or psychological study could, the unconscious emotional and psychic consequences of slavery. The novel reveals how the condition of enslavement in the external world, particularly the denial of one's status as a human subject, has deep repercussions in the individual's internal world. These internal resonances are so profound that even if one is eventually freed from external bondage, the self will still be trapped in an inner world that prevents a genuine experience of freedom. As Sethe succinctly puts it, "Freeing yourself was one thing; claiming ownership of that freed self was another" (95). The novel wrestles with this central problem of recognizing and claiming one's own subjectivity, and it shows how this cannot be achieved independently of the social environment.

A free, autonomous self, as Jessica Benjamin argues in *The Bonds of Love*, is still an essentially relational self and is dependent on the recognizing response of an other. *Beloved* powerfully dramatizes the fact that, in Benjamin's words, "In order to exist for oneself, one has to exist for an other" (53); in so doing, it enacts the complex interrelationship of social and intrapsychic reality. For Morrison's characters, African-Americans in a racist, slave society, there is no reliable other to recognize and affirm their existence. The mother, the child's first vital other, is made unreliable or unavailable by a slave system which either separates her from her child or so enervates and depletes her that she has no self with which to confer recognition. The consequences on the inner life of the child—the emotional

hunger, the obsessive and terrifying narcissistic fantasies—constitute the underlying psychological drama of the novel.

"124 was spiteful. Full of a baby's venom." The opening
lines of the novel establish its psychic source: infantile rage. A
wounded, enraged baby is the central figure of the book, both literally, in the character of Beloved, and symbolically, as it struggles beneath the surface of the other major characters. Even the
elderly grandmother is significantly named "Baby," and the ferocity of a baby's frustrated needs colors the novel's overt
mother-child relationships as well as the love relationship between Sethe and Paul D and that between Beloved and her sister
Denver. "A baby's frustrated needs" refers here not to physical
needs but to psychic and emotional ones. The worst atrocity of
slavery, the real horror the novel exposes, is not physical death
but psychic death. The pivotal event, or crisis, of the novel is
Sethe's murder of her baby daughter Beloved. The reader is allowed to feel, however, the paradoxical nature of the murder.
Sethe, having run away from the sadistic slave-master
Schoolteacher, is on the verge of being recaptured. Her humanity has been so violated by this man, and by her entire experience
as a slave woman, that she kills her daughter to save her from a
similar fate; she kills her to save her from psychic death: "if I
hadn't killed her she would have died and that is something I
could not bear to happen to her" (200).

Psychic death, as the novel makes clear, involves the denial of one's being as a human subject. The infant self has an essential, primary need to be recognized and affirmed as a whole
being, as an active agent of its own legitimate desires and impulses, and the fulfillment of this need is dependent on the human environment, on other selves. The premise of the object
relations school of psychoanalysis, as Jessica Benjamin notes, is
that "we are fundamentally social beings" (17). According to this
theory, human beings are not innately sexual or aggressive; they
are innately responsive and relational.[1] As Harry Guntrip explains, the "need of a love-relationship is the fundamental
thing" in life, and "the love-hunger and anger set up by frustration of this basic need must constitute the two primary problems
of personality on the emotional level" (45). The experience of
one's cohesiveness and reality as a self is dependent on this primary relationship, on the loving response and recognition from
an other. This issue is repeatedly illustrated and explored in
Morrison's novels. Sula, for instance, speaks of the two most

formative experiences of her life: the first concerns her overhearing her mother state matter-of-factly that she simply doesn't
"like" her (Sula), and the second involves her having thrown a
child, seemingly by accident, into the river to drown. "The first
experience taught her there was no other that you could count
on; the second that there was no self to count on either. She had
no center, no speck around which to grow" (*Sula* 118-119). These
experiences are intimately related: the lack of an affirming, reliable other leads to an unconscious, murderous rage and the lack
of a coherent, reliable self.

In *The Bonds of Love*, a feminist psychoanalytic study of
the problem of domination in Western culture, Benjamin modi-
fies object relations theory to form what she calls "intersubjective theory." She maintains the primacy of relationship in self-
development but argues that the self grows through relationship
with another *subject* rather than through relations with its object. The child has a need to see the mother, or his or her most
significant other, "as an independent subject, not simply as the
'external world' or an adjunct of his ego" (23). The intersubjective view, which Benjamin sees as complementary to intrapsychic theory, conceives of self and other "as distinct but interrelated beings" (20) who are involved in an intricate dance of assertion and recognition. The essential need is for *mutual* recognition—"the necessity of recognizing as well as being recognized
by the other" (23). Benjamin also emphasizes the concept of attunement, a "combination of resonance and difference" (26) in
which self and other are empathically in tune while maintaining their distinct boundaries and separateness. When the
boundaries break down and the necessary tension between self
and other dissolves, domination takes root. The search for
recognition then becomes a struggle for power and control, and
assertion turns into aggression.

Beloved does not delve into the roots of white domination, but there is a suggestion of fear and inadequate selfhood
underlying the problem. The white farmer Mr. Garner, while
still sharing in the cultural objectification of blacks, nevertheless
boasts that his "niggers is men every one of 'em." When another farmer argues that there "Ain't no nigger men," Garner
replies, "Not if you scared, they ain't. . . . But if you a man yourself, you'll want your niggers to be men too" (10). A self wants
the recognition of another self; this form of mutuality is more
desirable, Garner implies, than mastery of an object. Garner,

however, dies—his perspective cannot prevail in a world in which domination and the denial of recognition are built into the social system.

Beloved explores the interpersonal and intrapsychic effects of growing up as a black person in such a system, one in which intersubjectivity is impossible. How can a child see self or mother as subjects when the society denies them that status? The mother is made incapable of recognizing the child, and the child cannot recognize the mother. As a young girl, Sethe had to have her mother "pointed out" to her by another child. When she becomes a mother herself, she is so deprived and depleted that she cannot satisfy the hunger for recognition, the longed for "look," that both her daughters crave. The major characters in the novel are all working out of a deep loss to the self, a profound narcissistic wound that results from a breakdown and distortion of the earliest relations between self and other. In the case of Beloved, the intense desire for recognition evolves into enraged narcissistic omnipotence and a terrifying, tyrannical domination.

The infantile rage in the novel is a form of frustrated, murderous love. The baby ghost of Beloved wreaks havoc in Sethe's home, prompting Denver to comment, "For a baby she throws a powerful spell," to which Sethe replies, "No more powerful than the way I loved her" (4). The power of Beloved's rage is directly linked to the power of Sethe's love. The intimacy of destructive rage and love is asserted in various ways throughout the book—Sethe's love for Beloved is indeed a murderous love. The violation or murder of children by their parents is a theme that runs throughout much of Morrison's work, from Cholly raping his daughter in *The Bluest Eye* to Eva setting fire to her son in *Sula*, and in these cases too the acts are incited by feelings of love.[2] If the infant is traumatically frustrated in its first love relationship, if it fails to receive the affirmation and recognition it craves, the intense neediness of the infant's own love becomes dangerous and threatening. The fear, as Guntrip (27) and others have discussed, is that one's love will destroy. The baby's enraged, destructive love is also projected outward onto the parent, which suggests one perspective on the strain of destructive parental love in Morrison's novels.

Because the first physical mode of relationship to the mother is oral, the earliest emotional needs in relation to the mother are also figured in oral terms in the child's inner world.

Frustration in this first oral stage of relationship leads to what object relations theorists call "love made hungry," a terrifying greediness in which the baby fears it will devour and thus destroy mother and, conversely, that mother (due to projection) will devour and destroy the self (Guntrip 35). A preponderance of oral imagery characterizes Morrison's novel. Beloved, in her fantasies, repeatedly states that Sethe "chews and swallows me" (213), while the metaphor of Beloved chewing and swallowing Sethe is almost literal: "Beloved ate up her life, took it, swelled up with it, grew taller on it" (250). Denver's problems of identity and self-cohesion, too, are often imaged in oral terms: leaving the house means being prepared to "be swallowed up in the world beyond the edge of the porch" (243). When Denver temporarily loses sight of Beloved in the shed, she experiences a dissolution of self—"she does not know where her body stops, which part of her is an arm, a foot or a knee"—and feels she is being "eaten alive by the dark" (123). Beloved, in the second part of the novel, is said to have two dreams: "exploding, and being swallowed" (133). Everywhere in the novel, the fantasy of annihilation is figured orally; the love hunger, the boundless greed, that so determines the life of the characters also threatens to destroy them.

Sethe repeatedly asserts that the worst aspect of her rape was that the white boys "took my milk!" (17). She feels robbed of her essence, of her most precious substance, which is her maternal milk. We learn that as a child, Sethe was deprived of her own mother's milk: "The little whitebabies got it first and I got what was left. Or none. There was no nursing milk to call my own" (200). Sethe was not physically starved as a baby—she did receive milk from another nursing slave woman—but she was emotionally starved of a significant nurturing relationship, of which the nursing milk is symbolic. That relationship is associated with one's core being or essence; if she has no nursing milk to call her own, she feels without a self to call her own. Thus even before she was raped by the white farm boys, Sethe was ravaged as an infant, robbed of her milk/essence by the white social structure.

Beloved's first appearance in her incarnated form is marked by her excessive drinking, by her downing "cup after cup of water" (51), while Sethe, suddenly feeling her "bladder filled to capacity," lifts her skirts and "the water she voided was endless" (51). The dynamic suggests a mother being drained by the child's greedy, excessive need. Sethe's voiding is also associated with her own child-self in relation to her mother: "Not since she was a baby girl, being cared for by the eight-year-old girl who pointed out her mother to her, had she had an emergency that unmanageable" (51). One might rather expect Sethe to experience thirst upon seeing her mother, but perhaps that thirst is so extreme, so potentially violent and destructive, that the more urgent need is to void, to empty oneself completely of this unmanageable hunger and rage. Sethe must drain herself in order to avoid draining, and therefore destroying, her mother. This is the fearful fantasy so central to the book; it is precisely what Beloved almost succeeds in doing to Sethe. The nursing dynamic also characterizes Denver and Beloved's relationship: "so intent was her (Denver's) nursing" of Beloved, "she forgot to eat" (54), and she hides Beloved's incontinence. Paul D, as I will discuss more fully later, also plays a maternal, nurturing role in relation to Sethe. When he arrives, Sethe feels "that the responsibility for her breasts, at last, was in somebody else's hands" (18).

The primal nursing relationship is so fraught with ambivalence that frequently in the novel satiation leads to disaster. The most obvious example is the grand feast Baby Suggs prepares for ninety people—"Ninety people who ate so well, and laughed so much, it made them angry" (136). The feast is the prelude to the abandonment of the community, the return of Schoolteacher, and Sethe's consequent murder of her baby. Melanie Klein has discussed the baby's extreme "envy" of the withholding breast (183), and this projected envy may underlie the anger of the neighbors at the maternal bounty of Baby Suggs—she has "given too much, offended them by excess" (138). Similarly, the prelude to Beloved's appearance in the flesh and the ensuing disruption of Sethe's relationship with Paul D is the festive plenitude of the carnival at which Paul D plies both Sethe and Denver with candy and sweets. Paul D's abandonment of Sethe, too, is preceded by a special dinner that Sethe, feeling confident that "she had milk enough for all" (100), prepares for him.

The rage and ambivalence surrounding the love hunger in the novel is illustrated again in the scene in which Sethe, while sitting in the Clearing associated with Baby Suggs and her sermons on love, experiences fingers touching her throat. The fingers are first soothing and comforting but then begin to choke and strangle her, and the hands are associated with those of both

Baby Suggs and Beloved, of both mother and child. When Denver accuses Beloved of choking Sethe, Beloved insists that she "fixed" Sethe's neck—"I kissed her neck. I didn't choke it" (101). The incident, of course, parallels Sethe's murder of Beloved by sawing through her neck, the oral associations once more enforced by mention of the "teeth" of the saw (251) having chewed through the skin. After denying that she choked Sethe's neck, Beloved adds, "The circle of iron choked it" (101), and the image recalls the collars locked around the necks of the black slaves. Her statement is thus true in that the slave system has choked off the vital circulation between mother and child so crucial to the development of the self. Some of the most vivid, disturbing passages in the novel describe the experience of having a horse's bit forced into one's mouth; the sense of deep, searing injury to one's humanity that these descriptions evoke is perhaps compounded by unconscious resonances of violation at the earliest oral roots of our human identity.

The oral imagery in the novel is also closely associated with ocular imagery, with images of eyes and seeing. Sethe is described as being "licked, tasted, eaten by Beloved's eyes" (57); when Sethe lies hidden in the field, anticipating the approach of one of the white boys, she "was eager for his eyes, to bite into them; . . . 'I was hungry,' she told Denver, 'just as hungry as I could be for his eyes'" (31). For Denver, "looking" at Beloved "was food enough to last. But to be looked at in turn was beyond appetite; it was breaking through her own skin to a place where hunger hadn't been discovered" (118). In the logic of the unconscious world, the desire to get and "drink in" with the eyes is akin to the oral wish to consume. Psychoanalyst Heinz Kohut has written about the oral-visual relationship. If the mother is physically and emotionally distant from the child, if she withholds her body, he says, the visual will become "hypercathectic" for the child (116). One can also understand the connection from Benjamin's perspective in that the real hunger in this first relationship between self and other is the hunger for recognition—the desire to be, in Denver's words, "pulled into view by the interested, uncritical eyes of the other" (118). The gaze of the beloved other recognizes and affirms the wholeness and intrinsic value of one's being. Denver describes the quality of being looked at by Beloved: "Having her hair examined as a part of her self, not as material or a style. Having her lips, nose, chin caressed as they might be if she were a moss rose a gardener paused

to admire" (118). The look takes Denver to a "place beyond appetite," to where she is "Needing nothing. Being what there
was" (118). To be recognized by the beloved is all the nourish-
ment one needs; it brings one into coherence, into meaningful
existence. Before Beloved's arrival, Denver craved this look
from Sethe: none of the losses in her life mattered, she felt, "as
long as her mother did not look away" (12).

Sethe's eyes, however, are described as "empty"; Paul D
thinks of Sethe's face as "a mask with mercifully punched-out
eyes. . . . Even punched out they needed to be covered, lidded,
marked with some sign to warn folks of what that emptiness
held" (9). Her eyes reflect the psychic loss and denial of self she
has experienced on all levels in her life. The face of Sethe's
mother was also mask-like, distorted into a permanent false
smile from too many times with the bit. Sethe comments that
she never saw her mother's own smile (203). Sethe's mother,
deprived of her authentic selfhood, her status as a human subject, cannot provide the recognition and affirmation that her
child craves. The cycle is vicious, and thus Sethe's children,
Beloved and Denver, will suffer the same loss. Beloved's eyes
too are remarkable for their emptiness: "deep down in those big
black eyes there was no expression at all" (55).

The craving for mutual recognition—for simultaneously
"seeing" the beloved other and being "seen" by her—propels the
central characters in the novel. Beloved says she has returned in
order to "see" Sethe's face, and she wants "to be there in the
place where her face is and to be looking at it too" (210). When,
as a child, Sethe is shown the brand burned into her mother's
skin and is told that she will be able to "know" her by this mark,
Sethe anxiously responds, "But how will you know me? How
will you know me? Mark me, too, . . . Mark the mark on me
too" (61). Love is a form of knowing and being known. Beloved
repeatedly commands Paul D, "I want you to touch me on the
inside part and call me my name" (116). The hunger is to be
touched, recognized, known in one's inner being or essential
self. This yearning is poignantly captured in the image of two
turtles mating. Denver and Beloved observe the turtles on the
bank of the river: "The embracing necks—hers stretching up toward his bending down, the pat pat pat of their touching heads.
No height was beyond her yearning neck, stretched like a finger
toward his, risking everything outside the bowl just to touch his
face. The gravity of their shields, clashing, countered and

mocked the floating heads touching" (105).

The yearning of Beloved, Sethe, and Denver to touch faces with the beloved other, to know and be known, is, like that of the turtles, obstructed and mocked by the shields or shells each has constructed. The shell, however, is a necessary defense; it attempts to preserve the self from a culture that seeks to deny it, As Joseph Wessling argues in an article on narcissism in *Sula*, narcissistic defenses, such as "self-division" and an inability to empathize or experience human sympathy, may be "the price of survival" (286) in an oppressive, unjust society. The shell also serves to protect the self and its boundaries from the intensity of its own frustrated desire. The hunger for recognition, as discussed, may be so overwhelming that it threatens to swallow up the other and the self, destroying all boundaries in one total annihilation.

The novel as a whole is characterized by a fluidity of boundaries, by a continuously altering narrative perspective that slides in and out of characters' minds, by a mutable, nonsequential time structure, and by an absence of the conventional lines between fantasy and reality. Such fluidity, as Nancy Chodorow and Carol Gilligan have argued, is characteristic of female, as opposed to male, modes of perception and expression. It derives from the preservation of an original identity and preoedipal bondedness between self and mother. The series of monologues by Beloved, Sethe, and Denver in Part 2 of Morrison's novel, however, suggest something more extreme and dangerous than mere fluidity of boundaries: the monologues reveal an utter breakdown of the borders between self and other, a collapse that is bound up with incorporative fantasies. Sethe's section begins, "Beloved, she my daughter. She mine" (200). Denver's opens, "Beloved is my sister. I swallowed her blood right along with my mother's milk" (205), and Beloved's with the line, "I am Beloved and she is mine" (210). After that sentence, Beloved's monologue is marked by a total absence of punctuation, highlighting the fantasy of merging and oneness at the essence of her plaintive ramblings: "I am not separate from her there is no place where I stop her face is my own." Her words reveal the psychic loss—the denial of recognition—at the core of the fantasy:

> there is no one to want me   to say me my name . . . she
> chews and swallows me   I am gone   now I am her face
> my own face has left me . . . Sethe sees me see her and I

> see the smile   her smiling face is the place for me   it
> is the face I lost   she is my face smiling at me   doing
> it at last   a hot thing   now we can join   a hot thing.
>   (212-213)

A similar merging fantasy also figures prominently in
Sula, in the relationship between Sula and Nel. The two characters are described as so close that "they themselves had difficulty
distinguishing one's thoughts from the other's" (83); for Nel,
"talking to Sula had always been a conversation with herself"
(95); and Sula eventually realizes that neither Nel nor anyone
else "would ever be that version of herself which she sought to
reach out to and touch with an ungloved hand" (121). Each is
compelled continually to seek the self through an other, and
such blurring of boundaries can lead to one of the forms of domination and submission Benjamin describes: the self can surrender totally to the will and agency of the other, or the self can consume and appropriate the other as part of itself, as an object of its
possession.

The repetition of the word "mine" in the monologues of
Sethe, Denver, and Beloved suggests exactly this sort of possession and incorporation of the other as an object. "Mine" is the
haunting word that Stamp Paid hears surrounding Sethe's
house in ghostly whispers and is stressed again in a lyrical section following Beloved's unpunctuated monologue. In this section the voices of Beloved, Sethe, and Denver are joined (the
identity of the speaker in each line is sometimes unclear) while
at the same time each voice remains essentially isolated (the
voices speak to but not *with* each other):

> Beloved
> You are my sister
> You are my daughter
> You are my face; you are me
> I have found you again; you have come back to me
> You are my Beloved
> You are mine
> You are mine
> You are mine   (216)

This form of possessing and objectifying the other, however,
cannot satisfy—it imprisons the self within its own devouring
omnipotence, its own narcissism. True satisfaction or joy, as
Benjamin explains, can only be achieved through "mutual

recognition" between self and other, between two subjects or selves.

Both sides of the power dynamic, both surrender to and incorporation of the other, are apparent in the relationship between Sethe and Beloved. Toward the end of the novel, Sethe relinquishes herself completely to the will and desire of Beloved. She neglects to feed or care for herself and becomes physically drained and emotionally depleted. Sethe literally shrinks while Beloved literally expands and swells; both are caught up in a mutually destructive, frighteningly boundless narcissism. The prelude to Sethe's decline is an incident that again stresses lack of recognition at the source of this narcissistic condition. Sethe has been abandoned once again, this time by Paul D (her previous abandonments include those by her mother, her husband Halle, Baby Suggs, and her two sons), and to cheer herself, she takes Denver and Beloved ice-skating on the frozen creek. The three are unable to keep their balance, and as they fall on the ice, they shriek with both pain and laughter. The scene is redolent of childhood and of childlike helplessness. "Making a circle or a line, the three of them could not stay upright for one whole minute, but nobody saw them falling" (174). The phrase "nobody saw them falling" becomes the dominant motif of the scene; the line is repeated four times in the two-page description. Sethe's laughter turns into uncontrollable tears and her weeping in the context of the scene's refrain suggests a child's aching sense of loss or absence, specifically the absence of the confirming, legitimizing gaze of the other.

Once it is asserted that "nobody saw" her falling, that there is no "other" to confer the reality of her own existence on her, Sethe falls prey to a consuming narcissism. Suddenly she consciously recognizes Beloved as the incarnation of her dead child and surrenders herself totally to her. Sethe now feels that "there is no world outside" her door (184) and that since her daughter has come back, "she can sleep like the drowned" (204). In psychological terms, she retreats from external reality and succumbs to her destructive, narcissistic fantasies, to her murderously enraged child-self as well as her insatiable need to make reparation for her murderous love. Paul D recognizes, and fears, the narcissistic nature of Sethe's love: "This here new Sethe didn't know where the world stopped and she began . . . more important than what Sethe had done was what she claimed. It scared him" (164).

Paul D is the one character in the novel who has the

power to resist and disrupt the destructive, narcissistic mother-child dyad. Sethe recalls, "There was no room for any other thing or body until Paul D arrived and broke up the place, making room, shifting it, moving it over to someplace else, then standing in the place he had made" (39). Sethe also tells Beloved that she would have recognized her "right off, except for Paul D" (203). Paul D is the external "other" who triangulates the dyad, as the image of the "three shadows" of Sethe, Denver, and Paul D "holding hands" as they walk to the carnival emphasizes (47). The excursion to the carnival is Sethe's first venture into the community since the murder; Paul D has the capacity to lead Sethe out of her narcissistic isolation and into relationship with the external world. The claims of the angry baby Beloved, however, are still too powerful to allow for these other attachments: she makes her first appearance in the flesh immediately following the excursion.

While Paul D plays the role of the saving other in contradistinction to Beloved and the narcissistic dyad, he does not represent the typical world of the father. He is not, for instance, a token of male rationality countering the irrationality of the female world. He too is deeply affected by Beloved's irrational power—she literally "moves" him, making him physically restless and forcing him to sleep with her in the shed outside the house. His power lies precisely in his maternal, nurturing quality; he is that "other" with the power to recognize and affirm the inner or essential self. He is described as "the kind of man who could walk into a house and make the women cry. Because with him, in his presence, they could" (17). The women see him and not only want to weep; they also want to confess their deepest secrets, to expose all the pain and rage bound up with their true selves. Sethe thinks of how he "cradled her before the cooking stove" and is deeply comforted by "the mind of him that knew her own" (99).

Paul D has the power to satisfy the craving that fuels the novel, the craving to be "known," to have one's existence sanctioned by the empathic recognition of the other. That Morrison bestows this quality on an African-American male character is an interesting, and unusual, point. A common criticism of black women novelists is that their portrayals of black males are often flat, stereotypic, or unempathic. For Morrison, the maternal nurturing quality is a form of love that is not restricted by gender; this view expands the possibilities, and is a liberating factor,

for her characters. Yet Paul D, too, is not a totally reliable other:
he temporarily retreats after learning of Sethe's murder of her
child. Like all of the other black characters in the novel, he must
work out of a condition of psychic fragmentation—his selfhood
has been severely impaired, his status as a human subject denied
by the slave culture. He feels that even the old rooster Mister
was allowed an essential integrity of being denied him: "Mister
was allowed to be and stay what he was. But I wasn't allowed to
be and stay what I was. Even if you cooked him you'd be cooking a rooster named Mister. But wasn't no way I'd ever be Paul
D again, living or dead" (72).

Only Denver does not see Paul D as the other women do;
for her he does not play the same nurturing role. She sees him
only as a threat, as an intruder into her intense, and deeply ambivalent, relationship with her mother. Denver is terrified of
Sethe's murderous love: she has "monstrous and unmanageable
dreams about Sethe" (103) and is afraid to fall asleep while Sethe
braids her hair at night. In her fantasies, "She cut my head off
every night" (206). For Denver, the idealized, saving other is her
father Halle, whom she calls "Angel Man." Yet the father is significantly incapable of playing the savior role. The "other"—
whether represented by mother or father—is always untrust-
worthy in Morrison's world, rendered thus by the social environment. As a result, the self remains trapped within its own
destructive narcissism.

Sethe regards Halle as the ultimate betrayer: he witnessed
her rape, she learns, but did not protest or try to protect her. His
absent presence is worse than mere absence, for it confirms an
essential hollowness and undependability of the other and of
love. Yet Halle is not simply a "bad guy"; again, Morrison extends her compassion equally to her male characters. The reader
is allowed to see Halle too as a deeply wounded child. Traumatized by the rape of Sethe and the maternal violation that it also
represents, Halle literally loses his mind—his selfhood shatters.
Paul D observes him later squatting by a churn, with "butter all
over his face" (69). He smeared that butter on his face, Sethe
thinks, "because the milk they took is on his mind" (70). The
image of Halle here recalls Beloved and the image at the psychological base of the book: it is the picture of a lost, greedy child
whose ravenous hunger/love is out of control.

Ultimately Denver is able to escape the narcissistic vacuum, and she is helped not, as she had fantasized, by Halle, but

by another maternal figure in the novel, Mrs. Jones. Denver is first propelled out of the house by literal hunger, for Sethe, locked in her obsession with Beloved, has become oblivious to food and to all external or physical considerations. Denver realizes that "it was she who had to step off the edge of the world and die because if she didn't, they all would" (239). Excluded from the Beloved-Sethe dyad, Denver is forced into the role of the outside other, and assuming that role is her salvation. She goes first to her former teacher Lady Jones, an old woman of mixed race who has long struggled with the contempt of the black community and, equally, with self-contempt. Lady Jones thus has a special "affection for the unpicked children" (247), an empathy with those, like Denver, who have never been recognized or "picked," who have never had their existence validated or confirmed. After Denver asks her for food, Mrs. Jones compassionately croons, "Oh, baby," and that empathic recognition of the hungry baby within finally frees Denver from the trap of her infantile needs: "Denver looked up at her. She did not know it then, but it was the word 'baby,' said softly and with such kindness, that inaugurated her life in the world as a woman" (248).

With this recognition, Denver for the first time begins to experience the contours of her own separate self. When Nelson Lord, an old school acquaintance, affectionately says, "Take care of yourself, Denver," Denver "heard it as though it were what language was made for," and she realizes that "It was a new thought, having a self to look out for and preserve" (252). Self-recognition is inextricably tied up with self-love, and this is precisely the message of the sermons that Baby Suggs preaches to her people in the Clearing. In a white society that does not recognize or love you, she tells them, you must fight to recognize and love yourself:

> 'Here,' she said, 'in this here place, we flesh; flesh
> that weeps, laughs; flesh that dances on bare feet in
> grass. Love it. Love it hard. Yonder they do not love
> your flesh. They despise it. They don't love your eyes;
> they'd just as soon pick em out. . . . Love your hands!
> Love them. Raise them up and kiss them. Touch others
> with them, pat them together, stroke them on your race
> 'cause they don't love that either. *You* got to love it,
> *you*!'   (88)

Baby Suggs continues to enjoin her people to love every ap-
pendage, every organ in their bodies, and especially to "love
your heart." This is the crucial lesson, but it cannot be learned in
isolation; self-love needs a relational foundation and a social
context. Thus even Baby Suggs is unable to sustain her convictions and heed her own teachings. After Sethe's murder, Baby
Suggs retreats and ceases to care about herself or others, showing
interest in nothing except "colors."

   Morrison's novel, however, is not hopelessly bleak or despairing. Her characters are wounded, but not all of them are ru-
ined. Denver and Paul D, by courageously facing their inner ter-
rors—Denver leaves the house even though she expects to be
"swallowed up," and Paul D returns to Sethe and her fearful,
murderous love—are able to salvage out of the wreckage a bol-
stering faith in both self and other. Paul D tries to pass this faith
on to Sethe at the end. He assumes again a maternal, nurturing
role. He holds Sethe, calls her "baby," and gently tells her not to
cry. Beloved is gone and Sethe feels bereft and lost: "She was my
best thing" (272), she tells Paul D. He "leans over and takes her
hand. With the other he touches her face. 'You your best thing,
Sethe. You are.' His holding fingers are holding hers" (273).[3]
While the word "thing" still suggests a sense of self as object (an
objectification of self that perhaps no black person in the slave
culture could ever totally escape), the scene between Sethe and
Paul D at the end comes closest to that state of mutual recognition and attunement that Benjamin describes. Paul D's gently
touching Sethe's face recalls the touching faces of the mating turtles; the relationship here is not one of merging or of domination but of resonating "likeness" and empathic understanding.
Paul D recalls Sixo's description of his mistress, the "Thirty-Mile
Woman": "She is a friend of my mind. She gather me, man.
The pieces I am, she gather them and give them back to me in all
the right order. It's good, you know, when you got a woman
who is a friend of your mind" (272-273). The beloved other has
the power to give to the self its own essential wholeness. The
role of the other here is neither as an object to possess nor even
as a mirror for the self; as a "friend of [the] mind," the other is a
subject in its own right, with an inner life that corresponds with
that of the self. In such correspondence, in that mutuality of inner experience and suffering, lies the self-confirming and consol-
ing power of the relationship.

   Paul D tells Sethe in this final scene that "He wants to put his story next to hers" (273). Throughout the novel, stories and storytelling are associated with the self and with the primary oral relationship at its root.[4] Beloved is tireless in her demand, in "her thirst for hearing" Sethe's stories: "It became a way to feed her . . . Sethe learned the profound satisfaction Beloved got from storytelling" (58). Denver too feeds Beloved's craving for stories about Sethe, "nursing Beloved's interest like a lover whose pleasure was to overfeed the loved" (78). Denver's storytelling, because of the empathic identification it involves, also allows her to feel a closer bond and oneness with her mother. As she narrates the tale of Sethe's escape to Beloved, "Denver was seeing it now and feeling it—through Beloved. Feeling how it must have felt to her mother" (78). Paul D does not want to merge or incorporate Sethe's story into his own at the end; rather, he wants to "put his story next to hers." This suggests again an essential maintenance of boundaries, a balance of two like but separate selves, an attunement.

The novel does not end, however, with the scene between Sethe and Paul D, but with one last lyrical section on Beloved. The refrain of the last two pages is the line, repeated three times: "It was not a story to pass on." The final section arouses a deep sense of pathos for that unrecognized, ravenously needy infant-self that is Beloved:

> Everybody knew what she was called, but nobody anywhere knew her name. Disremembered and unaccounted for, she cannot be lost because no one is looking for her, and even if they were, how can they call her if they don't know her name? Although she has claim, she is not claimed. In the place where long grass opens, the girl who waited to be loved and cry shame erupts into her separate parts, to make it easy for the chewing laughter to swallow her all away.
> It was not a story to pass on.   (274)

The poignancy of Beloved's story/self is that it is *not* a story/self. She has been denied the narrative of her being, the subjectivity and continuity of inner experience that should be everyone's birthright. Beloved's desolation, her sorrow, is a more extreme version of the same sorrow that all of the black characters in the novel experience. Thus Baby Suggs, finally freed from slavery, expresses not the elation of freedom but the deep sadness of not knowing her self, of not being able to read her own story: "The sadness was at her center, the desolated cen-

ter where the self that was no self made its home. Sad as it was
that she did not know where her children were buried or what
they looked like if alive, fact was she knew more about them
than she knew about herself, having never had the map to discover what she was like" (140). In the end, the novel is more
about Beloved than Sethe. Beloved's character is both the frame
and center of the book, and it is her story—or her desperate
struggle to know and experience her own story—that is the
pumping heart of the novel. Beloved's struggle is Sethe's struggle; it is also Denver's, Paul D's, and Baby Suggs's. It is the struggle of all black people in a racist society, Morrison suggests, to
claim themselves as subjects in their own narrative.

    Beloved demonstrates, finally, the interconnection of so-
cial and intrapsychic reality. The novel plays out the deep psychic reverberations of living in a culture in which domination
and objectification of the self have been institutionalized. If
from the earliest years on, one's fundamental need to be recognized and affirmed as a human subject is denied, that need can
take on fantastic and destructive proportions in the inner world:
the intense hunger, the fantasized fear of either being swallowed
or exploding, can tyrannize one's life even when one is freed
from the external bonds of oppression. The self cannot experience freedom without first experiencing its own agency or, in
Sethe's words, "claiming ownership" of itself. The free, autonomous self, *Beloved* teaches, is an inherently social self,
rooted in relationship and dependent at its core on the vital
bond of mutual recognition.

Notes

[1] Object relations theory began with Melanie Klein's pioneering work
on the earliest, preoedipal dynamics of the mother-child relationship. For a
good explication and overview of her work, see Segal. For other influential
perspectives in British object relations theory, see Fairbairn, Guntrip, and
Winnicott.

[2] Madonne Miner sees Cholly's rape of Pecola as arising out of his desperate desire for recognition, for "confirmation of his presence" (179). This
reading again supports Benjamin's thesis about the deep intertwining of love,
recognition, and domination. Miner also discusses identity issues in *The Bluest
Eye* in terms of a "constantly shifting balance between seeing and being seen"
and the "distortion of this visual balance" (184) that sexism and racism create.

[3] The emphasis here on Paul D's "holding" quality calls to mind D. W.

Winnicott's argument about the need for the mother to provide a reliable and protective "holding environment" for the infant. Such "holding" forms the basis for trust in both self and world. See Winnicott 43-44.

[4] Stories and storytelling figure prominently in the fiction of many black women writers, and their significance is rooted historically in the slave narrative and in the rich folk tradition of black culture. See Willis for a historically informed rhetorical analysis of how the black oral tradition shapes narrative form in black women's fiction; see Skerrett for a discussion of storytelling in *Song of Solomon*. My depth psychological analysis of the function of stories in *Beloved* is compatible with and can complement historical, sociological, and rhetorical perspectives.

Works Cited

Benjamin, Jessica. *The Bonds of Love: Psychoanalysis, Feminism, and the Problem of Domination.* New York: Pantheon, 1988.

Chodorow, Nancy. *The Reproduction of Mothering: Psychoanalysis and the Sociology of Gender.* Berkeley: University of California Press, 1978.

Fairbairn, Ronald. *Psychoanalytic Studies of the Personality.* London: Routledge, 1952.

Gilligan, Carol. *In a Different Voice: Psychological Theory and Women's Development.* Cambridge: Harvard University Press, 1982.

Guntrip, Harry. *Schizoid Phenomena, Object Relations, and the Self.* New York: International Universities Press, 1969.

Klein, Melanie. *Envy and Gratitude and Other Works, 1946-1963.* New York: Dell, 1975.

Kohut, Heinz. *The Analysis of the Self.* New York: International Universities Press, 1971.

Miner, Madonne M. "Lady No Longer Sings the Blues: Rape, Madness, and Silence in *The Bluest Eye.*" *Conjuring: Black Women, Fiction, and Literary Tradition.* Ed. Marjorie Pryse and Hortense J. Spillers. Bloomington: Indiana University Press, 1985.

Morrison. Toni. *Beloved.* New York: New American Library, 1987.

—. *The Bluest Eye.* New York: Washington Square Press, 170.

—. *Sula.* New York: New American Library, 1973.

Segal, Hannah. *Introduction to the Work of Melanie Klein.* London: Hogarth and the Institute of Psycho-Analysis, 1973.

Skerrett, Joseph T. "Recitation to the Griot: Storytelling and Learning in Toni Morrison's *Song of Solomon.*" *Conjuring: Black Women, Fiction, and Literary Tradition.* Ed. Marjorie Pryse and Hortense J. Spillers. Bloomington: Indiana University Press, 1985. 192-202.

Wessling, Joseph. "Narcissism in Toni Morrison's *Sula.*" *College Language Association Journal* 31 (1988): 281-298.

Willis, Susan. *Specifying: Black Women Writing the American Experience.* Madison: University of Wisconsin Press, 1987.

Winnicott, D. W. *The Maturational Processes and the Facilitating Environment.* New York: International Universities Press, 1965.

"I Love to Tell the Story": Biblical Revisions in *Beloved*[1]

Carolyn A. Mitchell

> At first I said, "I will not bear
> His cross upon my back;
> He only seeks to place it there
> Because my skin is black."
> Countee Cullen,
> "Simon the Cyrenian Speaks"

> Who his own self bare our
> sins in his own body on the tree,
> that we, being dead to sins,
> should live unto righteousness:
> by whose stripes ye were healed.
> 1 Peter 2.24

> But a certain Samaritan, as he
> journeyed, came where he was: and
> when he saw him, he had compassion
> on him. . . .
> Luke 10.13

> For after that in the wisdom of God
> the world by wisdom knew not God,
> it pleased God by the foolishness
> of preaching to save them that believe.
> 1 Cor. 1.21

In Toni Morrison's novel, *Beloved*, three events, among others, compel the reader to think more deeply about the complex issues of African-American spirituality and Christianity. These events, crucial to my reading of the story, are the discovery of the "tree" Sethe carries on her back, the brief relationship between Sethe and Amy Denver (the white woman who discovers the tree), and the "Calling" of Baby Suggs to preach. These instances in the text raise important questions about the nature of African-American spirituality and religion, questions whose tentative answers address on one level the critical issue of African-Americans embracing Christianity, the religion of the slaveholders. The text suggests ways in which this same religion, refigured as heterodox through African-American suffering, is the source of liberation for the black community; and through Amy Denver's ministrations to the suffering Sethe, the white community's potential for liberation is also suggested.

The episodes mentioned above are seminal to the novel because Morrison refigures three gospel stories which are central to Christian hermeneutics: the carrying of the Cross (the tree on Sethe's back), the parable of the Good Samaritan (Amy Denver's healing of Sethe), and the call to preach the Gospel (the ministry of Baby Suggs).[2] Morrison, as I will argue, eliminates the distance between doctrine and practice by first telling of unspeakable things unspoken[3] is she revises the story of the life of Christ in the context of slavery. Christ's life provides a model for spiritual liberation which has continuing implications for understanding African-American history and the impact of this history on contemporary black life. Christ laid the foundation of a liberatory plan that must be activated and completed by us. This foundation is based on the interconnectedness of the spiritual and material, since our role as humans is to contain both spirit and flesh, and because we are bound by and to history as custodians of the earth. Morrison's revision presents a new perspective on an "old, old story" that has yet to be concluded.

The significance of this story has important implications for the past and present: *Beloved* reminds us that the Spirit is still among us, moving us in extraordinary ways; we are reminded, too, that the African-American story has not yet been fully told and that a major part of that telling rests in the interpretation of religion and spirituality in black life.

The distance between the "standard" version of the three New Testament stories and Toni Morrison's refiguring of them is the distance between religion and spirituality. My premise here is that religion is structured on doctrine and dogma, which is maintained by ritual. Religious belief and practice are subject to historical, social, and cultural change, and are tradition-bound. Spirit and spirituality, however, are the unchanging foundations of religion. Spirit is the nonanthropomorphic God and spirituality is godliness; religion is one way (but not the only way) to express the presence of both in human life.

The differences between religion and spirituality cannot be defined to suit all readers. Yet, the premise of this essay is that the distinctions are important. Religion is the worship of God; Spirit is God; spirituality is the individual manifestation of God in everyday life and experience. Spirituality creates an authentic relationship to one's own life, calling one to be wholly present in and accountable for this life. Thus, for example, Sethe, thinking she was on free ground, never expected to be apprehended by the slaveholder and returned to bondage. So palpable to her is freedom as life's only real option that she kills her daughter, Beloved. She later negotiates a tombstone for Beloved's grave— "Ten minutes for seven letters. With another ten could she have gotten 'Dearly' too?" (5). Though reprehensible on a religious level, Sethe's actions are profoundly spiritual, given the moral aberration of slavery, and Morrison dares the reader to condemn Sethe for her decisions. One may abhor the need Sethe feels of taking life to save life and decry the bartering of her body for a tombstone, but implicit in Sethe's actions is the understanding that simply to embrace physical life at any cost is not freedom. She knows that physical and spiritual freedom are inseparable and slavery violates both. Thus, spirituality can be perceived as a "sliding scale" and Sethe must negotiate her own soul's salvation based on her specific experiences. The paradox in this is that she must make choices where all the options are problematic.

Sethe's negotiations are examples of Cornel West's terms, "passionate physicality" and "combative spirituality" (28), terms which describe the tangible struggle between body and soul—not as the traditional religious battle of one to overcome the other, but the more challenging struggle of the two to work in tandem with each other. West's terms suggest the essential nature of spirituality as opposed to religion, where dogma and ritual circumscribe the heterodoxy that reveals the workings of Spirit in the exigencies and expediencies of everyday life. Religion is what one "does" on Sunday; spirituality is the extraordinary response to the demands of the unknown arising in daily life. Morrison refigures traditional Christian stories using the history of African-American enslavement; the reader must understand the concept of the Spirit still working in human life and history as a partial key to the complexity of Morrison's narrative.

The first scene that Morrison refigures is that in which Amy Denver discovers Sethe's mutilated back. Amy says,

> 'It's a tree, Lu. A chokecherry tree. See, here's the
> trunk—it's red and split wide open, full of sap, and this
> here's the parting for the branches. You got a mighty
> lot of branches. Leaves, too, look like, and dern if these
> ain't blossoms. Tiny little cherry blossoms, just as
> white. Your back got a whole tree on it. In bloom.
> What God have in mind, I wonder. . . .'   (79)

Amy prefaces her "reading" of Sethe's back with the words, "Come here, Jesus" (79). Her words link Sethe's tree to the cross of Christ, calling him to come and witness. If Christ's cross represents the sins of humankind, then Sethe's cross represents the sins of slavery. Since Sethe "carries" the cross, she is Christ. Morrison, in this narrative moment, redefines transubstantiation, making it more than the transformation of bread and wine into the body and blood of Christ, the ritual celebration of the Last Supper, as I suggest below.[4] The tree on Sethe's back unites the literal and figurative meaning of this commemoration, reminding us that the ritual is empty without "re-memory" (Morrison's own refrain used throughout the novel) of the suffering. Spiritual re-memory is acute for Sethe, whose pain physically re-members that of Christ. Her carrying the cross is different from that depicted in religious ritual because Sethe is "real" and both her spirit and body are permanently wounded. Amy's invocation, "Come here, Jesus," is a signal that she is a witness calling Jesus to see his cross reincarnated in and on Sethe. It is also Amy's involuntary invitation to the Christ-spirit to indwell in her as she aids Sethe. As I show later, Amy's action is the means by which she transcends the mores of the slavocracy that have tainted her life, too.

Morrison re-positions the journey to Calvary in the historical present, implying that the cross is carried by some humans as long as suffering exists. The conflation of Christ-life/human-life as a continuum is therefore suggested. Sethe's Calvary will be to murder her daughter, Beloved, for she certainly did die figuratively in her attempt to give Beloved life. In both instances, death is the price paid for freedom. This interpretation presents Christ's suffering as the suffering of a woman, conflating the two. Traditionally, the relevance of the Christ life

to the lives of women is so circumscribed by canonical interpretation that Mary Daly, the feminist theologian, eliminates Jesus
as a useful, relevant model for women. Daly writes:

> The qualities that Christianity *idealizes*, especially
> for women, are also those of a victim: sacrificial love,
> passive acceptance of suffering, humility, meekness,
> etc. Since these are the qualities idealized in Jesus
> 'who died for our sins,' his functioning as a model rein-
> forces the scapegoat syndrome for women. Given the
> victimized situation of the female in sexist society,
> these 'virtues' are hardly the qualities that women
> should be encouraged to have. Moreover, since women
> cannot be 'good' enough to measure up to this ideal, and
> since all are by sexual definition alien from the male
> savior, this is an impossible model. Thus doomed to
> failure even in emulating the Victim, women are
> plunged more deeply into victimization.   (77)

Daly's thoughts prompt me to consider the ways in which
African-Americans claim Christianity, suggesting new possibilities for doctrinal interpretation.

Contrary to Mary Daly's critique is the fact that for Sethe,
an African-American woman virtually broken by slavery, "emu-
lating the Victim" is not the issue. Sethe is the victim; the cross
she carries is at the same time literal and figurative. Her pain is
both enactment and reenactment, the merging of present and
past action, the price paid now by Sethe, embodying the price
paid then by Christ. This is what I mean by transubstantiation.
Two significant issues are evident here. One is the "materializ-
ing" of transubstantiation in the tree brutally whipped into
Sethe's back. The other is the co-joining of Sethe and Amy
Denver into a community of two, both now realized as the
Christ who "lives and dies" anew in each moment of human
suffering. Sethe and Amy are linked in different, but common
sufferings; their brief bond renews the Christ life as the life of
woman, two lives in which the horrors of racism and sexism
meld, providing them both with the opportunity for transcendence. Amy speaks to the extent of Sethe's beating by commenting on her own beating, thus joining female experiences—poor
white to poor slave, the example of transcending the slavocracy
mentioned earlier. Amy says,

> 'Your back got a whole tree on it. In bloom. What God
> have in mind, I wonder. *I had me some whippings, but I
> don't remember nothing like this.* Mr. Buddy had a
> right evil hand too. Whip you for looking at him
> straight. Sure would. I looked right at him one time
> and he hauled off and threw the poker at me. Guess he
> knew what I was a-thinking.'   (79, emphasis mine)

Another way, therefore, to look at Mary Daly's problems with
the "Victim" and victimization is to remember that in embodying suffering, Christians embody Christ who then becomes for
them more than an abstraction. Taken from the perspective of
an African-American woman like Sethe, this embodiment is not
symbolic, but literal. Though doctrine teaches us to believe that
the historical Christ was male and fully realized as depicted in
the Gospels, reviewing this text through Morrison's artistic eye
allows a broader spiritual reinterpretation which enhances the
orthodox religious interpretation.

Yet, doctrinal revision is central to *Beloved* because the
fictional rendering of African-American historical struggle conflates the secular and the sacred, a tradition that shapes significant moments in black life. Since Sethe is a slave and her suffering is uniquely female—she is robbed of her baby's milk by
schoolteacher's nephews, who force her to suckle them—she
bears the twin crosses of racism and sexism. The "cross" on her
back gains additional significance as she recounts her story for
Paul D, one of the slaves from the plantation, Sweet Home,
where schoolteacher is overseer. Sethe says,

> 'After I left you, those boys came in there and took
> my milk. That's what they came in there for. Held me
> down and took it. I told Mrs. Garner [the mistress of
> Sweet Home] on em. She had that lump and couldn't
> speak but her eyes rolled out tears. Them boys found out
> I told on em. Schoolteacher made one open up my back,
> and when it closed it made a tree. It grows there still.'
> 'They used cowhide on you?'
> 'And they took my milk."
> 'They beat you and you was pregnant?'
> 'And they took my milk!'   (16-17)

Paul D is fixated on the fact that Sethe was whipped, even
though she was pregnant; Sethe, herself, is more focused on the
violation of that which is the center of her female-
ness/womanness—the theft of her milk. This theft is testament

to how little the humanity of the slave woman and her child are valued. Yet, schoolteacher will punish the nephew responsible for scarring Sethe so badly because he has destroyed property and she is damaged goods, proof of which (according to schoolteacher) is in the murder of Beloved (149-151). What I interpret as an example of "combative spirituality" he interprets as cannibalism, justifying to himself the "moral discipline" of slavery. Ironically, the contradictions in his assessment of Sethe's lack of humanity are lost on him.[5] The tree on Sethe's back is the physical re-memory of her suffering, as well as that of her people. This tree is intended to help the reader understand why Beloved's death at her mother's hand is preferable to bondage. As Sethe so poignantly says to Paul D years later, "It grows there still" (17), suggesting again the Christ-human continuum of suffering.

Amy Denver is Christ, too; like Sethe, her life is not an emulation, but an embodiment of his. She is the Good Samaritan whose attention to the victim robbed and abandoned by the roadside earned him a place in biblical history. Amy does not falter when called to aid and abet a fugitive slave, or touch a mutilated black woman, or bring new black life into the world. She drags Sethe back to life, using spider-webs to ease her back, massaging circulation into her damaged feet, and delivering her baby. Proactive Christianity provides the tension that undercuts passive emulation and dissimulation. Amy's religion is eminently present, representing her sense of urgency and agency. Sethe owes her life to Amy, who is irreversibly linked to black life, both through her own suffering and through her surname, Denver, which the grateful Sethe gives to her newborn daughter.

Sethe's suffering is the site of renewal for Amy—a white woman who strikes an effective blow against slavery. Her action is another reason why Sethe knows the potential value of freedom, represented here in a healing touch and in human interaction with a white woman, who extends "loving kindness," actively accepting the challenge of the Christ example in her life.

The reasons why Amy is in flight are curious. On one level her journey to Boston to purchase velvet seems frivolous when compared to Sethe's quest for freedom. Yet, one of Morrison's strengths as a storyteller lies in her ability to suggest plausibility in a vignette such as this. Since Amy is the link between life and death for Sethe, the reader intuits that she must want more for herself than velvet because she gives so unstintingly to Sethe. She is not superficial, though her chatter may suggest this. Amy's life is circumscribed by gender and class, just as Sethe's is by gender and race. Though Amy seems to move more freely than Sethe, Morrison invites us to consider the ways in which Amy's life as a single, young white woman, a fugitive from indentured servitude, is comparable to (but not the same as) Sethe's. Morrison is positively lyrical in her description of the commonality between Sethe and Amy:

> On a riverbank in the cool of a summer evening two women struggled under a shower of silvery blue. They never expected to see each other again in this world and at the moment couldn't care less. But there on a summer night surrounded by bluefern they did something together appropriately and well. A pateroller passing would have sniggered to see two throw-away people, two lawless outlaws—a slave and a barefoot whitewoman with unpinned hair—wrapping a ten-minute-old baby in the rags they wore. But no pateroller came and no preacher. The water sucked and swallowed itself beneath them. There was nothing to disturb them at their work. So they did it appropriately and well.   (84-85)[6]

Amy's quest for velvet makes sense in the context of a Spirit which prompts her to action that is not "normal" for a white woman of her time. We simply cannot account logically for Amy Denver's fixation on velvet, but we do know that this fixation represents freedom for her. The important point is her decision to go to Boston in the first place. The ability to move from bondage to freedom is what Amy and Sethe have in common. On this manifestation of courage to step out in faith rests the mutuality in which we see them literally refigured as female Christs.

Toni Morrison slips into *Beloved* a refiguration from the story of Huckleberry Finn and Jim, the runaway slave, floating down the Mississippi River on the raft. Amy, however, is going East to Boston in search of velvet and all it connotes—not West to the territory, like Huck. The conflation of the two stories is suggested in Morrison's description of Sethe and Amy on the river, in Amy's innate sense of moral and ethical values which parallel Huck's decision to stand by Jim even though Huck believes he will go to hell, and in the spunk and determination of character reflected in Amy's parting words to Sethe.[7]

> Twilight came on and Amy said she had to go; that
> she wouldn't be caught dead in daylight on a busy river
> with a runaway. After rinsing her hands and face in the
> river, she stood and looked down at the baby wrapped
> and tied to Sethe's chest.
>   'She's never gonna know who I am. You gonna tell
> her? Who brought her into this here world?' She lifted
> her chin, looked off into the place where the sun used to
> be. 'You better tell her. You hear? Say Miss Amy Den-
> ver. Of Boston.'   (85)

Going to Boston to buy velvet is a trope for female adventure,
for the rite of passage, for the realization of larger aspirations.
The fact that rites of passage turn on moral/ethical dilemmas as
well as on physical adversity is important, and Amy passes both
tests.

Baby Suggs is Sethe's mother-in-law and though "un-
called, unrobed, and unanointed" (87) she preaches after answering the call of the Spirit. Slavery has "busted her legs, back, head,
eyes, hands, kidneys, womb and tongue" (87), leaving only her
heart. Following the call of her heart and acting out the "fool-
ishness" of the preacher alluded to in First Corinthians 1.21, she
collects the scattered members of the slave community, and restores them to themselves by teaching them first to love themselves anew and then to love one another. Baby Suggs gives the
people back the preciousness of their tears and laughter; she
gives them back their feelings—the first step toward restoration
of the human qualities stolen from them by slavery.[8] Baby
Suggs says,"'Let the children come!' and they ran from the trees
toward her" (87):

> 'Let your mother hear you laugh,' she told them,
> and the woods rang. The adults looked on and could not
> help smiling.
>   Then, 'Let the grown men come,' she shouted. They
> stepped out one by one from among the ringing trees.
>   'Let your wives and your children see you dance,'
> she told them, and groundlife shuddered under their
> feet.
>   Finally she called the women to her. 'Cry,' she told
> them. 'For the living and the dead. Just cry.' And with-
> out covering their eyes the women let loose.   (87-88)

Morrison is clear about the limits of religious dogma here as she tells us what Baby Suggs did and did not tell the people:

> She did not tell them to clean up their lives or to go and sin no more. She did not tell them they were the blessed of the earth, its inheriting meek or its glory-bound pure.
>
> She told them that the only grace they could have was the grace they could imagine. That if they could not see it, they would not have it.   (88)

Baby Suggs's ministry is a refiguration of Christ's public life, of his gift of life to the dispossessed of his time (and the model for our time). Though the faces of the dispossessed change, as do the specific circumstances of their poverty, their pain does not change. In Morrison's revisioning of this biblical moment, Baby Suggs provides what the letter of religious and civil law cannot. She gives the people the spiritual space to reclaim the Self, which is the God-Spirit that links each of them to their human selves, and to one another. In this, she assumes her own responsibility to be Christ and heal the people.

The story of Baby Suggs's ministry is, like the story of Amy Denver's healing ability, a vignette; its fullness is in what it alludes to, but does not say. Morrison chooses a woman to restore the spiritual lives of the ex-slaves, but she models her character after the life of the one person women (in most denominations) are told they cannot emulate in ordained ministry. However, Morrison suggests that the religion of the called, the robed, the anointed is insufficient to address the needs of those human beings who survived slavery.

Baby Suggs preaches "liberation spirituality," Vincent Harding's inspired term, which suggests the difference between "overcoming" as opposed to "just surviving" adversity. Harding sees the "resources of religion, freedom, justice [as] fundamental contextualizations of our [African-American] spirituality." According to Harding, liberation spirituality signifies the movement of God among the people, especially in the African-American context of Spirit possession kindled by congress and communion with others.[9] Baby Suggs, in appropriating the authority of the ordained minister, activates the spirit of God in and among the people, filling the void left in them by the prostitution of the Word in the aberration of slavery.

Baby Suggs restores the beloved community, and prepares

the people to withstand the pain experienced in the restoration of Self/self in re-memory.[10]   As Harding would say, she reteaches the people "the dance of life": they "enter in and out of one another's experience and as they pass through they are affected by and deeply altered by" the experience. Morrison's text supports Harding's exegesis:

> laughing children, dancing men, crying women and then it got mixed up. Women stopped crying and danced; men sat down and cried; children danced, women laughed, children cried until, exhausted and riven, all and each lay about the Clearing damp and gasping for breath. In the silence that followed, Baby Suggs, holy, offered up to them her great big heart.   (88)

In dancing and crying until "exhausted and riven," the people experience "the wildness of the divine," Harding's definitive explanation of liberation spirituality.

The irresolution at the conclusion of each of the stories revised by Morrison precludes strict comparison with the biblical stories cited, avoiding the danger of essentializing African-American history and religion. The lack of closure suggests that none of the stories has ended, neither the biblical, the historical, nor the fictional. The power in non-closure is that the dogmatism of the biblical paradigm is loosened by the fluidity of spiritual interception. The novel self-reflexively aligns with the Bible, challenging traditional interpretations by placing the secular and sacred in necessary tension. Indeed, the narrative structure of *Beloved* relies on this tension.

For example, if, as I suggest, Sethe's Calvary is the murder of Beloved, then the issue of Sethe's resurrection remains irresolvably vexed and the momentum of the novel depends on this and other physical/psychological/spiritual contradictions. We tend to forget in focusing on Beloved's death that Sethe attempts to kill all her children. However, she only wounds her sons, Howard and Buglar; and Stamp Paid manages to rescue the twenty-eight-day-old Denver. Sethe frees Beloved from slavery, but in the process imprisons Denver, Howard and Buglar (who leave home to escape the ghostly Beloved), Baby Suggs (from the end of her ministry up to her death), and herself in a house haunted by Beloved. Isolated freedom in a haunted house is better than chattel slavery, but it is hardly an ideal life and Morrison shows us the price each person pays for such vexed freedom.

Everyone at 124 Bluestone Road, literally enslaved by the ghost
of Beloved, pays an extraordinarily high price for freedom: psychological breakdown, spiritual isolation, and social marginalization. Though buried decently, Beloved refuses to stay buried;
Morrison asks implicitly: Who is to avenge her death? Paradoxically, only Sethe can avenge Beloved's death. But Sethe does
not succeed in doing so and Beloved's ghost is with us yet. She
is the unresolved remnant of slavery in the novel and in contemporary society. The people in the story try to forget her, but
she is not forgotten. Morrison speaks for Beloved, her family,
and for us:

> So they forgot her. Like an unpleasant dream dur-
> ing a troubling sleep. Occasionally, however, the rustle
> of skirt hushes when they wake, and the knuckles
> brushing a cheek in sleep seem to belong to the
> sleeper. . . .
> This is not a story to pass on.
> Down by the stream in back of 124 her footprints
> come and go, come and go. They are so familiar. Should
> a child, an adult place his feet in them, they will fit.
> Take them out and they disappear again as though no-
> body ever walked there.
> By and by all trace is gone, and what is forgotten is
> not only the footprints but the water too and what it is
> down there. . . .   (275)

Forgotten? Maybe, but "Beloved" is the last haunting word in
the novel.

      In all of this, Sethe comes perilously close to losing her
Self. The cross on her back is no hedge against such loss; yet, its
value as a spiritual emblem is not diminished. This is my point:
to receive of Spirit/spirituality does not promise the recipient
anything except the possibility of more suffering, which describes
a thin line between transcendence and despair. When transcendence happens, one experiences a moment when finitude is superseded by infinitude. The earthly is stripped away momentarily and we "know" the divine. The suffering implicit in the
human condition, as I see it, is defined by the paradox that transcendence is not a stable unchanging phenomenon, but is
known in the fleeting moments of spiritual and physical ecstasy
and even in the moments of mundane stability that we do experience—but can only hold permanently in memory, if we so
choose. Sometimes the only way to know we exist is through re-

memory, which is the point of Morrison's novel. The relationship between Paul D and Sethe, fragile as it is, and between Amy
Denver and Sethe, brief as it is, are examples of transcendence.
The experiences are human, but transformed by the touch of the
divine.

Closure is also precluded by the generational issues at
stake here, issues not easily resolved: Sethe's relationship to her
mother, Beloved's to Sethe, Denver's to Sethe. The thrice-told
story that begins the conclusion of the novel, the story beginning
with the words, "I am Beloved . . ." (210), is a haunting re-memory of the destruction of the African and African-American family. Conflated in these lines are the stories of Sethe's mother,
Sethe, and Beloved—intricate variations on the theme of the
motherless child. The refiguration of the tree on Sethe's back as
the cross of Calvary is one way to look at the idea that the complex freedoms (of consciousness, of spirit, of being) promised in
the Gospels have yet to be realized in actuality. Yet, Sethe's suffering does not end for having carried the cross. To the contrary,
she will carry it until the day she dies (as she says, "It grows there
still"), inheriting with it the psychic and spiritual wasteland between death and resurrection, which paradoxically is the part of
the Christ story that she cannot appropriate—since she has not
experienced physical death. Though Paul D and Sethe have an
extraordinary relationship which suggests reconciliation on
many levels, his presence in her life represents respite, not resolution. This is what I mean when I suggest that they share moments of transcendence but both of their lives have been permanently damaged by the experiences of slavery. Transcendence
allows respite; but while they are alive nothing can eradicate the
trauma caused by bondage.

Lack of closure also characterizes Amy Denver's story.
We do not know what happens to her—whether she reaches
Boston or finds her velvet. Her moment of interaction with
Sethe is one of Christian charity, but Amy's act of loving kindness does not guarantee her a better life. Morrison subtly stacks
the cards against Amy and the reader wonders: should Amy actually get to Boston, what of herself she might have to relin-
quish in order to obtain her velvet. Will she become a prosti-
tute? A kept woman? A factory girl? Or, will she be rewarded
in kind for her acts of mercy, her sense of empathy?

Last, Baby Suggs's story is equally vexed by lack of psychological and spiritual closure—after all that she does for her peo-

ple. The reader is left with a profound sense of injustice when the very people to whom Baby Suggs ministers turn on her after the lavish dinner which she prepares for them. Morrison is an astute observer of human nature and her description of Baby Suggs's intuition that her dinner was profligate in the eyes of the people is brilliant. Morrison refigures the parable of the loaves and fishes as Baby Suggs takes account of the disaster that follows her celebratory meal. Morrison writes,

> 124, rocking with laughter, goodwill, and food for ninety, made them angry. Too much, they thought. Where does she get it all, Baby Suggs, holy? . . .
> Now to take two buckets of blackberries and make ten, maybe twelve, pies; to have turkey enough for the whole town pretty near, new peas in September, fresh cream but no cow, ice and sugar, batter bread. . . . Loaves and fishes were His powers—they did not belong to an ex-slave who had probably never carried one hundred pounds to the scale, or picked okra with a baby on her back.   (137)

Baby Suggs knows the people are not so easily rid of slavery's taint (here seen as suspicion even of another black person) as she perceives the community weighing her slave experiences against theirs and finding hers less onerous. She tried, but the people are not healed, not whole. Worse, she is condemned by the very orthodoxy that she side-stepped in her preaching. The people do not know how close they are/were to Spirit and wholeness, and to restoration of the beloved community; instead they revert to rigid orthodox interpretations of Scripture that shield them in their condemnation of Baby Suggs.

In this interpretation of *Beloved*, I attempt to excavate the Christ story from centuries of racist and sexist interventions that obscure its power to renew and to redeem. My interpretation neither denies the problems implicit in the story for skeptics, nor extols the truth explicit in it for believers; both, in fact, might find it troublesome. The point I want to make, however, is that Christ's suffering informs the ways in which many African-Americans view their historical (and present day) suffering and Morrison is keenly aware of the power of these views.

Through "passionate physicality" and "combative spirituality," African-Americans have the choice to vitalize the Christ story, redeeming an "ideal" Christ from a position of distance and the role of passivity. This vitalization suggests that religious interpretation renders Christ the passive victim, safe and sanitized to preach about, but not to emulate. This is the truth of Mary Daly's observation: "Christianity *idealizes*." She is correct; the religion, Christianity, idealizes the life of Christ, separates it from us, and reifies it, making it inaccessible. But human life at its most tragic deidealizes Christ and paradoxically vitalizes the Christ who promises to be present in earthly suffering. This is Vincent Harding's premise in liberation spirituality. Sethe, Amy, and Baby Suggs assume the responsibility for vitalizing Christ in their lives, using their spiritual strength to answer the unforeseen demands of the moment. Their sacrifices elevate the beloved community as they become—briefly—the living Christ. Whatever we think of the authenticity of the Gospel stories, Morrison's (re)interpretation infuses them with new life.

Sethe, Amy Denver, and Baby Suggs each—through Toni Morrison's authorial agency—assume some manner of responsibility for restoring the beloved community, though, as with all things human, the restoration is momentary. Sethe gives the gift of freedom; Amy gives the gift of charity; Baby Suggs gives the gift of spiritual direction. The brilliance of the novel is in Morrison's bold retelling of the three Christian stories, suggesting as she does so, a new hermeneutics located not only in the intersection between spirituality and religion, but also in the intersection of fiction, history, and the contemporary present.

Notes

[1] "I Love to Tell the Story" is a line from a popular hymn. The words are:

> I love to tell the story of unseen things above
> Of Jesus and His glory, of Jesus and His love
> I love to tell the story because I know 'tis true
> It satisfies my longings as nothing else can do.

> Refrain
> I love to tell the story
> Twill be my theme in glory
> To tell the old, old story
> Of Jesus and His love.

[2] See Acts 5.30 and 10.30 for references to Christ hanged on a tree; Luke 10.33 for the parable of the Good Samaritan; and Luke 4.18-19 for the call to preach.

[3] See Morrison, "Unspeakable Things Unspoken." Note Morrison's early

focus on this topic in *Beloved* where Stamp Paid, the black abolitionist who ferries Sethe and the newborn Denver across the river to free territory, who saves Denver from death, and who is rebuffed in his efforts to help Sethe, stops trying:

> Stamp Paid abandoned his efforts to see about Sethe, after the pain of knocking and not gaining entrance, and when he did, 124 was left to its own devices. When Sethe locked the door, the women inside were free at last to be what they liked, see whatever they saw and say whatever was on their minds.
>
> Almost. Mixed in with the voices surrounding the house, recognizable but undecipherable to Stamp Paid, were the thoughts of the women of 124, *unspeakable thoughts, unspoken.*   (199, emphasis mine)

[4] According to *Webster's New Collegiate Dictionary*, to "transubstantiate" means to transmute. In Roman Catholic and Eastern Orthodox dogma, transubstantiation is "the miraculous change by which . . . the eucharistic elements at their consecration become the body and blood of Christ while keeping only the appearances of bread and wine."

[5] The fact that the overseer is schoolteacher (Morrison's use of the lower case "s" is deliberate) is crucial. His job as overseer is also his "research" opportunity and he teaches his nephews the "scientific" proof of African-American intellectual, moral, and aesthetic inferiority, proving that black people are sub-human; he, therefore, believes that he has a justification for slavery.

[6] The closing stanza of Adrienne Rich's poem, "Natural Resources" is especially relevant here. One is tempted to substitute the word "slaves" for "miners."

> The women who first knew themselves
> miners, are dead. The rainbow flies
>
> like a flying buttress from the walls
> of cloud, the silver-and-green vein
>
> awaits the battering of the pick
> the dark lode weeps for light
>
> My heart is moved by all I cannot save:
> so much has been destroyed
>
> I have to cast my lot with those
> who age after age, perversely,
>
> with no extraordinary power,
> reconstitute the world.   (67)

[7] Huck's tendency to listen to his own heart and to act accordingly regardless of the consequences is what I consider spirituality. Amy's words, "that she wouldn't be caught dead in daylight on a busy river with a runaway" remind the reader that she, like Huckleberry Finn, is still bound by the laws of her time, yet she has taken a great risk. Neither Amy nor Huck seems aware of how generous their actions are and how good they are. They are, however,

very much aware that civil and religious law would condemn them.

[8] Luke 4.18-19 is the passage that Morrison revises:

> The Spirit of the Lord is upon me, because he hath
> anointed me to preach the gospel to the poor; he hath
> sent me to heal the brokenhearted, to preach deliver-
> ance to the captives, and recovering of sight to the
> blind, to set at liberty them that are bruised,
> To preach the acceptable year of the Lord.

[9] Dr. Vincent Harding's thoughts were spoken in conversation with a gathering of students in Philadelphia, Pennsylvania, March 18, 1987. I am deeply indebted to Dr. Dwight Hopkins of the Department of Religion at Santa Clara University for sharing this tape with me. The concept of "liberation spirituality" was the breakthrough I needed to articulate fully my ideas about African-American spirituality. In this conversation, Harding differentiates between religion and theology, which he defines as Western, academic and abstract, and black liberation theology (spirituality), which, among other things, he defines as African, and as faith in the movement of God among the people.

[10] Dr. Joyce King, Department of Counseling, Psychology, and Education at Santa Clara University, suggested in conversation (March 6, 1990) that one explanation for African-Americans accepting Christianity is that it represented a spiritual alternative to the beloved community destroyed by the slave trade. Her point is that the concept of African community is located in religions which embrace the sacred and secular, which represents the harmony between Spirit and flesh. Central to this is the belief that Christianity, as African-Americans practice it, is different.

Works Cited

Daly, Mary. *Beyond God the Father: Toward a Philosophy of Women's Liberation*. Boston: Beacon Press, 1973.

Harding, Vincent. Taped conversation. March 18, 1987.

King, Joyce. Interview. March 6, 1990.

Morrison, Toni. *Beloved*. New York: Knopf, 1987.

—. "Unspeakable Things Unspoken: The Afro-American Presence in American Literature." *Michigan Quarterly Review* 28 (1989): 1-34.

Rich, Adrienne. "Natural Resources." *The Dream of a Common Language: Poems 1974-1977*. New York: Norton, 1978. 60-67.

West, Cornel. "Postmodernism and Black America." *Zeta Magazine* 1 (1988): 27-29.

Mixed Genres and the Logic of Slavery in Toni Morrison's *Beloved*

Carl D. Malmgren

At first reading Toni Morrison's *Beloved* strikes one as an unusually hybridized text—part ghost story, part historical novel, part slave narrative, part love story. Indeed, some of its genre forms seem to rub against one another, to co-exist uneasily, in a state of tension, if not antagonism. The relation between ghost story and historical novel is a case in point. The conventions of the former involve the partial cancellation of the mimetic contract and demand from the reader willing suspension of disbelief in the supernatural. The historical novel, on the other hand, is based on a respect for the reality principle, for the world of historical fact: its basic allegiance is to the world as it is or as it has been. Morrison somehow holds these two disparate forms together. At the same time, *Beloved* can be seen both as a tragedy, involving a mother's moment of choice, and as a love story, exploring what it means to be be-loved. How do these forms fit in with the others? It might be argued that another narrative form, the slave narrative, holds the key to the narrative's unity. It is the institution of slavery that supplies the logic underwriting the novel, the thematic glue that unifies this multifaceted text. In its opening sentences, *Beloved* announces part of its generic identity in no uncertain terms:

> 124 was spiteful. Full of baby's venom. The women in the house knew it and so did the children. For years each put up with the spite in his own way, but by 1873 Sethe and her daughter Denver were its only victims. The grandmother, Baby Suggs, was dead, and the sons, Howard and Buglar, had run away by the time they were thirteen years old—as soon as merely looking in

> the mirror shattered it (that was the signal for
> Buglar); as soon as two tiny handprints appeared in the
> cake (that was it for Howard). Neither boy waited to
> see more, another kettleful of chick peas smoking in a
> heap on the floor: soda crackers crumbled and strewn in
> a line next to the doorsill. Nor did they wait for one of
> the relief periods: the weeks, months even, when noth-
> ing was disturbed. No. Each one fled at once—the
> moment the house committed what was for him the one
> insult not to be borne or witnessed a second time.   (3)

Beloved is clearly a *ghost story*, dealing with the "spiteful"
or "sad" or "rebuked" spirit of a baby girl who died in a horrible
way some years previously. The girl, Beloved, manifests herself
initially as a poltergeist, haunting 124 Bluestone Road and those
who have in some way betrayed her. Despite the fact that the
spirit is a baby, she "throws a powerful spell" (4). But Paul D, the
last of the Sweet Home men, exorcises this ghost soon after his
arrival, and the restless and relentless spirit is forced to take
more drastic means. She assumes a human shape, at the age she
would have been had she lived, and returns to confront Sethe,
the mother who has wronged her in two ways, first by murdering her, second by denying her. For eighteen years Sethe has
been systematically "keeping the past at bay" (42), her days devoted to the "serious work of beating back the past" (73). The
reincarnation of Beloved compels Sethe to confront her personal
past, a past that up till then had been "unspeakable" (58), to come
to terms with the fact that she murdered her baby daughter. In
this novel, then, "nothing ever dies" (6), especially our private
ghosts, the skeletons we think safely locked in our closets, at
least until we put them to rest. Because "anything dead coming
back to life hurts" (35), what Sethe must undergo is an agonizing
private exorcism of her own.

   Seen in this light, the novel takes on a supernatural character; it is a ghost story about one beleaguered woman's struggle
with a real, but personal, demon. But *Beloved* is a novel that
straddles generic forms, as the opening paragraph makes clear. It
specifies that the novel's action takes place in the year 1873, at a
house outside Cincinnati that "didn't have a number then, because Cincinnati didn't stretch that far," in a state, Ohio, that had
been calling itself a state for only seventy years. The assignment
of a number to an unnumbered house, the precision of the historical specifications, the reference to the passage of time, and the
locus itself argue that this is a historical novel, obeying the con-

ventions of literary historiography, among them an acceptance
of the world of fact and a commitment to naturalistic interpretation. *Beloved* is very much situated in its historical time-frame;
it makes reference to the persecution of the Cherokee Indians in
the nineteenth-century (111), to the history of Cincinnati (155), to
the activities of the Ku Klux Klan in the 1870s, to the issues and
incidents that engaged slaves and ex-slaves in the middle part of
the last century—the Fugitive Bill, the Settlement Fee,
manumission, Dred Scott, Sojourner Truth, the underground
railway, the Colored Ladies of Delaware, Ohio. In chilling and
graphic detail, the novel renders the experience of African-
Americans before, during, and after the Civil War, in so doing
enabling its readers to "experience American slavery as it was
lived by those who were its objects of exchange" (Atwood 49). By
fashioning a concretely particularized account of that historical
experience, Morrison intends to make it come to life, to make it
real, especially for those who, removed in historical lime, "*can't*
imagine it, despite the greatest good intentions and sympathy"
(Schwartz B7). If Sethe must experience the "unspeakable" in
her private arena, then we readers must experience the unimaginable in the public sphere.

It might be argued, however, that these two genres resist
one another, that the concrete specificity of the historical dimension and its fidelity to the world of fact exert a kind of pressure
on the supernatural dimension, encouraging readers to find a
way to recuperate the text in naturalistic terms, to convert the
text, in Todorov's terms, from the *marvelous* to the *uncanny*.
The primary obstacle to this recuperation is, of course, the
eponymous character Beloved, whose initial appearance in the
novel is indeed miraculous—she is the "fully dressed woman"
who "walked out of the water" (50). Can her existence and appearance be accounted for in realistic, non-supernatural terms?
The evidence certifying her status as "real" ghost, as the preco-
cious, "already-crawling?" baby returned, is, after all, impressive.[1] She identifies herself immediately after her appearance as
"Beloved," the name that Sethe had had inscribed upon the unnamed baby's tombstone. She asks Sethe about the "diamond"
earrings she (Sethe) used to wear, earrings that had been confis-
cated from Sethe during her imprisonment eighteen years earlier. Beloved has the skin and complexion of a newborn despite
her eighteen years; her sole disfigurements—three parallel
scratches on her forehead and a neck scar, "the little curved

shadow of a smile in the kootchy-kootchy-coo place under her chin" (239)—would seem to be the stigmata left from Sethe's assault upon her. Finally, Beloved hums a song that Sethe had herself made up and sung to her children, a song no one else could possibly know. Hearing the song, Sethe becomes convinced of "a miracle that is truly miraculous," the return of her baby girl (176).

Until that point, however, Sethe believes that there is a naturalistic explanation for Beloved's appearance: "she believed Beloved had been locked up by some whiteman for his own purposes, and never let out the door. That she must have escaped to a bridge or someplace and rinsed the rest out of her mind" (119). Morrison's dedication of the novel, to the "sixty million and more," points out a way of following up on this line of reasoning. The dedication honors, Morrison says, "the number of black Africans who never made it into slavery—those who died either as captives in Africa or on the slave ships" (cited in Otten 83). The dedication suggests the possibility that Beloved might herself be one of those unfortunates who experienced the slave ship passage, presumably smuggled in sometime before the Civil War and the establishment of the Northern blockade.

This hypothesis proves to be a powerful instrument of naturalistic recuperation. For one thing, Beloved's previously obscure, if not opaque, monologue (210-213) becomes accessible, if not transparent. The monologue reveals that Beloved is haunted by the slave ship experience; for her "it is always now there will never be a time when I am not crouching and watching others who are crouching too" (210). Troubling references within the monologue—to the crouching, the men without skin (the white slavetraders), the dead man on Beloved's face, the rats, the iron circle on her mother's neck, the noisy clouds of smoke (from the slavetraders' guns)—can all be fitted into the passage experience. This reading also explains Beloved's "unnatural" attachment to Sethe. The monologue specifies that the woman with Beloved's face (her mother) quite literally abandoned her daughter by throwing herself into the ocean:

> I cannot lose her again my dead man was in the way
> like the noisy clouds when he dies on my face I can see
> hers she is going to smile at me she is going to her
> sharp earrings are gone the men without skin are mak-
> ing loud noises they push my own man through they do
> not push the woman with my face through she goes in

> they do not push her she goes in the little hill is gone
> she was going to smile at me she was going to   (212)

Beloved's mother goes in of her own accord; she chooses death before slavery (at about the same time Sethe is making a very different decision when confronted with very similar circumstances). Having been abandoned by her original mother, Beloved attaches herself to the reincarnation of that mother (Sethe) like a parasite.

Other references in the text fill in the rest of Beloved's history, confirming Sethe's original speculations about the girl. Beloved herself admits that she knew one white man (119). Presumably, he had kept her hidden and locked up her entire life, including a period of eight years *after* the end of the Civil War, using her for truly unspeakable purposes. This possibility is validated by a rumor Stamp Paid relates to Paul D: "Was a girl locked up in the house with a white man over by Deer Creek. Found him dead last summer and the girl gone. Maybe that's her. Folks said he had her in there since she was a pup" (235). The fact that the white man called her "beloved in the dark and bitch in the light" explains the name she chooses for herself. Other mysterious circumstances—the earrings, the scars, the song—can be accounted for by not-improbable incidents drawn from her personal history or from her close association with Denver in the days following her arrival at 124. In some such way, one can fully naturalize Beloved's existence, appearance, and behavior. Beloved is in this reading the ultimate victim of slavery, a living reminder of the brutality of the institution.[2]

And yet, the novel *Beloved* insists throughout that it is indeed a *ghost story*, that it must be read in those terms. The poltergeist haunting 124 is undeniably real, giving tangible proof of its existence: it turns over slop-jars, causes sideboards to move, projects a paralyzing pool of redlight, assaults Here Boy the dog, and envelops the house in a cacophony of voices. Elsewhere, Morrison has insisted upon the place of the supernatural in her work; she tries, she says, to blend

> the acceptance of the supernatural and a profound rootedness in the real world at the same time with neither taking precedence over the other. It is indicative of the cosmology, the way in which Black people look at the world. We are a very practical people, very down-to-earth, even shrewd people. But

> within that practicality we also accepted what I
> suppose could be called superstition and magic, which
> is another way of knowing things. . . . That kind of
> knowledge has a very strong place in my work.
>
> (Morrison, "Rootedness" 342)

Within the narrative ontology of the novel, one *must* acknowledge and accept the existence of ghosts. *Beloved* in fact
represents an example of Todorov's *fantastic*, a narrative form
inviting and validating both natural and supernatural readings
of it, preternatural phenomena.

Beloved is thus both ghost story and historical novel. Indeed, at the thematic level, Morrison finally makes the one form
reinforce the other, linking them through her reconception of
the institution of slavery. If, as part of the supernatural dimension of the novel, Sethe must come to terms with a very real
ghost from her personal past, something that forces her to deal
with the atrocity she committed in that past, then, too, within
the historical dimension, we readers must come to terms with
our own ghost, the spectre of a ruthless and dehumanizing institution whose legacy we have yet to acknowledge fully. In historical terms, slavery is a very real ghost from our collective past,
one that we must confront personally if we are to exorcise it.
The novel suggest that in some form "the slave past lives on,
raising havoc" (Snitow 25). By personifying slavery as history's
ghost, Morrison reimagines the institution and its legacy as a
kind of abnormal excess that finally defies rational explanation, a
ghastly figure from out of a nightmare. Indeed, she gives the
novel the name of a character who is the ultimate historical victim of slavery, someone totally brutalized and dehumanized,
someone reduced to a ghost of herself. And, the coda to the
novel tells us, Beloved's story is so horrific, so much a bad
dream, that within the black community it is deliberately repressed: "it was not a story to pass on" because in a case like this
"remembering seemed unwise" (274). The black community can
choose to forget Beloved, as perhaps America has chosen to forget the legacy of slavery, but for readers of the novel it is not that
simple; they hold in their hands the very document that rehearses for them the story of slavery and its aftermath, thus
memorializing Beloved's suffering and incarnating history's
ghost. In this way, the novel serves as a form of incantation, the
ritualistic calling forth of the spirits of the past.

If *Beloved* is both a ghost story *and* a historical novel, it can also be characterized as a love story, exploring what it means to be "be-loved." In various places the novel propounds a spectrum of possible relations between lover and loved one, between Self and Other. The hard-headed Ella tells Sethe, "If anybody was to ask me I'd say, 'Don't love nothing'" (92). For Paul D, the only safe alternative for slaves and ex-slaves is to "love small" (162): "The best thing, he knew, was to love just a little bit; everything, just a little bit, so that when they broke its back, or shoved it in a cracker sack, well, maybe you'd have a little love left over for the next one" (45). When Sethe confesses to Paul D what love made her try to do to her children, the shocked Paul D can only tell her that her kind of love is "too thick," to which she retorts, "Too thick? . . . Love is or it ain't. Thin love ain't love at all" (164).

The novel thus meditates upon and mediates between the various forms that love takes. In this regard, its dominant theme is the problematics of love, particularly as regards the question of identity. The key love relation in this particular historical context is the maternal one; the novel consistently foregrounds the relation of mother and child and the dangers and delights of mother love. Morrison has admitted elsewhere an interest in this relation: "One of the nice things that women do is nurture and love something other than themselves—they do that rather nicely. Instinctively, perhaps, but they are taught to do it, socialized to do it, or genetically predisposed to do it— whatever it is, it's something the majority of women feel strongly about. But mother love is also a killer" (cited in Rothstein C17). The novel examines in what circumstances mother love can be a "killer" (cf. *Beloved* 132). Can we relate this thematic framework, this discourse on maternal love, to the logic informing the novel's multigeneric identity?

Central to the issue of maternal love, at the ethical heart of the novel itself, is the tragic action that Sethe takes against her children, her loved ones, an action that she feels was "right because it came from true love" (251). How finally do we judge this action? Morrison herself has been forthcoming but deliberately ambiguous about this aspect of the novel: "It was absolutely the right thing to do," she tells an interviewer, "but she [Sethe] had no right to do it" (cited in Rothstein C17). This sort of categorical and logical illogic is echoed in Sethe's own justification: "if I hadn't killed her she would have died and that is something I could not bear to happen to her" (200).

The normative dimension of the novel thus hinges upon our assessment of Sethe's action, about which there is certainly no critical consensus. Martha Bayles blasts the novel, just because it excuses Sethe from "lasting blame": "a slave commits a crime, but it is not really a crime because it was committed by a slave. The system, and not the slave, stands unjustly condemned for a deed that would possess another meaning if committed in freedom" (40). In a similar vein, Stanley Crouch argues that the novel tends to exonerate Sethe: it "explains black behavior in terms of social conditioning, as if listing atrocities solves the mystery of human motive and behavior. It is designed to placate sentimental feminist ideology, and to make sure that the vision of black women as the most scorned and rebuked of victims doesn't weaken" (40). Terry Otten, on the other hand, says that the novel insists upon the "necessity of personal responsibility" (81), that Sethe's deed is finally "understandable but not excusable" (82). And Carol Iannone argues that the novel is finally ambiguous in its "treatment of the moral dimensions of Sethe's initial act of child murder" (63), and that this ambiguity is a function of a general authorial retention to "take no clear stand on the appalling actions she depicts" (61).

I would argue that the novel does indeed take a clear stand on the issue, and that the stand is itself a function of the logic underwriting the novel's multigeneric identity, the logic of slavery. In this regard, slavery—its logic and its legacy—serves as the figure in the novel's carpet, the cloth that links love story to ghost story and ghost story to historical novel.[3] In the former linkage, love story to ghost story, the key notion is "possession." Its connection to slavery and the historical dimension is rather straightforward, as shall be seen.

The novel's treatment of slavery makes clear that the institution perverts the relation between Self and Other, master and slave, by thoroughly dehumanizing both parties:

> Whitepeople believed that whatever the manners, under every dark skin was a jungle. Swift unnavigable waters, swinging screaming baboons, sleeping snakes, red gums ready for their sweet white blood. . . . But it wasn't the jungle blacks brought with them to this place from the other [livable] place. It was the jungle whitefolks planted in them. And it grew. It spread. In, through, and after life, it spread, until it invaded the whites who had made it. Touched them every one. Changed and altered them. Made them bloody, silly,

worse than they wanted to be, so scared were they of
the jungle they had made. The screaming baboon lived
under their own white skin; the red gums were their
own.   (198-199)[4]

As Margaret Atwood has noted, slavery serves in the
novel as a "paradigm of how most people behave when they are
given absolute power over other people" (50). As the above passage graphically depicts, such power reduces people to animals, a
truth brought chillingly home to Paul D when he is forced to
wear a bit in his mouth after an aborted escape attempt. Sethe's
eyes are opened to the reality of her status at Sweet Home when
she realizes that to schoolteacher she is nothing but a creature
whose value is determined in an accounts ledger enumerating
her human and animal characteristics.

Slaves as animals, slaves as objects, slaves as commodities—the common denominator here is the denial of the selfhood of the slave, the conversion of the Other to Object, the re-
duction of human beings to checker pieces (23), counters, or
commodities. This motif is figured most forcefully in Baby
Suggs's personal history: in the way in which her seven children
are taken from her only to disappear forever; in the fact that for
most of her adult life she has no name but Jenny, the name on
her bill of sale. When her owner finally asks her what she calls
herself, her response is telling: "Nothing. . . . I don't call myself
nothing" (142). Insofar as she is characterized by a "desolated
center where that self that was no self [makes] its home" (140),
she is indeed nothing. The novel makes it clear that this denial
of humanity and selfhood takes place even under the more benign forms of slavery, such as Garner's, as Paul D comes to realize: "Garner called and announced them men—but only on
Sweet Home, and by his leave. Was he naming what he saw or
creating what he did not? . . . Did a whiteman saying make it so?
Suppose Garner woke up one morning and changed his mind?
Took the word away" (220). In the master/slave relation, "definitions belong to the definer—not the defined" (190), and there
can be for the latter no sense of self-definition. Such is the inex-
orable logic of slavery. In extreme circumstances, such logic
leads from personal degradation to self-annihilation, from debasement to extinction. It is an awareness of this extremity that
Sethe acts on when she tries to destroy her children: "That anybody white could take your whole self for anything that came to
mind. Not just work, kill, or maim you, but dirty you. Dirty you

so bad you couldn't like yourself no more. Dirty you so bad you
forgot who you were and couldn't think it up. And though she
and others lived through it and got over it, she could never let it
happen to her own" (251). And, the novel says, if one contests or
rejects the logic of slavery, as Sixo does, then one is quite literally
reduced to nothing.

A sense of self is thus contingent upon personal freedom
and autonomy. In this respect, Baby Suggs's son Halle, a slave
all his life, is instinctively wise; he knows that there is nothing
like freedom in this world, that it is the most precious gift he can
give his mother. When Baby Suggs at last breathes the air of
freedom, she looks at her hands and realizes that they belong to
her; she becomes aware, for the first time, of the beating of her
heart. In a very real sense she takes possession of herself; at the
same time she assumes her rightful name. Sethe experiences a
similar kind of ego formation immediately after her arrival at
124: "Bit by bit, at 124 and in the Clearing, along with the others,
she had claimed herself. Freeing yourself was one thing; claiming ownership of that freed self was another" (95). Indeed, Sethe
draws upon the agonies endured during her desperate escape attempt in order to construct and validate that selfhood, a selfhood
she identifies with those she has suffered for, as she later tells
Paul D:

> I did it. I got us all out. Without Halle too. Up till
> then it was the only thing I ever did on my own. De-
> cided. And it came off right, like it was supposed to.
> We was here. Each and every one of my babies and me
> too. I birthed them and I got them out and it wasn't no
> accident. I did that. I had help, of course, lots of that,
> but still it was me doing it, me saying *Go on* and *Now*.
> Me having to look out. Me using my own head. But it
> was more than that. It was a kind of selfishness I never
> knew nothing about before. It felt good. Good and
> right. I was big, Paul D, and deep and wide and when I
> stretched out my arms all my children could get in be-
> tween. I was *that* wide.   (162)

Given the circumstances, Sethe's is a story of personal triumph, but her telling of it is troubling.[5] The frequent recurrence
of forms of the first personal pronoun in the speech, for example, indicates the extent to which Sethe's identity is connected
with this experience. This identification of her selfhood with
the fates of her children, this "selfishness," determines Sethe's

subsequent actions and informs our judgment of them.

For the fact is that Sethe so identifies her Self with the well-being of her children that she denies their existence as autonomous Others, in so doing unconsciously perpetuating the logic of slavery. In effect, both parties of critics are correct. The root cause of Sethe's action is indeed the institution of slavery, whose most terrible legacy is an awful logic of human relationship. The novel "drives home the meaning of slavery," one critic notes, by showing how, within Sethe, "the roles of master and slave, mother and child, have been fused" (Thurman 179). And yet, as Paul D argues, Sethe's action was not only futile but also counterproductive: the novel acknowledges the awful power of slavery but finally holds Sethe responsible, insists that there had to be "some other way" (165). At one point Sethe says that she "wouldn't draw breath without her children" (203). It is this conflation of Self and Other that underwrites Sethe's justification of her actions: "The best thing she was, was her children. Whites might dirty *her* all right, but not her best thing, her beautiful magical best thing—the part of her that was clean" (251). The language Sethe uses here suggests that she has both appropriated and depersonalized her children. It is this aspect of Sethe's love that shocks Paul D, forcing him to condemn her: "This here Sethe talked about love like any other woman: talked about baby clothes like any other woman, but what she meant could cleave the bone. This here Sethe talked about safety with a handsaw. This here new Sethe didn't know where the world stopped and she began" (164).

Not to know where the World stops and the Self begins— this is to deny the separate and inviolable existence of the Other. This kind of love has been infected by the logic of slavery, a logic that converts the Other into an object to be owned, into a possession. The idea of possession, of being possessed by that which we think we possess, thus serves as the unifying motif of the novel. This notion recurs throughout the monologues that emanate from 124 after the house has been converted to a world of its own, a hermetically sealed world in which all sense of the boundaries between Self and Other has been obliterated:

> Beloved
> You are my sister
> You are my daughter
> You are my face; you are me
> I have found you again, you have come back to me

You are my Beloved
You are mine
You are mine
You are mine   (216)

To be loved in such a way is to have being only in relationship, a state of affairs that readily metamorphoses into the
idea of possession. The loved one, the be-loved, is convened
into a love object, a thing. To love in that way is truly to be possessed, to be haunted by a ghost. This kind of love is itself an abnormal excess, an unnatural spirit. As Baby Suggs wisely notes,
"Everything depends on knowing how much, good is knowing
when to stop" (87).

When Paul D condemns Sethe, telling her in no uncertain terms that "what you did was wrong," he adds that there
had to be "some other way" (165). Sethe denies the possibility of
alternatives, but other episodes in the novel tend to undercut
that blanket denial. The action of Beloved's mother on the slave
ship represents one such alternative—suicide, the extinction of
the Self. Sethe's own action at the end of the novel—attacking
the master who would deny the Selfhood of the Other—represents another alternative. Indeed, it has been argued that it is
just this action, Sethe's turning on the enslaver in order to save
"her best thing," that serves to exorcise her personal ghost and
enables her to get on with her life (Otten 94).

The alternative to "thick love," the kind of love that sub-
sumes the identity of the Other, is the love that Sethe manifests
for Paul D, love that respects the integrity and inviolability of the
loved one. Sixo explains the kind of love he shares with Thirty-
Mile Woman as follows: "She is a friend of my mind. She
gather me, man. The pieces I am, she gather them and give
them back to me in all the right order. It's good you know,
when you got a woman who is a friend of your mind" (272-273).
This kind of love befriends the Other, gathers up the fragmented
pieces of the Other, restores the Other to itself. Only after Sethe
has learned the limits of love, the reciprocity of love, only then
do she and Paul D have a future; only then can they look forward and not backward. The two of them, Paul D says at the end
of the novel, have had too much yesterday and not enough tomorrow. They have been haunted by yesterday's ghosts, the
spectres of history and biography. They can only have a tomorrow when Sethe lays to rest the final ghost, the logic of slavery,
and accepts that she alone is "her own best thing"—a proposi-

tion to which she can only respond tentatively, interrogatively: "Me? Me?" (273).

Notes

[1] There are seven reviews of the novel reprinted in *Contemporary Literary Criticism, Yearbook 1988* that deal directly or indirectly with the question of Beloved's identity. All seven assume that Beloved is indeed the reincarnation of Sethe's long-dead baby girl. Otten proposes a naturalistic explanation for Beloved's appearance (84), but does not go into detail about it. The reading I'm about to develop was first suggested to me by my colleague Inge Fink. I am grateful to her for her help on this project.

[2] Morrison's own comments on the reality of the ghost are tantalizingly ambiguous: "I wanted that haunting not to be really a suggestion of being bedeviled by the past, but to have it be incarnate, to have it actually happen that a person enters your world who is in fact—you believe at any rate—the dead returned, and you get a second chance, a chance to do it right. Of course, you do it wrong again" (cited in Rothstein C17).

[3] Pursuing this line of argument, one might note how Morrison is careful to weave together her disparate generic strands: At one point she links love story to ghost story by comparing motherlove to magic (4); at another she links slave narrative to ghost story by imputing to the white masters a kind of occult power (244).

[4] Cf. Frederick Douglass's treatment of the relation between master and slave in *Narrative of the Life of Frederick Douglass, An American Slave,* chapter VII: "Slavery proved as injurious to [my mistress] as it did to me. When I went there she was a pious, warm, and tender-hearted woman. There was no sorrow or suffering for which she had not a tear. She had bread for the hungry, clothes for the naked, and comfort for every mourner that came within her reach. Slavery soon proved its ability to divest her of these heavenly qualities. Under its influence, the tender heart became stone, and the lamblike disposition gave way to one of tigerlike fierceness." In its depiction of slavery, Morrison's novel is clearly indebted to this and other slave narratives.

[5] Elsewhere Paul D notes that more important than what Sethe had done is the *claim* she made about what she had done (164).

Works Cited

Atwood, Margaret. "Haunted by Their Nightmares." Rev. of *Beloved. New York Times Book Review,* 13 September 1987, pp. 1, 49-50.

Bayles, Martha. "Special Effects, Special Pleading." *New Criterion* 6.5 (January 1988): 34-40.

Crouch, Stanley. "Aunt Medea." Rev. of *Beloved. New Republic,* 19 October 1987, pp. 38-43.

Douglass, Frederick. *Narrative of the Life of Frederick Douglass, An American Slave*. 1845; rpt. Garden City, New York: Anchor, 1973.

Iannone, Carol. "Tony Morrison's Career." *Commentary* 84.6 (December 1987): 59-63.

Morrison, Toni. *Beloved*. New York: New American, 1987.

—. "Rootedness: The Ancestor as Foundation." In *Black Women Writers (1950-1980): A Critical Evaluation*. Ed. Mari Evans. New York: Anchor, 1994. 339-345.

Otten, Terry. *The Crime of Innocence in the Novels of Toni Morrison*. Columbia: University of Missouri Press, 1989.

Rothstein, Mervyn. "Toni Morrison, in Her New Novel, Defends Women." *New York Times*, 26 August 1987: C17.

Schwartz, Amy B. "Beloved: It's Not a Question of Who Suffered More." *Washington Post*, 3 April 1988: B7.

Thurman, Judith. "A House Divided." Rev. of *Beloved. New Yorker*, 2 November 1987, pp. 175-180.

Todorov, Tzvetan. *The Fantastic*. Trans. Richard Howard. Cleveland, Ohio: Case Western Reserve University Press, 1973.

"Toni Morrison: *Beloved*." Survey of book reviews. *Contemporary Literary Criticism* 44 (1988): 194-213.

Narrative Control and Subjectivity: Dismantling Safety in Toni Morrison's *Beloved*

Andrew Schopp

> Mixed in with the voices surrounding the house, recognizable but undecipherable to Stamp Paid, were the thoughts of the women of 124, unspeakable thoughts, unspoken. (Morrison, *Beloved* 245)

In the above epigraph, Toni Morrison illuminates the paradoxical nature of silence, or "the silenced." For the women of 124, the unspeakable is to some degree spoken even while it ostensibly remains unvoiced. The women's unspeakable thoughts are "recognizable but undecipherable," and thus they constitute an articulated presence. Moreover, the four "chapters" that follow this passage provide the reader with access to these purportedly "unspeakable" thoughts. The idea that silence constitutes an "absence as presence" is hardly novel, especially in the postmodern text, and critics such as Barbara Hill Rigley have shown that Morrison's narrative voice is often informed as much by silence as by dialogue (*Voices* 7). Nonetheless, this "paradox of the unspoken" provides a useful tool for explicating Morrison's narrative practice in *Beloved*.

Of course, to speak the unspeakable, to articulate the culturally repressed, is to threaten the inherent "safety" provided by the maintenance of dichotomies such as speakable/unspeakable, known/unknown, etc. To some degree, the house at 124 seems to constitute a "safe" space within which Sethe, Denver and Beloved can speak what cannot be spoken elsewhere. This would seem incredibly ironic, since the house is also haunted. The house has its parallel in the novel itself, since a horrific history (that much of American culture would like to keep silenced) haunts this text and its characters. However, the idea that either the house or this text is exclusively "safe" is highly problematic, in part because the very notion of safety, especially as defined by Sethe, is vexed. When Sethe explains to Paul D why she killed her daughter, she claims, "I took and put my babies where they'd be safe" (*Beloved* 201). For Sethe, then, safety equals freedom from the control of, and subjugation to, a master; at the same time, safety equals death. According to Paul D, however, "what she wanted for her children was exactly what was missing in 124: safety" (201). He is horrified by the fact that "Sethe talked about safety with a handsaw" (202). Morrison's novel dramatizes the difficulty of negotiating a "safe" space, especially given the seeming omnipresence and omnipotence of the "master," and more specifically of master narratives that strive to shape and control one's sense of self and often even one's physical body. Morrison suggests that Sethe's answer is not a viable answer, since Sethe's "safe" daughter returns to haunt the house and drive her other children away. And, if Beloved is this dead daughter reincarnated, her physical return forces Sethe, Denver, and their community to confront a past and a set of experiences that are anything but safe.

The figure of Beloved represents a prime example of the unspeakable being spoken. However, as I shall eventually demonstrate, she is an unspeakable that is spoken in different ways by different characters to fulfill each character's specific needs. Beloved reflects all that is unknown, unspeakable, unsafe, and her existence speaks directly to the illusion of safety inherent in the "known" and the "norm"—those cultural "speakables" defined and empowered by the "master narratives" of western culture. Craig Owens has persuasively argued that such "master narratives" are essentially narratives of mastery (339), and the implication of dominance/subjection in his claim is crucial, for it reveals the ideological underpinnings of a culture that can and did endorse slavery. Morrison's novel reopens the wounds of slavery, articulates American culture's greatest unspeakable. At the same time, her text seems set on laying bare the power and potential horror of narrative itself, its ability to control, to define, to subjugate, and to disempower. While her text is to some degree a safe space in which unspeakables are spoken, her narrative practice strives at all points to dismantle this safety. Morrison accomplishes this in part via the identifications she establishes between reading subject and textual subject, reading subject and speaking subject. However, she also accomplishes this by revealing the horror inherent in narrative control, by constantly confronting the reading subject with the very processes of narrative control and coercion that strive to construct and shape this subject.

In this novel, the very substance of the traditional horror text—speaking the unspeakable—becomes the subject of interrogation. On the one hand, Morrison's narrative depicts characters who speak the unspeakable in order to construct a solid sense of subjectivity. Sethe, for example, continually retells the harrowing experience of her escape, and this act seems to reaffirm both her sense of self and Denver's. Significantly, Denver only really wishes to hear the part in which she is born—the events preceding her birth constituting a horrific history that she would rather keep repressed.

> This was the part of the story [Denver] loved. She was coming to it now, and she loved it because it was all about herself; but she hated it too because it made her feel like a bill was owing somewhere and she, Denver, had to pay it. But who she owed or what to pay it with eluded her.   (*Beloved* 95)

The unknown past of slavery haunts the present, yet there is a sense that, with enough retelling, understanding will arrive, and Denver will discover the truth about this "debt-to-he-paid." On the other hand, Morrison's narrative demands that the reader decipher the unspeakable as it is spoken. Morrison's characters strive to produce meaning by articulating a repressed past. Throughout the novel, they narrate over both the psychological and the physical wounds inflicted on them by slavery and by a white patriarchal culture that can perpetuate and reinflict the wounds of slavery even after the institution itself has been dismantled.

Much of the novel's action takes place during the Reconstruction, and as both Brian Finney and Rebecca Ferguson have suggested,[1] these characters spend the novel reconstructing their selves, their community and the relation between the two. In order to reconstruct a sense of subjectivity, these characters suture over their physical and psychic wounds by narrating events from their individual and collective pasts. Mae Henderson asserts that "the challenge of the slave as victim of enforced illiter-

acy is similar to that of the highly literate contemporary histo-
rian or novelist—and that is to discover a way of organizing
memory, of contriving a narrative configuration in the absence
of written records" (66). Thus, Morrison demonstrates the potential benefits of narration as she has her characters attempt to
articulate a repressed past, to "suture" over a "lack" with narrative. Paul D, for example, tells Sethe that Halle saw her being
abused, and he explains that he said nothing to Halle after Halle
broke down because he, Paul D, had a bit in his mouth. Paul D
then insists that he didn't intend to tell this story, but Sethe
knows that this is only partially true: "He wants to tell me, she
thought. He wants me to ask him about what it was like for
him—about how offended the tongue is, held down by iron,
how the need to spit is so deep you cry for it" (87). To some degree, Paul D and Sethe *need* to tell one another these narratives.
"Her story was bearable because it was his as well—to tell, to re-
fine and tell again" (121). Of course, they *need* to engage in a suturing process precisely because they have effectively been narrated out of the dominant culture.

I mention the term suture because Morrison's novel
lends itself to an analysis based on recent theories of cinematic
suture as they have been applied to literary studies. As critics
like Kaja Silverman have suggested, narrative methods which
indicate point-of-view "would seem to be equivalents for novels
and poems of the shot/reverse shot formation in cinema, and
like the latter would seem to both conceal all signs of actual production, and to invite identification" (236). The shot/reverse
shot formation produces an identification between the spectator
(reading subject) and a character within the text whose gaze
comes to represent that of the spectator. This internal gaze satisfies the displeasure produced by the implication of an external
gaze, that of the speaking subject. It is important to note that this
theory associates displeasure with a controlling gaze, with the
speaking (i.e., narrating) agent. Silverman explains that "the
speaking subject has everything which the viewing subject . . .
understands itself to be lacking," and this sense of lack "inspires
the desire for 'something else,' a desire to see more" (204).

Silverman's purpose, of course, is to delineate the process
by which the viewing subject comes to identify with a textual
subject, the process by which the spectator is drawn into the narrative space. Yet I find it crucial for this discussion especially
that this process is predicated upon satisfying a displeasure that

is specifically defined in terms of lack—lack of knowledge, lack
of control over narrative and the speaking of the subject, lack of
agency. Finney claims that there is

> considerable potentiality in the theory of suture for fur-
> ther exploration of the ways in which literary narra-
> tive interacts with the reader who is constituted by
> that narrative and whose pleasure in reading is depen-
> dent on satisfactorily suturing over the numerous vari-
> eties of cut or discontinuity that occur in all forms of
> narrative.   ("Suture" 144)

Finney's assertion exposes the inherent tension of the suturing
process. The reader is constituted by the narrative and thus inhabits an unpleasant position of little agency. At the same time,
the reader strives to suture over the various forms of "lack" in
the text in order to satisfy this displeasure. Yet it is this very process of suturing that perpetuates the reading subject being constituted by the narrative. The suturing process can only satisfy by
reinscribing the reading subject's displeasure.

At the core of this process is narrative control, and I
would argue that Morrison's novel self-consciously invites and
disrupts the suturing process while it also uses "suture" as a crucial metaphor that exposes narrative's horror and power. In fact,
Morrison's own narrative agency enables her to manipulate a
series of narratological mechanisms (e.g., shifts in focalization,
proairetic sequence, and hermeneutic codes), thereby revealing
to the reading subject his/her own subjugation to narrative control. However, it is her manipulation of suture, as both narrative process and metaphor, that constitutes the novel's most
significant use of displeasure and horror. In *Beloved*, the suturing process creates a disturbing dual identification between reading subject and textual subject (i.e., characters) and between reading subject and speaking subject (i.e., the processes of narrative
control). The tension between these identifications disrupts the
"safety" of the narrative space while it lays bare the subject's inevitable power struggle with those narrative processes that
would shape and constitute it, a struggle that serves as a frightening metaphor for the social subject's subjection to cultural inscription.

In *Beloved*, Morrison's characters enact a version of suture in order to repair the wounds inflicted, directly or indirectly,
by oppressive cultural narratives. The textual subjects, what Sil-

verman has termed the "spoken subjects," reflect the horror inherent in being spoken, in being forced into a cultural space and
thus prohibited from control over the "speaking of the subject."
Morrison's novel suggests that, though these characters have
been set free from the institution of slavery, they are still very
much "subject" to the narrations and narrative definitions constructed by white patriarchal culture and its various laws (e.g.,
Paul D's struggle with definitions of manhood, Sethe's struggle
with definitions of motherhood). At the same time, Morrison's
own narrative discourse demands that the reading subject engage in a suturing process in order to make meaning. While
Finney has suggested that all forms of narrative require that the
reader engage in such a process, at least to some extent,[2] Morrison's novel is self-conscious in its ripping open of gaps that
must be sutured over with narrative if meaning is to be attained.
In the novel's opening sections, for example, we learn that
Sethe's children fear "the baby," but we don't immediately learn
why; we learn the baby is dead, but we don't learn how; we learn
that Paul D knows more about Halle than he tells Sethe—"'I
don't know any more than I did then.' Except for the churn, he
thought, and you don't need to know that" (*Beloved* 9)—but we
don't know why the churn is important or why she needs to be
protected from this knowledge.

Because Morrison's narrative demands that the reader
engage in a process of suture, and because this demand has its
parallel in the representation of textual subjects engaged in a
similar process, the narrative invites a particularly intense form
of identification between reading subject and textual subject.
This identification would seem to offer the promise of narrative
"safety." However, it is an identification with subjects who are
the victims of culturally sanctioned horror and oppression, and
thus the reader's path to safety is much like Sethe's; it is an alternative horror.

More importantly perhaps, *Beloved*'s narrative also invites an identification between reading subject and speaking subject. Finney has emphasized the many ways that narrative texts
can produce the "cuts" or "gaps," the sense of castrating lack, that
"leads the viewer to desire the next shot or sequence, tying him
to the chain of narrative signification" ("Suture" 133). Here
Finney echoes Stephen Heath's concern that we not limit a study
of suture to one narrative device—in the case of film, the
shot/reverse shot formation, in the case of literary narrative,

shifts in focalization? Morrison's novel deploys numerous narrative tactics to produce the cuts and gaps that create the desire
for suture. In fact, her novel is so rife with ruptures in the signifying chain that it foregrounds the very processes of narrative
play and control that it enacts. This is especially the case in the
chapter in which Beloved "speaks the unspeakable," and the
narrative style—"the leaves are not for her she fills the basket
she opens the grass . . ." (259)—reflects the disrupted narrative
that constitutes the novel.

To an extent, such foregrounding would seem to thwart
the suturing process since it potentially exposes the speaking
subject, which in theory must remain hidden. However, in her
analysis of Hitchcock's *Psycho*, Silverman explains that such
foregrounding forces the viewer "into oblique and uncomfortable positions both vis-à-vis the cinematic apparatuses and the
spectacle which they produce" (206). It thus forces the reading
subject into a dual identification with both speaking subject and
spoken subject. This dual, destabilized identification ultimately
produces a greater threat of castration and loss, a greater desire
for a suturing narrative that will produce an internal identificatory gaze. Thus, Silverman concludes that "the whole operation
of suture can be made *more* rather than less irresistible when the
field of the speaking subject is continually implied" (208).

Morrison's narrative may promise the safety of an intense
identification with the textual subjects, but it also continually
works against such "safety" by implicating the reading subject in
the position of the speaking subject—i.e., the master narrative(s).
Morrison has acknowledged her desire to create both a sense of
identification between reading subject and textual subject and a
sense of confusion in the reading subject: "I wanted the compelling confusion of being there as they (the characters) are; suddenly without comfort or succor from the 'author,' with only
imagination, intelligence, and necessity available for the journey" ("Unspeakable Things" 33). The author may remain
masked, unable to provide succor. Yet the reading subject becomes implicated in the practice of narrative play and control, a
practice that has its parallel in the novel's representations of patriarchal culture and its concomitant ideologies and laws.

Morrison's frequent disruptions, cuts, and gaps push conventional narratological mechanisms to their limit. Shifts in focalization, for example, become so complex that a suturing identification becomes nearly impossible. The disjuncture between

proairetic sequence and hermeneutic codes becomes so great that meaning becomes obscured and the horror of specific instances is momentarily obfuscated, only to be revealed later and to produce an increased sense of horror. Such a disjuncture often precipitates a repetition, a rereading of the narrative in order to clarify the meaning. Not only are such narrative processes foregrounded, but in all cases the reading subject's experience with Morrison's narrative has parallels in the characters' experiences with personal or cultural narratives. Morrison manipulates the reading subject's "identification" most explicitly via her novel's shifts in localization, its manipulation of proairetic sequence and hermeneutic codes, and its construction of what Finney calls "temporal defamiliarization." Morrison thus manages to produce a disturbing identification for the reading subject; more importantly, however, she exposes the fact that narrative exists to control and subjugate.

The novel's primary method of producing ruptures in the signifying chain, and the method most closely aligned with cinematic suture, would be its frequent shifts in focalization. Barbara Hill Rigley has suggested that an identifiable narrator seems to disappear in this novel as one character or another steps forward to tell the story from another point of view (37). In fact, according to Rigley, Morrison's text provides various "narrative pictures" that exist as "cinematic clips" (79). Rigley's concept of a contained "narrative picture" necessarily implies a shift between pictures/clips—a shift in identifying gaze. The reading subject shifts into the fictional gaze of Sethe, Denver, Beloved, Stamp Paid, Paul D. Sometimes a "shift" in focalization is mediated by the external narrator (e.g., when we are given the account of Paul D's experience on the chain gang), sometimes the "shift" results in a narrative presented in direct discourse between characters (an embedded narrative—e.g., Sethe telling Paul D why she killed her child), and sometimes the narrative is appropriated by the focalizing agent (e.g., the sections narrated by Sethe, Denver, and Beloved, respectively). Such shifts in localization, whether in or between chapters, necessarily rupture the narrative. Ironically, these shifts can function as the narration required to suture over cuts inflicted by other narrative devices (e.g., when Sethe tells about killing her child, this narration sutures over one of the novel's largest gaps).[4] Therefore, the suturing process itself would seem to produce new gaps that must be repaired.

While the entire narrative, then, seems quite reliant on
shifts in focalization, perhaps the most significant shifts occur in
the final of those four chapters that articulate the "unspeakable
thoughts." In this chapter, it becomes virtually impossible to
identify the focalizing agent. As Rebecca Ferguson suggests, the
narrator's "mediation is withdrawn" (116), and this lack creates
a desire to accept the subject position of the fictional gaze.
Nonetheless, in this particular chapter, the reading subject cannot clearly identify a stable "I" that speaks. The desire to accept
the fictional subject position is both reinforced and frustrated,
and this forces the reading subject to repeat a narrative that is itself reliant on repetition:

> Beloved
> You are my sister
> You are my daughter
> You are my face; you are me . . .
> You are mine
> You are mine
> You are mine   (*Beloved* 266)

In this chapter and the chapter that precedes it, the shifts in focalization become so complicated that they call attention to themselves as a narrative process, and the repetition also foregrounds
itself. The very style of "Beloved's" narrative (i.e., in the third of
these four chapters) is one of gaps ("I am standing in the rain
falling the others are taken I am not taken I am falling like the
rain is . . ." [262]), and thus "Beloved's" narrative voice serves as
a metaphor for the novel's narrative structure.

That this chapter comes fairly late in the novel is not surprising. In many ways, the visible gaps in this chapter make explicit the lack of direct connections evident in much of the text
preceding this section. In fact, gaps in information, the disjuncture between proairetic sequence and hermeneutic codes, (the
latter being defined as "the questions and answers that structure
the story" [Brooks 287]), seem to characterize much of Morrison's
novel.[5] In Morrison's narrative, the reader may recognize that
an event or sequence of events is significant; however, her
reader often lacks the hermeneutic codes—the plot, according to
Brooks—that enable a determination of signification. This is especially true in the first third of Morrison's novel, for as Ferguson has argued, "with the abrupt entry into the house, the reader
is confronted with a network of allusions from which full mean-

ing is withheld, with constant intimations that sinister, even traumatic referents lie beyond them" (112).

And yet, the novel as a whole contains many missing "plots" that must be furnished before meaning can be determined. Consider, for example, Sethe's act of violence, the mystery surrounding what has prevented Halle from seeking out Sethe, the events that have led Paul D to close up the tin box in his chest, Beloved's entire past. Many of these plots take the entire novel to be revealed, many are not revealed, and Morrison's point would seem to be that many cannot be revealed. Still, this missing information is often crucial for understanding the significance of events that occur in the early portions of the text. The novel's opening paragraph, for example, explains that Howard and Buglar have run away, each one fleeing "the moment the house committed what was for him the one insult not to be borne or witnessed a second time" (*Beloved* 3). The narrator provides the specific incident that compels each boy to leave (the shattering of a mirror, tiny handprints in a cake). Since the reader does not yet know that the "baby" is dead (this information is first indicated on page 5), however, the reader cannot fully comprehend why two tiny handprints could signify something dreadful enough to force a child to leave home. Certainly, of course, the indication that the house "committed" something unspeakable produces a strong sense of the sinister and the horrific, even if the specific act committed remains a mystery.

However, by the novel's end, that "one insult" that cannot be "borne or witnessed a second time," multiplies in its significance. The reader eventually learns that Sethe killed her child and learns of Denver's perpetual fear that "the thing that happened that made it all right for my mother to kill my sister could happen again" (252). Given this knowledge, the reading subject can finally understand that the specific incidents merely functioned as signifiers to Howard and Buglar of the "one insult," the ultimate horror that refuses to stay repressed—that, in fact, manifests itself physically to them as a constant reminder of a past that could happen again. The insult that cannot be borne or witnessed a second time is revealed to be slavery, the socially sanctioned oppression from which only another horror, the handsaw, can provide safety. The initial confusion, the unresolved gap in Morrison's narrative, primes the reading subject for a suturing narrative that horrifies rather than reassures. Yet, this is quite typical of Morrison's manipulation of narrative structure and sequence.

One crucial effect of the disjuncture between proairetic sequence and hermeneutic codes is the concomitant disjuncture it produces between "benign" and horrific images. In the novel's initial pages, long before the reader has any clear knowledge of the horrors perpetrated at Sweet Home, Sethe chides herself for only remembering the beauty of Sweet Home. Sethe thinks of the "boys hanging from the most beautiful sycamores in the world. It shamed her—remembering the wonderful soughing trees rather than the boys. Try as she might to make it otherwise, the sycamores beat out the children every time . . ." (7). The narrative repeatedly indicates Sethe's shame at not being able to see beyond the "benign" trees. At this point, however, the reader has none of the ensuing plot that provides the necessary context in which boys hanging from trees signifies slaves being executed. The horrific significance of "boys hanging from the most beautiful sycamores" is initially obscured by the potentially "benign" image of children playing in trees.

Similarly when Sethe "spends" ten minutes to "purchase" the word "Beloved" on her daughter's tombstone, the "benign" is almost immediately stripped away to reveal the horrific truth of what occurred. When the engraver tells Sethe, "You got ten minutes I'll do it for free" (5), one can reasonably assume that he is making a generous offer: if you can wait ten minutes, I'll engrave your daughter's name for free. In the very next paragraph, however, the narrator disrupts this meaning by conveying Sethe's concern that if she had offered "twenty minutes, a half hour, say, she could have had the whole thing" (7). Even then, the complete significance of the situation remains hidden. It is not until the narrative describes her "rutting among the headstones with the engraver" that the reader sees the horrific truth behind the "benign" initial image. It may sound here as if I am assuming a rather naive reader, and to some degree I am. This incident occurs on page 5, just after the reader has been thrust into this "unknown" world. In short, Morrison manipulates the reader's "innocence," an innocence that she will later expose as resistance and/or willful blindness. Such moments constitute cultural unspeakables that strive to remain hidden despite the cultural history one might bring to the text.

Still, the most intriguing effect of this narrative's split between proairetic sequence and hermeneutic codes is its imposed repetition—i.e., the reading subject must frequently repeat immediate passages or entire prior sections of the novel in order to be sure of meaning. Brooks has suggested that "narrative always makes the implicit claim to be in a state of repetition, as a going over again of a ground already covered" (97). Brooks grounds this claim in Freudian theory, suggesting that repetition is thus "the movement from passivity to mastery," the attempt to go over the same ground as a means of asserting some sort of control over an imposed ending (which under Freudian theory would necessarily be linked to death) (98). In Morrison's text, the compulsion to repeat as a means of gaining mastery suggests a connection between reading subject and textual subject—both are offered a promise of agency/mastery, yet this is a promise left relatively unfulfilled. Also, it is not insignificant that mastering one's ending is equated with death. For Sethe, taking a position of mastery meant the death of her child who, not surprisingly, returns from beyond, much as the repressed must return.

Brooks describes the "compulsion to repeat" as "the work of the unconscious repressed" (99). He explains that in analysis the compulsion to repeat gives patients a sense of being pursued "by a demonic power," and Brooks immediately equates this demonic feeling with what one experiences when reading the literature of the uncanny—"texts of compulsive recurrence" (99). Michel De Certeau has described the "return of the repressed," the "uncanny" impulse to repeat a repressed past, as cannibalistic—"the past: it 're-bites' [il remord] (it is a secret and repeated biting)" (3). De Certeau's comment seems especially relevant to a narrative in which one character "feeds" stories of her past to another, yet is consumed in the process. While the reading subject's experience of the compulsion to repeat clearly differs in degree from the textual subjects' compulsion to repeat—and while it is hardly the same type of repressed "past" that is repeated— Morrison's narrative does compel an unpleasant and uncomfortable need for repetition. The reader must to some degree consume and re-consume this text, a fact that has a striking parallel in Beloved's obsessive devouring of Sethe's stories. Beloved grows fat on Sethe's stories and one must wonder whether this reflects a monstrous consumption or a gap so large it cannot be fulfilled; it can only produce more desire and thus require more repetition.

Brooks's reading of Freud suggests both a certain displeasure in being forced to repeat and the necessity of repetition not only to attain the "mastery" of one's ending (illusory as the mas-

tery must be), but also as a means of remembering, especially
"when recollection properly speaking is blocked by resistance"
(98). In Morrison's novel, the profusion of gaps and undecipherable information at the novel's beginning can construct an
effective resistance to "recollection." I am clearly manipulating
the meaning of Brooks's (Freud's) terms here. Nonetheless,
what I hope to suggest is that this narrative imposes the need for
repeated readings. In some cases, an imposed repetition can occur within the span of a few paragraphs. For example, the narrative describes Paul D's experience on the chain gang, the prisoners "kneeling in the mist [as] they waited for the whim of a
guard, or two, or three. Or maybe all of them wanted it"
(*Beloved* 132). The "it" is a gap not clearly defined. The narrative next presents a dialogue in which the guards ask the prisoners if they want breakfast to which the prisoners reply, "Yes, sir."
Then the narrative declares, "Occasionally a kneeling man chose
gunshot in his head as the price, maybe, of taking a bit of fore-
skin with him to Jesus" (132). This extremely jarring sentence
ultimately forces the reading subject to back up and reassess the
proairetic sequence of events s/he has just read to confirm the
meaning that is implied by that sentence (i.e., that the guards are
sodomizing the prisoners). By doing so, the reader recognizes
the perverse double entendre of the guards' words when they
ask the prisoners if they want breakfast. The narrative is structured in such a way that the reader *must* return and repeat the
passage to confirm meaning, perhaps because the narrative itself,
through its vague allusions, sets up a resistance to the actual
meaning. Nonetheless, in moments like this Morrison manipulates her implied reader's[6] own resistance, her/his "desire" to
construct a reading of "breakfast" that denies the message implied by prisoners kneeling before guards who want "it." At
moment's like this, Morrison exposes "innocence" as "resistance" or willful blindness.

It would seem, then, that such an imposed need to repeat
could function as another method of producing lack, since the
need to repeat necessarily signifies that "mastery" over the ending (plenitude, fulfillment) has not yet been achieved. More
importantly, however, the narrative again places the reading
subject in a position that parallels that of the textual subjects.
The reader knows, for example, that when Sethe tells the story of
Denver's birth, it is a story that has been told often—it is the part
of Sethe's story that Denver liked best (37). The novel details the

characters' desire to resist remembering, to resist repeating the story of their lives. Sethe claims that "the future was a matter of keeping the past at bay" (52), and Paul D refers to the tobacco tin in his heart in which he has closed off his memories. Nonetheless, the novel exposes the difficulty of maintaining such repression. After Paul D relates his knowledge of what happened to Halle, he says, "I didn't plan on telling you that," to which Sethe replies, "I didn't plan on hearing it" (87). These characters are compelled to repeat, to bypass their own resistance and confront the displeasure inherent in such involuntary repetition.

Henderson has effectively argued that the "return of the repressed" is a theme that preoccupies Morrison's text (74). Citing De Certeau's claim that "if the past . . . is *repressed*, it *returns* in the present from which it was excluded . . . ,"[7] she explains that the "figuration of the 'detour-return,' and its consequences in the lives of individual characters as well as the community as a whole, structures Morrison's novel" (74). For Henderson, then, Beloved represents the ultimate site of the return of the repressed—she figures as everything from Sethe's personal past to Denver's fears of an unknown past to the history of slavery. As I shall discuss shortly, Beloved, as monstrous fusion of past in present, is a wound that must be sutured over. Sethe attempts this repair through a compulsive repetition of her past. Morrison's narrative thus establishes an effective identificatory parallel between the reading subject's need to bypass resistance and repeat in order to make meaning and the textual subject's need to suture over wounds by repeating a repressed past.

The novel's concern with repeated pasts has obvious and important connections to the question of history, and specifically the history of slavery. The history of slavery is, paradoxically, the greatest spoken and the greatest unspoken of this text. Certainly, the figure of Beloved seems to represent the horrors of slavery, a horrific past that, if repressed, always threatens to return. Nonetheless, the novel's concern with repeated pasts and its manipulation of what Finney terms "temporal defamiliarization" speak to the vexed issue of repeating a past, either personal or cultural.

Finney explains that in this novel, "the distance between what the Russian Formalist called the *fabula* (the chronological ordering of events) and the *syuzhet* (the order in which events are actually presented in the narrative) . . . is about as great as can be tolerated by most modern readers" ("Temporal" 21). Finney offers a painstakingly detailed account of the chronology of events in the novel (the fabula), but explains that "as readers, we piece together the *fabula* from a *syuzhet* that coils about itself" (24). The novel's syuzhet repeats events from the fabula over and over again because, he argues, "the past is placed at the disposal of the present" (24).

Morrison's narrative stretches the gap between fabula and syuzhet to its limit, effectively producing a temporal defamiliarization, at once effacing distinctions between past and present (an implicitly ominous move since this would make manifest Denver's fear that the circumstances of the past can occur yet again) and insisting that we make sense of the gap between past and present. In short, when the past intrudes in the present in the form of narrated memory, it functions to suture over the lack that has been constructed by the repression of these past events. Morrison again enacts through her narrative practice what she depicts in her representations. The interplay of fabula and syuzhet establishes a temporal defamiliarization that parallels for the reading subject the sense of loss experienced by the textual subject. The textual subjects' pasts are kept at bay, creating desire in the reading subject for narrations of these pasts that can enable the construction of meaning, and that can be brought into the present to satisfy both the reading and textual subject's desire for plenitude.

Nonetheless, for the textual subjects, the reinscription of past in the present potentially horrifies and threatens; thus, the narrative depicts Sethe's attack on Bodwin when she sees him heading toward her house. Afraid that the past is in the process of repeating itself (that schoolteacher has yet again come to take "her best thing"), Sethe lashes out against Bodwin, the current representative of her oppressive past. But it is only after confronting this fear that Sethe can begin to heal. Morrison suggests that confronting the repressed past is both horrifying and necessary, and the implication of Morrison's novel is that for wounds to heal they must often be reopened, or at least reexamined, otherwise one risks forgetting one's history, falling into complacency, and abdicating whatever agency one might have gained. The inherent threat of suturing over wounds, then, is that it will somehow contain the horror associated with such wounds.

Morrison's foregrounding of narrative practice manipulates the reading subject's displeasure and produces a coercive identification with the process of narrative control; however, by implicating the reader in the suturing process while also constantly disrupting this process, Morrison's narrative forces the reading subject to experience the vexed status of narration. Narrating over wounds, retelling the past, is both necessary and horrifying. The text establishes a parallel between the reading subject's desire to suture over the many narrative discontinuities and the spoken subject's *need* to suture over both the physical and psychological wounds inflicted by the master narratives of white patriarchal culture—that which figures in this text as the most powerful and oppressive speaking subject. For these textual subjects, the need to suture is directly produced by their *lack* of power to "narrate," by their disempowered position vis-à-vis language, culture, and control of subjectivity. Thus, while the reading subject is drawn into a strong identification with these characters striving to suture over their own wounds, the reading subject is continually implicated in the position of the speaking subject, in the threat of the dominant, controlling narrative. Such a dual perspective allows (forces) Morrison's reader to more dramatically experience the pain and horror of the wounds that her characters experience and strive to heal.

Perhaps the most explicit physical wound that a character sutures over is the "tree" on Sethe's back—the "tree" that becomes a metaphor providing Sethe with comfort, but that potentially functions to contain the horror of the abuse inflicted on Sethe's body. When Sethe first mentions the tree on her back, she describes it to Paul D and explains that a white girl called "it" a tree. Once again, the narrative does not immediately explain what the "it" might be. Paul D remains in a similar state of confusion as Sethe goes on describing the chokecherry tree on her back, a tree she has never even seen (19). Sethe then narrates the incident when schoolteacher's boys took her milk. She explains that she told Mrs. Garner about the incident, the boys discovered that she told and then they beat her, inflicting the physical wound that became the chokecherry tree. According to Henderson, the scars from the beating "function as signs of ownership inscribing her as property, while the mutilation signifies her diminishment to a less than human status" (68). Schoolteacher, as representative of white patriarchal culture and thus as speaking subject, literally writes Sethe by writing her body.[8] In this first mention of the tree, it comes to signify a wound that must be explained and that thus forces Sethe to repeat a narrative from her past, a painful memory that, like all of her past, she would prefer to keep at bay. Nonetheless, the symbolic referent "tree" itself functions as a form of narrative that sutures over the physical wound.

I mentioned earlier that the disjuncture between proairetic and hermeneutic codes in Morrison's narrative often results in a seemingly benign image obscuring a darker truth. To an extent, Sethe's tree metaphor functions in the same way. When Sethe narrates the moment in which the white girl (Amy) first faces Sethe's wound, her descriptions detail Amy's attempt to suture over the horror of that wound with benign imagery. When Amy first sees Sethe's back she exclaims, "Come here, Jesus," and Sethe reasons that what Amy saw must be bad because "after that call to Jesus Amy didn't speak for a while" (*Beloved* 97). When Amy finally does speak, she offers a detailed description of Sethe's wound, a description that strives to cover over the horror, but that cannot quite do so:

> 'It's a tree, Lu. A chokecherry tree. See, here's the trunk—it's red and split wide open, full of sap, and this here's the parting of the branches. You gotta mighty lot of branches. Leaves, too, look like, and dern if these ain't blossoms. Tiny little cherry blossoms, just as white.'   (97)

Amy's metaphor comes off as more gruesome than comforting. Details like "full of sap" and "a mighty lot of branches" would indicate health, fertility and lushness if they were used to describe an actual tree. Here, however, each detail merely illuminates the extent of the damage inflicted on Sethe's body. Sap and cherry blossoms do not cover over, but instead emphasize, the body's process of healing, the blood and pus and the initial scarring taking place. Morrison lays bare, here, narrative's ability to obscure.

Sethe clings to the tree metaphor much as she clings to her memory of the "soughing sycamores" that block out the hanging slaves. Just as Amy "needed" to transform the horror before her eyes into a "natural" and more benign image, Sethe receives comfort in having mentally transcribed this physical wound into an image of strength and beauty. At the same time, Morrison implies that there is danger in such an act, for Sethe's metaphor in many ways obscures and contains the emotional and psychological wound that her physical wound signifies—namely, the abuse of her body when the boys forced her down and took her milk and the lack of personal agency, the lack of control over one's own body and definition of self, that this abuse signifies.

Paul D's reaction to Sethe's "tree" is worth noting. He can only see a "revolting clump of scars" (26). Paul D might admit that it has the shape of a tree, but it is "nothing like any tree he knew because trees were inviting; things you could trust and be near; talk to if you wanted to as he frequently did since way back . . ." (26).[9] Of course, Paul D's reaction to Sethe's tree is informed by his own conception of what a tree should be, and this conception is informed by his attempts to heal a personal psychological wound, a rupture in his sense of self as "man." The narrative immediately connects Paul D's inability to perceive Sethe's wound as a tree with his own anxiety about his manhood. And, of course, as Paul D alone knows, Sethe's abuse is directly connected to Halle's loss of manhood. After describing many of Sixo's accomplishments, Paul D explains "Now *there* was a man, and *that* was a tree. Himself lying in the bed and the 'tree' lying next to him didn't compare" (27). To an extent, Paul D cannot accept Sethe's wound as a tree because he associates "tree" with masculinity—it is strong and enduring like Sixo; the tree is a companion whom Paul D identifies as Brother, again emphasizing that for Paul D the tree signifies masculinity, or at least one definition of masculinity.

Paul D's struggle with conceptions of "manhood" reflects the struggle to suture over a psychological wound. According to Deborah Ayer Sitter, "Morrison dramatizes Paul D's enslavement to an ideal of manhood that distorts his images of self and others" (18). Morrison represents Paul D's need to negotiate various definitions of manhood: as Sitter suggests, the western ideals manifested in the ideology of Mr. Garner and schoolteacher, and the African ideals embodied in Sixo (21, 23), but also what it means to be a man as opposed to a commodity, what it means to be a man as opposed to an animal.

Paul D frequently questions the definition of manhood that he learned from Garner, and most especially when his experience threatens this definition. Paul D "grew up thinking that, of all the Blacks in Kentucky, only the [Sweet Home men] were men" (*Beloved* 154). But he immediately questions this notion, demanding whether manhood rests in possessing, purchasing, inventing, or whether it resides "in the naming done by a whiteman who was supposed to know" (154). Significantly, this entire questioning process takes place as Paul D ponders his removal from 124. Paul D's only strength was in "knowing that schoolteacher was wrong" (155) and that Garner was right, in knowing that he was not a "gelded workhorse" or a "rag doll," not an animal or object. Nonetheless, Paul D equates his "being moved" by Beloved with an affirmation of schoolteacher's definition of Paul D as not-man. Beloved's power over Paul D effectively emasculates him, placing him in a passive position, and his immediate response is to "document his manhood and break out of the girl's spell" by impregnating Sethe (156). We can see here that, as Sitter claims, "the qualities that Paul D associates with manliness originate in the dominant culture of the white slaveholder" (Sitter 24). Paul's attempt to reassert his masculinity necessitates a literal wielding of the phallus.

It should not be surprising that the threat of emasculation is represented as so horrifying. The theory of suture is predicated upon a displeasure associated with lack and with the threat of symbolic castration. Paul D's investment in patriarchal definitions of masculinity would necessitate his horror at having his (male) agency stripped away. Morrison's text suggests, however, that a return to normative/dominant ideological definitions of masculinity will not suffice. As Paul D pieces his story together, Morrison's narrative dramatizes the fabricated nature of Western constructions. Though he had long "believed schoolteacher broke into children what Garner had raised into men," he comes to question whether Garner was "naming what he saw or creating what he did not" (*Beloved* 271), whether a whiteman saying it made it so. He wonders what he would have been "in Sixo's country, or his mother's" (271). Implicit in this questioning is the recognition that such definitions are constructions, the manifestations of power.

By the novel's end, Paul D's conception of manhood has radically changed. It is not surprising that, just after Paul D articulates a new conception of manhood, he "wants to put his story next to [Sethe's]" (335). It has been through the process of placing his story next to hers, of listening to her story, sharing his own, and sharing in their story that he has been able to suture over the wounds inflicted by Garner, schoolteacher, and white patriarchal culture. Paul D's process has been one of negotiating cultural narratives—master narratives—and learning to construct his own, to construct a position of potential agency in a world in which freedom from schoolteacher does not mean freedom from a Master.

Paul D's struggle to construct a subject position vis-à-vis masculinity is perhaps an encapsulated reflection of Sethe's negotiation of a subject position vis-à-vis the cultural definitions of both motherhood and womanhood. (Of course, Paul D's stakes are clearly different from Sethe's, given his more privileged position vis-à-vis culturally sanctioned gender hierarchies.) David Lawrence has argued that, "whites 'spoke' on their slaves tirelessly, and, in the exploration of political power in the novel, ownership of body and authorship of language are shown to be insidiously linked," and thus "authority over one's own body is consistently related to . . . authority over discourse" (190). Thus we should not find it surprising that healing the wounds of slavery requires narration and specifically a set of narrations that reconfigure definitions of manhood, womanhood, African, etc. Morrison represents this task as difficult, if not impossible, and certainly continual. At the same time, Morrison exposes the patriarchal basis of such narratives and definitions. Finding a space in which to reconfigure such narratives requires a retreat into the domestic space (Sethe, Denver) or a retreat from patriarchal authority (Paul D). In all cases, the controlling figure is signified not just by race, but also by gender. The master, speaker of master narratives and controller of subjectivity, is clearly the idealized representative of patriarchy. Resisting or defying this "master" is difficult precisely because the only means available still requires narrative, a system that both heals and oppresses, a process that seems inextricably bound up in patriarchy.

By examining the figure of Beloved, we can see Morrison's insistence that the drive to redefine and reconstitute subjectivity may have its necessary place, but the inherent danger in suturing over painful wounds is a containment of horror and what that horror signifies. The figure of Beloved represents an absence present in the lives of these characters. She is an unknown that must be made known, and thus these characters strive to narrate her into meaning. For Sethe, Beloved begins as a "real" woman. Sethe tells Denver that "she believed Beloved had been locked up by some whiteman for his own purposes, and never let out the door" (*Beloved* 146). Only after Sethe has articulated the painful memory of killing her daughter does she come to believe that Beloved is that daughter resurrected.

To some degree, Sethe seems to speak Beloved into existence. In Sethe's first person narrative in part 2, she narrates

Beloved into the figure that she needs her to be. In a most telling moment, Sethe "reads"—and effectively "writes"—the wounds on Beloved's forehead as her own fingerprints, placed there when she held her daughter's head down to kill her. Of course, Morrison again demonstrates a literal example of narrating over a wound. Sethe's shift from viewing Beloved as other human woman to viewing Beloved as reincarnated daughter results from Sethe having recently opened the wound of her past by telling Paul D how she "saved" her daughter. From this point on, Sethe spends her time feeding Beloved stories in order, as Denver suggests, to make up for the handsaw. The past is a horror that devours if it returns. Still, Morrison's novel also implicitly asks what would/will happen if the past did/does not return? Can one realistically expect this past to stay repressed? Should one desire such repression?

From Beloved's first appearance, however, Denver has read Beloved as her dead sister come back to life. As soon as Paul D removes the ghost from the house, Denver sees a vision of a woman in a white dress helping her mother (36). Thus, when Sethe offers her initial explanation for Beloved, Denver rejects it for "she was certain that Beloved was the white dress that had knelt with her mother in the keeping room, the true-to-life presence of the baby that had kept her company most of her life" (147). Beloved, as both ghost and reincarnated daughter, satisfies Denver's own psychological wound, her desperate "need to love another" (128).

Though Beloved figures as ghost-made-flesh for Sethe, Denver, Ella, and the other women of the community, the novel also offers ample indications that Sethe's first "speculation" may be correct. Stamp Paid explains that "there was a girl locked up in the house with a whiteman over by Deer Creek. Found him dead last summer and the girl gone. Maybe that's her. Folks say he had her in there since she was a pup" (289). Since we know that Beloved arrived at 124 near the end of summer, this scenario would make sense. And, as Elizabeth House suggests, "this possibility would explain Beloved's 'new' skin, her unlined feet and hands" (20), and it would account for her apparent "lack" of memory concerning life prior to her appearance on the bridge, for her desperate need for Sethe, and for her often incongruent blend of childlike need and sexual sophistication. The idea that Beloved is an actual woman also correlates with much of Beloved's self-articulated experience. Though Beloved constantly confirms that she was "on the other side," that other side need not be read, as Sethe and Denver do, as death. Instead, it can be read as slavery, as the boat that brought her to America, or as Africa.

Information throughout the novel supports both possible explanations for Beloved. The narrative describes Beloved's concern that her tooth falling out foreshadows a future in which she will literally fly apart, and it is difficult not to read this as indicative of her supernatural condition (*Beloved* 164). This possibility seems to be reinforced by her disappearance at the novel's end: "First they saw it and then they didn't" (328). Beloved's insatiable hunger and her dramatic increase in size may seem supernatural effects; however, she might have been impregnated by the white man before she escaped—or by Paul D. Also, the description of her "supernatural" power over Paul D and his sex drive figures Beloved as a form of succubus—"Each time she came, pulled up her skirts, a life hunger overwhelmed him and he had no more control over it than over his lungs" (324). Of course, this power may very well be Paul D's projection onto Beloved of his own desire, Paul D's abdication of responsibility for controlling his sexual drives. In any case, Morrison configures Beloved as a monstrosity, yet a monstrosity directly linked to the horrific effects of slavery.

I would also note here that Beloved figures as what Drucilla Cornell has termed a "wild woman," a figure that is simultaneously absence and presence, and that is generally perceived as devouring. This woman cannot really be seen because she is everywhere yet nowhere, an embodiment of all that woman cannot be (Cornell). Clearly, then part of her monstrosity rests in her threat to definitions of sexual difference and, concomitantly, to patriarchal hierarchies. To know this woman is to destroy her, and this is essentially what happens to Beloved in the end. In the coda Morrison offers a description of Beloved that matches Cornell's wild woman:

> Everybody knew what she was called, but nobody anywhere knew her name. Disremembered and unaccounted for, she cannot be lost because no one is looking for her, and even if they were, how can they call her if they don't know her name? Although she has claim, she is not claimed.   (*Beloved* 336)

In the case of Beloved, the "wild woman's" absence as presence is figured, significantly, in linguistic terms—she is not named, or called. Nonetheless, the narrative also implies that she is everywhere and nowhere, unable to be seen even if she is sought after. Yet, if Beloved is a "wild woman," this may be in part because, having either been locked in a house for many years or struck down in childhood, she has not been narrated into patriarchal culture. She remains a blank, an unknown whose very existence defies the known and threatens to expose the "known's" fabricated status. She is more horrifying than the emasculated male or the appropriated phallus, and this is precisely because her strength rests in her ability to resist narration. She cannot be narrated *in* to culture; thus she must be narrated over, contained and forgotten.

As a result, Morrison's characters strive to narrate her and do so in accordance with their own needs. Not surprisingly, critics of the novel have done the same thing, striving to construct a definitive meaning for the Beloved character.[10] Beloved figures then as a wound that demands repair, yet as a wound that cannot be repaired. Whether she is the ghost of Sethe's dead daughter—killed as the direct effect of slavery—or an actual slave whose experience is too horrific to return from the repressed in any coherent form, Beloved signifies the horrors of slavery, horrors that must be repressed and rendered "unknown" for they inherently threaten the stability and "safety" of the "known."

Ultimately, however, Beloved's status as ghost or human is less significant than her status as neither and both. If *Beloved* is not a story to pass on, this is perhaps because to pass the story on is to contain the story. In the novel's coda, Morrison equates Beloved with the "loneliness that roams," that "is alive, on its own" (336), and she explains that the characters "forgot her like a bad dream. After they made up their tales, shaped and decorated them, those that saw her that day on the porch quickly and deliberately forgot her" (336). Morrison explicitly represents the suturing process as these characters suture over the loneliness with stories that contain and then repress the pain and horror of what Beloved signifies. And yet, despite the refrain that Beloved was and is not a story to pass on, Morrison's novel, by its very existence, insists that Beloved is a story that cannot be contained, that ultimately must be passed on, and that should not be forgotten. As Henderson suggests, "for Morrison, the absent (like the Historical) is only the 'other' of the present—just as the repressed is only the 'other' of the conscious" (83). Despite personal, communal, national attempts to contain the history of slavery, despite attempts to repress the horror of the past, it will return; the unspoken will be spoken.

It is hardly surprising to find that Morrison's novel constructs paradoxical messages. While the process of suturing over wounds is beneficial, even necessary if these characters are to "reconstruct" their subject positions and construct a position of agency in a culture that specifically denies them such agency, to engage in such a process is to potentially contain and repress (or re-repress) the horror and the horrific implications of the wounds themselves. Nonetheless, Morrison does not merely reveal the inherent dangers of containing past horrors. Because her narrative practice establishes a dual identification in the reading subject, the reading subject's experience parallels that of the textual subject striving to construct a position of agency; and at the same time, the reading subject becomes identified with the position of the "master" narratives, with the speaking subject that controls the processes of subject formation, of subjection. This disjuncture, this dual identification, is, much like Beloved, a wound that cannot be effectively healed or contained; thus Morrison's narrative perpetuates and manipulates the reading subject's displeasure while it exposes the cultural power dynamics that require and reinscribe repression, power dynamics that insist the unspeakable remain unspoken.

Morrison's novel manipulates monstrosity, exposing the cultural conditions from which a monstrous figure like Beloved comes to exist. At the same time, Morrison's text demonizes the very processes of cultural narration, the hierarchies of patriarchal culture perpetuated by narratives of gender, race, and power, and the systems that maintain sanctioned oppression by controlling and containing history, by determining what can and cannot be said. If, as Owens argues, "the postmodernist work attempts to upset the reassuring stability of [the] mastering position" (334), then Morrison's text certainly seems engaged in a postmodern narrative practice. Morrison constructs a narrative that is highly complicit with what it seeks to challenge. Her narrative dismantles the safety of the narrative space, but does so by offering the promise of such safety. While her text demonizes the processes of narrative control and subjection, it also demonstrates a sophisticated employment of narrative control. Morrison's text also prohibits the reader from placing him/herself outside the text. The reading subject cannot escape the mon-

strous narrative that seeks to draw the reader into its disturbing
world of ruptures and ambiguities. Significantly, however, the
reader finds this experience mirrored in the experience of the
novel' s characters who find they cannot really escape the processes of cultural inscription. They can, at best, struggle against
such processes and renegotiate definitions of self. To retreat into
a false safety, such as the house at 124, is perhaps even more
threatening than confronting the horror of an oppressive culture. Morrison thereby demonstrates that the unspeakable poses
profound challenges to the spoken, and she advocates embracing
the space of the unknown as a site of contest within the known.

Notes

[1] See Finney, "Temporal Defamiliarization," 22; Ferguson, "History,
Memory and Language," 111.

[2] Finney explains that according to Lacanian theory, "the subject is
bound to its discourse by its need to suture over gaps constantly opening up between it and its representation in discourse" ("Suture in Literary Analysis"
131).

[3] Heath argues that "lack" can be produced by numerous cinematic narrative devices—e.g., camera movement, movement within frame, off-screen
sound and framing (66), and Finney uses this as a basis for complicating the few
critical forays into the study of suture in literary narrative, most of which rely
on the premise that shifting focalization parallels the shot/reverse shot formation.

[4] In fact, this narrative sutures over what Andrew Levy posits as the
text's primary gap or "unspeakable" (114).

[5] Peter Brooks uses two of Barthes's five codes of narrative (as detailed
in *S/Z*) to establish his definition of "plot." Brooks sees plot as existing "in
some combination of Barthes's two irreversible codes . . . the *proairetic* and the
hermeneutic, that is: the codes of actions ("Voice of the Empirical") and the
code of enigmas and answer ("Voice of Truth") (18). For Brooks, then, plot can
be defined as the "'overcoding' of the proairetic by the hermeneutic, the latter
structuring the discrete elements of the former into larger interpretive wholes,
working our their play of meaning and significance" (18).

[6] In an extension of Harold Bloom's analysis, Seymour Chatman defines
the *implied reader* as a parallel construct to the *implied author*. Both mediate
the exchange between author and reader. The implied author is the narrative
construct "in the text, which invents it [the text] upon each reading," while the
implied reader is the construct "outside the text, which construes it upon each
reading" (76).

[7] See De Certeau.

[8] This writing of Sethe's body has its parallel in her milk being used for
the ink that schoolteacher uses to define her human and animal characteris-

tics. Henderson describes this writing of the body as a perverse fulfillment of Cixous's call for 'ecriture feminine'" (71).

[9] Henderson suggests that "the distance between these suggestively gendered readings . . . signifies the distance between the so-called 'natural' and culturally inscribed meanings attributed to the sign" (69).

[10] Beloved as ghost and representative of the unspeakable—Lawrence; Beloved as ghost and representative of a collectivity of African women— Deborah Horvitz; Beloved as actual African woman read by the characters as a ghost and representative of the individual slave history that strives to be told—Elizabeth House; and Beloved as both ghost and human, caught between two worlds and thus as absence in presence—Ferguson.

Works Cited

Brooks, Peter. *Reading for the Plot: Design and Intention in Narrative.* New York: Vintage Books, 1984.

Chatman, Seymour. *Coming to Terms: The Rhetoric of Narrative in Fiction and Film.* Ithaca: Cornell University Press, 1990.

Cornell, Drucilla. "Beyond Traditional Isms? Passing as a Liberal." American Literature Section. MLA Convention. New York, 28 December 1992.

De Certeau, Michel. *Heterologies; Discourse on the Other. Theory and History of Literature.* Vol. 17. Minneapolis: University of Minnesota Press, 1996.

Ferguson, Rebecca. "History, Memory and Language in Toni Morrison's *Beloved." Feminist Criticism: Theory and Practice.* Ed. Susan Sellers, Linda Hutcheon and Paul Perron. Toronto: University of Toronto Press, 1991. 109-127.

Finney, Brian. "Suture in Literary Analysis." *LIT: Literature, Interpretation, Theory* 2 (1990): 131-144.

—. "Temporal Defamiliarization in Toni Morrison's *Beloved." Obsidian II: Black Literature in Review* 5 (1990): 20-36.

Heath, Stephen. "Notes on Suture." *Screen* 18.4 (1977-1978): 48-76.

Henderson, Mae. "Toni Morrison's *Beloved*: Re-Membering the Body as Historical Text," *Comparative American Identities: Race, Sex and Nationality in the Modern Text.* Ed. Hortense Spillers. New York: Routledge, 1991. 63-86.

Horvitz, Deborah. "Nameless Ghosts: Possession and Dispossession in *Beloved." Studies in American Fiction* 17 (1989): 157-167.

House, Elizabeth. "Toni Morrison's Ghost: The Beloved who is not Beloved." *Studies in American Fiction* 18 (1990): 17-26.

Lawrence, David. "Fleshly Ghosts and Ghostly Flesh: The Word and the Body in *Beloved." Studies in American Fiction* 19 (1991): 189-201.

Levy, Andrew. "Telling *Beloved." Texas Studies in Language and Literature* 33 (1991): 114-123.

Morrison, Toni. *Beloved.* New York: Signet, 1991.

—. "Unspeakable Things Unspoken: The Afro-American Presence in American Literature." *Michigan Quarterly Review* 28.1 (1989): 1-34.

Owens, Craig. "The Discourse of Others." *The Post-modern Reader*. Ed. Charles Jencks. London: Academy Editions, 1992. 333-349.

Rigley, Barbara Hill. *The Voices of Toni Morrison*. Columbus: Ohio State University Press, 1991.

Silverman, Kaja. *The Subject of Semiotics*. New York: Oxford University Press, 1983.

Sitter, Deborah Ayer. "The Making of a Man: Dialogic Meaning in *Beloved*." *African American Review* 26 (1992): 17-29.

Giving Body to the Word:
The Maternal Symbolic
in
Toni Morrison's *Beloved*

Jean Wyatt

In *Beloved* Toni Morrison puts into words three orders of experience that Western cultural narratives usually leave out: childbirth and nursing from a mother's perspective; the desires of a preverbal infant; and the sufferings of those destroyed by slavery, including the Africans who died on the slave ships. The project of incorporating into a text subjects previously excluded from language causes a breakdown and restructuring of linguistic forms; to make room for the articulation of alternative desires, Morrison's textual practice flouts basic rules of normative discourse.

Through the device of the ghost story, Morrison gives a voice to the preverbal infant killed by a mother desperate to save her child from slavery: the dead baby, Beloved, comes back in the body of a nineteen-year-old, able to articulate infantile feelings that ordinarily remain unspoken. Her desire to regain the maternal closeness of a nursing baby powers a dialogue that fuses pronoun positions and abolishes punctuation, undoing all the marks of separation that usually stabilize language. Beloved also has a collective identity: she represents a whole lineage of people obliterated by slavery, beginning with the Africans who died on the Middle Passage, the "Sixty Million and more" of the novel's epigraph. She describes conditions on the slave ships in fragmented images without connective syntax or punctuation, capturing the loss of demarcation and differentiation of those caught in an "oceanic" space between cultural identities, between

Africa and an unknown destination (Spillers 72).

The mother figure, Sethe, defines herself as a maternal body. Her insistence on her own physical presence and connection to her children precludes an easy acceptance of the separations and substitutions that govern language: she will not, for example, use signifiers to represent her nursing baby, so she cannot tell the story of the baby's murder. The novel's discourse also tends to resist substitution, "the very law of metaphoric operation" (Rose 38): when the narrative focuses on either the maternal body or the haunted house, metaphors abandon their symbolic dimension to adhere to a baseline of literal meaning. For instance, a figure of speech in which *weight* usually means "responsibility" turns out to describe only the physical weight of Sethe's breasts (18). A similar "literalization" of spatial metaphors mimics the materializations in the haunted house: the phrase "she moved him" indicates not that Beloved stirred Paul D's emotions but that she physically moved him, from one location to another (114).[1] The continual shift from the abstract to the concrete creates the illusion of words sliding back to a base in the material world, an effect congruent with Morrison's emphasis on embodiment—on both the physical processes of maternity and the concrete presence of the ghost: "Usually [slavery] is an abstract concept. . . . The purpose of making [the ghost] real is making history possible, making memory real—somebody walks in the door and sits down at the table, so you have to think about it" (qtd. in Darling 6).

Describing a child's entry into language as a move from maternal bodily connection to a register of abstract signifiers, Lacan inadvertently sums up the psychological prerequisites for belonging to a patriarchal symbolic order. I invoke his paradigm to point out Morrison's deviations from dominant language practices and from the psychological premises that underlie them; I use the term *maternal symbolic* to discuss not only an alternative language incorporating maternal and material values but also a system that, like Lacan's symbolic, locates subjects in relation to other subjects. While Sethe operates within her own "maternal symbolic" of presence and connection, it is Denver, Sethe's surviving daughter, who in the end finds a more inclusive replacement for Lacan's paternal symbolic: a social order that conflates oral and verbal pleasures, nurtures her with words, and teaches her that caring is "what language was made for" (252).[2]

The Maternal Body in Language:
A Discourse of Presence

The mother figure of *Beloved* occupies a contradictory position in discourse. On the one hand, Sethe's self-definition as maternal body enables Morrison to construct a new narrative form—a specifically female quest powered by the desire to get one's milk to one's baby—that features childbirth as high adventure. On the other hand, this same self-definition forecloses Sethe's full participation in language.

In presenting Sethe's journey from slavery in Kentucky to the free state of Ohio as a maternal quest, Morrison is elaborating the figure of the heroic slave mother that in many female slave narratives replaces the figure of the heroic male fugitive. Harriet Jacobs's *Incidents in the Life of a Slave Girl*, for example, turns the rhetoric of heroic resolve common to male slave narratives into a text of courage drawn from a mother's love for her children: "I was resolved that I would foil my master and save my children, or I would perish in the attempt"; "Every trial I endured, every sacrifice I made for [the children's] sakes, drew them closer to my heart, and gave me fresh courage" (84, 89-90). If Jacobs (and other female slave narrators, like Lucy Delaney) appropriates the conventions of male heroism for the celebration of motherhood,[3] Morrison in turn reconstructs the acts of maternal heroism as the reproductive feats of the maternal body. Both Sethe and Jacobs find the courage to escape because they want their children to be free—"It was more for my helpless children than for myself that I longed for freedom," writes Jacobs (89)—but Jacobs's spiritual and emotional commitment becomes in Sethe a physical connection to the nursing baby she has sent on ahead: "I had to get my milk to my baby girl" (16). Sethe, like Jacobs, experiences the wish to give up the fight for survival and die, but while Jacobs says she was "willing to bear on" "for the children's sakes" (127), the reason that Sethe gives for enduring is the physical presence of the baby in her womb: "[I]t didn't seem such a bad idea [to die], . . . but the thought of herself stretched out dead while the little antelope lived on . . . in her lifeless body grieved her so" that she persevered (31).

The central heroic feat of Sethe's journey is her giving birth in the face of seemingly insuperable obstacles. Alone in the wilderness in a sinking boat on the Ohio River, in a state of physical injury and exhaustion, Sethe has only Amy, a white runaway indentured servant, to help her. Breaking the silence that has surrounded birth in Western narrative, Morrison provides a physically detailed account of childbirth, and—also new in Western cultural discourse—she gives labor its due as good work: Sethe and Amy "did something together appropriately and well" (84).

When Sethe finally wins through to Ohio, the text celebrates not the achievement of freedom but togetherness; a confusion of prepositions reflects the multiplicity of connections between mother and children: "Sethe lay in bed under, around, over, among but especially with them all" (93). At the triumphant close of her maternal quest, Sethe reports, "I was big, Paul D, and deep and wide and when I stretched out my arms all my children could get in between. I was *that* wide"; "she had milk enough for all" (162, 100). Thus the "nurturing power of the slave mother" (Gates xxxi) celebrated in women's slave narratives becomes literal in Morrison's account: Sethe's monumental body and abundant milk give and sustain life. But in spite of its mythic dimensions, the maternal body seems to lack a subjective center. During the journey, Sethe experiences her own existence only in relation to her children's survival; she is "concerned" not for herself but "for the life of her children's mother." She thinks, "I believe this baby's ma'am is gonna die" and pictures herself as "a crawling graveyard for a six-month baby's last hours" (30-31, 34).

Sethe maintains this roundabout self-definition through the many images of nursing that picture her as the sustaining ground of her children's existence; even after the children are weaned, her bond with them remains so strong that she continues to think of it as a nursing connection (100, 162, 200, 216). While celebrating the courage and determination that Sethe draws from this attachment, Morrison's narrative also dramatizes the problems of Sethe's maternal subjectivity, which is so embedded in her children that it both allows her to take the life of one of them and precludes putting that act into words.

When Sethe tries to explain her attempt to kill herself and her children to prevent their reenslavement, she finds speech blocked: "Sethe knew that the circle she was making around . . . the subject would remain one. That she could never close in, pin it down for anybody who had to ask."[4] A gap remains at the heart of her story, which the omniscient narrator subsequently fills in:

> [W]hen she saw [the slave owner] coming [to recapture
> them, she] collected every bit of life she had made, all
> the parts of her that were precious and fine and beauti-
> ful, and carried, pushed, dragged them through the
> veil, out, away, over there where no one could hurt
> them . . . where they would be safe.   (163)

Sethe extends her fights over her own body—the right to use any
means, including death, to protect herself from a return to slavery—to the "parts of her" that are her children, folding them
back into the maternal body in order to enter death as a single
unit (though she succeeded in killing only one of her daughters).
The novel withholds judgment on Sethe's act and persuades the
reader to do the same, presenting the infanticide as the ultimate
contradiction of mothering under slavery. "It was absolutely the
right thing to do, . . . but it's also the thing you have no right to
do," Morrison commented in an interview (Rothstein).[5]

Sethe's sense of continuity with her children also makes it
difficult for her to take the position of narrating subject and tell
her story. Her troubled relation to language can be read as a
carryover from a nursing mother's attitude toward separation.
When she engineered her family's escape from slavery, Sethe
had to send her nursing baby ahead of her to Ohio: "I told the
women in the wagon . . . to put sugar water in cloth to suck from
so when I got there in a few days [the baby] wouldn't have forgot
me. The milk would be there and I would be there with it" (16).
Sethe would not compromise with absence, overlooking the potentially life-threatening lack of food for her baby "for a few
days" to insist on presence: the milk would be "there," and the
mother would be "there with it." The standpoint of nursing
mother precludes separation and the substitutions that any separation would require.

Sethe's embrace of a relational system of presence and
connection, her reluctance to accept the principle of substitution,
extends to her refusal to invest in words and helps explain the
link between her failure to tell the story of her baby girl's death
and that baby's embodiment in Beloved. Lacan's account of a
child's entry into language opposes bodily connection and verbal
exchange in a way that clarifies Sethe's choices. To move into a
position in language and the social order, according to Lacan, an
infant must sacrifice its imaginary sense of wholeness and continuity with the mother's body. (Sethe is of course in the
mother's position rather than the child's, but her physical con-

nection with her nursing baby resembles the infant's initial radical dependency on the mother's body.) Lacan later makes the repudiation of maternal continuity an oedipal event, when the social law of the father prohibits the child's access to the maternal body. In "The Function and Field of Speech and Language in Psychoanalysis," however, he borrows from Freud an unmediated mother-child anecdote, perhaps to focus more intensely on the either-or choice between bodily presence and abstract signifier. Freud's grandson Ernst becomes a speaking subject in the same moment that he acknowledges his mother's absence. Throwing a spool out of his crib and bringing it back to the accompaniment of sounds ("ooo! aaa!") that Freud interprets as "Fort! Da!" ("Gone! There!"), the baby assumes a symbolic mastery over what he cannot control in reality—his mother's presence and absence (Freud, *Pleasure* 8-10). Lacan adds that the child "thereby raises his desire to a second power," investing desire in language (103). By acknowledging that he must put a signifier there, where his mother's body used to be, the child both recognizes absence and accepts loss. The word "manifests itself first of all as the murder of the thing" (104), or in John Muller's gloss, "the word destroys the immediacy of objects and gives us distance from them" (29).[6] It is this distance, this loss, that Sethe rejects. Just as she declined any mediation between her body and her nursing baby, insisting on presence, she now refuses to replace that baby with a signifier, to accept the irrevocability of absence by putting the child's death into words. Her denial of loss is fundamentally antimetaphorical—that is, the refusal to displace libido onto words is a refusal to let one thing stand for another and so impedes the whole project of speech.[7] Sethe remains without a narrative but with the baby ghost—there, embodied, a concrete presence.

Through Sethe's reluctance to substitute words for things, not just Beloved but all the painful events of the past that Sethe has not transformed into narrative are left there, where those events first occurred. "[W]hat I did, or knew, or saw, is still out there. Right in the place where it happened," Sethe tells Denver (36). The plot reflects this spatialized time, as incidents from the past occupy the various rooms in which they originally took place. In the shed, the murder replays, at least for Beloved; in the keeping room, an injured and demoralized Sethe once more gets bathed "in sections" by loving hands; and a white man "coming into [Sethe's] yard" triggers a repeat of her murderous

attack—with a saving difference (123-124, 272, 262). The plot—
present time—cannot move forward because Sethe's space is
crammed with the past:

> When she woke the house crowded in on her: there was
> the door where the soda crackers were lined up in a
> row; the white stairs her baby girl loved to climb; the
> comer where Baby Suggs mended shoes . . . the exact
> place on the stove where Denver burned her fingers. . . .
> There was no room for any other thing or body. . . .   (39)

There are no gaps in Sethe's world, no absences to be filled in
with signifiers; everything is there, an oppressive plenitude.
    Language reinforces the sense that materializations clog
the haunted house: spatial images that usually function as figures of speech take shape as actions. For example, when Paul D,
a former slave from the same plantation as Sethe, finds her
again after an absence of eighteen years, he feels out his chances
for establishing a relationship with her by asking if "there was
some space" for him (45). While his expression seems natural in
the circumstances, the situation in the house causes Paul D to
make a space for himself more literally than any suitor in literature: "[H]olding the table by two legs, he bashed it about, wreck-
ing everything, screaming back at the screaming house" (18).
Evidently Morrison wants the opening statement of the novel—
that "124 was spiteful. Full of a baby's venom" (3)—to be taken
quite literally. Before the dead baby takes the shape of Beloved,
her amorphous spirit haunts the house, filling it so completely
with her spite that "[t]here was no room for any other thing or
body until Paul D . . . broke up the place, making room, . . . then
standing in the place he had made" (39).
    After Paul D exorcises the ghost from the house and it re-
turns in the shape of Beloved, spatial metaphors continue to reflect the materialization of things that belong by rights in a spiritual realm. The sentence "She moved him," for example, opens
a chapter about Beloved's domestic relations with Paul D (114).
Because the grammatical object of *moved* is a human being—
him rather than *it*—the phrase seems at first glance to operate
figuratively, as in "she affected him emotionally." But the spiritual meaning quickly gives way to physical actuality as it becomes clear that Paul D "was being moved" literally (126)—out
of Sethe's bed, out of the living room, finally out of the house altogether—by Beloved's jealous desire to expel her rival.

Textual practice similarly seconds Sethe's emphasis on presence by rejecting metaphorical substitutions for the maternal body. In the opening scene, after Sethe has told Paul D about her quest to get her milk to her baby in Ohio, he cups her breasts from behind in a display of tenderness: "What she knew was that the responsibility for her breasts, at last, was in somebody else's hands" (18). The reader does a double take: the phrase "in somebody else's hands" usually functions as a metaphor meaning "someone else's responsibility"; here the hands are literally there, and what rests in them is not an abstract concept but flesh. The same slippage occurs in the next sentence, as Sethe imagines being "relieved of the weight of her breasts" (18). Because *weight* appears within the usually figurative phrase "relieved of the weight of," readers assume that it is a metaphor for care or responsibility, but the modifying phrase "of her breasts" gives *weight* back its literal meaning. When the maternal body becomes the locus of discourse, the metaphorical becomes the actual, a move that reinforces Sethe's definition of motherhood as an embodied responsibility: there are no substitutes, metaphorical or otherwise, for her breasts.

In the same passage, Paul D "reads" the story of slavery engraved on Sethe's back by a final savage beating. Because the scar tissue is without sensation—"her back skin had been dead for years" (18)—Sethe's back is, in a sense, not her own; it has been appropriated and reified as a tablet on which the slave masters have inscribed their code. She cannot substitute for this discourse of violence her own version of the event, in spite of Paul D's insistence (over the space of three pages) that she tell him about it. Sethe refuses, repeating instead Amy Denver's description of the wound left by the whipping as "a whole tree . . . in bloom": "I got a tree on my back. . . . I've never seen it and never will. But that's what she said it looked like. A chokecherry tree. Trunk, branches, and even leaves" (79, 15-16). The metaphor masks suffering and puts it at the distance of a beautiful image—an act of poetic detachment appropriate, perhaps, to Amy's position of onlooker after the event but not to Sethe's subjective experience of pain.[8] Unable to seize the word and thus become master of her own experience, Sethe remains "a body whose flesh . . . bears . . . the marks of a cultural text" that inscribes her as slave (Spillers 67).[9] Sethe's problematic relation to language results from her position as body not only in a maternal order but also in a social order that systematically denied the subject position to those it defined as objects of exchange.[10]

In the absence of a speaking subject, Morrison makes the most of body language, as the passage I have been analyzing, quoted in full, shows:

> Behind her, bending down, his body an arc of kindness, he held her breasts in the palms of his hands. He rubbed his cheek on her back and learned that way her sorrow, the roots of it; its wide trunk and intricate branches. . . . [H]e would tolerate no peace until he had touched every ridge and leaf of it with his mouth, none of which Sethe could feel because her back skin had been dead for years. What she knew was that the responsibility for her breasts, at last, was in somebody else's hands.
>
> Would there be a little space, she wondered, a little time, some way to . . . just stand there a minute or two, . . . relieved of the weight of her breasts . . . and feel the hurt her back ought to. Trust things and remember things because the last of the Sweet Home men was there to catch her if she sank?   (17-18)

On Sethe's back, the extreme of a patriarchal symbolic order "recast . . . in the terms of cultural domination" (Abel 187), a "hieroglyphics of the flesh" (Spillers 67); on her front, the locus of a maternal system of relations based on presence and connection: Paul D, flexible man, "reads" both stories through touch, quickly becoming a participant in Sethe's discourse of bodily connection. Implicit in the space Paul D's kind body protects is the possibility of yet a third relational system: Sethe thinks that with him there she might feel safe enough to "go inside," "feel the hurt her back ought to," and thus replace the outside language the slave owners imprinted on her body with an inner language of articulate memory; she might be able to tell her story (46, 18). But the potential for reclaiming her past along with its pain is not realized till Paul D re-creates this holding space in the last scene, enabling Sethe to move into the position of narrating subject from a base in physical intimacy. First she has to live out the unspeakable drama of the past that possesses the house—a symbiosis with her daughter that would only have been appropriate eighteen years before, when Beloved was a nursling in body as well as in spirit.

Who Is Beloved?

In part 2, Sethe lives out the dream of sustaining her
ghostly daughter with her own substance—a nursing fantasy
writ large. On the personal level, Beloved is the nursing baby
that Sethe killed. But in the social dimension that always doubles the personal in *Beloved*, the ghost represents—as the
generic name Beloved suggests—all the loved ones lost through
slavery, beginning with the Africans who died on the slave
ships. In one sense, then, the pain that haunts Sethe's house is
nothing special: "Not a house in the country ain't packed to its
rafters with some dead Negro's grief" (5).   Accordingly,
Beloved's message means one thing to those within the family
circle and another thing altogether to those who listen from outside the house, from the vantage point of the community.[11]
Morrison introduces the conversation of Sethe, Beloved, and
Denver that takes up most of part 2 as "unspeakable thoughts,
unspoken" (199): in its drive toward unity, the mother-daughter
dialogue wipes out all the positions of separation necessary to
language, and it is in this sense "unspeakable." But Stamp Paid,
who listens from outside, from social ground, hears in Beloved's
speech a whole chorus of "the black and angry dead," a communal "roaring" that is "unspeakable" because the accumulated sufferings under slavery overwhelm the expressive possibilities of
ordinary discourse (198-199, 181). What cannot be encompassed
within the symbolic order continues to haunt it, hovering on
the edge of language.
  Beloved herself ends up outside social discourse, wandering, after the narrative's conclusion, in a limbo where she is
"[d]isremembered and unaccounted for" (274). Her position in
the epilogue is symmetrical with that of the "Sixty Million and
more" of Morrison's epigraph. Having perished on the slave
ships midway between a place in African history and a place in
the history of American slavery, these lost souls never made it
into any text. Lost still, they remain stranded in the epigraph,
where their human features are erased beneath a number; they
are quantified in death, as they had been in life by a property system that measured wealth in terms of a body count. Morrison's
"and more" indicates the residue left over, left out, unaccounted
for by any text—like Beloved at the end. Denver gestures toward
the larger dimension of Beloved's identity when she responds to
Paul D's question "You think [the ghost] sure 'nough your sis-

ter?" with an echo of the epigraph: "At times. At times I think
she was—more" (266).

Morrison is unwilling, apparently, to leave the historical
parallel at the level of suggestion. She links Beloved to the
"Sixty Million and more" by joining her spirit to the body of a
woman who died on one of the slave ships. But first, in a
monologue that comes out of nowhere, Beloved gives an account of slave ship experience:

> I am always crouching   the man on my face is dead . . .
> in the beginning the women are away from the men and
> the men are away from the women   storms rock us and
> mix the men into the women and the women into the
> men   that is when I begin to be on the back of the man
> for a long time I see only his neck and his wide shoul-
> ders above me . . . he locks his eyes and dies on my face
> . . . the others do not know that he is dead.   (211-212)

Since Morrison does not identify these scattered perceptions as
observations of life on a slave ship or tell how Beloved came to
be there or give any coordinates of time and place, readers are
baffled: they have no idea where they are. Their confusion thus
imitates the disorientation of the Africans who were thrown
into the slave ships without explanation, suspended without
boundaries in time and space, "in movement across the Atlantic
but . . . also nowhere at all . . . inasmuch as . . . the captive[s] . . .
did not know where [they were]." The fragmented syntax and
absence of punctuation robs the reader of known demarcations,
creating a linguistic equivalent of the Africans' loss of differentiation in an "oceanic" space that "unmade" cultural identities
and erased even the lines between male and female; living and
dead (Spillers 72).

Readers who try to understand these unsettling images as
metaphors for Beloved's passage from death to life can find a basis for doing so in the African-American narrative tradition,
which pictures the Middle Passage as a journey toward a horrific
rebirth. (Robert Hayden calls the Middle Passage a "voyage
through death to life upon these shores" [48, 54]; Richard Wright
remarks, "We millions of black folk who live in this land were
born into Western civilization of a weird and paradoxical birth"
[12].) The nightmare collage of bodies piled on bodies in the slave
ship, where it is hard to tell the living from the dead, would
then figure Beloved's difficulty in discerning, in her transitional

state, whether she is alive or dead, traveling toward death or toward life. But Morrison everywhere demands that readers confront the horrors of slavery "in the flesh" rather than at the comfortable distance of metaphor (qtd. in Darling 5). "I wanted that haunting not to be really a suggestion of being bedeviled by the past," she comments, "but to have it be incarnate" (qtd. in Rothstein). What at first appears symbolic becomes actual in a characteristic collapse of metaphor into literal reality—a slippage that accompanies the central materialization of the novel, Beloved's embodiment. Scattered through Beloved's monologue are fragments that form the following sequence. Beloved becomes attached to the face of a woman actually on the slave ships, follows the woman's body into the sea after the sailors throw it overboard, and "joins" with it: the woman's "face comes through the water . . . her face is mine . . . I have to have my face . . . she knows I want to join   she chews and swallows me   I am gone   now I am her face" (211-213).[12] Beloved returns, then, in the body of one of the original "disappeared," and all her gestures are shadowed by a larger historical outline. Or, as she herself sees it, "All of it is now   it is always now": the unnumbered losses of slavery are collected in Beloved, in a temporal space outside the linear time of history (210).[13]

But Beloved is also the one-year-old baby that Sethe killed. Morrison skillfully exploits the parallels between a spirit in search of a body and a preoedipal child who desires a merger with her mother. To both, the boundaries between persons are permeable, permitting a "join," and both project this identity confusion as a dialectic of faces. As disembodied spirit, Beloved says, "I need to find a place to be," with the words "to be" taking on all the urgency of their literal meaning. Neither her language nor her need to find a support for her existence changes, however, when it is her mother's face that she needs: "I need to find a place to be . . . [Sethe's] smiling face is the place for me" (213). The ghost's insistence on becoming embodied blends, in Morrison's song of desire, with the preverbal child's dependence on the maternal face as a mirror of her own existence.[14]

Beloved wants from words the verbal equivalent of a face that reflects her exactly as she is, reassuring her of her own existence and of her identity with her mother. In the mother-daughter dialogue that follows her monologue, language bends to Beloved's desire. While a spoken dialogue (ideally) moves toward something new, with the difference voiced by one speaker moving the other speaker away from his or her original position, the dialogue among the three women imitates a mother-infant dialectic: it is motivated not by difference but by the desire to ascertain that the other is there and that the other is the same. It "moves" only toward the stasis of interreflecting mirrors, ending in identical statements wherein like mirrors like:

> You are mine
> You are mine
> You are mine.   (217)

What happens to language here reflects what happens in the female family circle, as Sethe (and Denver, for a time) is persuaded by Beloved's preoedipal understanding that the mother is an extension of the self: "I am not separate from her   there is no place where I stop" (210).   Punctuation disappears, leaving the sentence of each participant open to the sentence of the next speaker, and the personal pronouns *I* and *you* move toward each other, losing their difference first to become interchangeable and then to mesh in the possessive *mine*.   Initially, some difference remains.   Sethe and Denver say:

> You are my sister
> You are my daughter

to which Beloved responds:

> You are my face; you are me.   (216)

In Sethe's and Denver's lines, normative language reflects normative family life.   Separate pronouns correspond to the separate positions of family members who are connected only in the circumscribed ways authorized by conventional kinship structures.   Beloved's statement, though, overthrows the classifications that locate persons in cultural space, insisting on a closer relationship than either language or family law allows: "you are me."

"You are my face; I am you.   Why did you leave me who am you?" With this line, Beloved completes the limited and stubborn logic of the preoedipal: if I am you, there is no leeway for separation; you *cannot* leave me.   In the lines

> I have your milk . . .
> I brought your milk

the nursing connection erodes the distinctions of the symbolic by making the boundary between "you" and "me" soluble (216). Is the milk that the baby drinks part of the baby or part of the mother? Does the "I" in "I have your milk" refer to Sethe, who might be saying that she "has" (is carrying) Beloved's milk, or to Beloved, who could just as well be the "I" who speaks, saying that she "has" Sethe's milk inside her? The dedifferentiation of possessive pronouns dramatizes the impossibility of separating what belongs to the one body from what belongs to the other when the two are joined by the nipple or, rather, by the milk that flows between them, blurring borders.

Nursing serves as a figure for the totality and exclusivity of mother-daughter fusion: "Nobody will ever get my milk no more except my own children," says Sethe, turning inward, and Beloved completes the circle, "lapping devotion like cream" (200, 243). Since Beloved has moved Paul D out and thus demolished the shadowy oedipal triangle ("the three shadows [who] held hands" [47, 491] that threatened her hold on her mother, no father figure diverts Sethe's attention from her baby, and no "paternal signifier" points Beloved toward a larger symbolic order. She gets to live out the preoedipal wish "to be the exclusive desire of the mother" (Lacan, "Les formations" 14; qtd. in Rose 38).

The nursing paradigm does not work as the governing principle of family life, though. "Beloved . . . never got enough of anything: lullabies, new stitches, the bottom of the cake bowl, the top of the milk. . . . [W]hen Sethe ran out of things to give her, Beloved invented desire" (240). As preverbal infant, Beloved has not accepted the law of symbolic substitutions with which Freud's grandson made his peace, so no partial gift will do. She wants a total union with the mother, to have her and to be her. The text literalizes a nursing baby's fantasy of oral greed consuming the breast, the mother, and all (Klein 200-201): Sethe wastes away while Beloved becomes "bigger, plumper by the day" (239).[15] This drama of oral incorporation is also appropriate to Beloved's role as the past that sucks up all Sethe's energies, leaving nothing for "a life" with a present and future (46).

"You are mine" is of course what the slave owners said, and as in the larger social order, the disregard of the other as subject, the appropriation of the other to one's own desires, leads to violence. Although now Beloved's disregard of limits eats up Sethe's life, the logic of "You are mine" originally permitted Sethe to exercise life-or-death rights over the children she conceived as "parts of her" (163).

A Maternal Symbolic

It is Denver, Sethe's surviving daughter, who in part 3 initiates the breakup of this self-consuming mother-child circle. Impelled by the need to get food for her starving mother, she moves into the larger community, but the search for food is aligned with her own "hunger" for learning. Denver joins a social order of language and exchange that both feeds her and teaches her to read. Morrison thus rewrites the entry into the symbolic in terms that retain the oral and maternal, challenging the orthodox psychoanalytic opposition between a maternal order of nurturing and a paternal order of abstract signification.

From the beginning, Denver's development reverses Lacan's maturational sequence: what Morrison explicitly calls Denver's "original hunger" is not for the mother's body but for words (118, 121). At the age of seven, after a year of reading lessons, Denver abandons language to avoid learning the truth about her mother's murder of her sister. She becomes deaf and dumb for two years, "cut off by an answer she could not bear to hear." Since the period of silence follows the period of verbal exchange, Denver's nostalgia focuses not on a past of mute connection with the mother's body but on a time of verbal *jouissance*—delight in "the capital *w*, the little *i*, the beauty of the letters in her name, the deeply mournful sentences from the Bible Lady Jones used as a textbook" (102-103). Not for Denver the normal progress from oral to verbal, from the breast that fills the baby's mouth to verbal substitutes that never quite do so and always leave something to be desired. Instead, words give Denver the pleasures of the mouth, as the conflation of learning with eating implies: "sentences roll[ed] out like pie dough"; Lady Jones "watched her eat up a page, a rule, a figure" (121, 247).

What causes Denver to give up nourishing words for the hunger of not speaking? As a young girl, she lives out the unspeakable, as if to keep her mother's silence intact by locking it up in her body. Her empty ear and empty mouth reproduce in a corporeal language the empty place at the center of the text where her mother's story of the infanticide should be. In Freud's model of hysterical conversion, the symptom enacts the content of a repressed desire; here the paralysis of ear and throat represents not Denver's desire—her own primal hunger is for words —but her mother's wish that the story remain unspoken, the act unnamed, the memory repressed. Denver in effect closes herself up in her mother's silence. At the same time, she gives up her initial indifference to the ghost and begins to "fix [her concentration] on the baby ghost" (103). The complement of her mother's silence is the concrete presence of Beloved, the literalization of what Sethe refuses to abstract into words. When Denver goes "deaf rather than hear the answer, and [keeps] watch for the baby and [withdraws] from everything else" (105), she is retreating into her mother's world, making the rejection of speech and the obsession with the unnamed her own.

The paralysis of Denver's development shows how urgent is the need for a story that will make sense of the baby's death, mark the baby's disappearance, and lay her and the past she represents to rest. Even after Denver returns to speech and hearing, she lacks the narrative context to deal with the baby's death on a conscious level, so she processes it unconsciously in "monstrous and unmanageable dreams" about her mother: "She cut my head off every night" (103, 206). The unconscious, notorious for repetition without resolution, endlessly plays out dream derivatives of the repressed signifier. Meanwhile, the nonsignifying word *thing* marks the gap left by the signifier repressed from conscious thought: "certain odd and terrifying feelings about her mother were collecting around the thing that leapt up inside her" in response to questions about her mother. Freud remarks that the unconscious operates by means of "thing presentation" rather than "word presentation" ("Unconscious" 201). In Denver's idiom the unconscious marker "thing" fills the gap where conscious significance fails. It represents something in her own unconscious: "the thing that leapt up *in her* . . . was a thing that had been lying there all along" (102; my emphasis). Sethe's inability to confront and articulate her action— she hears primary process noises rather than conscious sequential thought when she tries to tell Paul D about the baby's death—results in the unsignified "thing" being lodged like a lump, undigestible and unsignifiable, in her child's unconscious, where it generates the repeated dream of decapitation.[16]

When Denver tries to leave the haunted house to get food for her mother and Beloved, she finds herself imprisoned within her mother's time—a time that, clinging to places, is always happening again: "Out there . . . were places in which things so bad had happened that when you went near them it would happen again. . . . Denver stood on the porch . . . and couldn't leave it." She crosses the threshold into social discourse only when the voice of Baby Suggs, the ancestor, speaks out: "You mean I never told you . . . nothing about how come I walk the way I do and about your mother's feet, not to speak of her back? I never told you all that? Is that why you can't walk down the steps?" (243-244). To a child afraid to step out into the world, the particulars of how that world damaged her grandmother and mother are hardly comforting. It is the speech act itself, the voice of the grandmother putting the past where it belongs, into oral history, that frees Denver to enter the present.

After Denver leaves the closed family circle, she goes straight to the place of verbal nurturance, the house of Lady Jones, the woman who had taught her to read some ten years earlier. However belatedly (she is by now eighteen), she takes the crucial step from the imaginary of mother-daughter fusions to the symbolic order of language and society. But this step does not entail abandoning maternal intimacy. "Oh, baby," says Lady Jones when Denver tells her about her starving mother, "[I]t was the word 'baby,' said softly and with such kindness, that inaugurated her life in the world as a woman." Lady Jones's maternal language indicates that Denver is a child of the community, not just of her mother: "Everybody's child was in that face." She bakes raisin loaves for Denver while teaching her to read Bible verses, and "all through the spring, names appeared near or in gifts of food" (248-250, 246). Morrison thus confounds the distinction between words and good things to eat, between oral and verbal pleasures.

Denver moves into the symbolic by leaving one nurturing maternal circle for another, but there is a difference. The community, which operates as a network of mutual aid (originally, the network helped slaves escape), takes offense at Sethe's claim of maternal self-sufficiency—that "she had milk enough for all"—and demands instead a reciprocal nurturing. "To belong to a community of other free Negroes [is] to love and be loved by them, . . . [to] feed and be fed." Denver enters into this nurturing reciprocity, "pay[ing] a thank you for half a pie," "paying" for help by telling her story (100, 177, 252-253).

Acts of maternal care also enable Sethe to move into an order of linguistic exchange. After the community of women intervenes and routs Beloved,[17] Sethe retreats into the keeping room in an imitation of Baby Suggs, who withdrew there to die. "I think I've lost my mother," Denver tells Paul D: the loss of Beloved entails the loss of Sethe, who is still attached to her baby (266). When Paul D offers to bathe her, taking the restorative maternal role once occupied by Baby Suggs (93, 98), Sethe can only protest that she is "nothing . . . now. . . . Nothing left to bathe." Then a consciousness of her body begins to emerge: "Will he [bathe her] in sections? First her face, then her hands, her thighs, her feet, her back? Ending with her exhausted breasts? And if he bathes her in sections, will the parts hold?" (272). Gone is her self-image as maternal life-giver (her breasts are "exhausted" now, after the ordeal of sustaining Beloved); she puts herself together anew, imitating in her fear of fragmentation the first infantile self-image, the body in pieces, that precedes the cohesion of the mirror stage and motor control (Lacan, "Mirror Stage" 4). After the body, the spirit revives. Suddenly freed from the "serious work of beating back the past," Sethe lets all the losses she has repressed flood into her mind: "that she called, but Howard and Buglar walked on down the railroad track and couldn't hear her; that Amy was scared to stay with her because her . . . back looked so bad; that her madam had hurt her feelings and she couldn't find her hat anywhere." Having confronted her grief consciously, Sethe quickly moves to put loss into words: "She left me" (73, 272). The act of acknowledging absence and saying "she" splits Beloved off, detaches her from the maternal body that has held the nursing connection static, entombed, and puts a signifier there, where the child's body had been.

In thus shifting from a subjectivity embedded in maternal connection to a subjectivity based on the separate positions of the linguistic register (*she* and *me*), Sethe indeed follows the Lacanian schema, in which taking the position of speaking subject requires a repudiation of continuity with the mother's body (or, for Sethe, with the nursing infant's body). But Morrison revises Lacan here, too, softening his opposition between bodily communion and the abstractions of verbal exchange: "She was my best thing," Sethe says of her lost daughter. Paul D "leans over and takes her hand. With the other he touches her face.

'You your best thing, Sethe. You are.' His holding fingers are holding hers." Sethe answers, "Me? Me?" expressing surprise and disbelief, perhaps, but also recognizing herself in the first-person singular (272-273).[18] Replacing Lacan's vision of the move into language—a move away from bodies touching to the compensations of abstract signifiers—Morrison makes physical contact the necessary support for Sethe's full acceptance of the separate subjectivity required by language systems.[19]

Though Paul D thus encircles Sethe physically, his intent is not to subsume her. The words "You are," standing alone, replace "You are mine," the hallmark of invasive identification in the mother-daughter dialogue. Paul D "wants to put his story next to hers"; the two stories may complement and complete each other (each person having lived out the missing fragment of the other's slave narrative), but they will lie "next to" each other—each whole, circumscribed, with its own beginning, middle, and end (273).[20] Difference can emerge within the space of relationship; a dialogue between self and other can replace the circular mother-daughter dialectic between same and same.

The hope at the end of the novel is that Sethe, having recognized herself as subject, will narrate the mother-daughter story and invent a language that can encompass the desperation of the slave mother who killed her daughter. Or will she? The heterosexual resolution, the enclosure of the mother in the symbolic, leaves out the preoedipal daughter, who wanders lost in the epilogue. She will not be remembered because "nobody anywhere knew her name"; she is "[d]isremembered and unaccounted for" because "they couldn't remember or repeat a single thing she said, and began to believe that . . . she hadn't said anything at all. So, in the end, they forgot her too." Outcast both as victim of slavery whose death is unspeakable and as preverbal infant who has not made her way into the symbolic order, Beloved remains outside language and therefore outside narrative memory. Her story is "not a story to pass on" (274-275). Of course, the sentence is ambiguous: Beloved's story, too terrible to find resolution in the logic of narrative, cannot be passed on from teller to teller, but it also cannot "pass on," or die (35). It continues to haunt the borders of a symbolic order that excludes it.[21]

Notes

[1] Margaret Homans's notion of literalization enabled me to see how Morrison's metaphors work. "Literalization," which "occurs when some piece of overtly figurative language, a simile or an extended or conspicuous metaphor, is translated into an actual event or circumstance," is in Homans's opinion a characteristic of women's writing (30). Homans uses Nancy Chodorow's theory to challenge Lacan: because men and women develop differently, women might not polarize body and word, signifier and absent referent, to the extent that men do; thus women writers are less likely to privilege the figurative over the literal and more likely to conceive of presence as commensurate with representation (14).

[2] As a white middle-class feminist who practices psychoanalytic theory, I come to this project burdened not only by the usual guilt about my own implication in the racist structures that Morrison uncovers but also by doubts about the suitability of psychoanalytic theory for analyzing an African-American text. Psychoanalytic theory is, after all, based on assumptions about family and language grounded in Western European patriarchal culture, while Morrison's novel comes out of African and African-American oral and written narrative traditions (see Christian, Holloway, Page, Sale, Sitter). Elizabeth Abel's essay "Race, Class, and Psychoanalysis?" performs an important service to feminist psychoanalysis by canvassing the difficulties of applying psychoanalysis to texts produced by other cultures and the possibilities for modifying object-relations theory and Lacanian theory to include "the roles of race and class in a diversified construction of subjectivity" (184). Reading Abel's essay both focused the limitations of my position as white middle-class female reader of an African-American woman's text and gave me the courage to "[k]now it, and go on out the yard" (Morrison 244)—to go on in spite of recognizing the hazards of venturing into a cultural space not my own.

[3] Hazel Carby points out that "slave narratives by women, about women, could mobilize the narrative forms of adventure and heroism normally constituted within ideologies of male sexuality" (38). Lucy Delaney, for instance, describes her mother's struggle to free her children in epic terms: "She had girded up her loins for the fight"; "others would have flinched before the obstacles which confronted her, but undauntedly she pursued her way, until my freedom was established" (35, 45). See also Claudia Tate's discussion of the idealized slave mother (the grandmother) in Jacobs's narrative (109-110).

[4] Sethe may hesitate to tell her story in part because the language available to her—a language structured by the logic of bipolar oppositions—cannot readily encompass the contradictions of motherhood under slavery. Had she access to it, Sethe would find in the discourse of actual slave mothers a language better suited to a world where "safe" from slavery can only mean "dead." Harriet Jacobs, writing from within the paradoxes of "the peculiar institution," indeed conflates maternal love and infanticide: "I would rather see [my children] killed than have them given up to [the slaveholder's] power"; "death is better than slavery" (80, 62).

Since Sethe cannot find a language of "motherlove" (132), her story remains in the rhetoric of the masters. As Mae Henderson points out, "the first [and, I would add, the only] full representation of the events surrounding the infanticide [is] figured from a collective white/male perspective, represented by schoolteacher and the sheriff" (78; see Morrison 149-151). Sethe's story is caught up in "the dominant metaphors of the master('s) narrative—wildness, cannibalism, animality, destructiveness" (Henderson 79).

⁵ Readers learn about the infanticide a bit at a time from different perspectives, a technique that prevents them from making simple judgments. Maggie Sale shows that Morrison's narrative strategy forces readers to see the event from multiple perspectives and to recognize that each version depends as much on the needs of the narrator and the listener as on the historical "facts." The lack of a single definitive account "challenges readers to examine their own responses" both to Sethe's act and to the circumstances that force her to it (44).

Stephanie Demetrakopoulos, comparing Sethe and Beloved to mythic counterparts, remarks that "Sethe attempts to return the babies to perhaps a collective mother body, to devour them back into the security of womb/tomb death . . . as the ultimate act of protection" (52). Demetrakopoulos focuses on the descriptive effects of Sethe's mothering, especially on her own growth as an individual.

⁶ Lacan returns to the *fort-da* anecdote in *Four Fundamental Concepts* only to contradict his earlier reading. Focusing on the spool instead of the accompanying words, Lacan says that it represents an *objet petit a*—an object that is only ambiguously detached from the subject. Because Ernst holds the string that can pull back the spool, "it is a small part of the subject that detaches itself from him, while still remaining his, still retained" (62). In this later text, then, Lacan locates the *fort-da* episode in a zone intermediate between mother-child fusions and the clear-cut separations of the symbolic order instead of naming it, as he did earlier, "the moment . . . in which the child is born into language" ("Function" 104). Kaja Silverman and Elisabeth Bronfen read this second Lacanian interpretation as a parable for the eclipse the subject undergoes on entering language: in *Four Fundamental Concepts* the spool stands for Ernst himself, and the game rehearses his absence; he plays out the fading of the subject as, entering the order of representation, he is replaced by a signifier (Silverman 168-171; Bronfen 27). Bronfen gives a comprehensive and valuable account of various theorists' uses of the *fort-da* episode (15-38), and she adds a new dimension to standard interpretations by considering all the implications of the game's enactment of death (including Freud's use of the anecdote to compensate for the death of Sophie—his daughter and Ernst's mother—during the writing of *Beyond the Pleasure Principle).*

⁷ Judith Butler helpfully summarizes the argument of Nicolas Abraham and Maria Torok, who distinguish between the work of mourning, which displaces libido onto words that "both signify and displace [the lost] object," and "incorporation," a refusal of loss in which one preserves the lost object as a (fantasized) part of one's own body (68). In *Black Sun* Julia Kristeva also identifies the melancholic's problem as a failure to transfer libido from the bodily connection with the mother to words; she or he maintains instead an undifferentiated sense of continuity with the maternal body.

⁸ Characteristically, Sethe can articulate only the part of the abuse connected with her maternal function: "[T]hey took my milk," she repeats (16-

17). In Anne Goldman's view, "schoolteacher orders [Sethe's milk] to be appropriated" because, as the one product of her labor that doesn't belong to the masters, it is the "signifier of an identity, a subjectivity, independent of white authorities" (324). Mae Henderson understands "the theft of her 'mother's milk'" as "the expropriation of [Sethe's] future—her ability to nurture and ensure the survival of the future embodied in the next generation. . . . Sethe must discover some way of regaining control of her story, her body, her progeny, her milk, her ability to nurture the future" (71). Barbara Christian points out that the nephews "milk" Sethe at the behest of schoolteacher, who wants to make the experiment as part of his "scientific observation" of slaves. Christian aligns schoolteacher, who measures slaves' body parts and observes their bodily functions with "apparently neutral" scientific curiosity, with the nineteenth-century white American intellectuals who buttressed slavery with various "scientific" treatises on the physiology of African-Americans (337-338).

[9] Hortense Spillers's essay helped me understand slavery as a system of domination that mandated slaves' "absence from a subject position" while imprinting the terms of their subjugation on their bodies (67).

By emphasizing the importance of language to a "used-to-be-slave woman," Morrison takes up a central theme of slave narratives (45). "[O]nly by grasping the word" could slaves, who were considered "silently laboring brutes," take part in speech acts that would help them achieve selfhood and give shape to their subjective reality (Baker 243, 245; see also Gates xxiii-xxxi).

Mae Henderson observes, "[B]ecause it is her back (symbolizing the *presence* of her *past*) that is marked, Sethe has only been able to read herself through the gaze of others. The challenge for Sethe is to learn to read herself—that is, to configure the history of her body's text. . . . Sethe must learn how to link these traces (marks of her passage through slavery) to the construction of a personal and historical discourse" (69).

[10] Cathy Caruth summarizes theories of trauma and memory that can explain not only Sethe's inability to put the baby's death into narrative form but also the problems that other characters (notably Paul D and Baby Suggs) have in integrating the trauma of slavery. In the syndrome known as posttraumatic stress disorder, overwhelming events of the past "repeatedly possess, in intrusive images and thoughts, the one who has lived through them" (418). The original event escaped understanding even as it was happening because it could not "be placed within the schemes of prior knowledge. . . . Not having been fully integrated as it occurred, the event cannot become . . . a 'narrative memory' that is integrated into a completed story of the past" (418-419). Morrison's narrative form brilliantly recaptures traumatic memory: the past comes back in bits—a fragment here, a fragment there. Since the "truth" of the experience "may reside not only in its brutal facts, but also in the way that their occurrence defies simple comprehension," Morrison's text needs this pointillism, this fragmentation, to remain true both to the events and to "their affront to understanding" (Caruth 418-420). Philip Page shows how the circularity and fragmentation of Morrison's narrative structure parallels the indirect, piecemeal remembering of the characters. Gayle Greene also analyzes the way memory functions in *Beloved*.

[11] For a summary of Beloved's multiple relations to language and for a

different view of the female family circle, see my *Reconstructing Desire* (195-200).

[12] Deborah Horvitz thinks that it is Sethe's mother who speaks in these passages, wanting to "join" with the body of her own mother (162-163). Others have speculated that the face Beloved claims as her own is that of Sethe's mother, who indeed came over on the slave ships (though she, of course, survived the voyage). These interpretations are useful in suggesting the range of what Beloved may represent: a whole line of daughters desperately wanting to "join" with the mothers wrenched away from them by slavery.

[13] Linda Anderson describes Morrison's "exploration of history's absences, of how what is unwritten and unremembered can come back to haunt us" (137). Karla Holloway points out that these absences are not accidental, that "the victim's own chronicles of these events were systematically submerged, ignored, mistrusted, or superseded by 'historians' of the era. This novel positions the consequences of black invisibility in both the records of slavery and the record-keeping as a situation of primary spiritual significance" (516-517).

[14] Morrison's account is true to a one-year-old's way of thinking, according to D. W. Winnicott. A baby looking into its mother's face imagines that it sees there the same thing its mother is looking at: its own face. The baby's still precarious sense of existence depends on the mother's mirroring face ("Mirror-Role" 112). Rebecca Ferguson also uses Winnicott's essay to explain Beloved's fixation on her mother's face (117-118). Barbara Mathieson cites Winnicott as support for her claim that Beloved's monologue mirrors the preoedipal child's conviction that its identity and its mother's identity "flow into one another as interchangeably as their faces" (2).

[15] Barbara Schapiro discusses the novel's images of orality and the gaze in the context of slavery, pointing out that "the emotional hunger, the obsessive and terrifying narcissistic fantasies" are not Beloved's alone; instead, they belong to all those denied both mothers and selves by a slave system that "either separates [a mother] from her child or so enervates and depletes her that she has no self with which to confer recognition" (194). Thus when Sethe complains, "There was no nursing milk to call my own," she expresses her own emotional starvation in the absence of her mother, and that emptiness in turn prevents her from adequately reflecting her own daughter Denver (200, 198).

[16] Nicolas Abraham cites similar cases, in which an unarticulated secret passes directly from a parent's unconscious to a child's unconscious. The child does not consciously know what the secret is but nevertheless acts it out, driven by a thing lodged in its unconscious that fits in with neither its conscious wishes nor its unconscious fantasies. "What haunts are not the dead, but the gaps left within us by the secrets of others" (75).

[17] Missy Dehn Kubitschek identifies yet another maternal discourse in *Beloved*: she reads the women's roar that casts Beloved out as an imitation of "the sounds accompanying birth" (174). Morrison's text replaces the biblical verse, "In the beginning was the Word, . . . and the Word was God" (John 1.1), with the line, "In the beginning there were no words. In the beginning was the sound, and they all knew what that sound sounded like" (259). The women's communal groan recalls women's creation of life, not God's, and overthrows the male authority of the word. Kubitschek's chapter on *Beloved* addresses

Sethe's need to change the static conception of motherhood she developed under slavery.

[18] As Marianne Hirsch writes, Sethe's "subjectivity . . . can only emerge in and through human interconnection" (198). I differ with Hirsch because she ignores the hiatus in the middle of Sethe's narrative and regards Sethe as a mother who tells her story throughout (6). But Hirsch also says that Sethe's "maternal voice and subjectivity" emerge only in the concluding scene, where her "Me? Me?" implies that "she questions, at least for a moment, the hierarchy of motherhood over selfhood on which her life had rested until that moment" (7).

[19] Morrison may have D. W. Winnicott's maternal "holding environment" in mind. Like Morrison, Winnicott pictures development as a joint project of self and other (mother) rather than as a movement toward increasing separation. Only in the presence of the mother can the infant be truly "alone," in Winnicott's terms. That is, the mother's protective presence releases the infant from survival needs and enables it to claim its impulses as authentically its own—hence to catch the first glimpse of an ongoing subjectivity ("Capacity" 34). Just so, Paul D's holding guarantees a space in which Sethe can safely think any thought, feel any feeling, and finally take the leap into a different subjectivity, one grounded in language. Morrison's idea of heterosexual relations fits the "holding fantasy" that Jessica Benjamin claims women retain from experiencing that early maternal presence: "the wish for a holding other whose presence does not violate one's space but permits the experience of one's own desire, who recognizes it when it merges of itself" (96).

[20] Deborah Sitter describes the dialogic relation between Paul D's story and Sethe's story, showing how Paul D comes to a new definition of manhood. Kate Cummings also traces Paul D's development from a definition of masculinity that enslaves him to the white slave master who named him to an identification with Sixo's different model of manhood—a shift that culminates in his "taking on the job of mothering" Sethe. Cummings lists mothering as one of three modes of resistance, along with menacing and naming: "Mothering provides the final and most fundamental opposition, for through it the subject is reconstituted and the body reborn in the flesh" (563-564).

[21] I am grateful for the generous help of Elizabeth Abel in cutting this essay down to size; I also thank Frances Restuccia and John Swift for readings that enabled me to make new connections and Richard Yarborough for sharing his knowledge of Morrison's works.

Works Cited

Abel, Elizabeth. "Race, Class, and Psychoanalysts? Opening Questions." *Conflicts in Feminism*. Ed. Marianne Hirsch and Evelyn Fox Keller. New York: Routledge, 1990. 184-204.

Abraham, Nicolas. "Notes on the Phantom: A Complement to Freud's Metapsychology." *The Trial(s) of Psychoanalysis*. Ed. Françoise Meltzer. Chicago: University of Chicago Press, 1987. 75-80.

Abraham, Nicolas and Maria Torok. "Introjection—Incorporation: Mourning or Melancholia." *Psychoanalysis in France.* Ed. Serge Lebovici and Daniel Widlocher. New York: International University Press, 1980. 3-16.

Anderson, Linda. "The Re-imagining of History in Contemporary Women's Fiction." *Plotting Change.* Ed. Anderson. London: Arnold, 1990. 129-141.

Baker, Houston A., Jr. "Autobiographical Acts and the Voice of the Southern Slave." Davis and Gates 242-261.

Benjamin, Jessica. "A Desire of One's Own: Psychoanalytic Feminism and Intersubjective Space." *Feminist Studies/Critical Studies.* Ed. Teresa de Lauretis. Bloomington: Indiana University Press, 1986. 78-101.

Bronfen, Elisabeth. *Over Her Dead Body: Death, Femininity, and the Aesthetic.* New York: Routledge, 1992.

Butler, Judith. *Gender Trouble: Feminism and the Subversion of Identity.* London: Routledge, 1990.

Carby, Hazel. *Reconstructing Womanhood: The Emergence of the Afro-American Woman Novelist.* New York: Oxford University Press, 1987.

Caruth, Cathy. Introduction. *Psychoanalysis, Culture and Trauma: II.* Special issue of *American Image* 48 (1991): 417-424.

Christian, Barbara. "'Somebody Forgot to Tell Somebody Something': African-American Women's Historical Novels." *Wild Women in the Whirlwind: Afra-American Culture and the Contemporary Literary Renaissance.* Ed. Joanne M. Braxton and Andrée Nicola McLaughlin. New Brunswick: Rutgers University Press, 1990. 326-341.

Cummings, Kate. "Reclaiming the Mother('s) Tongue: *Beloved, Ceremony, Mothers and Shadows.*" *College English* 52 (1990): 552-569.

Darling, Marsha. "In the Realm of Responsibility: A Conversation with Toni Morrison." *Women's Review of Books* March 1988: 5-6.

Davis, Charles T. and Henry Louis Gates, Jr., eds. *The Slave's Narrative.* New York: Oxford University Press, 1985.

Delaney, Lucy. *From the Darkness Cometh the Light; or, Struggles for Freedom.* C. 1891. *Six Women's Slave Narratives.* Schomburg Library of Nineteenth-Century Black Women Writers. New York: Oxford University Press, 1988. 1-64.

Demetrakopoulos, Stephanie. "Maternal Bonds as Devourers of Women's Individuation in Toni Morrison's *Beloved.*" *African-American Review* 26.1 (1992): 51-60.

Ferguson, Rebecca. "History, Memory and Language in Toni Morrison's *Beloved.*" *Feminist Criticism: Theory and Practice.* Toronto: University of Toronto Press, 1991. 109-27.

Freud, Sigmund. *Beyond the Pleasure Principle.* Trans. James Strachey. New York: Norton, 1961.

—. "The Unconscious." 1915. *The Standard Edition of the Complete Psychological Works of Sigmund Freud.* Ed. and trans. James Strachey. Vol. 14. London: Hogarth, 1953-1974. 159-215. 24 Vols.

Gates, Henry Louis, Jr. "Introduction: The Language of Slavery." Davis and Gates xi-xxxiv.

Goldman, Anne. "'I Made the Ink': (Literary) Production and Reproduction in *Dessa Rose* and *Beloved.*" *Feminist Studies* 16 (1990): 313-330.

Greene, Gayle. "Feminist Fictions and the Uses of Memory." *Signs* 16 (1990): 1-32.

Hayden, Robert. "Middle Passage." *Collected Works*. New York: Liveright, 1985. 48-54.

Henderson, Mae. "Toni Morrison's *Beloved*: Re-membering the Body as Historical Text." *Comparative American Identities: Race, Sex, and Nationality in the Modern Text*. Ed. Hortense Spillers. London: Routledge, 1991. 62-86.

Hirsch, Marianne. *The Mother-Daughter Plot: Narrative, Psychoanalysis, Feminism*. Bloomington: Indiana University Press, 1989.

Holloway, Karla. "*Beloved*: A Spiritual." *Callaloo* 13 (1990): 516-525.

Homans, Margaret. *Bearing the Word: Language and Female Experience in Nineteenth-Century Women's Writing*. Chicago: University of Chicago Press, 1986.

Horvitz, Deborah. "Nameless Ghosts: Possession and Dispossession in *Beloved*." *Studies in American Fiction* 17 (1989): 157-167.

Jacobs, Harriet. *Incidents in the Life of a Slave Girl*. Cambridge: Harvard University Press, 1987.

Klein, Melanie. "Some Theoretical Conclusions regarding the Emotional Life of the Infant." *Developments in Psychoanalysis*. Ed. Klein, et al. London: Hogarth, 1952. 198-236.

Kristeva, Julia. *Black Sun*. Trans. Leon Roudiez. New York: Columbia University Press, 1989.

Kubitschek, Missy Dehn. *Claiming the Heritage: African-American Women Novelists and History*. Jackson: University of Mississippi Press, 1991.

Lacan, Jacques. Ecrits: *A Selection*. Trans. Alan Sheridan. New York: Norton, 1981.

—. "Les formations de l'inconscient." *Bulletin de psychologie* 2 (1957-1958): 1-15.

—. *The Four Fundamental Concepts of Psychoanalysis*. 1973. Trans. Alan Sheridan. New York: Norton, 1981.

—. "The Function and Field of Speech and Language in Psychoanalysis." 1953. Lacan, Ecrits 30-113.

—. "The Mirror Stage as Formative of the Function of the I." Lacan, Ecrits 1-7.

Mathieson, Barbara O. "Memory and Mother Love in Morrison's *Beloved*." *American Image* 47 (1990): 1-21.

Morrison, Toni. *Beloved*. New York: Knopf, 1987.

Muller, John. "Language, Psychosis, and the Subject in Lacan." *Interpreting Lacan*. Ed. Joseph Smith and William Kerrigan. New Haven: Yale University Press, 1983. 21-32.

Page, Philip. "Circularity in Toni Morrison's *Beloved*." *African American Review* 26.1 (1992): 31-40.

Rose, Jacqueline. "Introduction II." *Feminine Sexuality: Jacques Lacan and the Ecole Freudienne*. Ed. Juliet Mitchell and Rose. New York: Norton, 1982. 27-57.

Rothstein, Mervyn. "Toni Morrison, in Her New Novel, Defends Women." *New York Times* 26 August 1987: C17.

Sale, Maggie. "Call and Response as Critical Method: African-American Oral Traditions and *Beloved*." *African American Review* 26.1 (1992): 41-50.

Schapiro, Barbara. "The Bonds of Love and the Boundaries of Self in Toni Morrison's *Beloved*." *Contemporary Literature* 32 (1991): 194-210.

Silverman, Kaja. *The Subject of Semiotics*. New York: Oxford University Press, 1983.

Sitter, Deborah Ayer. "The Making of a Man: Dialogic Meaning in *Beloved*." *African American Review* 26.1 (1992): 17-30.

Spillers, Hortense. "Mama's Baby, Papa's Maybe: An American Grammar Book." *Diacritics* 17 (1987): 65-81.

Tate, Claudia. "Allegories of Black Female Desire; or, Rereading Nineteenth-Century Sentimental Narratives of Black Female Authority." *Changing Our Own Words*. Ed. Cheryl A. Wall. New Brunswick: Rutgers University Press, 1989. 98-126.

Winnicott, D. W. "The Capacity to Be Alone." *The Maturational Processes and the Facilitating Environment*. New York: International University Press, 1965. 29-36.

—. "Mirror-Role of Mother and Family in Child Development." *Playing and Reality*. London: Tavistock, 1971. 111-118.

Wright, Richard. *Twelve Million Black Voices*. New York: Thunder's Mouth, 1988.

Wyatt, Jean. *Reconstructing Desire: The Role of the Unconscious in Women's Reading and Writing*. Chapel Hill: University of North Carolina Press, 1990.

Pain and the Unmaking of Self in Toni Morrison's *Beloved*

Kristin Boudreau

torture consists of acts that magnify the way in which
pain destroys a person's world, self, and voice. . . .
                                        Elaine Scarry
                                    The Body in Pain

He that shall humble himself shall be exalted.
                                    Matthew 23:12

When Toni Morrison's *Beloved* opens with a house "full
of baby's venom," it announces the prominent place of pain in
the lives of these ex-slaves. The reification of pain as venom—
intended to destroy the woman who had slit her baby girl's
throat rather than return her child to the slavery by which she
herself had been violated—suggests that pain may not point the
way to redemption but will instead perpetuate the process of violence in which it found its origin. The novel thus takes to task a
tradition of romantic suffering, a tradition that valorizes suffering as the pivotal experience whereby an individual becomes
fully human. This formulation of pain predates romanticism,
beginning as early as the Christian contemplative tradition, and
extends, in a different form, to the African-American blues tradition. As Arthur C. Clements notes, contemplation moves an
individual through a state of abject mortification and pain to "a
radical transformation of self, called 'regeneration' or 'rebirth'"
(10). "Regeneration," according to Clements, "is not merely verbal or intellectual grasp of certain principles nor a merely superficial conversion, but rather that deeply realized, radical, and
thoroughgoing change in one's mode of consciousness which is
both the true beginning and center of the mystic life" (10-11).

The sacred model, which Clements describes as a "central paradox of gain through loss, of life through death" (11), is secularized, I want to suggest, in two distinct traditions of literature and music that sublimate and celebrate physical and psychological pain: European romanticism and African-American blues.

Why, we might ask, has this recuperative account held such sway over our attempts to understand pain? To be sure, the celebration of suffering as a means of gaining full subjectivity may provide a palatable means of acknowledging the seemingly inevitable agony of the human condition. But the significant transition from acknowledging pain to depending on it for our own validation is dramatic and by no means inevitable. Nevertheless, we make that leap repeatedly, as John Keats demonstrates: "Do you not see how necessary a World of Pains and troubles is to school an Intelligence and make it a soul? A Place where the heart must feel and suffer in a thousand diverse ways!" (2:102).

In spite of a long tradition in Western culture of romanticizing and thereby almost embracing pain, it is nevertheless astonishing to note the prominent place occupied by a similar reading of pain in the writings of groups long victimized by bodily, economic, sexual, and psychological violence. I am thinking in particular of the creative and critical writings within African-American literature. The blues tradition, of course, shifts the emphasis of romanticism from the importance of pain to the effort at transcendence. As Houston Baker notes, blues is an "affirmation of human identity in the face of dehumanizing circumstances" (190). Many of James Baldwin's writings demonstrate this progression from pain to its artistic, humanizing effects. The end of "Sonny's Blues," for instance, signals the entrance of two brothers into their full humanity through the only passage available to them—the unfolding pain of their own and their ancestors' lives. As the narrator watches his brother on stage, he begins to understand how that pain serves his own subjectivity:

> there was no battle in his face now. I heard what he
> had gone through, and would continue to go through un-
> til he came to rest in earth. He had made it his: that
> long line, of which we knew only Mama and Daddy.
> And he was giving it back, as everything must be given
> back, so that, passing through death, it can live for-
> ever. I saw my mother's face again, and felt, for the

> first time, how the stones of the road she had walked
> on must have bruised her feet. I saw the moonlit road
> where my father's brother died. And it brought some-
> thing else back to me, and carried me past it, I saw my
> little girl again and felt Isabel's tears again, and I felt
> my own tears begin to rise. And I was yet aware that
> this was only a moment, that the world waited outside,
> as hungry as a tiger, and that trouble stretched above
> us, longer than the sky.   (122)

In order to rise, fully human, above the "world . . . outside, hungry as a tiger," the narrator, like Sonny, must make it his—the
long historical chain of suffering that binds him to his family
and to his race.

The blues tradition, of course, differs in at least one crucial
way from the romantic tradition that valorizes pain. Baldwin's
Sonny, we recall, must come to terms with his suffering not in
any private examination, but in the communal space of the bar,
surrounded by sympathetic friends. As Sherley A. Williams explains: "The particularized, individual experience rooted in a
common reality, is the primary thematic characteristic of all
blues songs no matter what their structure. The classic song
form itself internalizes and echoes, through the state-
ment/response pattern, the thematic relationship between individual and group experience which is implied in these evoca-
tions of social and political reality" (127). The blues articulation,
then, expands into a public realm what had hitherto been a private experience of suffering, taking the individual outside of
himself and his private pains, which might otherwise make the
self so achingly present that the world disappears. Romantic
treatments of emotion, on the other hand, depend upon "recollect[ion] in tranquillity" (Wordsworth 266), which requires privacy, for the sake of contemplation.

In his now famous description of the blues, Ralph Ellison
underscores another apparent distinction between this tradition
and Western uses of suffering. "The blues," he writes, "is an
impulse to keep the painful details and episodes of a brutal experience alive in one's aching consciousness, to finger its jagged
grain, and to transcend it, not by the consolation of philosophy
but by squeezing from it a near-tragic, near-comic lyricism. As a
form, the blues is an autobiographical chronicle of personal
catastrophe expressed lyrically" (78-79). In opposing the "near-
tragic, near-comic lyricism" to the "consolation of philosophy,"

Ellison suggests that the blues is not a Western response to pain: transcendence for the blues singer comes not from intellectual reflection on pain, as Boethius counseled, but from the distillation of something passionate into something artistically formed. Unlike Boethius's Lady Philosophy, whose first act of consolation was to drive the muses of poetry into exile, Ellison's blues singer squeezes poetic essences from the painful event.

But it might be a mistake to exaggerate the distance between the blues and romanticism. In spite of the differences between individual and community, contemplation and raw emotion, both the blues and romanticism depend upon the process whereby human suffering is transformed into an art form that validates the experience. If Lady Philosophy drives away the muses of poetry, romanticism summons them in to reformulate the horrific into the tragically beautiful. And if we turn to treatments of suffering in African-American literary texts, we discover that Western and non-Western art forms often seem indistinguishable. As Gayl Jones argues, "Modern African-American writers began to shape and modify their literature using models not only from European and European American traditions, but also from their own distinctive oral and aural forms. . . . When the African-American creative writers began to trust the literary possibilities of their own verbal and musical creations and to employ self-inspired techniques, they began to transform the European and European American models and to gain greater artistic sovereignty" (1). I am arguing here that the African-American literary tradition is replete with treatments of suffering that, while they certainly partake of the blues tradition, also reshape European romanticism with its claims for the centrality of suffering to any genuinely human experience. In a statement that seems equally derivative of romanticism and the blues, Baldwin implies that pain alone does not offer salvation; one must not stop short of embracing and reformulating suffering: "Most people had not lived—nor could it, for that matter, be said that they had died—through any of their terrible events. They had simply been stunned by the hammer. They passed their lives thereafter in a kind of limbo of denied and unexamined pain" (*Another Country* 112). To acknowledge and examine pain, Baldwin suggests, is to enter into a process whereby one gains one's full humanity.

Given both the historical continuity of violence in the African-American past and the Christian influence on slave communities, it is easy to see how an oral tradition like the blues would make productive use of physical and emotional suffering. Yet productive use might without notice evolve into something more troubling—the elevation, even the valorization of suffering. If one claims, that is, that suffering makes one fully human, might not this very assertion glorify the pain traditionally deployed against the enslaved body and mind? Might not the use of pain at times resemble the strategy of antebellum Christianity, whose promises of a redemptive after-life actually forestalled resistance to earthly oppression? As if in response to such doubts, Missy Dehn Kubitschek muses on the possibility that "the pain of acknowledging the historical past and its influences on the present may immobilize a heroine rather than energizing her" (144). Indeed, this is a central problem posed by Morrison's fictional meditation on slavery; while still taking part in a dialogue figured through blues language, *Beloved* suggests a radical revision of romantic and blues assessments of pain, asking, instead, *Can* one be fully human without having suffered? And the more troubling question: Does suffering do more or less than make one real? Although it seems too obvious to mention that the uses of pain I have described should not be taken as representative of all African-American utterances, many critics nevertheless seem nearly to celebrate pain even when reading works which, like *Beloved*, discourage such interpretations.[1] Most readings of *Beloved* suggest that suffering can heal and humanize, provided that one can reorganize the painful events of the past and retell them in one's own language. A crucial problem arises, however, when these readings must confront the narrative's emphatic final assertion: "This is not a story to pass on" (275). Most critics resolve the problem by claiming that the story should, in fact, be passed on.[2] But why not take the narrative at its word and heed its caution that this story should *not* be passed on? Why not ask what accounts for its untellability? Contrary to most readings of *Beloved*—and contrary even to some of Morrison's own comments on the novel—that suffering makes one real, suffering in fact makes one a great deal less than real.[3] Suffering, as *Beloved* seems to cry in repeated anguished moments, *unmakes* the self and calls violent attention to the practice of making and unmaking selves.[4]

　　The most extreme condition of physical and psychological pain is, of course, the pain of torture. As Elaine Scarry claims in her remarkable discussion of this particular category of physical pain, torture destroys both the subject and his or her body:

> what the process of torture does is to split the human
> being into two, to make emphatic the ever present but,
> except in the extremity of sickness and death, only la-
> tent distinction between a self and a body, between a
> 'me' and 'my body.' The 'self' or 'me,' which is experi-
> enced on the one hand as more private, more essentially
> at the center, and on the other hand as participating
> across the bridge of the body in the world, is 'embodied'
> in the voice, in language. The goal of the torturer is to
> make the one, the body, emphatically and crushingly
> *present* by destroying it, and to make the other, the
> voice, *absent* by destroying it.   (48-49)

I consider Scarry's analysis of torture an appropriate point of departure for a discussion of a novel that has located its narrative
space in the memories of slavery. *Beloved* returns repeatedly to
sites of physical, psychological, and sexual victimization, suggesting that these characters, scarred in an unfolding variety of ways,
represent the product of a system of torture. Unlike the slave
narrative, which typically presents a reasoned argument in favor
of abolition—punctuated, of course, by scenes of violence, but
seldom deviating from logical and rhetorically controlled con-
demnations of slavery—the characters in Morrison's novel have
no access to the methods of ordered narrative.[5] Their language,
their reasoning powers, even their sense of self have been dismantled by the process of torture. Because it acknowledges the
incapacitating effects of slavery, the novel refuses to celebrate the
pain that has produced these fragmented figures.

Slavery, of course, did not affect all African-Americans in
the same way, and we should be careful not to overstate the destructive power of the institution. Indeed, as Eugene Genovese
and others have shown, much independent and original production took place even under the burden of slavery. But it is
also clear that *Beloved* takes to task any nostalgia about slavery
days. One need not grant absolute authority to the oppressive-
ness of slavery, but *Beloved* cautions us against confusing gestures of creativity and self-reliance on the part of slaves with the
extremely different act of romanticizing the ugliness of slavery.

Certainly *Beloved* offers moments in which it approaches
a romantic, beautified version of pain. Remembering her last
days at Sweet Home, Sethe finds, to her dismay and astonish-
ment, that the violent events on the slave plantation have no

place in her memory, replaced, as they are, by a pastoral vision of
Sweet Home:

> Nothing else would be in her mind. . . . Nothing. Just
> the breeze cooling her face as she rushed toward water
> . . . and suddenly there was Sweet Home rolling,
> rolling, rolling out before her eyes, and although there
> was not a leaf on that farm that did not make her want
> to scream, it rolled itself out before her in shameless
> beauty. . . . Boys hanging from the most beautiful
> sycamores in the world. It shamed her—remembering
> the wonderful soughing trees rather than the boys. Try
> as she might to make it otherwise, the sycamores beat
> out the children every time and she could not forgive
> her memory, for that.   (6)

The problem is not, as we later discover, that Sethe beautifies the
pains that she herself does not experience. Even the sign of her
own pain presents itself to Sethe in "shameless beauty": she
cannot help repeating a white girl's vividly beautiful description
of the lash marks on her back. "I've never seen [the scar] and
never will," Sethe tells Paul D, "But that's what she said it
looked like. A chokecherry, tree. Trunk, branches, and even
leaves. Tiny little chokecherry leaves" (16). Even Sethe's
mother-in-law, Baby Suggs, arrives at a similar, aesthetically
charged description of the wound when she observes "Roses of
blood blossom[ing] in the blanket covering Sethe's shoulders"
(93). But Baby Suggs "hid her mouth with her hand," as if to
suggest that she, unlike Sethe, cannot find "shameless beauty" in
this sight. And Paul D, taken in at first by Sethe's metaphorical
description of her scar, soon rejects that description. The mark,
he decides, is "in fact a revolting clump of scars. Not a tree, as
she said. Maybe shaped like one, but nothing like any tree he
knew because trees were inviting; things you could trust and be
near; talk to if you wanted to as he frequently did since way back"
(21). The novel, in fact, quickly chastises its own impulse to
beautify pain. Even momentary attempts to recuperate a violent
past for the sake of transcendence are met with the implied accusation that such interpretive gestures occlude the horrific moments of slavery.

    Likewise, the novel raises the possibility of communicat-
ing pain only to mock that attempt. In a Baldwinian moment,
Sethe suggests that pain can, in fact, be articulated, and that the
effort to communicate pain can heal rifts between individuals.

To acknowledge and examine pain, as Baldwin implies—as well
as to convey that pain—might rescue these people from what
Baldwin calls the "limbo" of their failed lives. Such, at least, is
Sethe's feeling when she voices a hope for her murdered child's
return: "if she'd only come, I could make it clear to her" (4). But
this opening announcement—that the novel will dramatize the
communication of pain—is belied repeatedly by the dizzying effects of the narrative. Pain communicates nothing if not its own
incommunicability.

Not only is pain ineffable, but, as Sethe should know, the
experience of vivid pain dismantles language itself, so that pain
results in the impossibility of any intelligible utterance. After
Sethe sees the body of her dead mother, lynched and burned, her
language breaks down and remains incapacitated for a number
of years: "Stuttered after that. Didn't stop it till I saw Halle"
(201). One might argue that Sethe stutters still—indeed, that the
novel itself stutters in its Lavinian struggle to render pain lin-
guistically.[6] Sethe's own attempt to communicate her pain to
Paul D mirrors the larger narrative, made "recognizable but undecipherable" (199) to those who have not participated in the
particular pain being uttered:

> It made him dizzy. At first he thought it was her spin-
> ning. Circling him the way she was circling the subject.
> Round and round, never changing direction, which
> might have helped his head. Then he thought, No,
> it's the sound of her voice; it's too near. Each turn she
> made was at least three yards from where he sat, but
> listening to her was like having a child whisper into
> your ear so close you could feel its lips form the words
> you couldn't make out because they were too close. He
> caught only pieces of what she said.   (161)

Sethe tells her tale because she's convinced that "the words [in
the newspaper] she did not understand hadn't any more power
than she had to explain" (161). But in fact her own word, unsupported by the authority of the newspaper, is pallidly impo-
tent: "Sethe knew that the circle she was making around the
room, him, the subject, would remain one. That she could
never close in, pin it down for anybody who had to ask. If they
didn't get it right off—she could never explain" (163). Although
Paul D cannot read words, he understands the language of
newspapers, a language whose dangerous conventions carry a
force for him that Sethe's own words cannot:

> there was no way in hell a black face could appear in a
> newspaper if the story was about something anybody
> wanted to hear. A whip of fear broke through the
> heart chambers as soon as you saw a Negro's face in a
> paper, since the face was not there because the person
> had a healthy baby, or outran a street mob. Nor was it
> there because the person had been killed, or maimed or
> caught or burned or jailed or whipped or evicted or
> stomped or raped or cheated, since that could hardly
> qualify as news in a newspaper. It would have to be
> something out of the ordinary—something whitepeople
> would find interesting, truly different, worth a few
> minutes of teeth sucking if not gasps.   (155-156)

If the spoken word of individual experience offers an alternative center of meaning, Paul D nonetheless refuses that alternative in favor of an apparently more objective account: rightly or wrongly, Sethe has already been judged by the community of whitepeople, and nothing she tells Paul D can commute that judgment. Having heard Sethe's story and accepted the newspaper's unreadable "signs" rather than Sethe's own account, Paul D passes his own judgment and leaves.

Beloved challenges the romantic notion of beautiful, communicable, and humanizing pain by calling attention to the role of pain in unmaking language—not just the language of pain, but any language whatsoever. But if pain cannot be clearly conveyed, can it at least be examined privately, in order to validate the self to itself? If not publicly utterable, can suffering be comprehended and contemplated? The novel suggests a vexed relation between memory and desire, an interaction that makes contemplation all but impossible. When Stamp Paid attempts to tell Paul D of Sethe's violent past—to tell the very story she can render only in vertiginous language—he falters at the sight of Paul D's desire for an uncomplicated past. The problem for Stamp Paid—who had been present at the event—is not how to tell the story to Paul D, but finally, and more unsettlingly, how to remember it at all: "Stamp looked into Paul D's eyes and the sweet conviction in them almost made him wonder if it had happened at all, eighteen years ago, that while he and Baby Suggs were looking the wrong way, a pretty little slavegirl had recognized a hat, and split to the woodshed to kill her children" (158). In the blues tradition, Sethe's call and Paul D's response would lead to a dialogue of shared and transcended pain. But here, the anticipated response not only silences any articulation of pain but also dissolves the memory bearing these blues. If desire alters once vivid memories here, at other times it is unable to keep memory at bay. When Paul D calls attention to the inaccuracy of language, reminding Sethe that Sweet Home "wasn't sweet and it sure wasn't home," Sethe answers, "But it's where we were. . . . Comes back whether we want it to or not" (14). Sethe has already shown us that her memory is *not* accurate—that the "Sweet Home" that returns unbidden to her imagination is not the Sweet Home she had occupied during slavery—and now, in announcing that memory competes with desire, she suggests the impossibility of contemplation as well. Contemplation, that is, demands a sequestered space, remote from the conflicted workings of desire and denial. In figuring her memory as a battleground between desire and "factual' accuracy, Sethe calls attention to the futility of reflection. Not only is she unable to gain access to whatever painful events she has endured in the past, but her memory—far from healing and reordering the pain of her Sweet Home days—merely replicates the violence of that past.

The unmaking of language and memory, however, points to a more alarming unmaking of selfhood and signals Morrison's most radical revision of romantic, "humanizing" accounts of pain. *Beloved* persistently asks its readers where selfhood is located and seems to imply that language and memory, already dissolved by pain, bear responsibility for constructions of self. As Paul D puzzles over the source and status of his manhood, he wonders whether it wasn't invented and destroyed in the language of white men:

> Was that it? Is that where the manhood lay? In the naming done by a whiteman who was supposed to know? Who gave them the privilege not of working but of deciding how to? No. In their relationship with Garner was true metal: they were believed and trusted, but most of all they were listened to.   (125)

Manhood is constituted, Paul D concludes, not in language but in the "metal" of reality; language merely represents that metal. But after Garner's death and schoolteacher's arrival at Sweet Home, Paul D learns differently. After all, as schoolteacher makes clear, "definitions belonged to the definers—not the defined" (190). Only when Paul D arrives at Sethe's home and cannot help being seduced by a young girl does he begin to doubt the metal of his manhood: "If schoolteacher was right it explained how he had come to be a rag doll—picked up and put back down anywhere any time by a girl young enough to be his daughter. Fucking her when he was convinced he didn't want to" (126). His inability to resist this young girl drives him to interrogate the process whereby he inherited his "manhood," and finally to doubt the very metal of that manhood:

> Now . . . he wondered how much difference there really was between before schoolteacher and after. Garner called and announced them men—but only on Sweet Home, and by his leave. Was he naming what he saw or creating what he did not? . . . It troubled him that, concerning his own manhood, he could not satisfy himself on that point. Oh, he did manly things, but was that Garner's gift or his own will? . . . Did a whiteman saying it make it so?   (220)

Paul D discovers, then, that his identity is produced in the perceptions of others and rendered "real" to him through linguistic mechanisms—a slaveholder's descriptions, definitions, and boasts about his slaves. If his manhood seemed more stable and authentic when he was owned by the fair-minded Garner, that very stability was a fiction produced by consistent linguistic references to manhood. He only comes to doubt his manhood when those consistent signs are supplanted by a different rendering of the slave self. "Suppose Garner woke up one morning and changed his mind?" Paul D wonders, "Took the word away" (220). The self, he comes to understand, is located in the word, so that when that word changes, so, too, does identity.

Can freedom replace that instability with consistency and restore the fiction of autonomous selfhood? Baby Suggs, at one time a convincing advocate of self-reliance, learns the futility and slipperiness of such fictions. Just released from slavery and become a self-ordained preacher, she speaks for an almost Emersonian belief in the self: "She told them that the only grace they could have was the grace they could imagine. That if they could not see it, they would not have it" (88).[7] But self-reliance requires a self, and Baby Suggs soon discovers that imagination is impossible without this self, which she has never been granted:

> the sadness was at her center, the desolated center where the self that was no self made its home. Sad as it was that she did not know where her children were

> buried or what they looked like if alive, fact was she
> knew more about them than she knew about herself,
> having never had the map to discover what she was
> like.   (140)

Baby Suggs's slippery language betrays the unlocatable status of
selfhood: because she cannot decide whether hers is a self, no
self, or an undiscoverable self, she cannot accurately say that she
has a self at all, or if self can exist without being identified or
identifiable. Would she recognize her children if she saw them?
Would she recognize her *own* self if she could see it? If she can
neither see nor recognize her own interiority, how does she
know she is a self at all? Baby Suggs's skepticism about her own
selfhood presages the failure of her doctrine of self-reliance.[8]
Denver tells the story of Baby Suggs's disillusionment, of "how
she made a mistake. That what she thought about what the
heart and the body could do was wrong. The whitepeople came
anyway. In her yard. She had done everything right and they
came in her yard anyway" (209). Like Paul D, seduced against his
will by a young girl, Baby Suggs discovers that even the "grace
[she] could imagine" is impossible because her "desolated center"
is no self at all. The violence of slavery, like the changing linguistic code at Sweet Home, has unmade her fiction of autonomous selfhood.
      Having discovered the process whereby self is unmade,
are we to trust the remaking of self? Morrison offers us the possibility of recuperating the self when, near the close of the novel,
Denver discovers herself in her family's dependence on her:

> Somebody had to be saved, but unless Denver got work,
> there would be no one to save, no one to come home to,
> and no Denver either. It was a new thought, having a
> self to look out for and preserve. And it might not have
> occurred to her if she hadn't met Nelson Lord leaving
> his grandmother's house as Denver entered it to pay a
> thank you for half a pie. All he did was smile and say
> 'Take care of yourself, Denver,' but she heard it as
> though it were what language was made for. The last
> time he spoke to her his words blocked up her ears.
> Now they opened her mind.   (252)

Nelson's words "opened her mind": how are we to read this passage? Do Nelson's words, as Denver believes, call attention to a
self that had been present all along, the mere idea of which

"might not have occurred to her"? Does his language represent
the "metal" of selfhood, a real presence to which Denver had
previously been blind? Or should we rather believe, to modify
Paul D's insight, that a young boy's "saying it makes it so"? In
Denver's experience we see the real significance behind Paul D's:
the power of self-definition does indeed reside with the definers,
not the defined, and the definers are not necessarily white folks.
As Denver fails to recognize, but the novel seems to insist, identity is located in the perceptions and definitions of anyone or
anything external to the self. Even without language or cultural
power, the rooster named Mister fills the role of definer, as Paul
D discovers:

> He sat right there on the tub looking at me. I swear he
> smiled. My head was full of what I'd seen of Halle a
> while back. I wasn't even thinking about the bit. Just
> Halle and before him Sixo, but when I saw Mister I
> knew it was me too. . . .
>   . . . I was something else and that something was
> less than a chicken sitting in the sun on a tub.[9]   (72)

In seeing a "free" rooster smile at him, Paul D discovers his own
contrasting enslavement and arrives at a definition of himself
imposed by his internalization of the rooster's gaze. "Mister was
allowed to be and stay what he was," Paul D says. "But I wasn't
allowed to be and stay what I was" (72). Paul D resents not so
much the particular definition of selfhood imposed by the
rooster and the master but, more precisely, the transient, shifting
definitions of self that depend upon the gaze of his audience:
"When he looks at himself through Garner's eyes, he sees one
thing. Through Sixo's, another. One makes him feel righteous.
One makes him feel ashamed" (267). Though we might be
tempted to believe in either Paul D's "righteous" or Denver's
newly discovered self, the novel cautions against such a reading.
Identity, constructed according to one's audience, is liable to shift
as soon as the audience changes. The self remade in admiration
and kindness, though more palatable, is no more real than the
self made in violence, and one can only believe in it at the peril
of forgetting how easily self is made and unmade. Here the
novel seems to call attention to the pernicious flip side of a coin
minted in the call and response tradition. If, for that tradition,
self and community are mutually dependent and contingent, if
Sonny, for example, must find himself in the ritualized space of

communal suffering, here we see that the self can be dissolved in that same space.

Indeed, Paul D attempts to protect a fictional self from the violent remaking of this (perhaps sympathetic) audience. For this reason, he cuts short his account of Mister, even though Sethe, victim to pains of her own, has offered a nonjudgmental hearing. "Saying more might push them both to a place they couldn't get back from. He would keep the rest where it belonged: in that tobacco tin buried in his chest where a red heart used to be. Its lid rusted shut" (72-73). If he has no heart, Paul D implies, he at least has a heartless self that needs protecting, a self composed of unspeakable memories: "Alfred, Georgia, Sixo, schoolteacher, Halle, his brothers, Sethe, Mister, the taste of iron, the sight of butter, the smell of hickory, notebook paper" (113). But when, in a lonely moment, "His tobacco tin, blown open, spilled contents that floated freely and made him their play and prey" (218), the contents of the tin are revealed to be nothing but a metaphor for what Baby Suggs has called "the self that was no self." The tin opens, finally, to release not a self but merely a scattering of dry tobacco leaves (218). To protect the self from its audience, we learn, is to cause the disintegration of that self.

What, then, can we say about pain? Sethe wants to grant a reality to her painful memories, if only to invest them with meaning:

> If a house burns down, it's gone, but the place—the picture of it—stays, and not just in my rememory but out there, in the world. What I remember is a picture floating around out there outside my head. I mean, even if I don't think it, even if I die, the picture of what I did, or knew, or saw is still out there. Right in the place where it happened.
> . . . Someday you be walking down the road and you hear something or see something going on. So clear. And you think it's you thinking it up. A thought picture. But no. It's when you bump into a rememory that belongs to somebody else. (36)

If selfhood is rendered a fiction, Sethe wants to believe, at least the experience of suffering can be invested with meaning and made substantial. Sethe offers this reading of pain as an alternative to romanticism, as a means of making pain mean something without seeming, as Emerson says, to "court suffering, in the hope that here at least we shall find reality, sharp peaks and edges of truth" (48). If the self is neither real nor permanent, perhaps the pains endured by that "self" can be experienced empirically. If language cannot render the experience of suffering, at least, Sethe believes, that experience can continue to occupy physical space in the world, so that a stranger may "bump into a rememory that belongs to somebody else."

Sethe's reified memory merely highlights the tenuous status of selfhood: her memory is more real, more present and lasting, than the agent of that memory. Likewise, the reified desire embodied by Beloved points to the fictionality of subjectivities. The question posed by the novel's conclusion is not why Beloved disappears, but rather how anything short of disappearance could be possible for an individual who loses her desirability. Beloved, it must be noted, appears only after Sethe expresses a desire for the return of her dead child. "But if she'd only come," Sethe says, "I could make it clear to her" (4). Beloved's disappearance only literalizes what happens to all selves: constructed in terms of audience, she can exist only as long as her audience chooses to acknowledge her:

> Everybody knew what she was called, but nobody anywhere knew her name. Disremembered and unaccounted for, she cannot be lost because no one is looking for her, and even if they were, how can they call her if they don't know her name? Although she has claim, she is not claimed. In the place where long grass opens, the girl who waited to be loved and cry shame erupts into her separate parts, to make it easy for the chewing laughter to swallow her all away.   (274)

Like the "self that was no self" until constituted in language and acknowledged by an audience, this "self" disappears when the people among whom she lived no longer look for her or call her name. If the people in this community enjoy any agency over their lives, that agency consists of the ability to choose their own point of focus, to look away when desire dissipates or fear becomes too oppressive. Beloved's literal, corporeal disappearance prefigures her disappearance from memory—the vehicle of the real, according to Sethe:

> They forgot her like a bad dream. After they made up their tales, shaped and decorated them, those that saw her that day on the porch quickly and deliberately forgot her. It took longer for those who had spoken to

Pain and the Unmaking of Self
in Toni Morrison's *Beloved*
273

her, lived with her, fallen in love with her, to forget,
until they realized they couldn't remember or repeat a
single thing she said, and began to believe that, other
than what they themselves were thinking, she hadn't
said anything at all. So, in the end, they forgot her
too. (274)

Beloved, I would argue, is a model for all selves: if she is ghostly
and ephemeral, she only literalizes what occurs to all other characters in Morrison's novel. They, like Beloved, exist at the pleasure of other selves. Once one takes the word away, selfhood inevitably vanishes. The definers are not simply slaveholders and
schoolteachers, but anyone who threatens individual autonomy
by including the individual in his or her language and gaze.
And to revoke name and gaze, further, is to abolish the self.

Pain, finally, cannot make us real: if empirical reality is re-
served for (re)memory and desire, it can, like the acknowledgment of a self's existence, be revoked at any time. The most pain
can do, as the novel suggests, is call attention to the violent and
necessary process whereby self is constructed by other. If we
choose to seize on more attractive versions of self and believe
them to be "real"—or, in the romantic account, "fully human"—we take the dangerous risk, in Emerson's words, of
"courting suffering" in order to verify our humanity. Of course,
healthy-minded denials of pain pose an opposite threat to our
conceptions of history and perhaps the traditions I have been
discussing have gained such ground precisely as a corrective to
healthy-mindedness. However, if we wish to persist in our belief that pain does make us fully human, we need to reevaluate
our definition of "human." Perhaps here we find Morrison's
most radical reevaluation of Baldwin and other voices from the
blues heritage. To be human, *Beloved* suggests, is no different
from being ghostly: to be human means to be as likely spectral as
substantial, fictional as real, and to be ontologically as well as
emotionally contingent on one's audience, to occupy an ever
shifting identity.

Notes

[1] As Gayl Jones reminds us, "Some black writers and critics have rejected
the blues. For Ron Karenga blues is bound to the past; it teaches resignation and
acceptance of reality" (196).

[2] Deborah Horvitz writes that this conclusion "paradoxically appears to belie the crucial theme of the book, that it is imperative to preserve continuity through story, language, and culture" (165). David Lawrence writes that "While the painful heritage of slavery cannot simply 'pass on,' cannot die away . . . enslavement to that heritage, Morrison implies, must 'pass on,' must die away in order to undertake the task of remembering and rearticulating the individual and the communal body" (200). Rebecca Ferguson contends that, in spite of its claim, the narrative "*is* passing the story on" (123-124), and Karen E. Fields writes that *Beloved* "is not a story to be retold in only one way" (169).

[3] The pervasiveness of the readings that I am challenging here is evident even in Morrison's own reflections on her work. In a *New York Times* article by Mervyn Rothstein, she suggests that the pain dramatized in *Beloved* unmakes rather than makes humanity: "I don't know if that story came because I was considering certain aspects of self-sabotage, the ways in which the best things we do so often carry seeds of one's own destruction." But in the same article she intimates that pain—whether self-propelled or derived from outside forces—can in fact be overcome: "I wanted it to be our past, which is haunting, and her past, which is haunting—the way memory never really leaves you unless you have gone through it and confronted it head on."

[4] I am using the word "unmake" as Elaine Scarry introduces it in *The Body in Pain*: "Physical pain," Scarry writes, "does not simply resist language but actively destroys it, bringing about an immediate reversion to a state anterior to language, to the sounds and cries a human being makes before language is learned" (4). More dramatically in *Beloved*, pain destroys not merely language but selfhood—which is founded, of course, on language. Morrison's novel, I want to suggest, owes less to European traditions of romanticized pain than to Scarry's insight that pain unmakes the world.

[5] See, for instance, Henry Louis Gates, Jr.'s discussion, in *Figures in Black*, of rhetorical control in Frederick Douglass's *Narrative* (80-97).

[6] When Shakespeare's Titus Andronicus turns to the dismembered Lavinia who, deprived of hands and tongue, cannot communicate her rape, he laments his daughter's inability to convey her story: "Thou map of woe, that thus dost talk in signs!" (3.2.12). Likewise, Sethe speaks as if deprived of a tongue, for she, too, must "talk in signs" when language fails.

[7] Missy Dehn Kubitschek notes the sustaining power of Baby Suggs's self-reliance without addressing its failure: "Emphasizing preparedness rather than protection, Baby Suggs's method of mothering promotes, through historical examples, the same self-valuing and self-reliance as her preaching" (173).

[8] If I have suggested that Baby Suggs voices an Emersonian version of self-reliance, here she resembles the skeptical Emerson of "Experience," who discovers that skepticism regarding other selves might essentially lead to skepticism about one's own self. Emerson's suspicion that perhaps the world is a product of one's own mind, that "perhaps there are no objects" in fact "threaten[s] or insult[s] whatever is threatenable and unsuitable in us" (76). Emerson resolves the problem of skepticism by proposing an expediency of surfaces: "We live amid surfaces, and the true art of life is to skate well on them" (59). Baby Suggs, too, resorts to an attentiveness to surfaces when she announces her intention to do nothing and to think of nothing but colors: "What I have to do is get in my bed and lay down. I want to fix on something harmless in this

world. . . . Blue. That don't hurt nobody. Yellow neither" (179).
   [9] The rooster's name implies the cultural power of both class and the slaveholding system: "Mister" is a term of respect, only a vowel away from "master." But in assigning this name to a barnyard animal (even the king of the livestock), Morrison suggests the arbitrary status of power and selfhood.

Works Cited

Baker, Houston A. *Blues, Ideology, and Afro-American Literature: A Vernacular Theory.* Chicago: University of Illinois Press, 1984.

Baldwin, James. *Another Country.* New York: Dell, 1962.

—. "Sonny's Blues." 1957. *Going to Meet the Man.* New York: Dell, 1968. 86-122.

Clements, Arthur L. *Poetry of Contemplation: John Donne, George Herbert, Henry Vaughan, and the Modern Period.* Albany: SUNY Press, 1990.

Ellison, Ralph. "Richard Wright's Blues." 1945. *Shadow and Act.* New York: Random, 1964. 77-94.

Emerson, Ralph Waldo. "Experience." 1844. *Centenary Edition of the Complete Works of Ralph Waldo Emerson.* 1903. Vol. 3. New York: AMS Press, 1968. 43-86. 12 Vols.

Ferguson, Rebecca. "History, Memory and Language in Toni Morrison's *Beloved.*" *Feminist Criticism: Theory and Practice.* Ed. Susan Sellers. Toronto: University of Toronto Press, 1991. 109-127.

Fields, Karen E. "To Embrace Dead Strangers: Toni Morrison's *Beloved.*" *Mother Puzzles: Daughters and Mothers in Contemporary American Literature.* Ed. Mickey Pearlman. Contributions in Women's Studies 110. New York: Greenwood, 1989. 159-169.

Gates, Henry Louis, Jr. *Figures in Black: Words, Signs, and the "Racial" Self.* New York: Oxford University Press, 1987.

Genovese, Eugene D. *Roll, Jordan, Roll: The World the Slaves Made.* 1974. New York: Vintage, 1976.

Horvitz, Deborah. "Nameless Ghosts: Possession and Dispossession in *Beloved.*" *Studies in American Fiction* 17 (1989): 157-167.

Jones, Gayl. *Liberating Voices: Oral Tradition in African-American Literature.* Cambridge, Massachusetts: Harvard University Press, 1991.

Keats, John. *Letters of John Keats.* Ed. Hyder Edwards Rollins. Vol. 2. Cambridge, Massachusetts: Harvard University Press, 1958. 2 Vols.

Kubitschek, Missy Dehn. *Claiming the Heritage: African-American Women Novelists and History.* Jackson: University Press of Mississippi, 1991.

Lawrence, David. "Fleshly Ghosts and Ghostly Flesh: The Word and the Body in *Beloved.*" *Studies in American Fiction* 19 (1991): 189-201.

Morrison, Toni. *Beloved.* New York: Knopf, 1987.

Rothstein, Mervyn. "Toni Morrison, in Her New Novel, Defends Women." *New York Times* 26 August 1987, late ed.: C17.

Scarry, Elaine. *The Body in Pain: The Making and Unmaking of the World.* New York: Oxford University Press, 1985.

Shakespeare, William. *Titus Andronicus. The Riverside Shakespeare.* Ed. G. Blakemore Evans. Boston: Houghton, 1974. 1019-1054.

Williams, Sherley A. "The Blues Roots of Contemporary Afro-American Poetry." *Chant of Saints: A Gathering of Afro-American Literature, Art, and Scholarship.* Ed. Michael S. Harper and Robert B. Stepto. Urbana: University of Illinois Press, 1979. 123-135.

Wordsworth, William. Preface to the 1800 *Lyrical Ballads.* Ed. R. L. Brett and A. R. Jones. London: Methuen, 1963.

Missing Peace in Toni Morrison's
Sula and *Beloved*

Rachel C. Lee

From her earliest fictional work *The Bluest Eye* (1970) to her latest, *Jazz* (1992), Toni Morrison cultivates an aesthetic of ambiguity. Placing Morrison in a "postmodernist" context, Robert Grant, for instance, describes both the "labor" of interpreting *Sula* and the richness evoked by its narrative "gaps." Clearly, Morrison's emphasis on absences and indeterminate meanings casts an interpretational bone in the direction of readers and critics who, as urged by Grant, transform "absence into presence." However, I would argue that the more productive endeavor may be to read the ambiguities of Morrison's texts not as aporia to be "filled . . . by the reader" (Grant 94) but as signifiers of an unattainable desire for stable definitions and identities.

This essay, accordingly, explores the relationship between the slippage of words and the informing voids (desires) of Morrison's novels by examining two of her most critically recognized works, *Sula* (1973) and *Beloved* (1987). Though all of Morrison's novels play upon the variability of language, *Sula* especially throws into disequilibrium that exemplar dichotomy, good and evil, and by extension all Manichean systems which undergird traditional linguistic and ethical orders. By bringing to light the relativity of meaning, *Sula* broaches the subject not only of semantic integrity (how we can convey what we mean) but also of epistemological integrity (how can we know anything since there is no objective perspective and no objective essence or truth to know). While the aforementioned questions bristle under each of Morrison's texts, in *Sula*, Morrison offers to her readers a main character who telescopes that scandal of epistemology. How can we understand or know Sula, who is not only egoless or without a self (and hence undeterminable) but who also is unable to know anything herself?

By contrast, *Beloved*, set almost a century earlier (c. 1852-1873), deals less with the metaphysical premises of good and evil to focus instead upon the institution of slavery and its over-whelming perversion of meaning. Inspired by a newspaper clipping from the 1850s (Davis 151), *Beloved* reconstructs the nuances of a black woman's killing of her infant daughter in re-sponse to the Fugitive Slave Act. Symbolic and discursive sub-stitutions become emblematic in this latter narrative, where a ghost stands in for the lost living, where memory only approxi-mates event, and where gestures and words struggle to fill the gaps of unvoiced longings. In *Beloved*, Morrison again high-lights the variability of meaning and identity, yet in this case she links approximations of meaning to the historical condition of being enslaved.

Taking the cue from Eva's suggestion that there are no such things as innocent words or gestures—"'How you gone not mean something by it'" (*Sula* 68)—I engage in close readings of Morrison's texts with an eye toward the overdetermined nature of each sign. In addition, by looking at two of her works in con-junction, I hope to shed light on the different levels of language manipulation occurring in each book as well as conjecture the possible implications of these differences. How do the words of 1987 supplement, qualify, or reinforce their 1973 predecessors?

* * * * *

Sula begins with two gestures: a dedication and an epi-graph. In the dedication, Morrison reconfigures a traditional signifier of loss and elegiac retrieval, to one of desire: "It is sheer good fortune to miss somebody long before they leave you. This book is for Ford and Slade, whom I miss although they have not left me." Instead of invoking the dead, Morrison places "Ford and Slade" into a "missed" situation, rewriting their future ab-sence into the present and applying associations of loss and pro-found appreciation (usually reserved for the dead) to persons not yet defined by this absence. In effect, Morrison conveys a height-ened sense of the variability of Ford and Slade, their probable mortality, their easy slippage into alter identities. How does the writer, then, who in essence "embalms" or fixes her subject, inscribe this changeableness of character?   Does not every descriptive endeavor risk "missing" an essential, uncapturable quality (hence Morrison's play on the other meanings of to *miss*: 'to not quite capture,' 'to arrive too late,' 'to render inaccurately'—as in missing a piece, missing a train, or missing the point).   With this dedication, Morrison unsettles the very sense of to *miss* and intimates the impossibility of any representation not informed by missing meanings.

The second sign in *Sula*, the epigraph drawn from Williams's *The Rose Tattoo*, foreshadows the replication of signs, the overdetermination of meanings, and the thematics of self in the subsequent text:

> Nobody knew my rose of the world but me. . . . I had too
> much glory.   They don't want glory like *that* in nobody's heart.

The Rose Tattoo inscribes its sign upon Morrison's novel, not unlike the birthmark destined for Sula's eye.   This birthmark remains an ambiguous sign variously esteemed; it appears "a rose" to the narrative voice, a stemmed rose to Eva and Nel, a "scary black thing" to Nel's children, "a copperhead" to Jude, "Hannah's ashes" to the community, and "a tadpole" to Shadrack.   As a mark of and on Sula/*Sula*, the epigraph foreshadows Sula's final isolation and incomprehensibility.   At her death, nobody "knows" Sula but herself.   The epigraph also attributes to the eponymous protagonist an excess of self-centeredness.   The words "I had too much glory" find a near correlative in Sula's later assertion "'I can do it all, why can't I have it all?'" (142).   Yet, this epigraphic suggestion of Sula's self-love enacts a further corruption of signs, for Morrison later suggests that Sula has no sense of self—"She had no center . . . no ego" (119).   Both Rose Tattoos (birthmark and epigraph) become for Sula/*Sula* symbols of contradictory meanings as well as marks of "missed" identification.

With those dedicatory and epigraphic signs, one enters the narrative body of *Sula*, where missed meanings between conversants proliferate.   After Sula's return to Medallion, she and Nel engage in familiar yet unfamiliar banter:

> 'You been gone too long, Sula.'
> 'Not too long, but maybe too far.'

'What's that supposed to mean?' . . .
'Oh, I don't know.'
'Want some cool tea?'   (96)

While the reader may variously interpret Sula's suggestion that she has gone "too far" (i.e., she has reached a different value system, or has over-stepped consensus boundaries), Nel doesn't conjecture these meanings. Rather, the conversation turns to the distancing etiquette of proffered "tea." Nel's puzzlement over what Sula "mean[s]" is, in itself, an oddity, for the two women's history has been marked by an uncanny unison of thinking and movement that does not require words. Most memorable of that synchronicity is the prelude to Chicken Little's death, where the two girls "in concert, without ever meeting each other's eyes" dig two holes in the ground, furrowing deeper and deeper "until the two holes were one and the same," finally "replac[ing] the soil and cover[ing] the entire grave with uprooted grass [all during which] neither one had spoken a word" (58-59). This ensemble performance significantly occurs in silence, the implications being that words would disrupt the unity of action and, correlatively, that the necessity for words indicates a lesser degree of intimacy. Imbedded in the textual appeal to wordlessness, then, is the notion of language as the site and symptom of difference. Thus, when Nel recalls her former closeness with Sula, she describes them as "two throats and one eye" (147), emphasizing both perceptual "sameness" and discursive "difference." That is, even during the period in which the two girls shared "one eye," their means of articulating themselves were differentiated as "two."

In addition to the slips in language occurring *between* speakers, Morrison shows the schism between word and delayed/deferred significance that transpires within an individual's mind. When Eva describes her reasons for killing Plum, she speaks "with two voices. Like two people were talking at the same time, saying the same thing, one a fraction of a second behind the other" (71). The two voices say the "same thing"—but with a difference, one articulating, for Hannah, Plum's decline and Eva's response to it; the other translating for Eva, herself, the same scenario but with all the unsaid qualifications of motive and recollected vividness which encompass that "fraction of a second" delay. The "ambiguities of mercy" (Spillers 314), intoned but not made explicit in either Eva's act or her subsequent explanation, suggest that the "two voices" have not adequately justified her killing of Plum; perhaps the clarification required to assess Eva's act as a mercy killing or not lies in the reserve of that delayed moment—in the missing or sublimated text.

Contending with language's slippage presents a dilemma not only for Morrison's characters, but also for the author/narrator. For instance, the words "pig meat" (50) remain inadequate to describe the flavor of Ajax's utterance, the implicit "compliment" of his stylized delivery. The significance of pig meat lies less in the literal content of the term than in

> the way [Ajax] handled the words. When he said "hell" he hit the *h* with his lungs and the impact was greater than the achievement of the most imaginative foul mouth in the town. He could say "shit" with a nastiness impossible to imitate. So, when he said "pig meat" as Nel and Sula passed, they guarded their eyes lest someone see their delight.   (50)

This qualification acknowledges the distance between the words at the writer's disposal and the nuances conveyed in the hissing of a particular *h*. While Morrison elaborates on the *h*'s transformative effects on the word *hell*, she leaves absent how Ajax utters *pig meat* to give it a complimentary texture; like *shit* it remains "impossible to imitate." Thus, despite the supplement that Morrison provides, *pig meat* as Ajax delivers it, remains missing from the text, only associatively colored by the description of Ajax's hissing *hell*.

Through such proximal associations, Morrison manages to absent the utterance and, through such absence, deliver the sense. That is, Ajax says aloud what was "in all their minds" yet difficult or prohibitive to express (e.g., "the taste of young sweat on tight skin," or the "mystery curled" beneath "cream-colored trousers" [50]). The emphasis on the way in which Ajax mouths the words subordinates their referential function to highlight instead the process of meaning's construction. More important than the referent of "pig meat" is the utterance's capacity to inspire for the men in front of the pool hall and for the two walking girls a breeze of sexual (re)awakening. Moreover, the very slips and deviances in both Ajax's intonation and Morrison's description of it provide a stylistic correlative to Sula's and Nel's burgeoning sense of sexuality: They were "like tightrope walkers, as thrilled by the possibility of a slip as by the maintenance of tension and balance" (51). The playfulness in both Ajax's and

Morrison's words simultaneously create and avoid the desire for sexual and semantic gratification.

The absence of Ajax's "pig meat" utterance, yet its evocation through supplemental conceit, reveals its simultaneous properties as both missed yet not missing from the narrative. This liminal straddling between absence and presence becomes characteristic of the metonymic device which Morrison shows operating for herself as well as her characters. For instance, Jude's tie and Ajax's license evolve into metonyms for persons with whom they are associated. For Nel, Jude's tie becomes both the sign of his absence and the single remnant of all that he took: ". . . you walked past me saying, 'I'll be back for my things.' And you did but you left your tie" (106). Jude's tie remains liminally situated, as a signifier of absence, only through being present and metaphorically bringing into presence the remembered Jude.

It would seem that Ajax's license would likewise provide Sula with a "tie" to her former lover; however, in this instance, Morrison reflects on the relevance of linguistic error to one's sense of knowing. As Sula searches for signs of Ajax's former presence, she eventually stumbles across physical evidence, which ironically negates Ajax's identity as Sula knows it:

> Then one day . . . she found . . . proof that he had been there, his driver's license. . . . But what was this? Albert Jacks? His name was Albert Jacks? A. Jacks. She had thought it was Ajax . . . when for the first time in her life she had lain in bed with a man and said his name involuntarily or said it truly meaning *him*, the name she was screaming and saying was not his at all.
>
> (135-136)

Although she truly "means *him*," Sula misses saying Albert Jacks's name with its inscribed difference. This mistake leads Sula to question her knowledge in general: "'. . . there is nothing I did know and I have known nothing since the one thing I wanted was to know his name . . .'" (136). Her conclusion on knowing nothing applies beyond herself—how can anyone know anything when the purveyors of meaning slip, deviate, and deceive?

A correlative question—How can anyone convey anything when words limit and elude?—bristles under Morrison's text. Instead of released verbal expression, Morrison often presents only the gestures toward possible expressions:

> The body *must* move and throw itself about, the eyes
> *must* roll, the hands *should* have no peace, and the
> throat *should* release all the yearning, despair and
> outrage that accompany the stupidity of loss.
>
> (107; italics added)

The imperative thrust of *must* declines into its subjunctive *should*, a pattern which defers mandatory urgency. Desire and purpose replace definitive action, as Morrison thwarts her character's attempt to "release all yearning": "Nel waited . . . for the oldest cry . . . her very own howl. But it did not come" (108).

The inadequacy of words and the desire for meaningful expression infuse Morrison's novel. Yet Sula's statement on "know[ing] nothing" presents an even graver problem. In the silence of one's interior consciousness, meaning becomes variable or meaningless—knowledge a mere ruse. Variability of meaning, whether articulated or silent, derives from a relativity of perspective. If one could stabilize for a moment the relational connotations of the word *bottom*, one could not fix the variable viewpoint from which it refers. That is, the Bottom remains "'high up for us,' said the master, 'but when God looks down, it's the bottom. That's why we call it so. It's the bottom of heaven—best land there is'" (5). The white farmer argues from God's "viewpoint" not because he deems it right, but because it allows him to swindle his black slave out of valley or "bottom" land. However, genuine investment in God's point of view informs Eva's judgments of right and wrong as well as communal assessments of good and evil. It remains for Sula to question that fundamental reliance upon God's authority, bringing into focus the implied perspective from which consensus meaning derives:

> 'Bible say honor thy father and thy mother that
> thy days may be long upon the land thy God giveth
> thee,' [says Eva].
>   'Mamma must have skipped that part. Her days
> wasn't too long,' [responds Sula].
>   'Pus mouth! God's going to strike you!'
>   'Which God? The one watched you burn Plum?' (93)

By asking "Which God?" Sula poses the relativity of even this monolith and questions both Eva's version of good and evil and good and evil in general. Additionally, Sula flaunts "falling," saying "'What the hell do I care about falling?'" since falling/

Falling no longer *means* the descent into evil implied in Eva's Biblical aphorism ("'Pride goeth before a fall'") (93). Sula accepts this slippage, this fall (in language), and opposes the community's investment in a monolithic God as determiner of meaning.

Interestingly, while Sula here undermines God as monolith, she later seeks an unfallen language to describe the loneliness she seeks in coition—

> a loneliness so profound the word itself had no meaning. For loneliness assumed the absence of other people, and the solitude she found in that desperate terrain had never admitted the possibility of other people.   (123)

Sula and Morrison seek to describe an absence that antedates presence—a loneliness existing without relation to another. Yet language falls short. Morrison can only approximate Sula's loneliness through a catalog of "lost" items:

> She wept then. Tears for the deaths of the littlest things: the castaway shoes of children; broken stems of marsh grass battered and drowned by the sea; prom photographs of dead women she never knew; wedding rings in pawn-shop windows; the tidy bodies of Cornish hens in a nest of rice.   (123)

This list supplements the idea of loneliness-as-void, yet does not achieve it and, paradoxically, erases it by filling it in.

Morrison later makes more explicit this loneliness defined by another against a loneliness which is "mine." In response to Nel's implicit condemnation of Sula's self-reliant lifestyle ("'Lonely, ain't it?'"), Sula replies, "'Yes. But my lonely is *mine*. Now your lonely is somebody else's. . . . Ain't that something? A secondhand lonely'" (143). Although Sula has slipped into a "secondhand lonely" for Ajax, the loneliness she describes to Nel consists of a yearning or missing without object. In effect, Sula wishes to describe and achieve an Adamic loneliness, an unfallen, originary loneliness.

Sula / *Sula* thus exhibits a desire for absolute meaning, though only briefly. Shortly after Nel's departure, Sula contemplates her own lack of permanence and her correlative lack of meaning:

> 'If I live a hundred years my urine will flow the same way, my armpits and breath will smell the same. . . . *I*

> *didn't mean anything. I never meant anything.* I stood
> there watching her burn and was thrilled. I wanted
> her to keep on jerking like that, to keep on dancing.'
> (147; italics added)

Sula describes her unvariability (what one would think implies
a stable identity), but also her meaninglessness (perhaps confirming de Sausserian notions of meaning's contingency upon
differences [Derrida 140]). Despite this self-evaluation, Sula,
rather than meaning nothing, produces an excess of meanings.
Her words "I didn't mean anything" can be variously interpreted: Sula cannot intend meaning since meaning and the purveyors of meaning remain corrupt, or Sula hasn't made an impact on the world other than being "a body, a name and an address" (173). The latter interpretation confirms Sula as egoless or
only a striving toward identity rather than a completion or, as
Deborah McDowell phrases it, "character as *process*" rather than
"character as *essence*" (81). The context in which Sula "speaks"
these thoughts compound their overdetermination. As the last
quoted words before her death, these thoughts take on a confes-
sional tone, especially in juxtaposition to her recollection of
Hannah's burning. Sula's "I never meant anything" may refer
to her gesture of ambivalence, of looking at Hannah's fiery
dance, feeling neither remorse nor delight. Thus, Sula reaffirms
her non-relation to another, while also denying any substantive
presence unto herself. Rather than "never mean[ing] anything,"
Sula's meanings are endless, incomplete—always missed.

The seeming contradiction of Sula as neither in relation
to another nor defined as present unto herself resolves itself in
the notion of Sula as open-ended or "never achiev[ing] completeness of being" (McDowell 81). That is, to pose Sula's relation to another (effectively writing in what she desires) would be
to project a closure to her identity. In *Sula*, however, closure
consistently eludes both author and title character. For instance,
the narrative closing of Chicken Little's life, initially described as
"the closed place in the water," quickly transforms into "something newly missing" (61), as if closure were always informed by
some missing piece (and thus not closed or complete at all).
Chicken Little's "ending" oddly remains unseen by most of the
community; and because his remains are withheld from viewing by the "closed coffin" (64), closure paradoxically creates a
void in perception—a new lack in the text.

Sula's death creates similar gaps in the text. Her narrative continues beyond her last breath, and her post-mortem thoughts "'Well, I'll be damned . . . it didn't even hurt. Wait'll I tell Nel'" (149) not only write her beyond her own ending but also reinforce Sula's striving after supplementation. Sula/*Sula* asks the reader to "wait" until a doubtful future moment (since she is dead, she cannot tell Nel), deferring infinitely the closure of both book and "self."

Not surprisingly, then, *Sula* concludes with an openended description which re-emphasizes the ambiguous borders of personal and discursive definitions. Nel's contemplation of the Peace gravestones conflates people, words, and desires:

> Together they read like a chant: PEACE 1895-1921,
> PEACE 1890-1923, PEACE 1910-1940, PEACE 1892-1959.
> They were not dead people. They were words. Not
> even words. Wishes, longings.   (171)

The associative ambiguity of "Peace" clues the reader into the thematic suggestion that Peace, both the people and the word, remains missing and that this missing Peace (piece) inspires desire. Morrison takes the conventional sentiment of "rest-in-peace" out of equilibrium and overlays grave, book, language, and identity with inconclusiveness. Nel's final cry "'O Lord, Sula . . . girl, girl, girlgirlgirl'" (174) echoes this triple intersection of words, people, and desires. The variable referent of "girl" (Nel's invocation to Sula or to herself) points to language's plurisignifying potential to evoke missed people (others), the missed self, missed meanings, and all the desire encompassed in those yearnings for the "missed." The novel's inconclusiveness, then, reiterates Sula's identity as desire without object, as the narrative itself embodies that same sense of desire for the reader.

* * * * *

Whereas, in *Sula*, words fail to explain conversational objects (a restroom) or concepts (God), in *Beloved*, language and expression in general fall short because the experiences they strive to capture are peculiar—always circumscribed by the legacy of having been owned. In her later work, Morrison highlights the lack of vocabulary to speak the experience of the enslaved self as well as the often perilous relation of the former enslaved to a historically specific language which commodifies African-Americans. *Beloved*, then, redefines the duplicity of language with an eye toward its historical warping.

One might begin to define the "something missing" in *Beloved* through language and its often incomprehensible meanings. Morrison shows that the mutations of time often place language out of reach, so that former words cannot be recollected:

> What Nan told her [Sethe] had forgotten, along with
> the language she told it in . . . she was picking meaning
> out of a code she no longer understood.   (62)

Facing near hieroglyphs in memory, Sethe must bypass the language and the words for the meaning behind them. Thus, Morrison presents a gap in what Nan says, and instead proposes what Nan "means:"

> [Nan] told Sethe that her mother and Nan were to-
> gether from the sea. Both were taken up many times by
> the crew. 'She threw them all away but you. The one
> from the crew she threw away on the island. . . . With-
> out names, she threw them. You she gave the name of
> the black man. She put her arms around him. The
> others she did not put her arms around.'   (62)

Morrison switches from third-person paraphrase of Nan's "meaning" to direct quotations—fabricated quotations, however, since the original words and language have been lost. In Sethe's distillation of meaning from a forgotten "code," Morrison implies the dual construction of meaning. The words here are as much fabricated by Sethe as they are delivered by Nan, who, in turn, wishes to convey some elusive meaning from Sethe's mother. This last meaning finally surfaces through a series of deferrals, leaving the reader uncertain as to how to interpret Nan's "words." Are they indicators of Sethe's relative importance to her mother (since she has not met the fate of her half-siblings)? Do they create a threatening picture of mother-love, as Sethe's killing of Beloved has done for Howard and Buglar?

The difficulties of interpreting meaning pose dilemmas not only for those recollecting the past, but also among characters sharing the same narrative present. When Stamp Paid goes to visit the women of 124, he encounters an incomprehensible language:

> Out on Bluestone Road he thought he heard a confla-
> gration of hasty voices—loud, urgent, all speaking at
> once. . . . All he could make out was the word *mine*. The
> rest of it stayed outside his mind's reach.   (172)

Though Stamp Paid "couldn't describe [this speech] to save his
life," the narrator (through Stamp Paid's perspective) supplements this initial description with yet another approximation of
these "sounds":

> [It was] like the interior sounds a woman makes when
> she believes she is alone and unobserved at her work; a
> *sth* when she misses the needle's eye; a soft moan when
> she sees another chip in her one good platter; the low,
> friendly argument with which she greets the hens.
> Nothing fierce or startling. Just that eternal, private
> conversation that takes place between women and their
> tasks.   (172)

One wonders whether Morrison, here, portrays more about the
perceiver than the perceived. That is, the male figure, representative of the public workplace, glances in the window of the female privatized home, and sees an alien space defined by domestic tasks and an exclusive female presence (down to the hens).
To him, the sounds remain unintelligible, the significance of the
"argument with which she greets the hens" unfathomable.

As these two examples attest, slippage of language in
Beloved occurs between persons who have lost contact. Unlike
Sula and Nel, the main characters of this later novel, with the
exception of Beloved, remain discrete entities, none having
achieved the closeness implied in "two throats and one eye."
Even family members do not realize an affinity like Sula's and
Nel's. Sethe only knows her mother through two gestures: her
mother's revealing to Sethe her circle and cross brand, and the
slap Sethe receives upon requesting a similar mark (61);
Joshua/Stamp Paid displaces his emotional attachment to his
wife Vashti by changing his name rather than snapping her neck
(233). In both cases, the distance between mother-daughter and
husband-wife must be maintained, for in the pressurized atmosphere of slavery, close ties risk implosion. Thus, Morrison implies how historical realities perpetuate a system that precludes
intimate contact: As Denver later articulates, "Slaves not supposed to have pleasurable feelings on their own; their bodies not
supposed to be like that . . ." (209). Language's slippage and

missed meanings take place across migratory (and chronological) stretches, allowing Morrison to contextualize the corruption of signifiers within the historical exigencies of slavery and its aftermath.

In particular, Morrison shows how certain symbols become overdetermined in meaning. Sethe's breasts, for instance, begin as signifiers of nurturing. Sethe, who is pregnant with Denver but still has '"milk for [her] baby girl,"' must get to Ohio where her daughter awaits her. Yet, before Sethe leaves Sweet Home, Schoolteacher's nephews forcibly "rape" her milk (16-17), reinscribing her breasts as sites of violation and instruments through which to deprive her children of sustenance; they also epitomize how "private" body parts become commodified, public, and un-"own"-ed by the self. The overdetermined meaning of Sethe's breasts results, in part, from the lack of an appropriate language to speak the outrage of slavery. How can one describe the multiple injustices and rage which slavery yields—the "unspeakable thoughts, unspoken" (199)? Thus, tropes such as Sethe's breasts come to approximate the confluence of emotions (guilt, shame, rage, grief, insecurity, terror, numbness . . .) begotten from the "Peculiar Institution."

Likewise, Paul D's rooster becomes the only way for him to express a degradation so severe that it remains unnamed by the narrative's conclusion. In a conversation which begins reluctantly, with intentions both not to tell and not to hear, Paul D finally tells Sethe of the roosters:

> 'Mister [the rooster], he looked so . . . free. Better than me. Stronger, tougher. Son a bitch couldn't even get out the shell by hisself but he was still king and I was. . . .' Paul D stopped and squeezed his left hand with his right. . . . 'Mister was allowed to be and stay what he was. But I wasn't allowed to be and stay what I was. Even if you cooked him you'd be cooking a rooster named Mister. But wasn't no way I'd ever be Paul D again, living or dead. . . . I was something else and that something was less than a chicken sitting in the sun on a tub.'   (72)

The ellipses and hesitations throughout Paul D's speech tell of gaps and deferrals in meaning. Paul D doesn't know whether he can "say it right," or say it fully, and, in fact, as the narrative reveals, ". . . what he was telling her was only the beginning" (72).

Morrison further compounds the meaning of roosters by

associating Mister's comb with Paul D's missing or buried "red heart": ". . . there was no red heart bright as Mister's comb beating in him" (73). Red heart and rooster approximate each other, even as they trope toward some more ambiguous meaning. That meaning becomes further complicated by Paul D's chanting "'Red heart'" as he touches Beloved "'on the inside part'" (117) —an act which further shames him.

Morrison finally articulates a clearer image of Paul D's unnamed hurt through a catalog of items:

> A shudder ran through Paul D. . . . He didn't know if it was bad whiskey, nights in the cellar, pig fever, iron bits, *smiling roosters*, fired feet, laughing dead men, hissing grass, rain, apple blossoms, neck jewelry, Judy in the slaughterhouse, Halle in the butter, ghost-white stairs, chokecherry trees, cameo pins, aspens, Paul A's face, sausage or the loss of a *red, red heart.*
>
> 'Tell me something, Stamp,' Paul D's eyes were rheumy. 'Tell me this one thing. *How much is a nigger supposed to take?*' (235; italics added)

A shudder and exasperation flavor Morrison's "meaning," which one might conjecture as the degradation of having no agency, of being transformed or moved at will by another. The breasts and roosters, as overdetermined metaphors for the "weight" of being black in America during the late nineteenth-century, hint at how this "burden" cannot be expressed simply or singularly. Techniques such as cataloging and metaphorical substitution, displacement, and approximation aid Morrison in conveying the lack of vocabulary to describe fully the degradation of slavery.

Not only words but also gestures become subject to slippage; and often gestures (in themselves a comment on the need for supplements to words) remain the expression of choice for those who have no access to the "master language." Beloved, who returns from the dead, relies heavily upon gesture to supplement her words. In response to Denver's question "'What's it like over there, where you were before?'" Beloved replies, "'Dark . . . I'm small in that place. I'm like this here.' She raised her head off the bed, lay down on her side and curled up" (75). Beloved's gesture seems to indicate a womb of darkness, but her later assertions of her "crouching" with a "dead man on my face" (211) carry suggestions of slave ship passage. More simply, the place "over there" could be death, pre-birth, or void. To say that Beloved's words exhibit missing pieces would be not only to state the obvious but also to overlook Morrison's more masterful troping by gesture. Instead of supplementing Beloved's meaning through additional words, Morrison leaves Beloved's gesture literally *at rest*—not closed in meaning but accepting of the gaps that already exist in memory and that widen during the conveyance of meaning.

Beloved's "massage-stranglehold" of Sethe's neck becomes another gesture of ambivalent meaning. Denver insists that Beloved has "'choked [Sethe's] neck,'" whereas Beloved claims that she has "'kissed her neck'" (101). Beloved's counterstatement does not necessarily negate Denver's words. A too-strong kiss may strangle, just as a "too-thick love" can result in "'unmotherly'" acts. Interestingly, Paul D characterizes Sethe's love as "'too thick,'" to which Sethe responds, "'Love is or it ain't. Thin love ain't love at all'" (164). Sethe denies any texture or variable quality to love, while Paul D shows that "love" inadequately describes the emotional relation one has to another. He, thus, exposes "love" as a synecdoche of sorts that only partially names Sethe's relationship to her children. Likewise, the different interpretations of the "massage" as either chokehold or kiss emerge from a similarly reductive (is or ain't) determination of benevolent or malevolent intent. Yet Morrison consistently undermines this benevolent/malevolent dichotomy, showing how love for the captive female can manifest itself in both.

Morrison also shows how characters besides Beloved choose approximating gestures over words. For instance, after Sethe discovers Beloved's identity (as her returned "ghost" daughter), Sethe falls into a flurry of mothering activity: playing with Beloved, braiding her hair, feeding her "fancy food," and clothing her in "ribbon and dress goods" (240). Presumably trying to make up for lost time, Sethe condenses her gestures of care into two months, yet succeeds only in making Beloved, Denver, and herself look "like carnival women with nothing to do" (240). The narrative voice reveals the disjunction between Sethe's pattern-making and the shallowness of result. Instead of the "real thing," one has carnivalesque trappings without substance—the displaced substitute of some unrealizable desire.

The scapegoating of Sethe by various members in the community enacts a similar substitutive gesture. Instead of accusing themselves, Ella and Paul D, for instance, transfer self-censure onto the already publicly identified "criminal," Sethe. Ella, who shuns Sethe after the Misery (as Stamp Paid calls the Fugitive Slave Act and Sethe's desperate response to it [171]), has herself orchestrated a child's death, "a hairy white thing, fathered by 'the lowest yet,'" whom she "delivered, but would not nurse" (258-259). Likewise, Paul D displaces his own shame onto Sethe's recorded public act. As he listens to her explanation of the newspaper article, Paul D judges Sethe's action as "'wrong.'. . . 'You got two feet, Sethe, not four.'. . . Later he would wonder what made him say it. . . . How fast he had moved from his shame to hers" (165). The two displacements allow Ella and Paul D, and by extension the community, to voice the violence engendered by slavery in an already constructed language. That is, they use the language of the white judiciary, white newspapers, and white opinion to assess and fix judgment upon Sethe's act. Instead of arriving at a new discourse to express, encompass, and comprehend (but not necessarily mitigate) Sethe's act, Ella and Paul D misappropriate Sethe's "crime" in order to overlook and keep silent what they have no alternative words for.

"Missing" from the community, then, is a discourse for and about public/private shame. Sethe has ruptured secreted guilt by displaying "on the lawn"[1] the communally shared guilt over child abandonment, malevolent love, and infanticide. Sethe's killing of Beloved remains an inconceivable gesture whose meaning *Beloved* spends its entire length trying to approximate. In Schoolteacher's nephew's reaction to Sethe's killing in the woodshed, Morrison highlights the mistaken meanings derived from decontextualized judgments:

> What she go and do that for? On account of a beating?
> Hell, he'd been beat a million times and he was
> white. . . . 'What she go and do that for?'   (150)

The nephew reduces Sethe's act to a response to a whipping. He compares it to his own projected reaction, that "no way . . . could [he] have" done what she did (150). Not being a slave, he cannot grasp the meaning of Sethe's action, as perhaps that meaning may never be grasped through forgotten agony and "official" versions of history.

Perhaps what is desired, then, is a language to explain and absolve, to encompass all the nuance and ambiguity of motive and emotion—a language which allows the women of 124 "to be what they liked, see whatever they saw and say whatever was on their minds" (199). Morrison approximates this desired language in the lyric section running from pages 200 to 217, a rendition of interior consciousness, for, as Sethe asserts, she doesn't need to vocally explain herself because Beloved "understands everything already" (200). Only an unfallen language would exhibit a unity of thought and word that would render verbalization obsolete—a language in the beginning: "In the beginning there were no words. In the beginning was the sound, and they all knew what that sounded like" (259). Morrison allows that unfallen sounding to become realized for an instant, which recalls the healing work of the Clearing:

> For Sethe it was as though the Clearing had come to her with all its heat and simmering leaves, where the voices of women searched for . . . the sound that broke the back of words. . . . It broke over Sethe and she trembled like the baptized in its wash.   (261)

Morrison presents the "roaring" of the unspoken, which spiritually blesses and absolves. Yet, this triumphant moment of wordless song lasts only briefly, perhaps a glimpse of Paradise after the Fall. Morrison makes clear that this type of language, though desired, cannot often be realized—that the women of 124, for instance, can "say whatever was on their minds. *Almost*" (199; italics added). Amongst Sethe, Beloved, and Denver, much remains "unspeakable thoughts, unspoken" (200). Sethe's monologue, for instance, projects into an indeterminate future her "telling" of a specific knowledge: "I know what it is to be without the milk that belongs to you. . . . I'll tell Beloved about that; she'll understand" (200). Like Paul D's rooster, Sethe's stolen milk signals such inexpressible emotions that Sethe defers voicing them, even as she desires to make the incident "under stand[able]."

Morrison soberly returns the narrative to language's limitations. Words, akin to the "spores of bluefern growing in the hollows along the riverbank," have the potential to "live out [their] days as planned" (84); i.e., to express authentically. Instead of realizing that intent, however, the spore collapses and the certainty of its expression—its full bloom— "lasts no longer than [a moment]; longer, perhaps than the spore itself" (84).

Morrison does not simply refer to language here. The spore also represents the promise of human life and the fragility of that promise for the enslaved. As former slave Harriet Jacobs observed while watching "two beautiful children playing together" (one a "fair white child," the other her slave), "I foresaw the inevitable blight that would fall on the little slave's heart. I knew how soon her laughter would be changed to sighs" (Jacobs 29). The slave, denied possession of her body, will never realize the promise implied by and borne out in the fruition of her white counterpart. Possessed by another, the enslaved suffers from a fragmentation of self (literal as well as figurative),[2] or as Paul D phrases it, not being able "'to be and stay what I was" (72). Morrison's characters can only obliquely refer to the situation of being denied a self. For instance, Sethe mentions that "there was no nursing milk to call my own" (200), referring to the shared milk she took as a child from Nan's breasts and her own milk forcibly taken from her by Schoolteacher's nephews. After escaping to Ohio, she claims her post-slavery sense of self by reappropriating her milk for no one but "my own children" (200); through reclaimed agency over her milk, Sethe points to herself as no longer the possession of another.

However, Sethe still evokes her self through others: For Sethe, "the best thing she was, was her children" (251). Even when she earlier conjectures her possible death, Sethe couches it in terms of her baby, "'I believe this baby's ma'am is gonna die in wild onions on the bloody side of the Ohio River.'. . . And it didn't seem such a bad idea . . ." (31). Yet, because she is the "baby's ma'am," Sethe attempts to survive, a decision born of concern not for herself but for her baby. Thus, akin to Morrison's Sula, whose identity remains incomplete, Sethe, too, only proceeds toward an investment in herself as her own, "'best thing'" (273). Nel's voiced realization of herself as separate from her mother's influence "'I'm me. . . . Me'" (*Sula* 28)—becomes echoed in Sethe's concluding remarks which indicate a recognition of the self—but with a difference: "'Me? Me?'" (273). This faux-conclusion to Sethe's narrative revises the stable self implied in Nel's "'I'm me. . . . Me,'" emphasizing the striving toward rather than any realized definition of self.

Beloved's other conclusion (an epilogue?) also thematizes an open-endedness to words, narrative, and desires. In one phrase, "This is not a story to pass on" (275), Morrison seemingly closes her story as well as gestures toward unwriting her narrative. Like the "footprints" by the stream which "come and go, come and go," her narrative seems to imprint and efface itself—

much as Beloved has done within collective memory. The community deliberately forgets her "like a bad dream" (274), actively absenting her from their recollections; however, the narrative announces her as the final word of the text—"Beloved"—that which is desired, missing, yet elusively present.

* * * * *

While *Sula* appears overtly to thematize the notion of signification's duplicity, *Beloved* grounds language's slippage to the not so distant history of slavery in America. Perhaps Morrison signifies[3] on the earlier text, attempting a redefinition or respecifying of postmodernism's general emphasis on the instability of meaning; that is, whereas *Sula* capitalizes on the notion of language as aprioristically corrupt, *Beloved* does not take for granted that there is only one language (i.e., that defined by semioticians or that practiced by Schoolteacher and his nephews). Morrison contextualizes "corrupt" language as historically specific, even against deconstructionist theories which atemporalize and universalize language. Her historicization in *Beloved* thus speaks on some level about the limits of poststructuralist findings for African-American writers who remain doubly circumscribed by a language which can no longer convey authentically, but which has hitherto effectively constructed black subjects as less than human. Her grounding of discursive slippage to historical circumstances thus offers a praxis of resistance to these theories which would subsume all narratives as corruptions, just when alternate narratives taking the formerly enslaved as their subjects are beginning to emerge. Thus, whereas in *Sula*, language's slippage exists a priori, in *Beloved*, gaps and missed meanings evolve from specific sites of corruption due to historical circumstances. In neither text, however, are lapses elided or desires achieved. In effect, Morrison wishes to indulge two seemingly contradictory gestures: to make "Peace" a longing, and to make people "at rest" with this longing piece.

Notes

[1] In *Thinking Through the Body*, Jane Gallop describes Joanne Michulski's 1974 killing and dismemberment of her two children as bringing "violence by and to the mother—out of the home and onto the lawn, into the public eye . . . [effectively] reinscrib[ing] it in the world of work and meaning, power and knowledge" (2). Likewise, Sethe, rather than having fallen away from a community's mores, has actually enacted a public spectacle of the community's already shared, secreted history. She effectively reinscribes private crime onto public space.

[2] Morrison symbolizes this literal fragmentation in Schoolteacher's dissection of his slaves' body parts: their division into animal characteristics on the right side of the page and human characteristics on the left (*Beloved* 193).

[3] The practice of "Signifyin(g)," according to Henry Louis Gates, Jr., is "repetition and revision, or repetition with a signal difference" (*Monkey* xxiv). Gates expands the purview of "signifyin(g)" to include African-American intertextuality or the activity of "black writers read[ing] and critiqu[ing] other black texts as an act of rhetorical self-definition" (*Figures* 242). I suggest that Morrison, in *Beloved*, signifies on the very work of signification in *Sula*. That is, she repeats with a signal difference the thematics of language slippage so apparent in *Sula*, the difference being the grounding of that language slippage to historical event.

Works Cited

Davis, Christina. "Beloved: A Question of Identity." *Presence Africaine* 145 (1988): 151-156.

Derrida, Jacques. "Difference." *Speech and Phenomena and Other Essays on Husserl's Theory of Signs*. Evanston: Northwestern University Press, 1973. 129-60.

Gallop, Jane. *Thinking Through the Body*. New York: Columbia University Press, 1988.

Gates, Henry Louis, Jr. *Figures in Black: Words, Signs, and the "Racial" Self*. New York: Oxford University Press, 1987.

—. *The Signifying Monkey: A Theory of African-American Literary Criticism*. New York: Oxford University Press, 1988.

Grant, Robert. "Absence into Presence: The Themetics of Memory and 'Missing' Subjects in Toni Morrison's *Sula*." McKay 90-103.

Jacobs, Harriet. *Incidents in the Life of a Slave Girl*. Ed. Jean Fagan Yellin. Cambridge: Harvard University Press, 1987.

McDowell, Deborah. "'The Self and the Other: Reading Toni Morrison's *Sula* and the Black Female Text." McKay 77-89.

McKay, Nellie Y., ed. *Critical Essays on Toni Morrison*. Boston: Hall, 1988.

Morrison, Toni. *Beloved*. New York: Knopf, 1987.

—. *Sula*. 1973. New York: Plume, 1982.

Spillers. Hortense J. "A Hateful Passion, A Lost Love." *Feminist Studies* 9.2 (1983): 293-323.

The Force Outside/The Force Inside: Mother-Love and Regenerative Spaces in *Sula* and *Beloved*

Laurie Vickroy

Relationships between mothers and children in Toni Morrison's *Sula* and *Beloved* provide a compelling examination of the extent to which the exercise of power determines the workings of intimate relationships and even constructs versions of self-definition. In these two novels we witness mothers' passionate love for their children channeled into murderous acts. From such distorted misrenderings of love arise many questions: First, what compels a mother's will-to-dominate and the destructiveness which accompanies this? Secondly, is the traditional notion that the basis of love is a feeling of oneness or symbiosis a threat to the children's individuality? Also, to what degree is it in the nature of love, particularly mother-love, to refuse boundaries and to assume one can speak for or act on behalf of the other who is the object of one's love? *Sula* and *Beloved* address these questions by exploring how external threats distort mothers' love. Further, these texts offer, through daughters' embrace of personal spaces, new possibilities for reaching beyond those structures of domination which governed their mothers' behavior and conceptions of selfhood.

Mother-love

In Morrison's fiction the intimate love between Black mothers and their children is infiltrated by oppressive forces.

Slavery, racism, and poverty dominate the circumstances of these Black families, as these forces are internalized into, and in effect damage personal relationships. When the consequences are examined, Morrison's work illustrates what John Brenkman refers to as social mediation of the ego (169), where subjectivity and human interactions become reified and distorted within social systems. The once-protective love of mothers like Eva Peace in *Sula* and Sethe in *Beloved* becomes desperate and possessive in a hostile environment. As mediators between their children and the world, these mothers experience what Marianne Hirsch describes as a "double identity" or "self-division," wherein their ambivalent relationship to the world affects their motherly roles (1990, 421). In reacting to their own victimization by social forces, Eva and Sethe extend that victimization to their children.[1] Eva fears the possible return of this bond, dreaming that Plum wants to reenter her womb (*Sula* 71-72). Eva feels so strongly threatened by her grown child's need for *her* that she feels the need to eliminate *him* because his needs had become associated in the past with her own powerlessness and inability to provide for her children. It was after her night in the outhouse with the baby Plum that she left her children and took desperate action to bring them all financial security. However, in *Beloved* Sethe embraces this symbiosis and still feels strong connections to her children's bodies (through suckling and kissing) as the slavemaster approaches and therefore this connection reinforces Sethe's confidence in acting on their behalf, as they are "a part of her." For both characters this combination of symbiosis and the intervention of social forces makes their intense love destructive.

The conflicted interests of the motherly role are evident in the many parallels between Eva and Sethe: each is absorbed by forces beyond her control and each ends up harming her children in trying to protect them. They are compelled to make unilateral decisions concerning their children's lives in circumstances so adverse any choice they make would have tragic consequences. However, textual evidence and Morrison's own statements suggest that though done with good intentions, these mothers victimize their children and appropriate their rights. Each mother murders one of her four children. The murders are also the extreme consequence of over-identification between mother and children.[2] However, it is also evident that the over-identification becomes destructive *because* it is socially driven.

Vowing to resist her desperate poverty after the night in the outhouse with her baby Plum, Eva leaves the next day and returns eighteen months later with money but missing one leg. Though she has given up part of herself, she has taken control of her own and her children's lives. This, and her attempt to save her daughter Hannah from the fire, indicate Eva's willingness to sacrifice herself for her children. However, the destructive side of this denial of separation between her and her children is apparent when she murders the nineteen-year-old drug-addicted Plum. She defends her actions to her daughter Hannah by explaining that she wanted him to die like a man. However, because she had also dreamt that he wanted to crawl back into her womb, issues of control, the demands of intimacy, and the forces impinging on these are significant issues here. Even though she rationalizes her actions as done out of love, she violates his right to live his own life (Morrison herself has said that Eva "played God" in this instance [Syracuse lectures 1988]). She believes he needs the kind of control over his life with which she has defined her own life—being able to act on her own and others' destinies. Also, her dream is evidence that Eva herself was fearful of Plum's possible violation of *her*, that he wants to extend his childhood and her role as the nurturing mother. In effect, she desires his separation from *her*, but not hers from him—she can violate his boundaries but he is not allowed to violate hers. Moreover, she does not want to be reminded of the time she was powerless, during Plum's infancy.

Sethe of *Beloved* has much in common with Eva Peace: they share a fierce love for their children which leads each to murdering one of them. They are linked in Morrison's use of bird imagery. Depicted as an eagle, Eva's wild ferocity is apparent as she is pouring gasoline on Plum. He sees her huge "wing" above him, that wing which should protect rather than destroy. Birds also appear at that key moment in *Beloved* when Sethe is driven to protect her children from the approaching slavemaster: "Little hummingbirds stuck their needle beaks right through her headcloth into her hair and beat their wings" (163). Here there is a similar wildness to the association, suggesting an instinctual, perhaps self-preservatory action (Sethe intended to kill herself, too—she and her children were one and the same). There is a qualitative difference in the usage of these metaphors, however. Eva becomes a bird figuratively, implying this ferocity is within her, while Sethe is more impelled by outside forces. An attack by usually solitary and gentle humming-birds is abnormal as though nature has been turned topsy-turvy—like Sethe's gentle nature.[3] Her decision, to kill her children so that they might not live in slavery, is the outcome of a brutal system that warps the most natural of relationships and the greatest of loves. Eva and Sethe both suffer greatly, and each reaches a point where she cannot endure anymore and refuses her victimization: each repeats "No.   No. Nonono. . . ." as pre-lude to a violent, but to her mind, life-affirming act—for Sethe the murder of her children, for Eva the sacrifice of her leg.

Morrison's depiction of mother-love is not singly deter-mined, but fraught with irresolvable conflicts and difficulties. As each of these mothers is willing to give, so she asserts the right to take with an intensity that can be murderous and which appears extreme and even "monstrous" to some of the more moderate characters in these novels. Neither mother can main-tain an equilibrium between herself and her children.   They cannot acknowledge their children as separate subjects because they cannot be freely acting subjects themselves. "How can a child see self or mother as subjects when the society denies them that status? The mother is made incapable of recognizing the child, and the child cannot recognize the mother" (Schapiro 197). Mother-love and motherly responsibility are turned into bondage by oppression.

In *The Bonds of Love*, Jessica Benjamin discusses how a will-to-dominate becomes part of interpersonal relationships be-cause western thought functions in a dialectical paradigm of self and other, which inevitably leads to domination (33). Internal-ization, where an individual absorbs the traits or desires of an other (or of a larger culture) into their being, is a function of this dialectic. This is because in internalization there is not an ac-knowledgment of both separation and connection—one is either absorbed and same, or different and other. Benjamin views this as the model for all forms of political, social, and personal dom-ination.

The three generations of women in *Beloved* are inti-mately connected in their internalizations of one another's ex-perience, and because of this absorption of the other into oneself without acknowledging the separate, subjective existence of the other, dominance mars these connections. Again, the values, needs and patterns passed from mothers to daughters are strongly contingent upon social forces: in this case, the brutal influence of slavery. Though very young when her mother is killed, the events of her mother's life become deeply infused within Sethe's to the point where much of her mother's experience is repeated, though with differences in circumstances and motivations. We learn that Sethe has recreated (but for very different reasons) her own mother's acts of infanticide. Both Sethe's and her mother's milk is "taken" for or by white children. The re-creation of Sethe's own situation as an infant establishes in her mind the equivalence of her own and her children's needs: "I know what it is to be without the milk that belongs to you . . . I'll tell Beloved about that; she'll understand" (200). Beloved should understand because when Sethe ran away from Sweet Home she was hurrying to meet her children, including the nursing baby, Beloved.

The perception of abandonment also conflates the experiences of the three. Sethe alone survives the loss of her mother and her daughter, and the reappearance of Beloved symbolizes Sethe's wish to regain what has been lost. Sethe resists the knowledge of why her mother was hanged and she tries to deny it was for trying to escape (another act of her mother's she repeats with a difference) because "she was my ma'am and nobody's ma'am would run off and leave her daughter, would she?" (203). This issue continues to haunt Beloved, who also feels abandoned by her mother: "Sethe's is the face that left me" (213). These repetitions are one representation of "the deep psychic reverberations of living in a culture in which domination and objectification of the self have been institutionalized" (Schapiro 209). Nevertheless, daughters take control to feel their own agency. When Sethe makes the decision to condemn her children to death rather than let them suffer as she has done, she refuses boundaries between her and them—they are "the best part of her" without a separate existence and separate interests. Similarly, out of love and guilt, Sethe will allow the grown Beloved to exercise control over her and to ignore any differentiation between them. Both extremes exclude the notion of a separate, but connected and realized self, the possibility of which has long since been lost, because slavery has "choked off the vital circulation between mother and child so crucial to the development of the self" (Schapiro 199-200).

Beloved's presence can be read as a metaphor for Sethe's need to come to terms with the past, but when all boundaries disappear between past and present and between mother and daughter, a destructive process begins between them. Much as Sethe did not distinguish Beloved from herself at the time of the murder, Beloved also has no sense of boundaries between them upon reentering her mother's life: "I am not separate from her there is no place where I stop" (210). The two were one during Sethe's pregnancy and this assumption of symbiosis continues—Beloved is still the needy infant. They become "locked in a love that wore everybody out" (243), where no resolution or fulfillment can be reached, and their relations deteriorate because Sethe is too compliant—she is physically diminished by Beloved's bodily and emotional greed. Ella and the other townswomen are also mindful of the past, but put up resistance when it "invades" the present (257). The role of the community is more positive in *Beloved* than in *Sula* because it helps liberate Sethe from self-imposed guilt and exile. Beloved, amongst other things, represents the suffering and loss of all Blacks under slavery. As such, she cannot be recovered and in the novel she never finds a way out of the system of subjugation (though she reverses her own positioning in it temporarily). When the townswomen challenge the ascendancy of the past over the present (i.e., Beloved's dominance of Sethe), they help Sethe confront what slavery has wrought: the murder of her child. This is accomplished when the murder scene is reenacted, and this time Sethe refuses victimization. She can now externalize her situation and attack what she perceives are the forces of oppression rather than her children. In this resolution the townswomen and Sethe move beyond self-destructive internalization of oppression to confrontational action against it.

This reenactment enables some reconciliation with the past for Sethe. Throughout the novel she has broken familial patterns by taking her children with her out of slavery, and by wishing for Beloved's return, thereby refusing the brutality of slavery evidenced in her daughter's death and in the inheritance of abandonment by her own mother. Beloved, however, will always remain the victim of slavery, as we are reminded in the last pages of the novel as her heartbreaking and unsettling presence continues to linger.

In *Beloved* and *Sula*, mothers' histories especially consist in struggles with patterns of dominance. They need to act, to be acknowledged as actors in their own lives and on their children's behalf, but controlled by circumstances, their actions can only take on destructive forms. Always at risk, there is no op-

portunity to see their children as separate or to enjoy them as autonomous individuals. Consequently, their children have not
had the opportunity to grow in relationship to another who is
seen as an "independent subject, not simply as the 'external
world' or an adjunct of his [/her] ego" (Benjamin 23). As we will
see, Denver associates her mother with the dangers of the
external world, and for Beloved, Sethe is part of herself. What is
missing is the opportunity for relationships based on mutual interaction and recognition, the notion of balance—to be able to
simultaneously acknowledge connection and difference, and
thereby recognize an other's full subjectivity (Benjamin 25).
This formulation, based in object relations psychology, offers an
alternative to dominance whereto individuals can offer both
identification and something "other" to one another. An example is Winnicott's emphasis on play and response as interactions
which bring out mutuality in child-adult relations (25). Considering Morrison's work in this context, it is significant when Eva
tells Hannah she was too busy taking care of them and insuring
their survival to play with them. In *Beloved* the community of
women and Paul D, having experiences similar to Sethe's, but
not the enmeshed attachments of Sethe's family, are able to offer
alternate perspectives of neutral third parties, which in effect
provide resistance to the psychic effects of oppression.

The most compelling evidence presented against love become hurtful and the denial of separate subjectivity is the toll
this takes on the children involved. Plum and Beloved are
murdered by their mothers. Denver and Sula survive their
mothering, but they are scarred by fear and alienation as a result.
While *Sula* and *Beloved* explore mothers' traumas and obses-
sions, these novels also focus at length on how the daughters
who survive search for different ways of being (Denver and Sula
particularly, but also Sethe). In doing this, Morrison is asserting
that the forces which compel violent and desperate acts must be
resisted, and that the daughters must struggle against what has
overwhelmed their mothers. The transitions leading away from
dominance are marked by the private spaces which these daughters adopt.

Spaces

In Toni Morrison's fiction spaces often function as metaphors for her characters' relationships to others and to the larger culture surrounding them. With the creation of spatial metaphors, Morrison measures the possibility of individuals to achieve different degrees of autonomy through escape, refuge or growth. Many of Morrison's central characters enact a need for private space as a response to personal interactions gone awry or to powerful social pressures like racial and sexual oppression. It is in the nature of these private spaces that we can see how the individual's relation to others and to the environment is negotiated.

As transitional phenomenon, metaphors can connect past and present events as well as individual and collective experience. This linkage is accomplished by metaphor's displacing function, i.e. a metaphor presents an interplay of closeness and distance because it is connected to an ordinary context but, by adding another element to the original term, it also reaches for associations and meaning beyond that context.[4] This notion of transition between past and present is significant to Morrison's use of metaphor, because it is by this displacement of past associations into the present that she is able to represent the struggle to coexist with or become reconciled to the insistence of the past within a new situation (particularly in *Beloved*). By emphasizing the interplay of past and present within shifting relations between characters and the contexts in which those relations occur, Morrison acknowledges the strength of the past as well as allowing for options to change or subvert it.

The contexts of spaces in *Sula* and *Beloved* reinforce Jessica Benjamin's notion that spatial metaphor allows for an "in-betweeness" which reflects early mother and infant relations where the "representation of self and other evolves in part through a play of distance and closeness, a shifting of spatial boundaries between two bodies" (127). The ability to achieve "in-betweeness" is inspired by D. W. Winnicott's idea of transitional space, that which is not sharply defined as outside or inside, and which Benjamin posits as the "basis of knowledge and recognition of the other" (192)—a possible means toward the practice of dynamic, intersubjective relations between individuals that avoid dominance. In Morrison's work, such transitional spaces are associated with connection to others, but also help to

keep recognition of others partial, unrealized, or forfeited out of
fear that the self may be diminished in some way. The other is
desired but suspect, and often appropriative or oppressive, and
so these spaces also act to reestablish boundaries which have
been dissolved between mothers and daughters. Providing a
means of self-assertion and defense against the claims of others,
solitary space enables privacy and self-examination. Morrison's
fictional daughters often seek out these private spaces when they
feel violated, or forced by the other to live by values, judgments,
or desires not in accord with their own wishes. These spaces are
metaphors of transition, appearing in times of turmoil, grief,
questioning or reevaluation, and are associated with processes of
self-discovery and growth.

Sula

Sula's embrace of space marks the forceful assertion of her
independence. When Sula has her grandmother Eva committed
and keeps her ancestral home to herself, she is rebelling against
her grandmother's attempt to control her, and acknowledging
her fear of the matriarch. I characterize this as a mother/daugh-
ter relationship because Eva is particularly important to Sula's
personal development, outliving Sula's mother Hannah but
also passing on many of her traits to Sula. The identification between Eva and Sula is strong, but they are not close and neither
will tolerate being dominated. They are both proud, and each
has committed self-mutilating acts in desperate situations which
Susan Willis has characterized as "confrontation(s) with oppressive social forces" (277). These acts indicate they are strong individuals who will resist victimization and attain autonomy and
control in their lives. Their bitter argument (91-94) indicates
that each is afraid of the other: Sula knows Eva has burned
Plum, and Eva knows Sula has watched her mother burn out of
curiosity. Eva crosses another boundary, this time between her
and Sula, by trying to impose her own and the community's will
on Sula: "You need to have some babies. It'll settle you . . . I'm a
tell you what you need" (92), and Sula, refusing to be dominated,
retaliates and escapes Eva's grasp by removing Eva from her
home and keeping it as her own independent space.

Eva's rigid stance is but one important example of the positioning and defining Sula must try to evade if she is to live a free life. However, she can only maintain her sense of self through refusal of connection to others, and there is a great loss for her in denying that connection. She is an example of someone, who in asserting self-control and freedom, is perhaps denying "the terror of having once been subjected to the control of others" (Benjamin 1977, 57), that is, in Hannah's rejection of her ("I love Sula. I just don't like her." [*Sula* 57]) and Eva's commands. Sethe's construction of autonomy necessitates she resist identification with the other—as she fights to preserve the notion that she is an autonomous, intact subject, she must guard against recognition of the other as part of herself. Sula, whose experience has taught her that to trust another means to be slighted (by Hannah) or to be threatened with domination (by Eva), is largely deprived of seeing herself in connection to others. In fact, the harsh self-indulgence that she has learned from Hannah and Eva, such as thinking "all men available" (119), destroys the closest, most successfully equal relationship she has, with Nel. Sula tries to live freely and to allow others their separate identities, but must sacrifice connection for freedom. Again, we see a lack of balance, but unlike the mother figures, with Sula the focus is on separation.

In Nel's situation, space is a refuge, a place where she can contain her grief. She needs the "small bright space" of the bathroom which holds only herself. This replaces that other space (her bed) once filled by her and her husband Jude and which she can no longer tolerate because he has introduced a third element, Sula. Grief over lost connection brings Nel to a private space "to a deeply personal cry for one's own pain" (108) that will resemble Sula's embrace of private space within sexual relations. Defining herself by her marriage, once it is over she lives in a self-constructed space of pain.

Unlike Nel, Sula does not see herself through men's eyes and in fact resists men within intimate relations—disconnecting herself even in the arms of her sexual partners. What she is usually able to bring away from sex is not connection, but "misery and the ability to feel deep sorrow," a loneliness and a "privateness" in which she is able to discover and examine herself (122). She finds

> . . . an eye of sorrow in the midst of all that hurricane
> rage of joy. There, in the center of that silence was not
> eternity but the death of time and a loneliness so pro-

> found the word itself had no meaning. For loneliness
> assumed the absence of other people, and the solitude
> she found in that *desperate terrain* had never admitted
> the possibility of other people.   (123, my emphasis)

Sula's sexuality expresses a deep need for connection, but
the act becomes a barren place for Sula because she is aware of
the lack of connection between her and her lovers even as their
bodies are intimately engaged. When she and Nel were children, no private spaces were necessary because each saw herself
in the eyes of the other. In Sula's adult relations, self and other
are disconnected. There is a failure of authentic subjective ac-
knowledgment on both sides, and Sula's response is to build her
own space which becomes a barrier to full interaction with the
other.

However, the space Sula embraces as she is dying offers a
way out of this character's isolation. Although the "finality" of
the boarded-up bedroom (which was once Eva's) gives her solitude and appears to be another refuge from appropriation, it is
also rendered in her imagination as an organic place of growth
and connection. Her acceptance of death can be interpreted as
resignation, but also as a desire to renew life; her fetal position
and the accompanying water imagery suggest a longing to return
to infancy, and the space of the bedroom transforms into the wet,
protecting and creative space of a womb in her imagination:

> The sealed window soothed her with its sturdy termi-
> nation, its unassailable finality. It was as though for
> the first time she was completely alone—where she
> had always wanted to be—free of the possibility of
> distraction. It would be here, held by this blind win-
> dow . . . that she might draw her legs up to her chest,
> close her eyes, put her thumb in her mouth and float
> over and down the tunnels, just missing the dark walls,
> down, down until she met a rain scent and would know
> the water was near, and she would curl into its heavy
> softness and it would envelop her, carry her, and wash
> her tired flesh always.   (148-149)

Sula is often described with water imagery ("her eyes were
as clean as rain"). Fluidity is indicative of her character, which is
presented as in process and not in stasis: she is "multiple, fluid,
relational and in a perpetual state of becoming" (McDowell 81).
In relation to Sula, water is associated with destruction (the river

into which she lets go of Chicken Little) as well as growth (she is water and Ajax is loam). In this context, the womb is associated with death and constriction, but also renewal. Sula looks to the past, not with nostalgia, but with a desire for another chance: the resumption of physical symbiosis with a mother who was not so soothing, and for rebirth, with all its possibilities and potential. This return to the womb reflects Sula's desire to reclaim her life as in process, not in positioning herself against others. When seen through the eyes and values of others (the town), or when she tries to preserve herself from Eva or the white boys, she acts destructively. However, when seen on her own terms (by Nel and Ajax) she is at her best. The imagery associated with her relations to Nel and Ajax, that of growth, sexual awakening, and fertility (57-59, 130-131), connect this image of rebirth to the two successful (if temporary) relationships Sula has—relationships that allow her freedom and encourage her uniqueness and creativity. These relationships are most rewarding when no positions are taken, where there is mutual identification, mutual recognition, and mutual pleasure in them.

Morrison's characterization of Sula also illustrates Abena Busia's point that Black women writers have needed to "reclaim" their own stories, to define and affirm themselves and their lives using writing strategies which involve "self-definition and therefore, cultural redefinition" (3). One of these strategies is the association of self-knowledge with place and "autonomy with space" (3). Although it has been argued elsewhere that Sula responds to her environment through narcissistic defenses,[5] one could also argue that she accepts the price of solitude to remain uninscribed in a world that has not welcomed her. Here, Morrison expresses a powerful need to create a place of one's own in a hostile world.

Beloved

For Sethe in *Beloved*, as with Sula, the embrace of a particular space expresses a powerful rejection of the world, self-affirmation, and accommodation to loss. After her triumphant escape from slavery with her children and after her trial, she has a strong need to stay in one place, to atone for the past through commitment. Sethe's attachment to 124 (which is haunted by the baby's ghost), represents her need to maintain contact with the past and the need for a space of her own. Her home is a metaphor for her relation to past and present: it displaces a part of her past which she desires to explore, but cannot yet confront directly. When asked why she does not move out of the eerie house, she tells Paul D, "I will never run from another thing on this earth. I took one journey and I paid for the ticket, but let me tell you something, Paul D. Garner: it cost too much!" (15). She is referring here to the sacrifices she has made for running to freedom, but she is also rejecting the dislocation of Paul D's life and that of other former slaves during Reconstruction (Ferguson 119) because by her residence of 124 she is resisting Paul D's (understandable) fears of staying too long or loving too much. Though her mind resists memory, it is significant, as Rebecca Ferguson notes, that at least physically, she does not evade the place where she killed her daughter (113). The house is a transitional place which can contain both the memory of a dead daughter and Sethe's ability to be independent in the present. For Sethe, who came from the dirt floors of the slave quarters, 124 is the only home she has ever had. Possession is an essential issue for Sethe, having experienced the condition of slavery, where one is never the owner of anything, not one's children, nor even one's own body. For Sethe, freedom is "a place where you could love anything you chose" (162) and seeking refuge to express that love is a political act, a means to establish her independence and refuse victimization by a repressive and racist society. Also, as Gaston Bachelard suggests, memory and imagination play a significant role in how we experience our homes (4-5), and in a similar way Sethe finds something familiar at 124 yet imagines its freeing possibilities as well. The house itself changes identity, as Sethe and her past (figured in the baby's ghost) take it over. As with Nel's and Sula's spatial withdrawals, Morrison depicts such action as self-preserving to the individual, but also limiting in terms of connection to others and to the world. Sethe's act of strength is mitigated by the community's perception of her selfishness; she is thought to shun those who share her suffering and to be too involved with the past.

In *Beloved* memory itself is also depicted as a place which allows the past to exist concurrently with the present. For Sethe, places and events remain as they were in memory and they are recollected whole, taking up space, so to speak. She says the past is "going to always be there waiting for you" (36). I would liken this formulation to those conflicts or events which have remained unresolved, surfacing from the unconscious. The concrete recreations of the past in *Beloved*, including Beloved herself, are eruptions from the past like Sethe's "rememory," which Marianne Hirsch interprets as memory plus repetition (1990)—pointing to the power of the past over Sethe. Much as in the workings of a transference process, where the powerful presence of the past emerges through the welling up of emotion in a new context, Sethe first responds to the past through affect rather than memory (that is, through emotion rather than consciousness).[6] The past surfaces via Sethe's flesh—i.e. her "water breaks" at Beloved's appearance (51). Also, Sethe is moved by hearing the name "Beloved" upon the girl's appearance, but at first consciously ignores the clues indicating who this girl might really be.

In the beginning of the novel 124 is a refuge for Denver, too. She is terrified of her mother, or of that which drove her to kill Beloved. The trauma of Beloved's death continues in Denver's nightmares, where Sethe "cut my head off every night" (206). Denver refuses to move far from the house because,

> All the time, I'm afraid the thing that happened that made it all right for my mother to kill my sister could happen again. I don't know what it is, I don't know who it is, but maybe there is something else terrible enough to make her do it again. I need to know what that thing might be, but I don't want to. Whatever it is, it comes from outside this house, outside the yard, and it can come right on in the yard if it wants to. So I never leave this house and I watch over the yard, so it can't happen again and my mother won't have to kill me too.   (205)

Though not confronted directly with racial oppression, Denver experiences its power to terrorize and destroy through her mother's violent response to slavery. It also seems particularly significant that it is outside the yard (in school) where Denver has learned the truth about her mother with traumatic consequences (Denver's hysterical deafness). However, as she grows, the limitations and the isolation of 124 become apparent to her and Sethe and her insular family situation are no longer sufficient for Denver.

When her grandmother (who she thought protected her

from Sethe) dies, Denver begins going to her "secret house" out-
doors, which appears to be a substitute for, but also an outgrowth
from, the safety of her grandmother's room.   Denver's attachment to her own space also resembles her mother's attachment
to 124 in that it represents a retreat from the world.   Her secret
house has particular significance for Denver in its privacy and as
her "playroom . . . refuge . . . closed off from the hurt" (28). This
place is associated with her physical and emotional growth,
where Denver keeps her cologne (a sign of womanhood, or a desire for it), which was first given to her by a white townswoman,
Miss Bodwin (whose brother will figure prominently in the resolution of Sethe's situation with Beloved).   Though an isolated
spot, the "closet" is also connected to others, e.g., it's bushes recall Baby Suggs who preached in the woods, reaching out personally and spiritually to the community around her.   Denver's
secret house is a transitional space between childhood and
adulthood.   In order to overcome the past, Denver must trust
the members of the town who are willing to help her, and enter
into the more open space of the town and leave the trauma-
filled enclosure of her mother's home, 124.

For Sethe and Denver personal spaces are part of a
(re)generation process, closely associated with discovery and assertion of selfhood amidst the pressures around them, but these
places also remain deeply connected to the past.   The change of
space alters the structure and patterns of life for them both: Sethe
escapes from slavery and Denver leaves her enmeshed family.
In inhabiting their own spaces, they try to fill the voids created
by their losses: of mother, of sister, of daughter.

Denver's home, "124," and her "emerald house," are both
enclosed spaces of desire and loneliness, in contrast to the more
open space of the town. I would characterize the first two spaces
as having repetitive and regressive (metonymic) connection to
Denver's past, representing partially a repetition of her mother's
withdrawal, a resistance to change, and a fear of the world incul-
cated by her mother's experience.   However, her entry into the
wider area of the town represents her need to reach out so as to
help her family, and to fulfill her own need to break away from
them and find her own life. The town is still connected with her
past, particularly her childhood schoolteacher, but it offers the
potential for change. What was once "outside," posing a threat
to her and her mother, has become a place offering openness and
growth.

Through Paul D, Morrison presents another option: space as an area to be shared. When he asks Sethe if there is a space for him in her life, too, we are offered a more optimistic and inter-subjective alternative, in contrast to Sethe's possessive idea of space. Paul D has already arrived at a point where he is able to share. It will take Denver until the end of the book to reach this point, and Sethe's growth in this area is yet to be accomplished by the end of the novel, for up until the end, the past has the strongest demands on her.

Morrison makes it very clear that disturbed relationships reflect and interconnect with a broader social context and that our ability to change the nature of our attachments to others de-pends on whether we evaluate the past and examine our behav-iors and relations in it. Morrison has indicated that it is selfish and unproductive to try to forget, that change can never occur without an analysis of the past (1984, 388). In her novels she evokes the reader's sympathy for any attempts at resistance pow-erless characters undertake. However, in examining the costs of their actions she asserts the need for alternatives. When Sethe turns her knife on Bodwin instead of Beloved, and when Den-ver lets the world in by embracing and being embraced by the town, Morrison is giving these characters self-affirming as well as other-affirming options.

According to Morrison, examining interests which are de-structive to the individual is an important project of all Black writers, whose mission, she says, is "the clear identification of what the enemy forces are, not this person or that person and so on, but the acknowledgment of a way of life dreamed up for us by some other people who are at the moment in power, and knowing the ways in which it can be subverted" (Morrison 1988, 146). Subversion usually comes at a high price in her fiction. However, through daughterly spaces and the intervention of the community in *Beloved*, there is an optimistic movement favor-ing the possibility of survival and change which exists to a lesser degree in her earlier fiction (e.g., *The Bluest Eye* and *Sula*).

In a world where social, racial and political dominance prevail, the exercise of power, even in its most destructive forms, becomes paradoxically a confirmation of the self, provid-ing an approximation of self-determination. The daughters of *Sula* and *Beloved* seek ways out of this paradigm. Their alterna-tives are sometimes solipsistic and unsuccessful, but given their separate spaces of place and of being, they are allowed the opportunity to renounce the patterns of dominance handed down from within and without the family.

Notes

[1] See Nancy Chodorow's *The Reproduction of Mothering*, Jessica Benjamin, et el. Michele Barrett, Chodorow, and Adrienne Rich also emphasize that the relations between mother and child are socially mediated.

[2] Overidentification is where children (particularly girls) and their mothers "experience themselves as overly attached, unindividuated, and without boundaries" (Chodorow 135).

3 Thanks to Anne Herbert for pointing out to me another reading of this image—in Mexican mythology a god who takes the form of a hummingbird is associated with the sacrifice of children.

[4] Metonymy is the signifying function where the part is taken for the whole, emphasizing continuity, and it is based in a word to word connection in the signifier. Metaphor is the conjunction of two, possibly disparate, signifiers, where one replaces or conflates the other. Generally, metaphor is regarded as the more creative figure, enlarging its context in the relation between the two images as one replaces the other in the signifying chain. However, these two figures are interrelated because the element replaced by metaphor also remains present as Lacan maintains, "through its [metonymic] connection with the rest of the chain" (1977, 157). My ideas about the connection between transference, metaphor and metonymy are influenced by my reading of Julia Kristeva, Jacques Lacan, Cynthia Chase and Maria Ruegg (works are listed below).

[5] See Wessling.

[6] I agree with Gloria Randle's contention that defenses such as repression are necessary for the psychic survival of victims of slavery or other forms of oppression. Morrison's work suggests we cannot merely write these defenses off as pathology or flaws.

Works Cited

Bachelard, Gaston. *The Poetics of Space*. Boston: Beacon Press, 1969.

Benjamin, Jessica. *The Bonds of Love: Psychoanalysis, Feminism, and the Problem of Domination*. New York: Pantheon Books, 1988.

Brenkman, John. *Culture and Domination*. Ithaca: Cornell University Press, 1987.

Busia, Abena P. B. "Words Whispered Over Voids: A Context for Black Women's Rebellious Voices in the Novel of the African Diaspora." *Studies in Black American Literature: Black Feminist Criticism*. Vol. 3. Eds. Joe Weixlmann and Houston A. Baker. Greenwood, Florida: The Penkevill Publishing Co., 1988. 1-36.

314 Laurie Vickroy

Chase, Cynthia. "Transference as Trope and Persuasion." *Discourse in Psycho-analysis and Literature*. Ed. Shlomith Rimmon-Kenan. London: Methuen, 1987. 211-229.

Ferguson, Rebecca. "History, Memory and Language in Toni Morrison's *Beloved*." *Feminist Criticism: Theory and Practice*. Eds. Susan Sellers, Linda Hutcheon and Paul Perron. Toronto: University of Toronto Press, 1991.

Freud, Sigmund. "The Dynamics of Transference" (1912). *Papers on Technique in Collected Works* Vol. 12. 99-108.

—. "Remembering, Repeating and Working-Through" (1914). *Standard Edition* Vol. 12. 147-156.

Hirsch, Marianne. Lecture on Toni Morrison's *Beloved*: "Maternity and Remem-ory." SUNY-Binghamton, Binghamton, New York, 8 February 1990.

—. "Maternal Narratives: Cruel Enough to Stop the Blood." *Reading Black, Reading Feminist*. Ed. Henry Louis Gates, Jr. New York: Meridian, 1990. 415-430.

Kristeva, Julia. *Tales of Love*. Trans. Leon S. Roudiez. New York: Columbia University Press, 1987.

Lacan, Jacques. "The Agency of the Letter in the Unconscious or Reason Since Freud." *Ecrits*. Trans. Alan Sheridan. New York: W. W. Norton and Com-pany, 1977. 146-178.

Laplanche, Jean and J. B. Pontalis. *The Language of Psychoanalysis*. Trans. Donald Nicholson-Smith. New York: Norton, 1974.

McDowell, Deborah E. "The Self and the Other: Reading Toni Morrison's *Sula* and the Black Female Text." *Critical Essays on Toni Morrison*. Ed. Nellie Y. McKay. Boston: G. K. Hall, 1988. 77-90.

Morrison, Toni. *Beloved*. New York: Knopf, 1987.

—. "Memory, Creation and Writing," *Thought* 59.235 (December 1984): 385-390.

—. *Sula*, New York: New American Library, 1973.

—. "Unspeakable Things Unspoken: The Afro-American Presence in American Literature." *Michigan Quarterly Review* 28.1 (Winter 1989): 1-34.

Randle. Gloria T. "Good-Enough Mothering and the Mechanisms of Defense in the World of *Beloved*." Diss. University of Chicago, 1992.

Ruegg, Maria. "Metaphor and Metonymy: The Logic of Structuralist Rhetoric." *Glyph* 6 (1979): 141-157.

Schapiro, Barbara. "The Bonds of Love and the Boundaries of Self in Toni Mor-rison's *Beloved*." *Contemporary Literature* 32.2 (1991): 194-210.

Wessling, Joseph H. "Narcissism in Toni Morrison's *Sula*." *College Language Association Journal* 31.1 (March 1988): 281-298.

Willis, Susan. "Eruptions of Funk: Historicizing Toni Morrison." *Black Litera-ture and Literary Theory*. Ed. Henry L. Gates, Jr. New York: Methuen, 1984. 263-283.

Winnicott, D. W. *Playing and Reality*. Harmondsworth, U.K.: Penguin Books, 1974.

A Blessing and a Burden:
The Relation to the Past in
Sula, Song of Solomon and *Beloved*

Deborah Guth

Among the many issues that inhabit Toni Morrison's fiction, one of the most absorbing is the multifaceted and often problematic relationship of the present to the past. Whether she explores a love-affair or a girlhood friendship, generational rupture or the meaning of freedom—whether she uses the model of communal story-telling to shape her work, reactivates a traditional myth or explores the dynamics of memory—the impact of the past remains a central issue, wending its way through theme and form. Clearly, for Morrison, the question: "Who am I?" and "Where are we going?" are inseparable from "Where do we come from?", and the two sides—the search for self-definition and an understanding of what the past is about—interact constantly throughout her work. "The reclamation of the history of black people in this country is paramount in its importance. . . . You have to stake out [your part of the work] and identify those who have preceded you," she says, but also adds that "resummoning them, acknowledging them is just one step in that process of reclamation" ("Interview," Davis 143).

Significantly, her purpose is never simply to recapture the texture of a world gone by, to document its details or recreate an idealized portrait for purpose of nostalgia. Rather, the impetus of her work is to explore and dramatize the complex interaction between a present in search of itself and a past that appears sometimes as nurturing cultural foundation, sometimes as a restrictive tradition to be fought off, and sometimes—in *Beloved* for example as a frightening nightmare that imposes itself between the present and a future of freedom and renewal. Morrison is aware of "both the burdens and the blessings of the past" ("An Interview," McKay 413); in light of this, I examine in this essay three different constructions of this relationship and three aspects of the problem—rejection, reclamation and the dynamics of the remembering imagination—in order to clarify the ramifications and cultural implications of her thought.

Sula has often been seen as a Bildungsroman which traces the development of the title character, her relationship with her childhood friend Nel and their very different lives within the community of Medallion.[1] The ostensible relation of present to past in this novel is one of rejection as Sula attempts to define for herself a new identity in contradistinction to the values of the community. Framed by Shadrack's tragic madness and shot through with death, Sula's path may thus be seen as an attempt to free herself from the traditions—and the suffering—of her community and to define a new mode of black womanhood.[2] However, significant patterns of repetition implicitly connecting Sula's life to that of her grandmother, Eva Peace, provide an alternative interpretive prism and suggest that the rejected ancestor, for all her destructiveness and tyranny, is in fact the freest, most integrated character, and a model which the text itself imposes in order to challenge the more "modern" definition of selfhood that Sula is trying to live out.

Sula herself is a complex figure, a "moral and psychological enigma" (Grant 92) that the narrative is careful to maintain.[3] Presented in the first part of the novel mainly through sporadic scenes of violence, her growth reflects a process of inner disengagement, a gradual decentering from the role of active participant to that of passive observer, and from there to conscious self exclusion. This process can be traced from the episode where she actively faces down Nel's tormentors by lopping off her own finger, through Chicken Little's drowning, where she is both initiator, swinging him around, and then helpless onlooker as his body flies out over the water; to the day when she stands by, watching with passive complicity, as her mother burns to death; and culminating when, at her best friend's wedding, she refuses even the implicit involvement of the observer, turns her back and leaves Medallion.

Her return after a ten-year absence marks no symbolic reintegration into the community, and her central position within it serves mainly to offset a total inner detachment both from others and, more disturbingly, from herself. Her refusal to

live according to the values of her community—to marry and
settle down—and the "distinctly different" quality about her
which causes the townspeople to see her as evil, have often been
seen as contributing to the picture of a young woman suffering
and fighting for the right to choose her own path in life. As the
narrator tells us, "hers was an experimental life" (102). However, the freedom and "difference" which she flaunts have little
meaning for her. She destroys her friend's marriage without
fore- or afterthought and without really desiring Jude. She has
her grandmother placed in an old age home simply because she
does not want her in the house; even sex gives her none of the
deep satisfaction it gave to her sensual mother. Her final conversation with Nel is a model of contemptuous disrelation, and
finally she experiences even her own death from some disembodied point outside her body: "she noticed that she was not
breathing, that her heart had stopped completely. . . . Her body
did not need oxygen. She was dead" (133). In all these instances
not unlike Camus' outsider Meursault, she simply refuses to attribute meaning or to relate to the implications of her behavior,
and although we are told by the narrator that she spent her time
"exploring her own thoughts and emotions, giving them full
reign" (102), there is little evidence of this in the text. "'I don't
want to make somebody else,'" she had said earlier to Eva, "'I
want to make myself'" (80). But this bid for selfhood has neither
center nor purpose. The unpunctuated, self reversing phrases
that she croons to herself after Ajax leaves—"*I have sung all the
songs all the songs I have sung all the songs there are*"—reflect
only world-weary stasis, and her defiant words to Nel—"'your
lonely is somebody else's . . . but my lonely is *mine*'" (123)—ring
as a last ditch effort to define selfhood through absence. Like the
closed place in the water where Chicken Little disappeared, Morrison's character is the trace of "something newly missing" (52),
a series of dramatic gestures that never coalesce either for the
reader or, it would seem, for herself."[4]

The comparison with Eva Peace helps to clarify the nature
of her failure and is based on striking similarities within the two
women's respective life-cycles. Both assert themselves through
an act of self-mutilation, Sula when she cuts off her finger to face
down Nel's tormentors, Eva when she loses her leg under a
train in order to provide for her children. They both cause the
death of another: Eva kills her son Plum, while Sula causes
Chicken Little's death in the river. Each one is abandoned by a

man—Eva by her husband BoyBoy, Sula by Ajax; and each disappears for a spell from Medallion—Eva when her children are
small, Sula after Nel's marriage. Both are figures of lawlessness,
and both are exiled: Sula within the community, and Eva outside it when Sula places her in an old age home.

Yet while both women are violent at times and both lay
claim to being self-created, Eva never negates the world around
her. Unlike Sula, she faces life head on, actively challenging the
forces of destruction that threaten and shape her life. In fact, the
communal saying that "[t]he only way to avoid the Hand of God
is to get in it" (56) may be seen as a metaphor for the position of
self-empowerment from which she constantly grapples with the
fearful contingencies of life. None of her actions is caused by
disconnectedness or by a refusal to attribute meaning; on the
contrary, her actions derive from an intense, although frightening definition of caring and commitment. In contrast to Sula's
thoughtless destruction of her friend's marriage, Eva's killing of
Plum is accompanied by passionate conviction: having fought so
hard to save and bring him up, she cannot countenance his own
surrender in the face of life. The action she takes may well be
terrible, but her horror and inability to accept his passive disintegration are both real and compelling. Nor is she simply destructive, for the same impulse that leads her to burn Plum causes
her, one-legged as she is, to jump from a third-floor window to
save her burning daughter, while Sula simply watches as her
mother's body twitches on the ground. Or again: whereas Sula
retreats behind self-pitying images of paper dolls when Ajax
walks out on her, passively crooning herself into unconscious-
ness, Eva responds combatively to her abandonment by BoyBoy
and mobilizes the full energy of her hatred to redefine herself
(Lounsberry and Hovet 127), reigning supreme from her upstairs
room.[5] And most significantly, unlike Sula who rarely tries to
understand even herself and who "never really comes to terms
with the limitations of her approach to life" (Munro 153), Eva's
insight and uncanny knowledge range beyond her singular self
to encompass the entire action of the novel.[6] Her dreams predict
the future, they give interpretive depth to the present. And it is
she who voices the most compelling insights into those around
her: she reveals Sula's response to her mother's death long before Sula herself admits it, she knows how Chicken Little died
although she was apparently not there, and she can trace the
hidden Sula-self in Nel back to its source by the river. Larger

than life in her knowledge and her capacity to act on her convictions, she exemplifies a deep self-possession that gives the lie to Sula's purely rejectionist definition of the term.[7] And so it is fitting that Eva's indomitable presence should reassert itself at the end, long after Sula has disappeared, forcing Nel to new self-awareness and releasing her in the pain and love which unravel backwards to reunite her with her friend. Indeed, through the narrative of Sula's failed journey to selfhood, it is in fact Eva's inner potency, her black ancestral knowledge and their loss that is being explored.

The overall structure of the novel underscores this conclusion. While the narrowing of the narrative focus from the first part, which spans the community, to the second devoted exclusively to Sula signifies the displacement of traditional communal values by the "mandates (modern) individualism" encodes (Morrison, "City" 36), Eva's uncanny return at the end reverses this trend and reinstates the full authority of the past. The decisive role she plays in Nel's renewal and the model implicit in her guidance—the need to reach back into the past in order to open up the future—retroactively clarify the shortcomings of Sula's methods and contrast the empowering solitude of the one with the barren, defiant isolation of the other which is to compare the gestures with the substance of self-hood.[8]

While in *Sula* the past serves as suppressed model, juxtaposed with the present in order to assess the nature of failure, *Song of Solomon* explores the reclamation of the past as a slow process of dismantling imposed cultural constructions and reconstructing from obscured remains a uniquely different world-picture.[9] Significantly, the vehicle Morrison uses for this exploration is language itself—names, words, fragmented phrases, a song—which, decoded from semantically distortive contexts and interpreted anew within their context of origin, cohere into a fully signifying narrative. "Language is holy. To destroy a culture you first denigrate its language. . . . You screen it and filter it until it accommodates itself to the presiding language" says Morrison ("Writers" 412), adding elsewhere that "one's job is to clear away the code and see what really is there in the language and what are the connections" ("Interview," Davis 143).[10] The discovery of Milkman's family past is thus not simply a retrieval of obliterated facts; rather, the actual process of reconstruction becomes a metaphor for his initiation into a different way of "reading" the world and constructing meaning which together constitute his cultural heritage. Peter Brooks' analysis of plot is here particularly relevant: insofar as plot, or the plotting of narrative, may be defined as a "dynamic of . . . interpretive ordering"—the "active process of *sjuzet* working on *fabula*" (25) of which the model is the detective working back through obscure clues to reconstruct a hidden sequence of events—what we see in this novel is precisely Milkman's slowly emergent new reading as *sjuzet* challenging the dominant reading in order to reveal the story of his past as *fabula*. The plot of this novel of restoration is thus the transformative act of reading itself, the repetition of the subtle "same-but-different" (Brooks 99) which underlies the uniqueness of each culture here figured through language and the story it creates.

The world that Milkman sets out from is a portrait of cultural alienation and internal disrelation. Macon Dead's all-consuming pursuit of status and property are too well-documented to need comment, as are the ramifications of his family name. Most significant, perhaps, in its implication is the uncanny similarity between him, as he evicts poor tenants who impede the growth of his wealth, and the white landowners who "evicted" his father (through murder) in order to increase their own. Similarly, Ruth Dead honors her father's contempt for the black community by carefully burying him "someplace other than the one where Negroes were all laid together" (123). Her debilitating sense of unreality and her sickly relationships with both her dead father and her young son; the Dead daughters' empty lady-like existences making "bright, lifeless flowers"; the ugly suspicions and rampant hatred that substitute for human warmth— all contribute to the analysis of a family which has denied its cultural heritage in favor of the acquisitive, status conscious values of the white urban middle-classes.[11]

Only Guitar and Pilate, the sister his father has disowned, offer Milkman the sense of alternative ways of life. Guitar's past and his dedication to secret reprisals make him appear at first as an image of daring and commitment, which appeals to Milkman. Later, however, as the logic of revenge spins out of control and blinding suspicion elides the distinction between friend and foe, the image of Guitar the hunter is collapsed into that of the prey—the dead cat whose eyes gleam revenge—and it becomes clear that the cycle of violence in which he is engaged is ultimately self-destructive. In short, just as Macon Dead has substituted the bond of generational continuity for a chain of possession encoded in the phrase "Own things. And let the things you own own other things" (55),[12] so also Guitar's definition of self-empowerment reflects his participation in the very world he seeks to oppose. In both cases, the attempt to overcome dispossession and suffering—to "wipe out the past"—in fact reiterates the oppressor's terms of reference and value system: while Macon seeks quite consciously to beat the white world by joining it, Guitar's apparently oppositional stance unwittingly adds up to the same thing, for through his system of hidden reprisals he does no more than inscribe himself invisibly into a society that has condemned him, and his people, to invisibility.

The figure of Pilate opposes both Macon's and Guitar's definitions of power with a model of inner strength and self-determination. Her birth from a dead woman's body, her uncanny lack of a navel—that mark of primal connection—and her decision to throw away "every assumption she had learned and [begin] at zero" (149) make her an image of self-creation. At the same time, her harkening back to her dead father's words, the bones which hang in her living room, the earring she wears, and the song she sings are all signs of a deep connectedness from which she gains both her charisma and her inner peace. As a double metaphor of freedom and rootedness, she fittingly serves Milkman as spiritual guide.[13] It is her footsteps that he retraces south, and her name will serve as a model for a different mode of reading. Indeed, as Ruth Rosenberg points out (213-214), while for literate readers Pilate's inappropriate cross-gender name evokes only the figure of a "Christ-killer," her preliterate father saw in the letters on the page the image of a great tree "hanging in some princely but protective way over a row of smaller trees" (Morrison, *Song* 18), a connotation of nurturing that is far more appropriate and used throughout the novel to characterize her.

The two stages of Milkman's journey—Danville, Pennsylvania, and then Shalimar, Virginia—reflect Milkman's initiation into this other mode of reading. "'You don't listen to people,'" Circe says to him when he misinterprets the reason for her presence in the decaying house. "'Your ear is on your head but it's not connected to your brain'" (249). Learning to "hear" in a different, more connective mode, to grasp a contextualized speaker-speech totality rather than the speech alone, leads Milkman first to understand Circe's presence not as loyalty but as an iron determination to oversee the destruction of an order that had so misused her; then to reinterpret his father's words about his own father, seeing love, respect and mutuality where before he had heard only empty boasting (236); and later to understand his own motives for seeking the gold as an exercise in self-deception. For the first time be understands that it is the tremor in the voice saying "my *people*" that gives the word its real meaning (231), how other words and names that had seemed like disused signposts pointing nowhere acquire substance and come alive with unsuspected meanings.

As he moves from place to place, he recovers a significant portion of his family history. He is sent from Danville to a place he thought was called Charlemagne but which is actually Shalimar, pronounced "Shalleemone" like Solomon, whose name later emerges as the original version of "Sugarman" in Pilate's song. He identities his grandmother's family name Byrd as Bird, a sign of Indian ancestry; the "Jay" in the children's song as Jake, the original name of his grandfather (who had been misnamed "Macon Dead"), this grandfather as the child carried away in flight only to be dropped, and Solomon the flying African as his own ancestor. The past thus emerges as a secret code obscured by language: discovering original names behind acquired ones, new phonetic associations and words that link up with other words or phrases, he suddenly understands that his grandfather's ghostly command to Pilate—"Sing"—which gave her the healing power of song, was in fact her mother's, his grandmother's, unknown name, making Pilate's song a double hidden referent to the past.[14] And that Jake's other message to Pilate—"You just can't fly on off and leave a body"—reread in its original context, was not as she believed an order to retrieve the body of the man her brother had killed; instead it was Jake's childhood appeal to his own father, the legendary Solomon, not to leave him behind when he flew away home to Africa.

Arguably Milkman's most significant experience in this context occurs during the night hunt in Shalimar when, lost in total darkness, he learns to "read blind" in the tradition of his forefathers. The stages of this process represent yet another restoration of hidden layers, a retracing of language back to its source: in the dark when no one speaks, he discovers first the complex expressiveness of sound and rhythm through which the men communicate with their dogs, and then the codes of silence that connect the men to the forest they stalk. "No, it was not language," he realizes, "it was what there was before language. Before things were written down" (281)—a fluid world of sound and the unmediated communication of touch that codified language has displaced and which he sees in Calvin as he touches the ground, not just looking for tracks but actually "pulling meaning through his fingers" (282).

For Milkman, the hunt becomes the paradigm of an entirely new mode of signification, as well as an experience of reintegration into his ground of origin: "he found himself exhilarated by simply walking the earth. Walking it like he belonged on it; like his legs were stalks, tree trunks, a part of his body that extended down down into the rock and soil, and were comfortable there . . ."(284). The lesson in reading he derives from this night is twofold: analytic and synthetic. In the first instance it enables him to break down immediate experience according to new vital criteria, "*to separate out*, of all the things there were to sense, the one that life itself might depend on" (280-281; my emphasis), and by preempting Guitar's attack to save his own life. Secondly, it teaches him to correlate various modes of signification: when after the hunt he juxtaposes Guitar's remembered words with the slow gutting of the bobcat, an entirely new meaning is generated through the dialogic interaction of word and physical gesture, phrase and context, past and present frames of reference.

> [Omar] and Calvin turned [the bobcat] over on its back. The legs fell open. Such thin delicate ankles.
> '*Everybody wants a black mans life.*'
> Calvin held the forefeet open while Omar pierced the curling hair at the point where the sternum lay. Then he sliced all the way down to the genitals. His knife pointed upward for a cleaner, neater incision.
> '*Not his dead life; I mean his living life.*'
> When he reached the genitals he cut them off, but left the scrotum intact.
> '*It's the condition our condition is in,*' etc.   (285)

Through this interaction, the hunt and slow dismembering of the prey become first a metaphor for the history of racial persecution in America and then, through the cumulative effect of choral phrasing and ceremonial gesture,[16] this historical plane itself is refracted as a ritual repetition of some far more ancient drama of male rivalry and lust for power. On another level, the closing shift which reveals Guitar the prophet of violence to be in fact its victim—dead as the cat but for the eyes glinting re-

venge[17]—shows Milkman's new capacity to move from literal
to broader metaphoric levels of meaning and to counterpoint
personal and historical readings.

The final phrase he hears—"'*It is about love. What
else?*'"—provides the culminating revelation at this scene. Juxtaposed as it is with the tearing out of the heart (the organ of
love itself), it dismantles all previous uses of the word: Hagar's
"killing passion" for Milkman, Guitar's systematic murder in its
name, Ruth's debilitating affection, the "loving kindness" that
masks white destruction like the candy Guitar was given after
his father died. As a result, it also points to the various functions of language itself: to name, to explain, but also—like the
names which obliterate identity—to hide, to distort, to mock, to
signify absence.

Finally, the various ways he has learned to reconstruct
language and meaning enable him to unscramble the children's
song and decode beneath the garbled sounds the narrative of his
ancestor, the flying African Solomon. As song and dance, fact,
legend and place unite to form a total signifying whole, he recovers the original meaning of the word "to act." Having seen
through the world of pretense and play-acting he had lived before, here innocently encoded in the "round game" that the
children perform without understanding, he can now transform
the whirling flight their game suggests into a fully meaningful,
self-expressive act. And in so doing he restores ritual repetition
to its true status as the re-actualization of an originary past.[18]

The words he has learned to read anew—freedom, self-determination, love, belonging—are no longer depleted signifiers,
traces of absence like the watermark left on his mother's dining-
table. They are the names of newly grounded experiences recon-
textualized within a different culture of feeling and value, vital
impulses that now translate directly into action as Milkman
rides out his growing euphoria to its natural climax—his ecstatic
flight from the edge of Solomon's Leap.[19] In this one moment
he finally repossesses his mythic heritage. More than that, he
gives it new meaning. For Solomon's original flight defined
freedom as an escape from the present: but as Milkman leaps
into the air and into the arms of the "brother" poised to kill him,
be embraces the present as well as the legendary past and defines
freedom as a complex connectedness.

The distance he has covered in his repossession of the past
can finally be assessed through the framing episodes of flight

which mark his evolution from a materialistic, object-oriented reading of life, encoded in Smith's belief that flying is a function of blue silk wings, to a final symbolic understanding of flight as the objective correlative of inner power and joy.[20] Ultimately, the process through which "collapsed" metaphors—Smith's failed flight or Pilate's partial song—are transformed into fully active vehicles of cultural transmission reflects Milkman's own journey into the past as a rebirth from the world of the Dead to an inner space of unimagined creative power.

Beloved, Morrison's most complex fictional achievement to date, presents yet another construction of the relation of present to past. Crafted as a fable of the dynamics of memory, it dramatizes the intersection of two warring impulses towards the past, the imperative to remember and the desperate need to forget, and encodes them in a tale where one woman's attempt to defy forget and to the encroachment of the past culminates in a fully symbiotic bond between the present, imaged as haunted mother, and the past, represented in the form of her murdered and resurrected child.

On the most immediate level, *Beloved* clearly presents itself as a novel of remembering.[21] Through a stream-of-consciousness technique that provides fragmented and frightening hints, the narrative meanders through the minds of various characters to slowly reconstruct a portrait of the past, both individual and communal. It finally closes in on the day of the killing, remembered consecutively by three different people, and then moves out again from there to draw the resurrected Beloved, Sethe and Sethe's long-dead mother into a closed circle of violence and loss manifested in the scars that mark each one.

Beneath the process of recall dramatized by the text, however, lies the far more potent and subversive dynamic of forgetfulness—Sethe's determination to remember "as close to nothing as was safe," to "beat . . . back the past" at the start of every day (7, 90). Clearly, it is not Sethe's memory that resurrects Beloved, nor does Beloved's progressive invasion of her mother's life reflect intensified recall. In fact the text acts as a foil: just as Sethe herself dances around Paul D when he finally questions her about the murder, so the initial sections of the novel circle evasively from Paul D's past to tales remembered by Denver, touching down obliquely on the dead child and then veering away to signify Sethe's suppression of memory. And it is this "disremembering," a denial reformulated in Paul D's expulsion of the ghost from the house, that precipitates the reappearance of Beloved in the flesh.

The uncanny disjunction between memory and the revival of the past is further emphasized after Beloved's return. In spite of the birth symbolism that accompanies her arrival (Sethe's water breaks when she sees her), her name, the scar on her neck and a knowledge of the past that no stranger could have, and although even Denver knows who she is, Sethe does not recognize her daughter for a very long time. Instead of memory reviving the past, then, it is the resurrected past—the actual presence of Beloved—that slowly summons memory in its wake. This inversion is significant: Beloved's return is no reflection on the shaping, revitalizing power of memory. On the contrary, she emerges in the flesh to challenge a continuous process of forgetting, refusal and evasion.

The ghostly resurrection of the past is thus mediated by two major forms of repetition. The first is the textual raising of the dead to dramatize the process, the tensions and the price of disremembering.[22] The second type of repetition creates a structural connection between the present and the past as Sethe, after finally recognizing Beloved, tries to relive with her the halcyon days of happiness that were cut short by her death. Beloved's appearance takes Sethe back to the moment of birth, as she feels her water about to break. Recognition occurs after the skating outing when Sethe gives her warm milk, reminiscent of the milk she had obsessively carried to freedom for her child. And their relationship culminates as Sethe, seeing in Mr. Bodwin the reappearance of schoolteacher who had precipitated the murder years ago, rushes once again to kill in order to protect her child.

However, although this second type of repetition implicitly connects the two time-frames, it primarily exposes the distance that separates memory from the past and dramatizes the distortion it imposes on the present. For Sethe, Beloved's resurrection signals the triumph of motherlove over time and death. "Mine," she chants as she recognizes her child. "You are my Beloved / You are mine / You are mine / You are mine" (266). Her surge of joy in the reunion is both poignant and defensive: just as earlier she remembered focusing on the beauty of the sycamore trees in order not to see the bodies hanging from them, so now she basks in the glory of present love in order to blot out the memory of the bleeding child she had held in her arms. "This here's all there is and all there needs to be . . . I don't have to remember nothing," she thinks (224).

The resurrected past, however, challenges this evasion. Beloved's disruptive influence denies any restoration of innocent joy, and the terrible memories of the "other side" with which she counters her mother's song of joy make clear that the death Sethe wants to forget is Beloved's central, (one could almost say) primal experience. Literally as well as figuratively, she is not the child from before the killing but the ghostly outgrowth of that experience, bearing the name she was given in its aftermath, and leading her mother back to the same terror and loss that she is trying to erase.

The scene in which Sethe attacks Mr. Bodwin fully dramatizes this tension between remembering and forgetfulness. In her unconscious attempt to undo and change the past, Sethe now attacks the source of the threat, the white man himself, rather than the child to be protected. She wants to triumph this time not by facing him with the mangled body of her child, as before, but by annihilating him and preserving the daughter she cannot bear to lose again. Tragically, however, this belated attempt to alter the course of events will be defeated by Beloved herself. From her own separate vantage point, Beloved sees her mother's rush away from her as a repetition of the desertion she had experienced before, and to avoid this, she disappears back to the land of the dead. For both, the attempt to escape the past leads inevitably to its repetition.

Like the dynamic of remembering and forgetting, the relation of the present to the past that emerges from this novel is complex. If one returns, as Sethe tragically does, to the day of the killing, then the extent of the conflict becomes clearer. For unlike any other moment in the novel, this one stands out as directly reformed by memory—of humiliation, of milk taken from her in contempt, of "animal" characteristics calmly listed, of skulls measured for anthropological reasons—memories that impel her to grab her baby and put her "where [she'd] be safe" (201). The ghostly revival of the past that Sethe experiences—the return of Beloved—may then well be the price of forgetfulness. But as that terrible day many years before and its spectral repetition make clear, remembering leads to murder.

Morrison's most amazing achievement, however, lies in the way she focuses the entire relation of present and past through the image of the mother. From the opening scene where Sethe stands with her legs wide apart "as any grave" to

buy a memorial for her child, through the memory of another
violation when her milk was taken from her: from the birthing
of Denver during her lonely escape and the periodicity of the
female cycle inscribed in the text—"4 days . . . 28 days . . . 3
months . . . 4 months . . ."—to the final image where Sethe herself has withered to the stature of a child, shrinking back as it
were to the womb of the ghostly daughter who stands beside her,
naked and pregnant, the motherbody pervades the entire text as
a paradigm of primal unity and its historic distortion. The symbiotic union of mother and child, the earthbond that allows no
separation even while it kills, and no reparation thereafter; the
mother whose terror and love lead to the most terrifying protection, through whom possession and dispossession acquire their
most fundamental meaning—these constitute the subtext, and
the substance, of *Beloved*.

Sethe's mother had an identifying mark, a circle with a
cross, which did not help her daughter identify the body hanging
from the tree. On Sethe's back is that same tree of death, a mass
of scarred flesh bearing fruit of pus: the figure of Beloved. And
Beloved herself carries the final scar, the jagged line of the knife
that was to cut her free but which actually locks all generations
into a closed cycle of destruction that unravels backwards into
the past. Thus past and present, the two faces of one same
motherbody, are created and destroyed in a continuous act of disremembering and re-imagining, an endless circle of flight from
and return to the source.

"Dearly Beloved," the phrase with which Sethe com-
memorates and names her dead child, provides the textual cross
of presence and absence, of memory and forgetfulness, within
this scarred circle of repetition. As her only memory of
Beloved's burial, this phrase is striking in its displacement, for it
is overwhelmingly associated with the opening of the Christian
marriage service: "Dearly Beloved. We are gathered together in
the sight of God to join in holy matrimony. . . ." Its appearance
in this context thus signifies absence on two separate levels. It
calls up the ghost of the marriage service Sethe herself was denied with Halle, the sanctified love and joy from which she was
excluded. And it points to the absent remainder of the marriage
text which now implicitly joins her and her dead child in an
(un)holy bond, a "mystical union" that "no man (may) put
asunder" and that no death can part. Frozen in a position of
birth inseparable from the violation she submits to—"her knees

wide apart as any grave"—Sethe herself posits womb and grave
as mirror images, birth as life collapsed into its negation and the
motherbody as the desecrated locus of African-American history:
its conception an act of violation, its unfolding a play of ghostly
reflections, remembering a testimony of tortured absence.

In Morrison, the discourse of memory and the past foregrounds many dynamics, from the implications of rejection in
Sula to the healing glory of return in *Song*. And then as though
to stem the sense of euphoric repossession, she reconvenes the
two impulses within the broader context of black history and
dramatizes in *Beloved* the power struggle between the re-cre-
ative imagination and an irreducible past of pain in order to de-
construct the idealization of recall. The problem of remembering and forgetting, of rejection and return, is thus problematized
by the fact that there are two pasts addressed in Morrison's work:
the black cultural heritage, with its distinctive artistic forms and
modes of awareness, and the historic past of outrage and suffering with all the compounded distortions it involved. The
reclamation of the past in terms of the first may best be clarified
through the final stages of Milkman's quest. For just as Milkman moves from the actual words of the song to their hidden
meaning, and from a passive to an active form of knowledge
seen in his ability to create the myth anew, so reclamation involves reaching beyond the letter of the past to the spirit that
moves it—literally moves Milkman to fly—and that, continually reconvened and shaped anew, provides the key to cultural
continuity within a changing world. This spirit of the past however is also Beloved, the demon of historic distortion which
cannot be simply bracketed away in the name of renewal as Morrison feels previous generations have tried to do, but demands
full recognition and understanding before it can be exorcized.[23]
As Pilate says, "'the dead you kill'"—or forget—"'is yours'"
(210). And the story of Sethe, whose attempt to disremember the
past exiles her into a no-man's-land of endless repetition, serves
here as a cautionary tale.

The relation of present to past in Morrison's work is thus
neither a question of simply "going back" to a traditional world
and denying the present, nor of sealing off an "unspeakable" past
to make way for a new order, but rather of continuously exploring the hidden intersections between the two time-spans, the
subtle similarities—wanted or unwanted—the disjunctions and
dislocations. Mainly, as her narrative constructions make clear,

the dialogical integration of the past into an ongoing narrative opens up semantic recesses which give depth and new direction to the understanding of the present. It restores an alienated present to itself and provides that sense of cultural self-possession which for her is the bedrock of identity.

For this reason, the figure of repetition is maybe the central feature of her work in all its intricate variety. Obliquely associating disparate moments through an expanding play of image and metaphor, creating strange phantasmagoric resemblances and resonances that echo back and forth, it charts the subtle "same-but-different" that connects present to past, the uncanny similarities that momentarily fuse the two time-spans as well as the slow transformation of meaning through which a temporal succession of events is envisioned as the constant reconfiguration and play of complex meanings.

In his now classic work on repetition, J. Hillis Miller outlines two basic types of repetition. The first so-called Platonic type presents repetition as an imitation of an original model and calls on us to view difference against a background of basic similarity. The second or Nietzschean type, on the other hand, is based on an awareness of the uniqueness of all things—and periods—and views similarity as arising against a background of fundamental difference. "Ungrounded doublings" he calls these similarities, ghostly likenesses or phantasms whose meaning occurs in some strange "empty space" between dissimilarity and real similarity which "the opaque similarity crosses" (Miller 5-9). Almost more than plot, these patterns of repetition form the textual energetics of Morrison's work and make repetition a primary metaphor of connectedness itself. While the phantasmal likenesses created by the second type collapse difference into shadowy similarity and elide the boundaries between present and past, the first—seen in Milkman's final flight—uses similarity to offset difference and foregrounds repetition as a vehicle for cultural transmission as well as the medium for its self-transformation and renewal.

Brooks provides us with an equally important insight. Repetition in narrative, he states, dramatizes the way in which the mind creates meaning and is itself a form of remembering—a series of "returns to and returns of, confounding the movement forward to the end with a movement back to origins, reversing meaning within forward-looking time . . . offering the possibility (or illusion) of 'meaning' wrested from 'life'" (98,

108). His analysis here clarifies the construction of meaning, both narrative and cultural, as intimately bound up with memory. It also foregrounds the internal self-reversing motions through which Morrison's imagination carves out its own unique space in defiance of "real" time, that same "empty space" of metaphoric play in which she recreates and transmits the distinctive modalities of meaning as well as the forms of knowledge which to her constitute her cultural heritage. Narrative, she says, "is one of the ways in which knowledge is organized," maybe the only place she adds, referring to *Beloved* "where [she] can take that information" ("Memory" 388; Toni Morrison 237).

In the last analysis, of course, Morrison's novels are themselves acts of repetition both as remembering and as transformation. Her extensive use of myth and folk belief to explore the meaning of the present, the open musical architecture of her work, the oral/aural narrative voice and communal storytelling techniques she deploys, all show the degree to which she herself draws on the past.[24] More important, they dramatize the act of imaginative transformation so central to her thought—the possibility, that is, of recreating various traditional forms within a modern, in this case narrative, context. On a broader level, of course, the very composition of *Beloved* shows this capacity not simply to descriptively "repeal" the past, but to actually transform the chaos of history into a fable of love and bereavement. By carefully maintaining the tension between these two extremes—past and present, history and its imaginative transformation—she balances the need for return with a constant awareness of historical distance, and redefines Du Bois's "double-consciousness" as a form of self-reflexiveness about the function and the functioning of memory.

The extent to which these various types of repetition inform her work may finally be seen as her response to a future- and achievement-oriented society whose linear concept of time as Progress, consciously distancing itself from the past,[25] is countered by her own constructions of periodic return: "Without a clear understanding of the past there's no way to confront the future," she states categorically. "It's vital for us to preserve the culture genes we have inherited. . . . Writers are the people— possibly the only people—who can do that" ("Person" 29).

Notes

[1] See, for example, Bakerman 548-554. For a much challenged analysis of the latent erotic dynamic between Sula and Nel, see Barbara Smith 165-170.

[2] A number of critics privilege her emblematic value, among them Willis, who views Sula as "a prophet of change on an imaginative and metaphoric plane" (213), and Middleton who sees her as an "audacious genius" whose example "changes the way we see the world" (378, 380-381).

[3] According to McDowell, "[t]he novel's fragmentary, episodic, elliptical quality helps to thwart textual unity, to prevent a totalized interpretation" (87). Butler-Evans comments in the same vein (87), as does Spillers, who sees in *Sula* "a novel whose formal strategies are ambiguous and even discomforting in their uncertainties" (298). For a masterly analysis of the "calculated indeterminacies" in the novel, see Grant.

[4] Critical assessments of Sula's achievement are varied. Among those who see Sula triumphing in her rebellion are Ogunyemi and Royster: Montgomery views the womb imagery in Sula's death as a sign of rebirth (135); for Stein, Sula's journey should be seen as a successful enactment of freedom because of the legacy of new understanding she leaves to Nel (148-149). Analyses of failure include McDowell, who unlike Montgomery, interprets Sula's final fetal position as sign that she "never achieves completeness of being" (81); Lounsberry and Hovet, for whom Sula fails to act on her vision and realize her potential (128-129); Lee, who cites her self-centered pursuit of whim and experience as ultimately impoverishing ("Quest" 352). For Davis, Sula falls short of being the "free" existential hero because she defines herself solely through exclusion from the community (332-333), while Christian sees her as dying of self-absorption, both because she rejects the community and because the community rejects her gift: "the leap into living, the insistence on knowing oneself, the urge to experiment" ("Community" 54; also "Contemporary Fables" 167).

[5] See Dixon: Sula's "physical and emotional paralysis . . . reverses the moment of moral strength Eva felt in her husband BoyBoy's desertion . . ." (157).

[6] See Morrison: "Eva is a triumphant figure, one-legged or not. She is playing God. She maims people. *But she says all of the important things*" (Parker 255; my emphasis).

[7] Morrison's own comment is relevant: "[T]he point is that freedom is choosing your responsibility. Its not having no responsibilities; it's choosing the ones you want" ("Conversation" 573)

[8] I am not claiming that Morrison simply affirms tradition at the expense of individualism, but that Sula errs in seeing the two as mutually exclusive. See Grant's conclusion that the novel "'privileges' *both* tradition and transgression" (91) and Morrison's own comment—"If we don't keep in touch with the ancestor . . . we are, in fact, lost. . . . I want to point out the dangers, to show that the nice things don't always happen to the totally self-reliant if there is no conscious historical connection" ("Rootedness" 344).

[9] Analyses of *Song* as a mythic quest include Davis, Fabre, Campbell, and Bruck.

[10] A similar point is made in "'The Language Must Not Sweat'" (27).

[11] As Skerrett has pointed out, this alienation is equally reflected in the function of storytelling in the Dead household where expressive communal

narratives are replaced by purely personal, self-justifying ones (194-195); see also Valerie Smith 140.

[12] Macon's obsession with property is also a clear misreading of his father's love for his land, and serves as an example of the distorted meanings that Milkman must undo. On the two types of relationship to ownership, see Mason 571-572.

[13] As Barbara Christian notes, Milkman "is even more Pilate's child than he is Macon's, for without her conjuring, he would not have been conceived or born" ("Community" 55).

[14] It connects her to her mother through the act of singing, to her father and his forebears through the text of the song.

[15] Pilate's apparent misreading of her father's words and her mistaken identification of the bones do not denote inner dispossession: rather, they clarify the specific type of connectedness that Morrison is exploring—the spirit rather than the letter of the word.

[16] For a detailed analysis of this scene, see Lee, "*Song*" 69. Morrison herself notes the similar function of song and chorus in Greek tragedy and African-American communal structures ("Unspeakable Things" 2-3).

[17] The fact that Guitar has been characterized throughout by his cat's eyes (7, 22, 85, etc.) paves the way for this identification.

[18] In this context, see Eliade: "A rite is always the repetition of an archetypal gesture accomplished *in illo tempore* by the ancestors or the gods. . . . Through this repetition, the rite *coincides* with its 'archetype,' and secular time is abolished. We witness, so to speak, *the same act* as that which was accomplished *in illo tempore*" while "the time which is commemorated or repeated by the rite is re-presented in the sense of *made present . . .*" (*Traite* 40, 331; my translation).

[19] O'Shaughnessy sees the various storytellers in the South as a chorus drawing the lost son, Milkman, back into the community (129). This reintegration is graphically encoded in Milkman's shift from outside spectator of the children's round game to central whirling figure in the final scene.

[20] In this context, see Bachelard's distinction between objective and symbolic constructions: in the real world, he says, we fly "because" we have wings. But in the world of dream and myth the process is reversed—there we have wings "because" we fly, the wings being an expression of the feeling of flying (90, 119).

[21] The actual incident on which this novel is based is discussed by Morrison in "Rediscovering Black History" (16, 18). Recent scholarship focuses on other commemorative aspects: Samuels and Hudson-Weems view it as a slave-narrative exploring "not what history has recorded . . . but what it has omitted," that is, the subjective impact and details of suffering that would have been considered "offensive" by the white audiences of the time (96-97). Christian also cites Morrison's comments on slave-narrators' self-censorship ("Somebody" 329). Both House and Horvitz point to Beloved's narrative of death as a commemoration of the Middle Passage, while Traylor suggests that the novel contains an emblematic memorial to Henry Dumas, mainly through the reference to Sweet Home, Dumas' birthplace (366 ff). See also Morrison's comment: "There is no place you or I can go, to think about or not think about, to summon the presences of, or recollect the absences of slaves. . . . There is no suit-

able memorial or plaque or wreath or wall or park. . . . And because such a place doesn't exist . . . the book had to" (qtd. in Denard 332).

[22] A number of recent studies deal with repetition in *Beloved*. Particularly relevant in this context is Holloway, who sees "the reclamation and revision of history . . . as both a thematic emphasis and a *textual methodology*," with repetition functioning as "a means of accessing memory and enabling its domination of the text" (516, 519). This does not contradict my thesis, which essentially views the text as remembering what Sethe wants to forget.

[23] Christian cites Morrison's comment that many African-Americans in the post-World War II era "X'd out" the painful past in order, as they thought, to free their children towards a new future ("Somebody" 326). On the recovery of the past in *Beloved* as a "ritual of healing," see Krumholz.

[24] According to Morrison, "If my work is faithfully to reflect the aesthetic tradition of Afro-American culture, it must make conscious use of the characteristics of its art forms and translate them into print antiphony, the group nature of art, its functionality, its improvisational nature, its relationship to audience performance . . ." ("Memory" 388-389). She expresses a similar idea in an interview with Nellie McKay (427-428), and on a broader level in "The Site of Memory": "The act of imagination is bound up with memory" (119). For an analysis of *Beloved* as "an extended blues performance," see Rodrigues 153; on the re-creation of folkloric forms in Morrison's works, see Harris' recent book.

[25] For a fascinating discussion of the cultural implications of repetition as well as its relation to black music, see Snead, in particular his comment that "Strangely enough . . . what recent Western or European culture repeats continuously is the belief that there is no repetition in culture but only difference, defined as progress and growth" (60).

Works Cited

Bachelard Gaston. *L'Air et les Songes: Essai sur l'Imagination du Mouvement.* 1943. Paris: Corti, 1981.

Bakerman, Jane S. "Failures of Love: Female Initiation in the Novels of Toni Morrison." *American Literature* 52 (981): 541-583.

Brooks, Peter. *Reading for the Plot.* New York: Vintage, 1985.

Bruck, Peter. "Returning to One's Roots: The Motif of Searching and Flying in Toni Morrison's *Song of Solomon* (1977)." *The Afro-American Novel Since 1960.* Ed. Peter Bruck and Wolfgang Karper. Amsterdam: B. R. Gruner, 1982. 289-305.

Butler-Evans, Elliott. *Race, Gender, and Desire: Narrative Strategies in the Fiction of Toni Cade Bambara, Toni Morrison and Alice Walker.* Philadelphia: Temple University Press, 1989.

Campbell, Jane. "Ancestral Quests in Toni Morrison's *Song of Solomon* and David Bradley's *The Chaneysville Incident*." *Mythic Black Fiction: The Transformation of History.* Knoxville: University of Tennessee Press, 1986. 136-153.

Christian, Barbara T. "Community and Nature: The Novels of Toni Morrison." *Black Feminist Criticism*. New York: Pergamon, 1985. 47-63.

—. "The Contemporary Fables of Toni Morrison." *Black Women Novelists: The Development of a Tradition 1892-1976*. Westport: Greenwood Press, 1980. 137-179.

—. "'Somebody Forgot to Tell Somebody Something': African-American Women's Historical Novels." *Wild Women in the Whirlwind: Afra-American Culture and the Contemporary Literary Renaissance*. Ed. Joanne M. Braxton and André McLaughlin. New Brunswick: Rutgers University Press, 1990. 326-341.

Davis, Cynthia A. "Self, Society and Myth in Toni Morrison's Fiction." *Contemporary Literature* 23 (1982): 323-342.

Denard, Carolyn C. "Toni Morrison." *Modern American Women Writers*. Ed. Elaine Showalter. New York: Scribner's, 1991. 317-338.

Dixon, Melvin. "Like an Eagle in the Air: Toni Morrison." *Ride Out the Wilderness: Geography and Identity in Afro-American Literature*. Urbana: University of Illinois Press, 1987. 141-169.

Eliade, Mircea. *Traité d'Histoire des Religions*. Paris: Payot, 1975.

Fabre, Genevieve. "Genealogical Archaeology or the Quest for Legacy in Toni Morrison's *Song of Solomon*." *Critical Essays on Toni Morrison*. Ed. Nellie McKay. Boston: G. K. Hall, 1988. 105-114.

Grant, Robert. "Absence into Presence: The Thematics of Memory and 'Missing' Subjects in Toni Morrison's *Sula*." *Critical Essays on Toni Morrison*. Ed. Nellie McKay. Boston: G. K. Hall, 1988. 90-103.

Harris, Trudier. *Fiction and Folklore: The Novels of Toni Morrison*. Knoxville: University of Tennessee Press, 1991.

Holloway, Karla F. C. "*Beloved*: A Spiritual." *Callaloo* 13 (1990: 516-525.

Horvitz, Deborah. "Nameless Ghosts: Possession and Dispossession in *Beloved*." *Studies in American Fiction* 17 (1989): 157-167.

House, Elizabeth B. "Toni Morrison's Ghost: The Beloved Who Is Not Beloved." *Studies in American Fiction* 18 (1990): 17-26.

Krumholz, Linda. "The Ghosts of Slavery: Historical Recovery in Toni Morrison's *Beloved*." *African American Review* 26 (1992): 395-408.

Lee, Dorothy H. "The Quest for Self: Triumph and Failure in the Works of Toni Morrison." *Black Women Writers (1950-1980)*. Ed. Mari Evans. Garden City: Anchor/Doubleday, 1984. 346-360.

—. "*Song of Solomon*: To Ride the Air." *Black American Literature Forum* 16 (1982): 64-70.

Lounsberry, Barbara and Grace Ann Hovet. "Principles of Perception in Toni Morrison's *Sula*." *Black American Literature Forum* 13 (1979): 126-129.

Mason, Theodore O., Jr. "The Novelist as Conservator: Stories and Comprehension in Toni Morrison's *Song of Solomon*." *Contemporary Literature* 29 (1988): 564-581.

McDowell, Deborah E. "'The Self and the Other': Reading Toni Morrison's *Sula* and the Black Female Text." *Critical Essays on Toni Morrison*. Ed. Nellie McKay. Boston: G. K. Hall, 1988. 77-90.

Middleton, Victoria. "Sula: An Experimental Life." *CLA Journal* 28 (1985): 367-381.

Miller, J. Hillis. *Fiction and Repetition*. Oxford: Blackwell, 1982.

Montgomery, Maxine Lavon. "A Pilgrimage to the Origins: The Apocalypse as Structure and Theme in Toni Morrison's *Sula*." *Black American Literature Forum* 23 (1989): 127-137.

Morrison, Toni. *Beloved*. New York: Signet/NAL, 1988.

—. "City Limits. Village Values: Concepts of the Neighborhood in Black Fiction." *Literature and the Urban Experience*. Ed. Michael C. Jaye and Ann Chalmers Watts. New Brunswick: Rutgers University Press, 1981. 35-43.

—. "A Conversation." With Gloria Naylor. *Southern Review* 21 (1985): 567-593.

—. "Interview with Toni Morrison." With Christina Davis. *Présence Africaine* 145 (1988): 141-150.

—. "An Interview with Toni Morrison." With Nellie McKay. *Contemporary Literature* 24 (1983): 413-429.

—. "'The Language Must Not Sweat: A Conversation with Toni Morrison." With Thomas LeClair. *New Republic* 21 March 1981: 25-29.

—. "Memory, Creation and Writing." *Thought* 59 (1984): 385-390.

—. "Person to Person: Toni Morrison." *Black Seeds* (Engl.) 1 (1980): 28-29.

—. "Rediscovering Black History." *New York Times Magazine* 11 August 1974: 14ff.

—. "Rootedness: The Ancestor as Foundation." *Black Women Writers (1950-1980)*. Ed. Mari Evans. Garden City: Anchor/Doubleday, 1984. 339-345.

—. "The Site of Memory." *Inventing the Truth: The Art and Craft of Memoir*. Ed. William Zinsser. Boston: Houghton Mifflin, 1987. 103-124.

—. *Song of Solomon*. New York: Signet/NAL, 1978.

—. *Sula*. New York: Bantam, 1975.

—. "Toni Morrison." Interview with Charles Ruas. *Conversations with American Writers*. Ed. Charles Ruas. New York: Knopf, 1985. 215-243.

—. "Unspeakable Things Unspoken: The Afro-American Presence in American Literature." *Michigan Quarterly Review* 28 (1989): 1-34.

—. "Writers Together." (Address given at the American Writers Congress, 9 October 1981). *Nation* 24 October 1981: 396ff.

Munro, Lynn C. "The Tattooed Heart and the Serpentine Eye: Morrison's Choice of an Epigraph for *Sula*." *Black American Literature Forum* 18 (1984): 150-154.

O'Shaughnessy, Kathleen. "'Life life life life': The Community as Chorus in *Song of Solomon*." *Critical Essays on Toni Morrison*. Ed. Nellie McKay. Boston: G. K. Hall, 1988. 125-133.

Ogunyemi, Chikwenye Okonjo. "*Sula*: A Nigger Joke." *Black American Literature Forum* 13 (1979): 130-133.

Parker, Bettye J. "Complexity: Toni Morrison's Women—An Interview Essay." *Sturdy Black Bridges: Visions of Black Women in Literature*. Ed. Roseann P. Bell, Bettye Parker and Beverly Guy-Sheftall. Garden City: Doubleday, 1979. 251-257.

Rodrigues, Eusesbio L. "The Telling of *Beloved*." *Journal of Narrative Technique* 21 (1991): 153-169.

Rosenberg, Ruth. "'And the Children May Know Their Names': Toni Morrison's *Song of Solomon*." *Literary Onomastic Studies* 8 (1981): 195-219.

Royster, Philip M. "A Priest and a Witch Against the Spiders and the Snakes: Scapegoating in Toni Morrison's *Sula*." *Umoja* 2.2 (1978): 149-168.

Samuels, Wilfred D. and Clenora Hudson-Weems. *Toni Morrison*. Boston: Twayne, 1990.

Skerrett, Joseph T., Jr. "Recitation to the *Griot*: Storytelling and Learning in Toni Morrison's *Song of Solomon*." *Conjuring: Black Women, Fiction and Literary Tradition*. Ed. Marjorie Pryse and Hortense J. Spillers. Bloomington: Indiana University Press, 1985. 192-202.

Smith, Barbara. "Towards a Black Feminist Criticism." *All the Women Are White, All the Blacks Are Men, But Some of Us Are Brave*. Ed. Gloria Hull, Patricia Bell Scott and Barbara Smith. New York: Feminist Press, 1982. 157-175.

Smith, Valerie. "Toni Morrison's Narratives of Community." *Self-Discovery and Authority in Afro-American Narrative*. Cambridge: Harvard University Press, 1987. 122-153.

Snead, James A. "Repetition as a Figure of Black Culture." *Black Literature and Literary Theory*. Ed. Henry L. Gates, Jr. London: Methuen, 1984. 59-79.

Spillers, Hortense J. "A Hateful Passion, A Lost Love." *Feminist Studies* 9 (1983): 293-323.

Stein, Karen. "Toni Morrison's *Sula*: A Black Woman's Epic." *Black American Literature Forum* 18 (1984): 146-150.

Traylor, Eleanor W. "Henry Dumas and the Discourse of Memory." *Black American Literature Forum* 22 (1988): 365-378.

Willis, Susan. "Black Women Writers: Taking a Critical Perspective." *Making a Difference: Feminist Literary Criticism*. Ed. Gayle Green and Coppelia Kahn. London: Methuen, 1985. 211-237.

Sula and *Beloved*:
Images of Cain in the Novels of Toni Morrison

Carolyn M. Jones

In *The Mark of Cain*, Ruth Mellinkoff rejects the single modern image of Cain she examines, Hesse's *Demien*, as an "intentionally distorted" treatment of the myth. In Hesse's novel, she claims,

> the interpreter has designed his interpretation to serve his own purpose—a self-conscious twisting to achieve personal ends. Clarification or elaboration of biblical texts is not the primary goal; rather, biblical elements are used to enhance the interpreter's particular point of view about something he is critical of in his contemporary society. (81)

Displacements of myth in contemporary fiction, however, are not distortions but are intertextual examinations of the place and function of myth in contemporary life. Myth as a point of reference is archetypal memory, fixed in time and space; but as writers utilize myth, they signify on it, displace its original meanings. This displacement, as Charles Long explains, "gains its power of meaning from the structure of the discourse itself without the signification being subjected to the rules of the discourse" (1). This allows "the community [to] undercut this legitimized signification with a signification upon this legitimated signifying" (2). Thus, the minority writer or community may emphasize a meaning or an implication of a myth that the "master narrative,"[1] the ideological script that the Western world imposes on "others," refuses to consider, and may signify the original meaning into the background, giving primary authority to the signification over the master's trope. Thinking and writing about myth in the modern world is, to use Henry Louis Gates's term, *double-voiced*, representing a process of both repetition and revision (22, 50, 60).

Thinking on Cain has been subject to this process of signification. Writers, working with the Biblical myth, have focused on the meaning and form of Cain's mark. Various answers for what the mark was have been offered—either a mark on Cain's forehead[2] or a blackening of Cain's face, connecting him with Ham as a father of the black race (Mellinkoff 77).[3] Cain himself has been called the mark, a pariah identifiable by his marked body—either his trembling, groaning, or incessant wandering.[4] Yet, what strikes me about the Cain myth, reading it in a hermeneutical and intertextual relationship to Morrison's *Sula* and *Beloved*, is Cain's complete refusal to remember and to mourn. Cain denies responsibility both for his brother and for his act: "Am I my brother's keeper?" (Genesis 4.9). And he seeks to protect himself: "Lord, my punishment is greater than I can bear" (Genesis 4.13). Cain, concerned with self, lets sin in the door, but more importantly, he refuses to acknowledge his effect on the "other"; he refuses to remember and to mourn his brother Abel. This refusal marks him, and tattoo becomes taboo: He is set apart as both dangerous and holy.

Sethe and Sula, both victims and victimizers, reenact the myth of Cain. Sethe is the beloved slave who is "remarked" as an animal when Schoolteacher's odious nephews drink her breast milk while Schoolteacher "remarks," writes down her reactions, using the ink that Sethe herself made. They then mark the experience on her body, whipping her and creating a chokeberry tree on her back. Sethe's mark limits her. It is the sign of her slavery, and with the return of Beloved, it traps her in 124 Bluestone. Sula, with her rose birthmark, is denied identity by her mother, and she murders a childhood friend, throwing him accidentally into the Ohio River. Yet Sula, in contrast to Sethe, claims absolute freedom, which is symbolized by her mark. Both Sethe and Sula commit Cain's act, although they do not act out of jealousy as Cain does. Sethe acts out of pure desperation, and Sula, who feels Cain's sense of rejection, kills accidentally. They also bear Cain's mark, a mark that sets each woman apart both from personal identity and from community, and each must undergo mourning and memory to find and define the self.

Understanding and transcending the mark has to do with coming to terms with the past. Memory is a special and essential category for Toni Morrison. To "rememory" is to make an act of the moral imagination and to shape the events of one's life into story. Even events that must be put behind one must be subjected to the formative power of memory then "disremembered," put into their proper place in the individual's life. The process of mourning is a special and essential kind of memory, because it creates a hermeneutic between the self and the "other." As Deborah E. McDowell says, "the process of mourning and remembering . . . leads to intimacy with the self, which is all that makes intimacy with the others possible" (85). Yet both Sethe and Sula forsake this intimacy. Sethe, alone at the grave of the child she murdered, trades ten minutes of sex for seven letters: Beloved. Later, at the funeral of Baby Suggs, Sethe refuses to accept the support of the community, and members of the community, in turn, abandon her. Sethe feels that she has no self, except in the role of mother.[5] Sula, a rejected child who becomes a woman who refuses to be defined by anyone except herself, sits apart as Chicken is mourned and, later, dies alone. Both women deny themselves and are denied a sense of self and a place in community. Sula finds her centered and unbounded existence is one of exile, and she seeks boundaries in herself, in the community of Medallion, and in her friend Nel; Sethe finds that motherhood is not an affirmation of her identity but another manifestation of her mark.

* * * * *

When Paul D, the man whose compassion is his blessedness (Beloved 272), stands behind Sethe, holding her breasts and kissing the chokeberry tree on her back, he is affirming Sethe's whole self, though the course of the novel is run before Sethe herself can make this affirmation. Sethe's sense of her identity comes from denying the chokeberry tree, which is completely dead to feeling, and from affirming her breasts, her role as mother, having "milk enough for all" (100, 198). The victim becomes victimizer as she, having enjoyed twenty-eight days of freedom, sees Schoolteacher coming to take her and her children back to Sweet Home plantation. A terrified Sethe takes her children to the coal shed at the back of 124 Bluestone Road and cuts the throat of her "almost crawling!" baby girl. The "lessons" of

Sweet Home and the murder are what Sethe avoids. She, thus, traps herself in time and in space, in a house haunted by her baby's ghost, keeping the past at bay and losing the future, "not having any dreams of her own" (20). Paul D begins to break apart this stagnation and to chase away the spirit, but he cannot do Sethe's rememory for her. Beloved, though she has many dimensions, is memory: The child that Sethe murdered comes to demand explanation, the child, that, as Mae Henderson says, Sethe must rebirth in her remarking on her own story.

Sethe thinks she is "junkheaped . . . because she loved her children" (174), but though her individual "sin" is murder, her community sin is her pride. Baby Suggs, Sethe's mother-in-law, begins the cycle of pride. Baby's motto is "'Good is knowing when to stop'" (87), but she violates that maxim when Sethe and Denver arrive safely at her house. Brought buckets of blueberries by Stamp Paid, she and Sethe make a feast for the entire community, and the satiated community becomes suspicious of the Suggs family. The animosity created by this excess is a second origin of Beloved. Baby Suggs smells the anger of the community, but behind it she smells Beloved, a ghost in black shoes (138). The community does not warn Baby that the slavecatchers are coming to her house and, thus, participates in the murder of the child.

Sethe compounds this sin of pride and alienation when Baby Suggs dies. The community will not enter the house, so Sethe refuses to go to the funeral. At the graveside, the community does not sing for Baby and to support Sethe, so Sethe does not eat their food, and they do not eat hers. A funeral is a ritual of mourning which binds the individual and the community in an act of remembrance and which, potentially, is a point of reconciliation. Here, both Sethe and her community deny themselves this opportunity. Each refuses to engage in the rememory that will articulate Baby Suggs's place in the public sphere and that will honor her spirit as an ancestor. Thus, the individuals are denied access to her power in their private lives. There is loss on both sides. By ostracizing Sethe, the community commits a sin of pride against Baby Suggs, and Sethe, in her pride, freezes memory and makes her life stagnant. In essence, both are marked; both become images of Cain. For Sethe, this mark is deep, for it completely isolates her. Ella, for example, understands Sethe's rage but not Sethe's decision to refuse the help of the black community. Neither does she understand

Sethe's act. Ella believes Sethe's rage to have been prideful and misdirected.

In Sethe's act, blood and breast milk, rage, pride, end love become one. When Sethe tells the story of her escape, she stresses that she did it alone, out of love for the children: Nobody could take care of them like she could. Nobody could nurse them like she could. Nobody else would mother them like Sethe. Like Odysseus, who cries "Nobody" and must become "Nobody," Sethe loses herself in her mother role. Morrison says that Sethe is a

> woman [who] loved something other than herself so much [that] she had placed all of the value of her life in something outside herself. . . . [This is] interesting because the best thing that is in us is also the thing that makes us sabotage ourselves, sabotage in the sense that our life is not as worthy, or our perception of the best part of ourselves . . . what is it that nearly compels a good woman to displace the self, herself?
> (Naylor and Morrison 584-585)

For Sethe, the tree on her back is nothing compared to the fact that Schoolteacher's boys took her milk, but we realize that the two emblems are the same. The primary, destructive connection of mark and milk is illustrated as Denver, the miracle child born while Sethe is running north, drinks from Sethe's breast right after the murder of Beloved, taking in her sister's blood with her mother's milk. Enacting her extreme and exclusive self-definition as mother, Sethe becomes what Schoolteacher defined her as: an animal without memory. Baby Suggs tells us that "'Good is knowing when to stop.'" Sethe's love, like Cain's for God, becomes one with Sethe's pride and rage. Sethe argues that, by killing her baby, she kept her safe from the dehumanization of slavery. The children are her only self, her "best things"—she claims she "wouldn't draw breath without [her] children" (203)—and she will destroy rather than surrender them. Paul D, listening to the story, thinks that more important than Sethe's act is her claim (164), that maybe there is something worse than slavery. And there is.

Stamp Paid tells us that whites so feared the black people that they enslaved that they had to deny completely the humanity of blacks. So whites, whom Baby Suggs says have no limits, are savages, and project onto the blacks that savagery:

> . . . it wasn't the jungle that blacks brought with them
> to this place from the other (livable) place. It was the
> jungle whitefolks planted in them. And it grew. It
> spread. In, through and after life, it spread, until it in-
> vaded the whites who had made it. Touched them ev-
> ery one. Changed and altered them. Made them
> bloody, silly, worse than even they wanted to be, so
> scared were they of the jungle they had made. The
> screaming baboon lived under their own white skin; the
> red gums were their own.
>
> Meantime, the secret spread of this new kind of
> whitefolks' jungle was hidden, silent, except once in a
> while when you could hear its mumbling in places like
> 124.   (198-199)

The "worse sin" is to let that jungle loose. What is worse than
slavery is to let the soul become so contorted that the only self
you are is the self that the master defines for you. Sethe stops
Schoolteacher, but she destroys her child and nearly herself.
Paul D tells Sethe that she has two legs, not four; she is human,
not animal. Accepting Schoolteacher's definition of herself creates Sethe's "thick love," the love that is "safety with a handsaw" and that keeps Sethe from knowing where the world stops
and where she begins. This love denies that the children are
true "others." Like Schoolteacher's "thick mind," the excess of
reason which allows him to deny the humanity of the human
beings on whom he conducts his experiments, Sethe's "thick
love" is an excessive love that allows her to destroy what she has
created, to deny the humanness of her own child.

Beloved is the child that Sethe has to rebear in order to
rememory the mother role and to grieve. In essence, what
marks Sethe as Cain is that she refuses to acknowledge the implications of her act and to mourn properly her child. Her pride
becomes a shield against her grief. Beloved shatters that defense;
she takes Sethe deep into the truth that, until she mourns, she is
still a slave. The three hand-holding shadows of Paul D, Sethe,
and Denver which make a tentative family are replaced by
Beloved, Sethe, and Denver—a mother and her children. The
silent jungle speaks in 124, and Sethe is isolated in her role as
mother and with her pain, denying there is a world outside her
door. Eventually, even Denver is excluded, as Beloved and
Sethe create anew the Cain image, the victim-victimizer/master-
slave relationship. Beloved seeks "the join" (213) to become
what Sethe says she is, her best self; she draws off Sethe all that is

vital until she is "pregnant" with Sethe, becoming the mother. Sethe, finally facing her memories, rejoices in the return of human feelings, yet she is as trapped in them as she was in her denial. She loses the remnants of her self and enjoys the pain.

Denver tells us that Sethe does not want to be forgiven (252). The relationship between the two becomes hostile, as Sethe is denied Beloved's forgiveness and as Beloved drives Sethe to self-destruction, Denver, frightened, ventures into the community. Wearing Beloved's shoes (243), she too makes a return from the grave that 124 has become. Denver, who was a child and innocent in Sethe's and the community's sin against Baby Suggs, can be touched by Baby's spirit. She is forced by Baby Suggs to give up her defense and face the future:

> But you said there was no defense.
> 'There ain't.'
> Then what do I do?
> 'Know it, and go on out the yard. Go on.'   (244)

Denver, who realizes that she has a self of her own to preserve (252), becomes the agent of reconciliation. She, the child who ingested blood and breast milk, is as much a symbol of Sethe's pride as is Beloved. Denver, too, has been exiled, trapped in Sethe's memories. But Baby's spirit tells Denver that life is risk, and only through risk, relationship, and rememory is the self formed. Armed with this knowledge, Denver acts. She practices what her mother could not at the funeral—humility—and does what her mother could not—she asks for help. Her humility causes the community, especially the women, to rally around the family in 124.

Ella, taking Baby Suggs's maxim to heart, recognizes that Beloved is excess, that, though the mother killed the child, "'. . . the children can't just up and kill the mama'" (256). What follows this recognition is a repetition of the past—a recreation of the moment of the murder and the flooding of memory into the present so that reconciliation can take place. The women go to 124 Bluestone. They remember the feast that Baby Suggs prepared for them; they remember themselves young. They make the primal sound that they did not make for Baby at her funeral: They mourn. Meanwhile, Mr. Bodwin, the abolitionist who has helped the Suggs family, drives toward the house. Sethe believes that he is Schoolteacher, come for Beloved, and runs towards him with an ice pick. This time, she attacks the master and not the child, and this time, the child saves the mother. Denver, the flesh-and-blood child nursed on blood and milk, throws her mother to the ground, and the women of the community collapse on them like a mountain, a symbol of solidity and endurance. This action honors Baby Suggs even as it saves Sethe and affirms Denver's independence. Thus, on the level of community, rememory is accomplished.

The reenactment of Sethe's memory and that of the community exorcises Beloved, restoring the Suggs family to its place in the order of things. Still, Sethe is not yet saved. She can hate the master, but she cannot love herself. She remains in exile. Like Baby Suggs before her, she takes to her bed, feeling that, without her child, there is no future, no possibility for living and for change:

> . . . 'Paul D?'
> 'What, baby?'
> 'She left me.'
> 'Aw, girl. Don't cry.'
> 'She was my best thing.'   (272)

Paul D, who has decided that he wants to put his story next to Sethe's, affirms verbally the action he made in the beginning of the novel when he held Sethe's breasts in his hands and kissed the scar on her back:

> 'Sethe,' he says, 'me and you, we got more yesterday than anybody. We need some kind of tomorrow.'
> He leans over and takes her hand. With the other he touches her face. 'You your best thing, Sethe. You are.'

Sethe cries, "'Me? Me?'" (273), a timid identification of her own self, but a bold step out of her exile. Paul D, who has made his own odyssey in the course of the novel acknowledges the link between Sethe's breasts and her back, and helps Sethe to see that they are not in opposition to one another but can be balanced if integrated into Sethe's identity. Paul D offers an alternative to the "thick love" of the victim-victimizer cycle. Thick love would rather destroy than mourn, rather face exile than put its story beside that of another. Sethe has to yield her fierce pride to become her true self. The end of the novel dramatizes Sethe's coming to wholeness, the first step in Cain's return.

Baby Suggs's spirit said to Denver, as the girl hesitated on the edge of the porch, that the life of a black person is not a battle; it is a rout. The whites have already won, and the only defense is to accept the defeat whites made on the terms of power and to claim another kind of victory. That victory comes when one takes the risk to suffer and to understand. The curse of Cain, of guilt and alienation, is broken when Sethe can mourn and when she can tell the tale with moral imagination and, thereby, find a truth different from the master's truth. The thick love, erupting from the jungle, has to be first remembered, then "disremembered," let be. The silent story, exemplified by *Beloved*, is "not a story to pass on" (274)—a story neither to ignore nor to forget.[6]

* * * * *

If Sethe is a woman trying to find herself, Sula Peace, at first, seems to be a complete self. Her birthmark seems to confirm this wholeness and difference, distinguishing her from other "heavy brown" (*Sula* 52) girls:

> [It] spread from the middle of the lid toward the eyebrow, shaped something like a stemmed rose. It gave her otherwise plain face a broken excitement and blue-blade threat. . . . The birthmark was to grow darker as the years passed, but now it was the same shade as her gold-flecked eyes, which, to the end, were as steady and clean as rain. (53)

As Sula develops, the birthmark on her eye changes. When she is thirteen, the rose develops a stem, and as Sula grows older, the mark grows darker.

Her mark is interpreted in various, mostly negative, ways throughout the novel: Nel's children think of the mark as a "scary black thing" (97-98), and Jude, Nel's husband, who gets angry when Sula will not participate in the "milkwarm commiseration" he needs to feel like a man, thinks that Sula has a copperhead over her eye (103). The community, indicting the evil Sula for every accident that befalls it, recognizes the mark as the sign of a murderer: They "cleared up for everybody the meaning of the birthmark over her eye; it was not a stemmed rose, or a snake, it was Hannah's [Sula's mother's] ashes marking her from the very beginning" (114). Nel thinks that the

mark gives Sula's glance "a suggestion of startled pleasure" (96).
Only Shadrack recognizes the mark as a sign of Sula's developing self: "She," he thinks, "had a tadpole over her eye" (156).

Like Sethe, Sula is both a victim and a victimizer, becoming both at the age of twelve, when her identity is forming. Sula
experiences two things that create her radical self. First, Sula
overhears her mother say that she loves Sula but does not like
her (57). After this incident, Sula and her friend Nel go to the
river and there encounter a friend, Chicken Little. While swinging him around, Sula accidentally throws him into the river:

> The water darkened and closed quickly over the
> place where Chicken Little sank. The pressure of his
> hard and tight little fingers was still in Sula's palms
> as she stood looking at the closed place in the water.
> They expected him to come back up, laughing. Both
> girls stared at the water. (61)

At Chicken's funeral, we realize that something is wrong in this
community. As Reverend Deal preaches, the members of the
community mourn not for the dead child, but for themselves:

> They did not hear all of what he said; they heard the
> one word, or phrase, or inflection that was for them the
> connection between the event and themselves. For some
> it was the term 'Sweet Jesus.' And they saw the Lamb's
> eye and the truly innocent victim: themselves.

This image of individuals mourning only for themselves is intensified in Nel. She stands even more removed from the
mourning process because she, afraid of being caught, separates
herself from Sula and casts herself as the innocent victim:
". . . she knew that she had 'done nothing'" (65). Though Nel
will reconcile with Sula after the funeral, during the ritual, she
leaves Sula completely alone for the first time: "Nel and Sula
did not touch hands or look at each other during the funeral.
There was a space, a separateness, between them" (64).

Sula, alone, "simply cried" (65). Yet, Sula's tears neither
heal the great pain that she has experienced nor do they signify
mourning for Chicken Little. Her inability to mourn marks her
as one set apart, like Cain. The rejection by her mother and the
death of Chicken, the events that Sula cannot rememory, make
Sula what she is:

> As willing to feel pain as to give pain, to feel pleasure
> as to give pleasure, hers was an experimental life—
> ever since her mother's remarks sent her flying up those
> stairs, ever since her one major feeling of responsibility
> had been exorcised on the bank of a river with a closed
> place in the middle. The first experience taught her
> there was no other that you could count on; the second
> that there was no self to count on either. She had no
> center, no speck around which to grow.   (118-119)

With nothing to depend on, not even herself, Sula patterns her life on being unsupported and unconventional, on the free fall that requires "invention" and "a full surrender to the downward flight" (120). Sula is, at once, all self and no self: an artist with no medium, energy without form (121). Refusing participation in community, Sula finds no "other" against whom she can define herself. Her energy and curiosity seek limits throughout the novel, finding the only real limit in death.

There are four temporary boundaries for Sula: the mad-man Shadrack and his promise, her best friend Nel, her beloved Ajax, and the community of Medallion. Shadrack's promise to Sula, along with her mother's rejection and the death of Chicken Little, becomes the basis of all her actions. Afraid that Shadrack saw Chicken Little drown, Sula runs to his house. There Shadrack makes Sula a promise: "'Always'" (62), answering "a question she had not asked [the promise of which] licked at her feet" (63). Shadrack promises Sula, who comes to him in his isolation and becomes "his visitor, his company, his guest, his social life, his woman, his daughter and his friend," that he, who controls death through National Suicide Day, will keep her safe from death:

> . . . he tried to think of something to say to comfort her,
> something to stop the hurt from spilling out of her eyes.
> So he had said 'always,' so she would not have to be
> afraid of the change—the falling away of skin, the
> drip and slide of blood, and the exposure of bone under-
> neath. He had said 'always' to convince her, assure
> her, of permanency.   (157)

Shadrack ensures that Sula never has to mourn or to re-member. Hers is a life of forward movement; for Sula, there is only the moment. This sense of her permanence, of her immor-tality, is Sula's true mark—her blessing and her curse. It frees her to experiment, to work through the range of experience, while it ensures that she will find only repetition because she cannot critically evaluate what she does. For Sula, ". . . doing anything forever and ever [i]s hell" (108). Yet in her incessant wanderings, Sula finds the same thing everywhere. The sense of her own permanence also takes away from her two essential things: fear and compassion. Lack of fear makes her hurt herself to save herself; for example, she cuts off the end of her finger to save herself and Nel—who misinterprets the act—from a group of white bullies (54-55, 101). Lack of compassion lets her interestingly watch her mother Hannah burn and enjoy her jerking and dancing. Sula says, "'I never meant anything'" (147), and she is honest and right. No experience, from the most trivial—someone's chewing with his mouth open—to the most important— her mother's death—has any ultimate meaning to Sula. The darkening and spreading of the birthmark is the symbol of the tyranny of Sula's eye/I. Because Sula cannot take the perspective of the "other," she can see neither herself nor anyone else clearly.

That tyranny of the eye/1 includes even Nel, Sula's best friend, who is "the closest thing to both an other and a self" that Sula finds. Sula cannot understand that, though they see together, are one eye, they are also two throats: They have different needs and are not "one and the same thing" (119). Sula forces Nel to define herself; Sula knows Nel's name as she will not know Ajax's (120). Sula, however, refuses to be defined, for she feels that she knows herself intimately (121). She demands that Nel want nothing from her and accept all aspects of her (119)— even her adultery with Nel's husband Jude. Sula's sleeping with Jude is not personal; it is merely another of Sula's "experiences." Sexuality, for Sula, is not the attempt to meet with an "other," but with herself. It is an attempt to find that center that she has lost:

> There, in the center of that silence was not eternity but the death of time and a loneliness so profound the word itself had no meaning. For loneliness assumed the absence of other people, and the solitude she found in that desperate terrain had never admitted the possibility of other people. She wept then . . . [in] the postcoital privateness in which she met herself, welcomed herself, and joined herself in matchless harmony.   (123)

Sexuality becomes a site of memory, but not one of meeting. Sexuality is, for Sula, a place where she recovers the self that her mother took away, the self on which she can depend. It is the way to experience and to mourn the death of her dislocated self that Shadrack promised she would never experience. It is a limit, and limitation is what Sula unconsciously seeks.

Sula's desire for boundaries is best illustrated in her love for Ajax. Only Ajax, a man as strong and as free as herself, makes her desire to join the self that she finds in the sexual act with an "other," to return from her Cain-like exile in taking responsibility for another person. With Ajax, Sula feels the desires of possession and of attempting to know a person other than herself. Their lovemaking is symbolized as a tree in loam—fertile, rich, and moist (130-131)—and Sula wants to look through all the layers of Ajax to find his center, to reach the source of that richness. Ajax, however, desires the Sula that is separate, complete in her solitude. He, like Sula, is a gold-eyed person, a true individual (Tate 125), and he leaves Sula when she wants to limit him by making him hers alone. When she says, "'Lean on me'" (133), Sula is asking Ajax to give up his freedom—to become bound to her, and to bind himself to him and to the community. Ajax rejects this relationship for the radical freedom that he has learned from his mother, another outsider: "He dragged [Sula] under him and made love to her with the steadiness and the intensity of a man about to leave for Dayton" (134).

Marriage, like mourning, is a ritual that binds the self to the beloved, to the community, and to God. The loss of Ajax, and with him Sula's one attempt at joining with another in marriage and with the community of Medallion, destroys Sula. When she finds his driver's license, she realizes that, in contrast to Nel, Ajax is someone whose name she did not know. She sees that, when she "said his name involuntarily or said it truly meaning *him*, the name she was screaming and saying was not his at all." A name indicates the essence of a human being, and Ajax has not given Sula that deep understanding of himself. Sula realizes that she would have had to destroy him to get it: "'It's just as well he left. Soon I would have torn the flesh from his face just to see if I was right about the gold and nobody would have understood that kind of curiosity'" (136). Faced with this loss, Sula becomes like the headless solider that Shadrack sees his first day in the war (8). Sula's body goes on, but she has lost her head, just like her paper dolls'. Sula's headless paper dolls indicate Sula's having lost herself, having given up her name, to Ajax and her being unable to "hold her head up," to maintain herself in the face of this loss: "'I did not hold my head stiff enough when I met him and so I.lost it just like the dolls'" (136). The image of paper dolls also suggests emptiness of body, mind, and soul, and that emptiness leads to Sula's death.

Medallion and her grandmother's room provide a final limit for the boundless energy that is Sula. Sula returns to Medallion because she has exhausted the experience of Nashville, Detroit, New Orleans, New York, Philadelphia, Macon, and San Diego (120). Toni Morrison has said that Sula returns because she simply cannot live anywhere else. Though Sula is recognized as evil, the community more than tolerates her, and, again, we see that something is wrong in Medallion. Medallion is only a community when it has Sula for a center, when her "evil" draws its members together in fear. Bad mothers take care of their children; wives love their husbands to keep them out of Sula's bed; and every disaster, large and small, has a reason—Sula. The community is bound in hate and refuses to mourn Sula after her death. The people accept the news of her death as good and attend the funeral only "to verify [the witch's] being put away" (150). They leave Sula to the white people, making her only "a body, a name, and an address" (173)—denying her essence and dishonoring her. Thus, the question of the hymn "Shall We Gather at the River?" is answered affirmatively, but in a deadly way, by Sula's spirit. The destruction of the community at the end of the novel is accomplished through Sula's element—water. That ruin comes because the community's refusal to mourn marks it. The power of her spirit indicates Sula's centrality, negative or not, in Medallion. Both are Cain, and each destroys the other. Sula takes the community with her in her return to the womb, her "sleep of water" (149).

Medallion and her grandmother's house and room are, for Sula, the end; they represent the closure of the circle of her experience. Left by Ajax, Sula thinks, "'There aren't any more new songs and I have sung all the ones there are'" (137). Sula refuses to look back, and there is no future for her. In contrast to Sethe at the end of *Beloved*, Sula will not yield. Unlike Baby Suggs, who goes to bed broken, Sula is defiant to the end, as her final conversation with Nel illustrates:

> [Nel] opened the door and heard Sula's low whis-
> per. 'Hey, girl.' Nel paused and turned her head but
> not enough to see her.
> 'How you know?' Sula asked.
> 'Know what?' Nel still wouldn't look at her.
> 'About who was good. How you know it was you?'
> 'What you mean?'
> 'I mean maybe it wasn't you. Maybe it was me.'
>   (146)

Sula—and we have to admire her—affirms her own mode of being in the world. All that is left for her to experience is death.
Dying, she faces a sealed window—the window from which her
grandmother threw herself while trying to save Hannah, Sula's
mother. The boarded window soothes Sula "with its sturdy
termination, its unassailable finality" (148). The closed room
represents the end of the tyranny of the eye/I, the closing off of
Sula's single perspective, and the womb, the place where Sula
can be completely alone, completely herself, free of distraction
and curled up in water. The promise of "Always," the promise
of permanence, can be fulfilled only in death, in "a sleep of water
always" (149).

For the living Sula, the mark becomes a sign of the completeness that is her incompleteness—the mark of the independent self who, like Cain, refuses to acknowledge the need for and
the importance of the "other." Even in dying, she will not apol-
ogize to and reach out for Nel, her Abel. For the dead Sula, the
mark is a sign of her permanence, her power, and her beauty.
Shadrack's promise, then, is broken in one sense, but in another
it is fulfilled. After her death, Sula recognizes that she needs
community—specifically, that she needs Nel:

> She was dead.
> Sula felt her face smiling. 'Well, I'll be damned,'
> she thought, 'it didn't even hurt. Wait'll I tell Nel.'
>   (149)

This need for the "other" is confirmed after death. Sula becomes
her sister's keeper; thus, Sula lives on as Nel feels the presence
of her dead friend. Nel realizes tint she never missed her husband Jude at all but that she did miss Sula: "'We was girls together. . . . O Lord, Sula, . . . girl, girl, girlgirlgirl'" (174). That
"girl" is Nel. Shocked into seeing herself by Eva's assertion that
Nel, too, is guilty and that Nel and Sula are alike, Nel realizes

that Sula was right: There was no difference between them (169). This recognition leads Nel to mourn her other self. Doing her rememory and mourning her friend, Nel finds her own eye twitching as she takes on the mark and is reborn.[7] After her childhood trip to New Orleans, Nel cried "me" five times, praying to be wonderful (28-29). Taking on Sula's mark, she begins to become that "me." Like Sethe at the end of *Beloved*, Nel finds that her story is bound with the story of another, and that connection, which transcends death, becomes the path to finding her identity.

Morrison has said that Sula and Nel make up one whole person: Sula is ship, the "New World Black Woman," and Nel safe harbor, the "Traditional Black Woman" (Moyers interview).[8] Neither is complete alone. That sense of our finitude and the necessity for contact with the "other" that is central to the Cain myth is what Toni Morrison retains in the stories of her marked women. She illustrates the sense of the risk of human life and human relationships that the Biblical myth contains, even as she signifies on the myth to affirm the healing power of memory and of ritual. She presents to us the human being, marked by oppression and/or by an act done in desperation and fear and set outside of the boundaries of community. That fallen human, however, cannot be sent "east of Eden" but must be reconciled to the self and to the community for the sake of both. In a community that has suffered through slavery and reconstruction, not a member can be lost. Cain cannot be banished forever but, somehow, must come home, lest both Cain and community be forever marked. The black community is a people in mourning, reconstructing itself through memory: This is not a story to pass on.

* * * * *

For Morrison, the mark must not be passed on, for it always carries possibility; it is not just a sign of alienation but one of latent beauty and wholeness. Sethe's chokeberry tree is potentially beautiful—the blood from her back makes roses on her bed (*Beloved* 93)—and organic—it might have cherries (17). When Sethe accepts her mark, she finds the true meaning of her name. She is no longer Cain, the exile, but is both Set, crucified by the tree on her back,[9] and Seth, the son who carries on the line of Adam and Eve and who foreshadows Christ.[10] The tree marks her as one of those cast out of Eden, yet the tree also connects her to her mother, marked with a cross, and the group of African slaves who were all marked in that way. Thus, the mark becomes a sign of community, identity, and wholeness; and Sethe, the chosen child, has to remember the stories and witness her people's history—and her own. The tree also becomes a symbol of Sethe's own power. Sethe's act, however brutal, signals individual defiance to the oppression of slavery and the beginnings of claiming and defining the self, of breaking the physical and psychological boundaries of oppression. Like the trees at Sweet Home and like Paul D's sapling, however, Sethe finally bends and, thus, survives—even prevails.

In contrast, Sula's mark is that of a self who is absolutely unbounded and free. The mark as rose and snake signifies the beauty and danger of Sula's kind of freedom. Ultimately, it symbolizes her absolute refusal to see life, to paraphrase Fitzgerald, from more than one window, from any perspective other than her own. This immense, unchecked power is destructive both for the self, as we see when Sula dies alone, and for the community, as we see when the people of Medallion refuse to recognize Sula's importance and are destroyed by the angry spirit of the dead Sula. Alone, Sula, as Morrison says, is a warning. Balanced after death, however, with the loving and stable power of Nel, who takes on the task of mourning and memory, the mark becomes tadpole and not snake. That is, it signals the development of the self and creates the compassion—the ability to be a self but also to see with the "other"—that is the basis of true community.

Both Sula and Sethe must embrace and even, finally, celebrate the mark of Cain which sets each apart but which also makes each unique—and so must their communities. Toni Morrison shows us in *Beloved* and *Sula* that we are bound together through story and through action. Memory, for the oppressed person, is a private story that must be understood, but it must also be shared. Thus, memory is also a public story made permanent as myth and reenacted through ritual—in these novels, the funeral. Myth and ritual bind the person to the group and to the sacred. Steinbeck, in *East of Eden*, says that the Cain story is "the symbol story of the [rejected, guilty] human soul" (240). The way out of that guilt and rejection, for Toni

Morrison, is to claim the mark as a symbol of the self and willingly to undergo what one has been forced to undergo in the past. The act of rememory is a private and a public act of homecoming; it is like water, forever moving, forever trying to get back to where it was ("Site" 119).

Notes

[1] Morrison used this term in an interview with Bill Moyers.

[2] "To protect [Cain] from the on-slaught of the beasts, God inscribed one letter of his Holy Name upon his forehead," writes Louis Ginzberg (112). Mellinkoff offers other examples: In Symmachus's *Life of Abel*, Cain returns home with a "terrible sign on his forehead" (30). See also Amoul Greban's "Mystere de la Passion" and Byron's "Cain." Others place the mark on the cheek or on the arm (Pirke de Rabbi Eliezer).

[3] The *Genesis* Rabbah says that God "beat Cain's face with hail, which blackened like coal, and thus he remained with a black face." Medieval art picks up this concept of blacks as evil. An alternate reading is found in Ginzberg, where Cain is given leprosy (112).

[4] ". . . the decree had condemned him to he a fugitive and a wanderer on the earth," observes Ginzberg (111). This is the origin of the idea of the Wandering Jew.

[5] For an interesting discussion of the mother-daughter issue in *Beloved*, see Horvitz.

[6] For a discussion of the last lines of the novel, see Holloway 517.

7 Munro (150-154) clearly connects Sula's mark with Nel as well as with Sula.

[8] See also Naylor and Morrison 577-578, and Stepto 216-217.

[9] "The *furka* or 'fork' was the cross on which the Egyptian god Set was crucified," notes Walker. "As the original of the Biblical Seth, the 'supplanter' of [Abel], Set ruled the alternating halves of the year in Egypt's predynastic sacred king-cult. . . . Annual rebirth of the world was said to be achieved by the blood of Set, which was spread over the fields" (36).

[10] Seth, observes Ginzberg, "was one of the thirteen men born perfect in a way. . . . Thus, Seth became, in a genuine sense, the father of the human race, especially the father of the pious" (121).

Works Cited

Gates, Henry Louis, Jr. *The Signifying Monkey: A Theory of African-American Literary Criticism.* New York: Oxford University Press, 1988.

Ginzberg, Louis. *The Legends of the Jews.* Vol. 1. Trans. Henrietta Szold. Philadelphia: Jewish Publication Society of America, 1968.

Holloway, Karla F. C. "*Beloved*: A Spiritual." *Callaloo* 13 (1990): 516-525.

Horvitz, Deborah. "Nameless Ghosts: Possession and Dispossession in *Beloved*." *Studies in American Fiction* 17 (Autumn 1989): 157-167.

Long, Charles H. *Significations: Signs, Symbols, and Images in the Interpretation of Religion*. Philadelphia: Fortress, 1986.

McDowell, Deborah E. "'The Self and the Other': Reading Toni Morrison's *Sula* and the Black Female Text." *Critical Essays on Toni Morrison*. Ed. Nellie Y. McKay. Boston: Hall, 1988. 77-90.

Mellinkoff, Ruth. *The Mark of Cain*. Berkeley: University of California Press, 1981.

Morrison, Toni. *Beloved*. New York: Knopf, 1987.

—. Interview with Bill Moyers. "The World of Ideas." 14 September 1990.

—. "The Site of Memory." *Inventing the Truth: The Art and Craft of Memoir*. Ed. William Zinsser. Boston: Houghton, 1987. 101-124.

—. *Sula*. 1973, New York: Plume, 1987.

Munro, C. Lynn. "The Tattooed Heart and the Serpentine Eye: Morrison's Choice of an Epigraph for *Sula*." *Black American Literature Forum* 18 (1984): 150-154.

Naylor, Gloria and Toni Morrison. "A Conversation." *Southern Review* 21.3 (1985): 567-593.

Steinbeck, John. *East of Eden*. New York: Bantam, 1952.

Stepto, Robert B. "'Intimate Things in Place': A Conversation with Toni Morrison." *Chant of Saints: A Gathering of Afro-American Literature, Art, and Scholarship*. Ed. Michael S. Harper and Stepto. Urbana: University of Illinois Press, 1979. 213-229.

Tate, Claudia. "Toni Morrison." *Black Women Writers at Work*. New York: Continuum 1983. 117-131.

Walker, Barbara G. *The Woman's Dictionary of Symbols and Sacred Objects*. New York: Harper, 1988.

Selected Bibliography

General

Abel, Elizabeth. "(E)Merging Identities: The Dynamics of Female Friendship in Contemporary Fiction by Women." *Signs: Journal of Women in Culture and Society* 6.3 (Spring 1981): 413-435.

Angelo, Bonnie. "The Pain of Being Black." *Time* 22 May 1989: 120-122.

Armstrong, Nancy. "Why Daughters Die: The Racial Logic of American Sentimentalism." *The Yale Journal of Criticism: Interpretation in the Humanities* 7.2 (Fall 1994): 1-24.

Awkward, Michael. *Inspiriting Influences: Tradition, Revision, and Afro-American Women's Novels*. New York: Columbia University Press, 1989.

Bakerman, Jane S. "Failures of Love: Female Initiation in the Novels of Toni Morrison." *American Literature: A Journal of Literary History, Criticism and Bibliography* 52.4 (January 1981): 541-563.

—. "The Seams Can't Show: An Interview with Toni Morrison." *Black American Literature Forum* 12 (1979): 56-60.

Barksdale, Richard K. "Castration Symbolism in Recent Black American Fiction." *College Language Association Journal* (June 1986): 400-413.

Bischoff, Joan. "The Novels of Toni Morrison: Studies in Thwarted Sensitivity." *Studies in Black Literature* 6.3 (1975): 21-22.

Bjork, Patrick. *The Novels of Toni Morrison: The Search for Self and Place Within the Community*. New York: Lang, 1992.

Blair, Barbara. "Textual Expressions of the Search for Cultural Identify." *American Studies in Scandinavia* 27.1 (1995): 48-63.

Byerman, Keith. "Beyond Realism: The Fiction of Toni Morrison." *Toni Morrison: Modern Critical Views*. Ed. Harold Bloom. New York: Chelsea House, 1990. 55-85.

Carmean, Karen. *Toni Morrison's World of Fiction*. Troy, New York: Whitston Publishing Co., 1993.

Christian, Barbara. "Community and Nature: The Novels of Toni Morrison." *The Journal of Ethnic Studies* 7.4 (Winter 1980): 65-78.

—. "The Concept of Class in the Novels of Toni Morrison." *Black Feminist Criticism* 1985: 71-80.

Collins, Patricia. "Learning from the Outsider Within: The Sociological Significance of Black Feminist Thought." *Social Problems* 33 (December 1986): 514-532.

Davis, Cynthia A. "Self, Society, and Myth in Toni Morrison's Fiction." *Contemporary Literature* 23 (1982): 323-342.

Dixon, Melvin. "Like an Eagle in the Air. Toni Morrison." *Toni Morrison: Modern Critical Views*. Ed. Harold Bloom. New York: Chelsea House, 1990. 115-142.

Edelberg, Cynthia. "Morrison's Voices: Formal Education, the Work Ethic, and the Bible." *American Literature* 58 (May 1986): 217-237.

Frederickson, George M. *The Black Image in the White Mind: The Debate on Afro-American Character and Destiny 1817-1914*. New York: Harper and Row, 1971.

Furman, Jan. *Toni Morrison's Fiction*. South Carolina: University of South Carolina Press, 1996.

Gates, Henry Louis, Jr. "Criticism in the Jungle." *Black Literature and Literary Theory*. Ed. Henry Louis Gates, Jr. New York: Methuen, 1984. 1-24.

Guerrero, Edward. "Tracking 'The Look' in the Novels of Toni Morrison." *Black American Literature Forum* 24 (Winter 1990): 761-773.

Hamilton, Cynthia. "Revisions, Rememories, and Exorcisms: Toni Morrison and Slave Narrative." *Journal of American Studies* 30.3 (December 1996): 429-445.

Harding, Wendy and Jacky Martin. "Subjective Correlatives as Correlations of Subjection in Toni Morrison's Fiction." *Profiles of Americans* 2 (1992): 103-111.

Harris, Trudier. *Fiction and Folklore: The Novels of Toni Morrison*. Knoxville: University of Tennessee Press, 1991.

Heinze, Denise. *The Dilemma of "Double-Consciousness" in Toni Morrison's Novels*. Athens: University of Georgia Press, 1993.

Holloway, Karla and Stephanie Demetrakopoulos. *New Dimensions of Spirituality: A Biracial and Bicultural Reading of the Novels of Toni Morrison*. New York: Greenwood Press, 1987.

House, E. B. "The 'Sweet Life' in Toni Morrison's Fiction." *American Literature* 56 (1984): 181-202.

Hovet, Grace Ann and Barbara Lounsberry. "Flying as Symbol and Legend in Toni Morrison's *The Bluest Eye, Sula,* and *Song of Solomon. College Language Association Journal* 27.2 (December 1983): 119-140.

Jones, Bessie W. and Audrey L. Vinson. *The World of Toni Morrison: Explorations in Literary Criticism*. Iowa: Kendell/Hunt, 1985.

Kelley, Margot Anne. "Sisters' Choices: Quilting in Contemporary African-American Women's Fiction." *Alice Walker: Everyday Use*. Ed. Barbara T. Christian. New Brunswick: Rutgers University Press, 1994. 167-194.

Kubitschek, Missy Dehn. *Claiming the Heritage: African-American Women Novelists and History*. Jackson, Mississippi: University Press of Mississippi, 1991.

Lange, Bonnie Shipman. "Toni Morrison's Rainbow Code." *Critique* 24 (1983): 173-181.

LeClair, Thomas. "'The Language Must Not Sweat': A Conversation with Toni Morrison." *The New Republic* 184 (March 21, 1981): 25-30.

Lee, Dorothy H. "The Quest for Self: Triumph and Failure in the Works of Toni Morrison." *Black Women Writers (1950-1980): A Critical Evaluation*. Ed. Mari Evans. Garden City, New York: Anchor Doubleday, 1984. 346-360.

Lewis, Desiree. "Myths of Motherhood and Power: The Construction of 'Black Women in Literature.'" *English in Africa* 19.1 (May 1992): 35-51.

Mbalia, Dorothea Drummond. *Toni Morrison's Developing Class Consciousness.* Selinsgrove: Susquehanna University Press, 1991.

McKay, Nellie. "An Interview with Toni Morrison." *Contemporary Literature* 24 (1983): 413-429.

McKay, Nellie Y., ed. *Critical Essays on Toni Morrison.* Boston: Hall, 1988.

Mickelson, Anne Z. "Toni Morrison." *Reaching Out: Sensitivity and Order in Recent American Fiction by Women.* Metuchen, New Jersey: Scarecrow Press, 1979.

Miller, Adam David. "Breedlove, Peace, and the Dead: Some Observations on the World of Toni Morrison." *Black Scholar* (March 1978): 47-50.

Morey, Anne Janine. "Margaret Atwood and Toni Morrison: Reflections on Postmodernism and the Study of Religion." *Toni Morrison's Fiction. Contemporary Criticism.* Ed. David L. Middleton. New York: Garland, 1997. 247-268.

Morrison, Toni. "Rootedness: The Ancestor as Foundation," in *Black Women Writers (1950-1980): A Critical Evaluation.* Ed. Mari Evans. Garden City, New York: Anchor Press/Doubleday, 1984.

—. "Unspeakable Things Unspoken: The Afro-American Presence in American Literature." *Michigan Quarterly Review* 28 (1989): 1-34.

—. *Playing in the Dark: Whiteness and the Literary Imagination.* Cambridge: Harvard University Press, 1992.

Myers, Linda Buck. "Perception and Power Through Naming: Characters in Search of a Self in the Fiction of Toni Morrison." *Exploration in Ethnic Studies* 7.1 (1984): 39-55.

Otten, Terry. *The Crime of Innocence in the Novels of Toni Morrison.* Columbia: University of Missouri Press, 1989.

Parker, Bettye J. "Complexity: Toni Morrison's Women—An Interview Essay." *Sturdy Black Bridges: Visions of Black Women in Literature.* Ed. Roseanne P. Bell, Bettye J. Parker and Beverly Guy-Sheftall. New York: Anchor, 1979. 251-257.

Parrish, Timothy. "Imaging Slavery: Toni Morrison and Charles Johnson." *Studies in American Fiction* 25.1 (Spring 1997): 81-100.

Randolph, Laura B. "The Magic of Toni Morrison." *Ebony* (July 1988): 100, 102, 104, 108.

Rigley, Barbara Hill. *The Voices of Toni Morrison.* Columbus: Ohio State University Press, 1991.

Rushdy, Ashraf H. A. "'Rememory': Primal Scenes and Constructions in Toni Morrison's Novels." *Contemporary Literature* 31.3 (1990): 300-323.

Samuel, Wilfred D. and Clenora Hudson-Weems. *Toni Morrison.* Boston: Twayne, 1990.

Smith, Barbara. "Toward a Black Feminist Criticism." *The New Feminist Criticism: Essays on Women, Literature, and Theory.* Ed. Elaine Showalter. New York: Pantheon, 1985. 32-40.

Staples, Robert. *From Behind the Veil: A Study of Afro-American Narrative.* Urbana: University of Illinois Press, 1979.

—. *The Black Woman in America.* Chicago: Nelson-Hall, 1973.

Stepto, Robert B. "'Intimate Things in Place': A Conversation with Toni Morrison." *Massachusetts Review* 8 (1977): 486-487.

Tate, Claudia. "Toni Morrison." *Black Women Writers at Work.* New York: Continuum (1983): 117-131.

Taylor-Guthrie, Danille, ed. *Conversations with Toni Morrison.* Jackson: University of Mississippi, 1994.

Thompson, Robert Farris. *Flash of the Spirit: African and Afro-American Art and Philosophy.* New York: Random, 1983.

Turner, Darwin T. "Theme, Characterization, and Style in the Works of Toni Morrison." *Black Women Writers (1950-1980): A Critical Evaluation.* Ed. Mari Evans. New York: Doubleday, 1984. 361-370.

Wade, Gayles Gloria. "The Truth of Our Mother's Lives: Mother-Daughter Relationships in Black Women's Fiction." *SAGE: A Scholarly Journal on Black Women* 1.2 (Fall 1984): 8-12.

Wall, Cheryl A., ed. *Changing Our Own Words: Essays on Criticism, Theory, and Writing by Black Women.* New Brunswick: Rutgers University Press, 1989.

Willis, Susan. "Black Women Writers: Taking a Critical Perspective." *Making a Difference: Feminist Literary Criticism.* Ed. Gayle Greene and Coppelia Kahn. New York: Methuen, 1985. 211-237.

—. "Eruptions of Funk: Historicizing Toni Morrison." *Black American Literature Forum* 16.1 (1982): 34-42.

Sula

Baker, Houston A., Jr. "When Lindbergh Sleeps with Bessie Smith: The Writing of Place in *Sula. Toni Morrison: Critical Perspectives Past and Present.* New York: Amistad Press (1993). 236-260.

Banyiwa, Horne Naana. "The Scary Face of the Self: An Analysis of the Character of Sula in Toni Morrison's *Sula.*" *SAGE: A Scholarly Journal on Black Women* 2.1 (Spring 1985): 28-31.

Basu, B. "The Black Voice and the Language of the Text: Toni Morrison's *Sula.*" *College Literature* 23.3 (October 1996): 88-103.

Bergenholtz, R. A. "Toni Morrison's *Sula*—A Satire on Binary Thinking." *African American Review* 30.1 (Spring 1996): 89-98.

Bogus, S. Diane. "An Authorial Tie-Up: The Wedding of Symbol and Point of View in Toni Morrison's *Sula.*" *College Language Association Journal* 33.1 (September 1989): 73-80.

Bryant, C. G. "The Orderliness of Disorder—Madness and Evil in Toni Morrison's *Sula.*" *Black American Literature Forum* 24.4 (1990): 731-745.

Coleman, Alisha R. "One and One Make One, A Metacritical and Psychoanalytic Reading of Friendship in Toni Morrison's *Sula.*" *College Language Association Journal* 37.2 (December 1993): 145-155.

De Weever, Jacqueline. "The Inverted World of Toni Morrison's *The Bluest Eye* and *Sula.*" *College Language Association Journal* 22 (June 1979): 402-414.

Delancey, Dayle B. "Mother Love is a Killer: *Sula, Beloved,* and The Deadly Trinity of Motherlove." *SAGE: A Scholarly Journal of Black Women* 7.2 (Fall 1990): 15-18.

Gillespie, Diane and Missy Dehn Kubitschek. "Who Cares? Women-Centered Psychology in *Sula.*" *Black American Literature Forum* 24.1 (Spring 1990): 21-48.

Grant, Robert. "Absence into Presence: The Thematics of Memory and 'Missing' Subjects in Toni Morrison's *Sula.*" *Critical Essays on Toni Morrison.* Ed. Nellie McKay. Boston: G. K. Hall, 1988. 90-103.

Hoffarth, Zelloe Monika. "Resolving the Paradox: An Interlinear Reading of Toni Morrison's *Sula.*" *Journal of Narrative Technique* 22.2 (Spring 1992): 114-127.

Hunt, Patricia. "War and Peace: Transfigured Categories and the Politics of *Sula.*" *African American Review* 27.3 (Fall 1993): 443-459.

Johnson, Barbara. "'Aesthetic' and 'Rapport' in Toni Morrison's *Sula.*" *Textural-Practice* 7.2 (Summer 1993): 165-172.

Jones, Carolyn M. "*Sula* and *Beloved*—Images of Cain in the Novels of Toni Morrison." *African American Review* 27.4 (Winter 1993): 615-626.

Lee, Rachael. "Missing Peace in Toni Morrison's *Sula* and *Beloved.*" *African American Review* 28.4 (Winter 1994): 571-583.

Lewis, Vashti Crutcher. "African Tradition in Toni Morrison's *Sula.*" *Phylon: A Review of Race and Culture* 48.1 (March 1987): 91-97.

Lounsberry, Barbara and Grace Ann Hover. "Principles of Perception in Toni Morrison's *Sula.*" *Black American Literature Forum* 13 (1979): 126-129.

Martin, Odette. "*Sula.*" *First World* 1 (1977): 34-44.

McDowell, Deborah E. "'The self and the other': Reading Toni Morrison's *Sula* and the Black Female Text." *Critical Essays on Toni Morrison.* Ed. Nellie Y. McKay. Boston: Hall, 1988: 77-90.

McKee, Patricia. "Spacing and Placing Experience in Toni Morrison's *Sula.*" *Modern Fiction Studies* 42.1 (Spring 1996): 1-30.

Middleton, Victoria. "*Sula*: An Experimental Life." *College Language Association Journal* 28 (1985): 367-381.

Montgomery, Maxine Lavon. "A Pilgrimage to the Origins: The Apocalypse as Structure." *Black American Literature Forum* 23 (Spring 1989): 127-137.

Munro, C. Lynn. "The Tattooed Heart and the Serpentine Eye: Morrison's Choice of an Epigraph for *Sula.*" *Black American Literature Forum* 18 (1984): 150-154.

Ogunyemi, Chikwenye Okonjo. "*Sula*: 'A Nigger Joke.'" *Black American Literature Forum* 13 (1979): 130-133.

Pessoni, Michele. "She-Was-Laughing-At-Their-God: Discovering the Goddess Within *Sula.*" *African American Review* 29.3 (Fall 1995): 439-451.

Ramsey, Deanna. "A Comparison of the Triads of Women in Toni Morrison's *Sula* and *Song of Solomon.*" *Mount Olive Review* 6 (Spring 1992): 104-109.

Reddy, Maureen T. "The Tripled Plot and Center of *Sula.*" *Black American Literature Forum* 22.1 (Spring 1988): 29-45.

Richard, P. M. "*Sula* and the Discourse of the Folk in African-American Literature." *Cultural Studies* 9.2 (May 1995): 270-292.

Royster, Phillip M. "A Priest and a Witch Against the Spiders and Snakes: Scapegoating in Toni Morrison's *Sula.*" *Umoja* 2 (1978): 149-168.

Schramm, Margaret. "The Quest for the Perfect Mother in Toni Morrison's *Sula*." *The Anna Book: Searching for Anna in Literary History*. Ed. Mickey Pearlman. Connecticut Greenwood, 1992: 167-176.

Seidel, Kathryn Lee. "The Lilith Figure in Toni Morrison's *Sula* and Alice Walker's *The Color Purple*." *Weber Studies: An Interdisciplinary Humanities Journal* 10:2 (Spring-Summer 1993): 85-94.

Shannon, Anna. "'We Was Girls Together': A Study of Toni Morrison's *Sula*." *Midwestern Miscellany* 10 (1982): 9-22.

Smith, Barbara. "Beautiful, Needed, Mysterious." *Freedomways* 14 (1974): 69-72.

Stein, Karen. "'I Didn't Even Know His Name': Name and Naming in Toni Morrison's *Sula*." *Names: A Journal of Onomastics* 28.3 (September 1980): 226-229.

Stein, Karen F. "Toni Morrison's *Sula*: A Black Woman's Epic." *Black American Literature Forum* 18.4 (Winter 1984): 146-150.

Stockton, Kathryn Bond. "Heaven's Bottom, Anal Economics and the Critical Debasement of Freud in Toni Morrison's *Sula*." *Cultural Critique* 24 (Spring 1993): 81-118.

Tonegawa, Maki. "Toni Morrison's Exploration of the Relational Self in *Sula* and *Beloved*." *Studies in American Literature* 29 (1992): 91-106.

Vickroy, Laurie. "The Force Outside/The Force Inside: Mother-Love and Regenerative Spaces in *Sula* and *Beloved*." *Obsidian II: Black Literature in Review* 8.2 (Fall-Winter 1993): 28-45.

Wessling, Joseph H. "Narcissism in Toni Morrison's *Sula*." *College Language Association Journal* 31.3 (March 1988): 281-298.

Wilson, Michael. "Affirming Characters, Communities, and Change: Dialogism in Toni Morrison's *Sula*." *Midwestern Miscellany* 24 (1996): 24-36.

Beloved

Aguiar, Sarah Appleton. "Everywhere and Nowhere: *Beloved*'s 'Wild' Legacy in Toni Morrison." *Notes on Contemporary Literature* 25.4 (September 1995): 11-12.

Askeland, Lori. "Remodeling the Model in *Uncle Tom's Cabin* and *Beloved*." *American Literature: A Journal of Literary History, Criticism, and Bibliography* (December 1992): 785-805.

Atlas, Marilyn Judith. "Toni Morrison's *Beloved* and the Reviewers." *Midwestern Miscellany* 18 (1990): 45-57.

Barber, Michael. "The Fragmentation and Social Reconstruction of the Past in Toni Morrison's *Beloved*." Ed. Anna Teresa Tymieniecka. *Allegory Revisited: Ideals of Mankind*. Dordrecht: Kluwer Academy 1994. 347-358.

Bardolph, Jacqueline. "*Beloved* as a Story of Telling." *QWERTY: Arts, Literatures, and Civilisations du Monde Anglophone* (October 1993): 161-167.

Berben, Masi Jacqueline. "Beloved as Protest Literature: Cultural Inter- and Intracontextuality." *QWERTY: Arts, Literatures, and Civilisations du Monde Anglophone* (October 1993): 175-180.

Berger, James. "Ghost of Liberalism: Morrison's *Beloved* and the Moynihan Report." (May 1996): 408-420.

Birat, Kathie. "Stories to Pass On: Closure and Community. Toni Morrison's *Beloved*." Ed. Versluys-Kristiaan. *The Insular Dream: Obsession and Resistance.* Amsterdam: VU VP, 1995. 324-334.

Boudmau, Kristin. "Pain and the Unmaking of Self in Toni Morrison's *Beloved*." *Contemporary Literature* 36.3 (Fall 1995): 447-465.

Bowers, Susan. "*Beloved* and the New Apocalypse." *Journal of Ethnic Studies* 18.1 (Spring 1990): 59-77.

Britton, Wesley. "The Puritan Past and Black Gothic: The Haunting of Toni Morrison's *Beloved* in Light of Hawthorne's *The House of the Seven Gables*." *Nathaniel Hawthorne Review* 21.2 (Fall 1995): 7-23.

Broad, Robert L. "Giving Blood to the [Scraps]: Haints, History, and Hosea in *Beloved*." *African American Review* 28.2 (Summer 1994): 189-196.

Caesar, Terry Paul. "Slavery and Motherhood in Toni Morrison's *Beloved*." *Revista de Letras* 34 (1994): 111-120.

Cooley, Elizabeth. "Remembering and Dis(Re)Membering: Memory, Community and the Individual in *Beloved*." *University of Mississippi Studies in English* 11-12 (1993-1995): 351-360.

Coykendall, Abby. "Resuscitating the Literal from the Spectral Figural: History and (Re)-production in Toni Morrison's *Beloved*." *Theory Buffalo* (Fall 1996): 107-122.

Cummings, Kate. "Reclaiming the Mother(s) Tongue: *Beloved*, Ceremony. Mothers and Silence." *College English* 52 (1990): 16-32.

Dahill-Bane, William. "Insignificant Monkeys: Preaching Black English in Faulkner's *The Sound and the Fury*, and Morrison's *The Bluest Eye* and *Beloved*." *Mississippi Quarterly: The Journal of Southern Culture* 49.3 (1996): 457-473.

Davis, Christina. "*Beloved*: A Question of Identity." *Presence Africaine: Revue Culturelle du Monde Noir Cultural Review of the Negro World* 145 (1988): 151-156.

Falling-rain, Sunny. "A Literary Patchwork Crazy Quilt: Toni Morrison's *Beloved*." *Uncoverings: Research Papers of the American-Quilt Study Group* 15 (1994): 111-140.

Ferguson, Rebecca. "History, Memory and Language in Toni Morrison's *Beloved*." *Feminist Criticism: Theory and Practice.* Ed. Linda Hutcheson, Susan Seller and Paul Perron. Toronto: University of Toronto Press, 1991. 109-127.

Fields, Karen E. "To Embrace Dead Strangers: Toni Morrison's *Beloved*," in *Mother Puzzles: Daughters and Mothers in Contemporary American Literature.* Ed. Mickey Pearlman. Westport, Connecticut: Greenwood, 1989. 159-169.

Finney, Brian. "Temporal Defamiliarization in Toni Morrison's *Beloved*." *Obsidian II: Black Literature in Review* 5.1 (Spring 1990): 20-36.

Fitzgerald, Jennifer. "Selfhood and Community: Psychoanalysis and Discourse in *Beloved*." *Modern Fiction Studies* 39:3-4 (Fall/Winter 1993): 669-687.

Fritz, Angela DiPace. "Toni Morrison's *Beloved*: "Unspeakable Things Unspoken, Spoken." *Sacred Heart University Review* 14.1-2 (Fall 1993-Spring 1994): 40-52.

Fulweiler, Howard W. "Belonging and Freedom in Morrison's *Beloved*: Slavery, Sentimentality, and the Evolution of Consciousness." *The Centennial Review* 40.2 (Spring 1996): 331-358.

Goldman, Anne E. "'I Made the Ink': (Literary) Production and Reproduction in *Dessa Rose* and *Beloved*." *Feminist Studies* 16.2 (Summer 1990): 313-330.

Guth, Deborah. "'Wonder What God Had in Mind': *Beloved*'s Dialogue With Christianity." *Journal of Narrative Technique* 24.2 (Spring 1994): 83-97.

—. "A Blessing and a Burden: The Relation to the Past in *Sula, Song of Solomon*, and *Beloved*." *Modern Fiction Studies* 39.3-4 (Fall/Winter 1993): 575-596.

Handley, William R. "The House a Ghost Built: Nommo, Allegory, and the Ethics of Reading in Toni Morrison's *Beloved*." *Contemporary Literature* 36.4 (Winter 1995): 676-701.

Harding, Wendy and Jacky Martin. "Reading at the Cultural Interface: The Corn Symbolism of *Beloved*." *MELUS: The Journal of the Society for the Study of the Multi-Ethnic Literature of the United States* 19.2 (Summer 1994): 85-97.

Henderson, Mae G. "Toni Morrison's *Beloved*: Re-Membering the Body as Historical Text." *Comparative American Identities: Race, Sex and Nationality in the Modern Text*. Ed. Hortense J. Spillers. New York: Routledge, 1991. 62-86.

Holloway, Karla F. "*Beloved*: A Spiritual." *Callaloo: A Journal of African American and African Arts and Letters* 13.3 (Summer 1990): 516-525.

Holton, Robert. "Bearing Witness: Toni Morrison's *Song of Solomon* and *Beloved*." *English Studies in Canada* 20.1 (March 1994): 79-90.

Horvitz, Deborah. "Nameless Ghosts: Possession and Dispossession in *Beloved*." *Studies in American Fiction* 17.2 (Autumn 1989): 157-167.

House, Elizabeth B. "Toni Morrison's Ghost: The Beloved Who Is Not Beloved." *Studies in American Fiction* 18.1 (Spring 1990): 17-26.

Jablon, Madelyn. "Rememory, Dream History, and Revision in Toni Morrison's *Beloved* and Alice Walker's *The Temple of My Familiar*." *College Language Association Journal* 37.2 (December 1993): 136-144.

Kelly, Robert W. "Toni Morrison's *Beloved*: Destructive Past Becoming Instructive Memory." *Griot: Official Journal of the Southern Conference on Afro-American Studies, Inc.* 14.2 (Fall 1995): 20-23.

Koolish, Lynda. "Fictive Strategies and Cinematic Representations in Toni Morrison's *Beloved*: Post Colonial Theory/Post Colonial Text." *African American Review* 29.3 (Fall 1995): 421-438.

Krumholz, Linda. "The Ghost of Slavery: Historical Recovery in Toni Morrison's *Beloved*." *African American Review* 26:3 (Fall 1992): 395-408.

Lawrence, David. "Fleshly Ghosts and Ghostly Flesh: The Word and the Body in *Beloved*." *Studies in American Fiction* 19.2 (1991): 189-201.

Leake, Katherine. "Morrison's *Beloved*." *Explicator* 53.2 (Winter 1995): 120-123.

Levy, Andrew. "Telling *Beloved*." *Texas Studies in Literature and Language* 33.1 (Spring 1991): 114-123.

Lewis, Charles. "The Ironic Romance of New Historicism: *The Scarlet Letter* and *Beloved* Standing in Side by Side." *Arizona Quarterly: A Journal of American Literature, Culture and Theory* 51.1 (Spring 1995): 32-60.

Linehan, Thomas M. "Narrating the Self: Aspects of Moral Psychology in Toni Morrison's *Beloved*." *The Centennial Review* 41.2 (Spring 1997): 301-330.

Liscio, Lorraine. "*Beloved*'s Narrative: Writing Mother's Milk." *Tulsa Studies in Women's Literature* II (1992): 31-46.

Luckhurst, Roger. "'Impossible Mourning' in Toni Morrison's *Beloved* and Michele Robert's *Daughters of the House*." *Critique: Studies in Contemporary Fiction* 37.4 (Summer 1996): 243-260.

Malmgren, Carl D. "Mixed Genres and the Logic of Slavery in Toni Morrison's *Beloved*." *Critique: Studies in Contemporary Fiction* 36.2 (Winter 1995): 96-106.

Mathieson, Barbara Offutt. "Memory and Mother Love in Morrison's *Beloved*." *American Imago: Studies in Psychoanalysis and Culture* 47.1 (Spring 1990): 1-21.

Mitchell, Carolyn A. "'I Love to Tell the Story': Biblical Revisions in *Beloved*." *Religion and Literature* 23.3 (Autumn 1991): 27-42.

Mobley, Marilyn Sanders. "A Different Remembering: Memory, History, and Meaning in Toni Morrison's *Beloved*." *Toni Morrison*. Ed. Harold Bloom. New York: Chelsea House, 1990. 189-199.

Mohanty, Satya P. "The Epistemic Status of Cultural Identity: On *Beloved* and the Post Colonial Condition." *Cultural Critique* (Spring 1993): 41-80.

Osagie, Iyunolu. "Is Morrison Also Among the Prophets? 'Psychoanalytical' Strategies in *Beloved*." *African American Review* 28.3 (Fall 1994): 423-440.

Park, Sue. "One Reader's Response to Toni Morrison's *Beloved*." *Conference of College Teachers of English Studies* 56 (September 1991): 39-46.

Perez Torres, Rafael. "Knitting and Knotting the Narrative Thread—*Beloved* as Postmodern Novel." *Modern Fiction Studies* 39.3-4 (Fall/Winter 1993): 689-707.

Pesch, Josef. "*Beloved*: Toni Morrison's Post-Apocalyptic Novel." *Canadian Review of Literature, Revue Canadienne de Litterature Comparee* 20.3 (September-December 1993): 397-408.

Phelan, James. "Toward a Rhetorical Reader-Response Criticism: The Difficult, the Stubborn and the Ending of *Beloved*." *Modern Fiction Studies* 39 (1993): 709-728.

Portelli, Alessandro. "Figlie e padri, Scrittura e assenza in *Beloved* di Morrison. *Acoma: Revista, Internazionale di Studi Nordamericani* 2.5 (Summer/Autumn 1995): 72-84.

Powell, Betty Jane. "'will the parts hold?': The Journey Toward a Coherent Self in *Beloved*." *Colby Quarterly* 31.2 (June 1995): 105-113.

Rand, Naomi R. "Surviving What Haunts You: The Art of Invisibility in Ceremony, the Ghost Writer and *Beloved*." *MELUS: The Journal of the Society for the Study of the Multi-Ethnic Literature of the United States* 20.3 (Fall 1995): 21-32.

Raphael, Heike. "A Journey to Independence: Toni Morrison's *Beloved* and the Critical Utopia." *Flip Sides: New Critical Essays in American Literature*. Ed. H. Klaus Schmidt. Frankfurt: Peter Lang, 1995. 43-60.

Rhodes, Jewell Poucker. "Toni Morrison's *Beloved*: Ironies of a 'Sweet Home' Utopia in a Dystopian Slave Society." *Utopian Studies* 1.1 (1990): 77-92.

Rimmon-Kenan, Shlomith. "Narration, Doubt, Retrieval: Toni Morrison's *Beloved*. *Narrative* 4.2 (May 1996): 109-123.

Rodrigues, Eusebio L. "The Telling of *Beloved.*" *Journal of Narrative Technique* 21.2 (Spring 1991): 153-169.

Rody, Caroline. "Toni Morrison's *Beloved*: History, 'Rememory,' and a 'Clamor for a Kiss.'" *American Literary History* 7.1 (Spring 1995): 92-119.

Rohrkemper, John. "'The Site of Memory': Narrative and Meaning in Toni Morrison's *Beloved.*" *Midwestern Miscellany* 24 (1996): 51-62.

Rushdy, Ashraf H. A. "Daughters Signifyin(g) History: The Example of Toni Morrison's *Beloved.*" *American Literature: A Journal of Literary History, Criticism, and Bibliography* 64.3 (September 1992): 567-597.

Scarpa, Giulia. "Narrative Possibilities at Play in Toni Morrison's *Beloved.*" *MELUS: The Journal of the Society for the Study of the Multi-Ethnic Literature of the United States* 17.4 (Winter 1991-1992): 91-103.

Schapiro, Barbara. "The Bonds of Love and the Boundaries of Self in Toni Morrison's *Beloved.*" *Contemporary Literature* 32.2 (1991): 194-210.

Schmudde, Carol E. "Morrison's *Beloved.*" *Explicator* 50.3 (Spring 1992): 187-188.

—. "Knowing When to Stop: A Reading of Toni Morrison's *Beloved.*" *College Language Association Journal* 37.2 (December 1993): 121-135.

Schopp, Andrew. "Narrative Control and Subjectivity: Dismantling Safety in Toni Morrison's *Beloved.*" *The Centennial Review* 39.2 (Spring 1995): 355-379.

Schreiber, Evelyn Jaffee. "Reader, Text, and Subjectivity: Toni Morrison's *Beloved* as Lacan's Gaze Hal Object." *Syle* 30:3 (Fall 1996): 445-461.

Sitter, Deborah Ayer. "The Making of a Man: Dialogic Meaning in *Beloved.*" *African American Review* 26 (Spring 1992): 17-29.

Teeter, N. "The Male Threat in *Beloved.*" *University of Mississippi Studies in English* 11-12 (1993-1995): 226-229.

Vickroy, Laurie. "*Beloved* and Shoah: Witnessing the Unspeakable." *The Comparatist* (1998): 225.

Waxman, Barbara Frey. "Changing History Through a Gendered Perspective: A Postmodern Feminist Reading of Morrison's *Beloved.*" Ed. Barbara Frey Waxman. *Multicultural Literatures Through Feminist/Poststructuralist Lenses.* Knoxville: University of Tennessee, 1993. 57-83.

Woidat, Caroline M. "Talking Back to Schoolteacher: Morrison's Confrontation with Hawthorne in *Beloved.*" *Modern Fiction Studies* 39.3-4 (Fall/Winter 1993): 527-546.

Wyatt, Jean. "Giving Body to the Word: The Maternal Symbolic in Toni Morrison's *Beloved.*" *PMLA* 108.3 (May 1993): 474-488.

Contributors to
Understanding Toni Morrison's Beloved and Sula

Edited by Drs. Solomon and Marla Iyasere

Kristin Boudreau teaches at the University of Georgia. She earned her doctorate at University of Rochester (1992) and published numerous studies of American authors, including Louisa May Alcott, Ralph Waldo Emerson, Henry James, Alice James, and Toni Morrison. Her 1997 article on "Early American Criminal Narratives and the Problem of Public Sentiments" appeared in *Early American Literature* and "Henry James's Inward Inches" is forthcoming in *The Henry James Review*. Dr. Boudreau recently completed a book entitled *The Age of Sympathy: American Sentiments from Jefferson to the Jameses*.

Howard F. Fulweiler, Professor of English at University of Missouri-Columbia, has published extensively since earning his Ph.D. in 1960 at University of North Carolina, Chapel Hill. Dr. Fulweiler's most recent publications are "'A Dismal Swamp': Darwin, Design and Evolution in *Our Mutual Friend* (*Nineteenth Century Literature*), "The Other Missing Link: Owen Barfield and the Scientific Imagination" (*renascence*) and *'Here a Captive Heart Busted': Studies in the Sentimental Journey of Modern Literature* for Fordham University Press.

Diane Gillespie, a Professor with The Goodrich Scholarship Program at the University of Nebraska at Omaha, authored *The Mind's We: Contextualism in Cognitive Psychology* (Southern Illinois University Press) as well as a variety of articles, including "From Student Narratives to Case Studies: Diversity from the Bottom Up" for *Journal on Excellence in College Teaching* and "When the Story Won't Write Itself" for *Reflections: Narratives* *of Professional Helping.* Dr. Gillespie earned her Ph.D. at the University of Nebraska at Lincoln in 1982.

Deborah Guth is Lecturer in English Literature at Tel Aviv University in Israel. With a Doctorate in Comparative Literature from the University of Paris-Sorbonne, Dr. Guth has published on a wide range of authors, such as Virginia Woolf, Joseph Conrad, John Fowles, George Eliot, and Friedrich von Schiller. Recent publications include "George Eliot and Schiller: The Case of *The Mill on the Floss*," "George Eliot and Schiller: Narrative Ambivalence in *Middlemarch* and *Felix Holt*," and "Submerged Narratives in Kazuo Ishiguro's *The Remains of the Day*." Professor Guth is currently completing a book-length study of Eliot and Schiller.

Carolyn M. Jones teaches religious studies and English at Louisiana State University where she is an Associate Professor. Dr. Jones is working on a book on Toni Morrison, *The Fiction and Criticism of Toni Morrison* for Macmillan Press, and has published widely on Morrison's fiction, including "Traces and Cracks: Identity and Narrative in Toni Morrison's *Jazz*" for *African-American Review* and "Nature, Spirituality and Home-Making," a chapter in *Home-Making: Women Writers and the Politics and Poetics of Home.* Dr. Jones completed her doctorate in 1991 at University of Virginia.

Missy Dehn Kubitschek is currently Professor of English, Women's Studies and Afro-American Studies at Indiana University-Purdue University at Indianapolis. Dr. Kubitschek earned her doctorate in 1979 at the University of Illinois. Among her many publications are two recent books, *Claiming the Heritage: African American Women's Novels and History* (University Press of Mississippi) and *Toni Morrison: A Companion Volume* (Greenwood Press).

Rachel Lee is an Assistant Professor in the departments of English and Women's Studies at UCLA. She has held a National Endowment for the Humanities Fellowship and a Chancellor's Postdoctoral Fellowship at the University of California, Berkeley. She is the author of *The Americas of Asian American Literature: Gendered Fictions of Nation and Transnation* (forthcoming from Princeton University Press). Her articles have been published in the journals *African American Review, Cultural Critique, boundary 2* (forthcoming Vol. 26) and the volumes *Revisioning Asian America* and *Interethnic Literacy*. Her work spans the fields of twentieth-century American literature, feminist theory, ethnic studies, and cultural studies.

Carl D. Malmgren, Professor of English at University of New Orleans, has just completed a book-length study, *Anatomy of Murder: Mystery, Detective, and Crime Fiction*, and an article, "Primers, Texts, and Voices in Toni Morrison's *The Bluest Eye*." Among Dr. Malmgren's other major publications are *Fictional Space in the Modernist and Postmodernist American Novel* (Bucknell University Press) and *Worlds Apart: Narratology of Science Fiction* (Indiana University Press). Dr. Malmgren earned his doctorate in 1979 at University of Oregon.

Carolyn A. Mitchell is currently Professor of English and Director of Women's Studies at Union College in Schenectady, New York. Dr. Mitchell's recent publications include a book co-authored with Dr. Joyce King, "After/Word" *Black Mothers to Sons: Juxtaposing African American Literature with Social Practice*, and two poems set to music, "Reveries: A Summer's Cycle," which premiered at the Plymouth Music Series in Minneapolis, Minnesota, and "Beach/Block," featured on NPR's "Pipe Dreams." She earned her Ph.D. at Boston College.

Betty Powell holds a Ph.D. in English from the University of Kentucky and specializes in nineteenth-century American (specifically women writers) and African-American literature. An Assistant Professor at Mars Hill College in North Carolina, Dr. Powell is Director of Women's Studies. Her most recent publication, on Sarah Orne Jewett, is titled "Speaking to One Another: Narrative Unity in Sarah Orne Jewett's *Old Friends and New*" (*Colby Quarterly*, June 1998). She is working on a book-length project, *The Women They Left Behind*, a documentary oral history of women who have suffered some loss due in the Vietnam War, to be published by Islewest Press.

Maureen T. Reddy, Professor of English and Women's Studies at Rhode Island College, recently completed *Traces, Codes, and Clues: Reading Race in Genre Fiction* for Rutgers University Press. Dr. Reddy' s other books include *Everyday Acts Against*

Racism (Seal Press) and *Crossing the Color Line: Race, Parenting and Culture* (Rutgers University Press). She earned her Ph.D. in 1985 at University of Minnesota.

Eusebio L. Rodrigues has taught contemporary American fiction at Georgetown University for more than twenty years. Dr. Rodrigues is presently completing a novel, *Love and Samsara*, set in sixteenth-century India. Professor Rodrigues has published a book on Saul Bellow's fiction and contributed an article on Toni Morrison's *Jazz* to *Modern Fiction Studies*. He completed his doctoral work at the University of Pennsylvania.

Caroline Rody teaches English at University of Virginia, where she completed her Ph.D. in 1995. Dr. Rody's recent articles include "The Mad Colonial Daughter's Revolt: J. M. Coetzee's *In the Heart of the Country*" (*South Atlantic Quarterly*) and "Burning Down the House: The Revisionary Paradigm of Jean Rhys's *Wide Sargasso Sea*," a chapter in *Famous Last Words: Changes in Gender and Narrative Closure*. She has also taught at Yale.

Barbara Ann Schapiro completed her Ph.D. at Tufts University. A Professor of English at Rhode Island College, Dr. Schapiro has published a number of books, including *Literature and the Relational Self* (NYU Press), *The Romantic Mother: Narcissistic Patterns in Romantic Poetry* (The Johns Hopkins Press), and *D. H. Lawrence and the Paradoxes of Psychic Life* (SUNY Press, forthcoming).

Andrew Schopp is Assistant Professor of English at University of Tennessee at Martin. His current projects include two books. One explores the social issues of fear in narrative and the other examines the absent father and constructions of masculinity in contemporary literature. Dr. Schopp published "Writing (with) the Body: Stephen King's *Misery in Literature, Interpretation, Theory*" while completing his Ph.D. from the University of Rochester.

Karen F. Stein earned her Ph.D. at University of Connecticut in 1982. She holds a position as Professor of English and Women's Studies at University of Rhode Island and is currently writing a reader's guide to Margaret Atwood for the Twayne World Authors Series. Dr. Stein's publications includes "Speaking in

Tongues: Margaret Laurence's *A Jest of God* as Gothic Narrative" in *Studies in Canadian Literature* and "The Handmaid's Tale: Margaret Atwood's Modest Proposal" in *Canadian Literature*.

Laurie Vickroy, an Assistant Professor at Bradley University, holds a Ph.D. in English from Binghamton University (SUNY). Among her recent publication are "Beloved and Shoah: Witnessing the Unspeakable" in *The Comparatist* and "The Drama of the Traumatized Child in Two Works by Toni Morrison and Marguerite Dumas" in *Mosaic*. She has just finished a manuscript exploring the multiple manifestations of trauma in the works of Morrison, Dumas, and other twentieth-century writers.

Jean Wyatt is Professor of English at Occidental College in Los Angeles, California. She is the author of *Reconstructing Desire* (University of North Carolina Press, 1990) on reader response and alternative family structures in contemporary novels by English and American women writers. Most recently, she has published articles on Sandra Cisneros ("On Not Being La Malinche: Border Negotiations of Gender in Cisneros's *Woman Hollering Creek* in *Tulsa Studies in Women's Literature*, Fall 1995) and Margaret Atwood ("I Want to be You: Envy, the Lacanian Double, and Feminist Community in Atwood's *The Robber Bride* in *Tulsa Studies*, Fall 1998). Professor Wyatt is completing a book on identification in contemporary novels by English and American writers. She earned her doctorate at Harvard University.

Index

380 Index